INTELLIGENT INFORMATION PROCESSING

IFIP - The International Federation for Information Processing

IFIP was founded in 1960 under the auspices of UNESCO, following the First World Computer Congress held in Paris the previous year. An umbrella organization for societies working in information processing, IFIP's aim is two-fold: to support information processing within its member countries and to encourage technology transfer to developing nations. As its mission statement clearly states,

IFIP's mission is to be the leading, truly international, apolitical organization which encourages and assists in the development, exploitation and application of information technology for the benefit of all people.

IFIP is a non-profitmaking organization, run almost solely by 2500 volunteers. It operates through a number of technical committees, which organize events and publications. IFIP's events range from an international congress to local seminars, but the most important are:

- The IFIP World Computer Congress, held every second year;
- open conferences;
- working conferences.

The flagship event is the IFIP World Computer Congress, at which both invited and contributed papers are presented. Contributed papers are rigorously refereed and the rejection rate is high.

As with the Congress, participation in the open conferences is open to all and papers may be invited or submitted. Again, submitted papers are stringently refereed.

The working conferences are structured differently. They are usually run by a working group and attendance is small and by invitation only. Their purpose is to create an atmosphere conducive to innovation and development. Refereeing is less rigorous and papers are subjected to extensive group discussion.

Publications arising from IFIP events vary. The papers presented at the IFIP World Computer Congress and at open conferences are published as conference proceedings, while the results of the working conferences are often published as collections of selected and edited papers.

Any national society whose primary activity is in information may apply to become a full member of IFIP, although full membership is restricted to one society per country. Full members are entitled to vote at the annual General Assembly, National societies preferring a less committed involvement may apply for associate or corresponding membership. Associate members enjoy the same benefits as full members, but without voting rights. Corresponding members are not represented in IFIP bodies. Affiliated membership is open to non-national societies, and individual and honorary membership schemes are also offered.

INTELLIGENT INFORMATION PROCESSING

IFIP 17th World Computer Congress —
TC12 Stream on Intelligent Information Processing
August 25-30, 2002, Montréal, Québec, Canada

Edited by

Mark Musen
Stanford Medical Informatics
Stanford University
USA

Bernd Neumann
FB Informatik
Hamburg University
Germany

Rudi Studer
Institute AIFB
University of Karlsruhe
Germany

KLUWER ACADEMIC PUBLISHERS
BOSTON / DORDRECHT / LONDON

Distributors for North, Central and South America:
Kluwer Academic Publishers
101 Philip Drive
Assinippi Park
Norwell, Massachusetts 02061 USA
Telephone (781) 871-6600
Fax (781) 681-9045
E-Mail <kluwer@wkap.com>

Distributors for all other countries:
Kluwer Academic Publishers Group
Post Office Box 322
3300 AH Dordrecht, THE NETHERLANDS
Telephone 31 786 576 000
Fax 31 786 576 474
E-Mail <services@wkap.nl>

Electronic Services <http://www.wkap.nl>

Library of Congress Cataloging-in-Publication Data

IFIP World Computer Congress (17th : 2002 : Montréal, Québec)
Intelligent information processing : IFIP 17th World Computer Congress—TC12 stream on intelligent information processing, August 25-30, 2002, Montréal, Québec / edited by Mark Musen, Bernd Neumann, Rudi Studer.
p. cm. — (International Federation for Information Processing ; 93)
Includes bibliographical references and index.
ISBN 978-1-4757-1031-1 ISBN 978-0-387-35602-0 (eBook)
DOI 10.1007/978-0-387-35602-0
1. Expert systems (Computer science)—Congresses. 2. Database management—Congresses. I. Musen, Mark A. II. Neumann, Bernd, 1943 May 17– . III. Studer, Rudi. IV. Title. V. International Federation for Information Processing (Series) ; 93.

QA76.76.E95 I388 2002
006.3'3—dc21 2002075993

Printed on acid-free paper.

Contents

Semantic Web Architecture

Knowledge-engineering Frameworks

Knowledge-system Structure

Data Mining

Implementing Problem Solvers

Poster Session

Foreword

The papers in this volume represent the program for the Conference on Intelligent Information Processing (IIP 2002) held in conjunction with the 17th World Computer Congress of the International Federation of Information Processing (IFIP), which convened in Montreal, Canada, August 26–29, 2002. The conference represents a major activity of IFIP Working Group 12.5, dedicated to "knowledge-oriented development of applications," of Technical Committee 12, on Artificial Intelligence. Working group 12.5 brings together an international community of scientists concerned with the use of knowledge-based techniques in the engineering of real-world software systems.

IIP 2002 emphasized discussions of knowledge-based system architectures and intelligent information management. Invited talks and panels highlighted important new topics, such as the use of ontologies to support knowledge-based applications, the emergence of knowledge-based techniques on the Web, agent-oriented architectures, and fundamental questions of knowledge representation.

The majority of the conference was devoted to presentation of the scientific results contained in this volume. Through oral presentations, panels and poster sessions, attendees discussed varied dimensions of intelligent information processing. All papers were refereed by at least two reviewers. Of the 44 manuscripts submitted to the conference, the program committee was able to accept 17 full papers and 12 posters. Two keynote presentations and five invited surveys constituted an important part of the conference:

- H. Akkermans (The Netherlands): Being Smart in Information Processing: Technological and Social Challenges and Opportunities
- B. Chandrasekaran (USA): Multimodal Representations as Basis for Cognitive Architecture
- N. Jennings (UK): Agent-Based Computing
- J. Hendler (USA): The Semantic Web

- E. Motta (UK): Architectures and Solutions for the Knowledge Web
- W. Nejdl (Germany): Semantic Web and Peer-to-Peer Technologies for Distributed Learning Repositories
- W. Wahlster (Germany): Personalized Web Interaction

IIP 2002 would not have been possible without the hard work of the scientific program committee. The program co-chairs are also grateful to Nenad Stojanovic and Eva Elliott for their expert assistance in handling manuscripts and assembling these proceedings.

We hope that you will find these proceedings a valuable collection of some of the most stimulating work taking place internationally in the area of intelligent information processing. The emergence of novel architectures for intelligent systems, the advent of the Semantic Web, and the maturation and widespread dissemination of techniques for the construction of intelligent systems make these exciting times for the knowledge-oriented development of software applications. These proceedings serve as a written record of the contributions made by the participants of IIP 2002 and of the promising new results of research in applied artificial intelligence.

Mark A. Musen, Stanford
Bernd Neumann, Hamburg
Rudi Studer, Karlsruhe

Conference and Program Committees

Conference Chair:

Bernd Neumann, University of Hamburg, Germany

Program Co-Chairs:

Mark Musen, Stanford University, USA
Rudi Studer, University of Karlsruhe, Germany

Program Committee:

Hans Akkermans (The Netherlands)
Salem Abdelbadeeh (Egypt)
Richard Benjamins (Spain)
B. Chandrasekaran (USA)
Paul Compton (Australia)
Monica Crubezy (USA)
John Debenham (Australia)
Yves Demazeau (France)
Rose Dieng-Kuntz (France)
Wolfgang Klas (Austria)
Deborah McGuiness (USA)
Robert Meersman (Belgium)
Tim Menzies (Canada)
Riichiro Mizoguchi (Japan)
Pavol Navrat (Slovakia)
Wolfgang Nejdl (Germany)
Erich Neuhold (Germany)
Natalya Fridman Noy (USA)

Henrik Eriksson (Sweden)
Boi Faltings (Switzerland)
Adam Farquhar (USA)
Dieter Fensel (The Netherlands)
John Gennari (USA)
Yolanda Gil (USA)
Asun Gomez-Perez (Spain)
Nicola Guarino (Italy)
Lynda Hardmann (The Netherlands)
Masahiro Hori (Japan)
Werner Horn (Austria)
Ian Horrocks (UK)
Nik Kasabov (New Zealand)
Larry Kerschberg (USA)
Dan O'Leary (USA)
Enric Plaza (Spain)
Alun Preece (UK)
Ulrich Reimer (Switzerland)
M. Sasikumar (India)
Guus Schreiber (The Netherlands)
Ana Garcia Serrano (Spain)
Nigel Shadbolt (UK)
Yuval Shahar (Israel)
Stuart C. Shapiro (USA)
Derek Sleeman (UK)
Steffen Staab (Germany)
Gerd Stumme (Germany)
Samson Tu (USA)

BEING SMART IN INFORMATION PROCESSING

Technological And Social Challenges And Opportunities

Hans Akkermans

Free University Amsterdam VUA, The Netherlands

Abstract: A very exciting development in current intelligent information processing is the Semantic Web and the innovative e-applications it promises to enable. This promise will not come true, however, if research limits itself to the technological aspects and challenges only. Both supply-demand sides and business-technology sides need to be investigated in an integrated fashion. This implies that we simultaneously have to address technological, social, and business considerations. Therefore, a comprehensive research strategy for the next decade of intelligent information processing must be of an integrated socio-technical nature covering different levels: (1) Definition and standardization of the baseline infrastructures, content libraries and languages that make up the Semantic Web; (2) The associated construction of generic smart web services that dynamically bridge the low-level (for the end user) infrastructures and the high-level user applications; (3) Designing and studying innovative e-services, information systems, and business processes at the domain, customer, and business level; (4) Understanding and influencing the business and market logics and critical success factors that will determine the social adoption of smart web-based innovations.

Key words: Keynote IFIP IIP-2002

1. EXCITING NEW TECHNOLOGIES

A very exciting development in current intelligent information processing is the Semantic Web (cf. [Berners-Lee et al., 2001] [Fensel et al., to appear]) and the innovative applications it promises to enable. The Semantic Web will provide the next generation of the World Wide Web. The current Web is a very interesting and successful, but also passive and rather unstructured storage place of information resources. This makes it increasingly difficult to quickly find the right information you need, a problem that becomes even more pressing with the scaling up of the Web. The vision of the Semantic Web is to make the Web from a passive information store into a proactive service facility for its users. This is done by equipping it with information management services, based on semantic and knowledge-based methods, that let the Web act - in the eyes of its users - as understanding the contents and meaning (rather than just the syntax) of the many information resources it contains and, moreover, as capable of knowledge processing these resources. In the words of Tim Berners-Lee: “The Semantic Web will globalise knowledge representation, just as the WWW globalised hypertext”. This globalised semantic approach offers concrete research lines how to solve the problem of interoperability between systems and humans in a highly distributed but connected world.

Designing the infrastructure of the Semantic Web poses major technical and scientific challenges. This is already evident if we look at the envisaged technical architecture of the Semantic Web (see Figure 1) that somewhat resembles a delicately layered cake made from a variety of cyberspace ingredients.

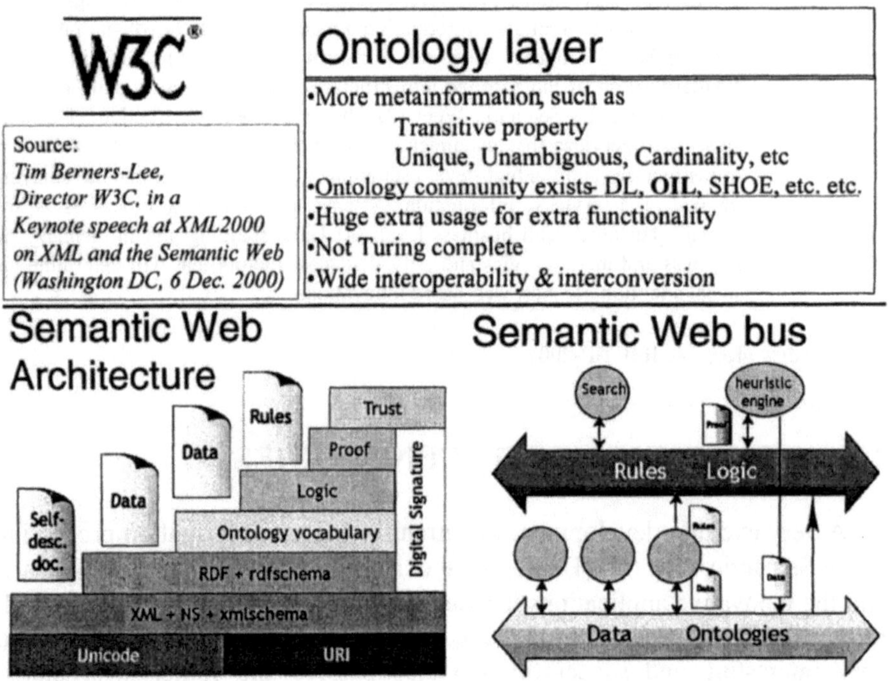

Figure 1. Ingredients and envisaged technical architecture of the Semantic Web.

Some of these ingredients are based on combining existing results and experiences that stem from research areas such as intelligent systems, knowledge representation and reasoning, knowledge engineering and management, or ontology and agent technology. Others are still in the process of invention. Recent progress is reported in the proceedings of this and other conferences and journals (e.g. [Harmelen & Horrocks, 2000], [Staab et al., 2001]).

Challenging and interesting as this is, it is a necessary but not yet sufficient condition to realize the full potential of the Web. For a comprehensive R&D strategy it is necessary to look at the broader picture (depicted in Figure 2) of the Semantic Web: how it is going to be useful in practical real-world applications, and how it will interact with and be beneficial to its users.

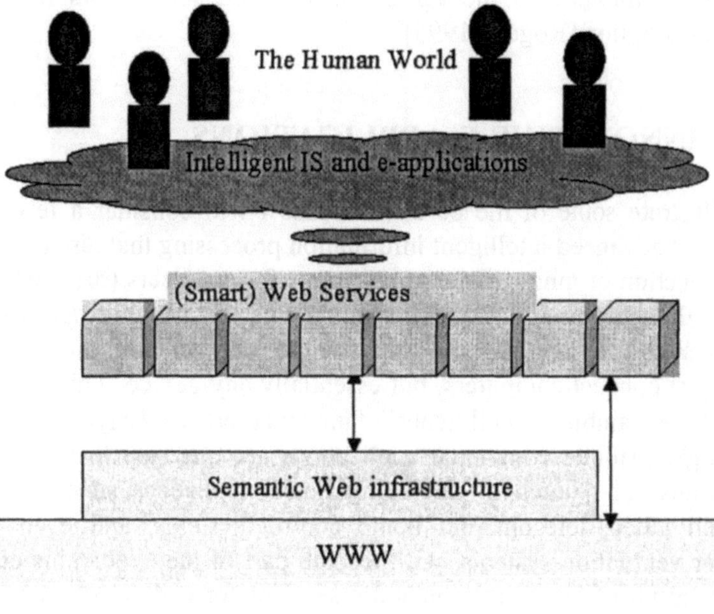

Figure 2. The broader picture: Semantic Web infrastructure, smart services, e-applications and their human-world context.

The ongoing worldwide research effort related to the Semantic Web currently shows an emphasis on those technological issues that are indicated in Figure 2 as web infrastructure and, to a lesser extent, smart web services. This is highly important research because generic semantic infrastructure (such as web ontology languages and content libraries) and associated generic smart web services (such as semantic search, semantic browsing, reasoning, knowledge processing and ontology management services – these services are highly non-trivial because they must be able to deal with the unavoidable evolutional dynamics of web-based knowledge) are a *conditio sine qua non* for the Semantic Web. Nevertheless, it is also important to look already from the start from an *outside-in* perspective. What are the new business, domain, or user/customer applications that are not yet possible today but will be tomorrow as a result of the Semantic Web? Why would businesses, markets or individuals be willing to adopt such innovations? After all, many great innovations fail or have very long lead times because of significant upfront investments. These are in many cases not just of a financial nature: in addition they require behavioural or -even more problematic- cultural changes from their adopters (whether individuals or organizations). We must recognize that the Semantic Web is such a great innovation. Consequently, there is no reason to assume that the new wave of intelligent information processing is immune to the age-old established social laws that govern innovation adoption [Rogers, 1995].

2. INNOVATIVE E-APPLICATIONS

To illustrate some of the pertinent issues I will consider a few specific examples of advanced intelligent information processing that aim the creation and introduction of innovative e-applications for end users (the third level in Figure 2). In addition to the Web becoming smarter (which is denoted by the Semantic Web effort), it will also become more universal in the sense that it will not just connect computers, but essentially any device. This is variously referred to as "ambient intelligence", "universal connectivity" or "pervasive computing". Mobile commerce applications are one step in this direction, but basically all equipment, including home appliances such as personal audio and video, telecom and home control systems, and even heaters, coolers or ventilation systems, will become part of the Web. This enables a broad spectrum of e-applications and e-services for end consumers in many different industry areas: home security, e-health, e-entertainment, e-shopping, distance learning, digital media services, and smart buildings that are able to manage themselves. All of these new imagined e-services are technically challenging, but will also require and induce different behaviours and attitudes from the end consumers as well as from the businesses delivering these e-services.

Figure 3. Smart building field experiment site at ECN, Petten, The Netherlands.

As a specific example, I take smart buildings. With several colleagues from different countries, we are researching how smart buildings can serve those who live or work in it [Ygge & Akkermans, 1999], [Gustavsson, 1999], [Kamphuis et al., 2001]. This work has progressed to the point that actual field experiments are carried out (Figure 3), whereby the social aspects are investigated as an integrated part of the research. One of the issues studied is comfort management: how buildings can automatically provide a optimally comfortable climate with costs and energy use that are at the same time as low as possible.

Technically, smart comfort management is based on intelligent agents (so-called *HomeBot* agents) that act as software representatives of individual building users as well as of various types of equipment that play a role in the energy functionality, usage and production in a building (e.g. heaters, sun-blinds, ventilators, photovoltaic cells). These *HomeBot* agents communicate with each other over Internet and PLC media, and negotiate in order to optimise the overall energy efficiency in the building. This optimisation is based on multi-criteria agent negotiations taking place on an electronic marketplace. These take place in the form of a multi-commodity auction, where energy is being bought and sold in different time slots. They are based on the current energy needs, local sensor data, model forecasts (e.g. weather, building physics), and the going real-time power prices. The e-market outcome then determines the needed building control actions in a fully distributed and decentralised way.

The calculation model optimises the total utility, which is a trade-off between cost and comfort, over the coming 24 hours, taking into account both the customer preferences and the actual energy prices. This optimisation is redone every hour, because expected energy prices, outside temperatures, etc. may change, which results in different optimal device settings. Needed forecasts of comfort aspects in a building are based on simple thermodynamic climate models. Energy prices are in general known a certain period (typically 24 hours) in advance. The system reacts on electricity prices, trying to use as little energy as possible when prices are high. In simulations we have concentrated on two dimensions: the economic aspect and the inside climate. The economic aspect is illustrated by a scenario featuring two archetypes: Erika, a yuppie who wants to make no concessions to her comfort level whatsoever irrespective of cost; and Erik, a poor student who wants to keep comfort levels acceptable when at home, but also needs to economise as much as possible. Some typical results are presented in Figure 4. They do show that significant savings without loss of comfort are possible in smart self-managing buildings.

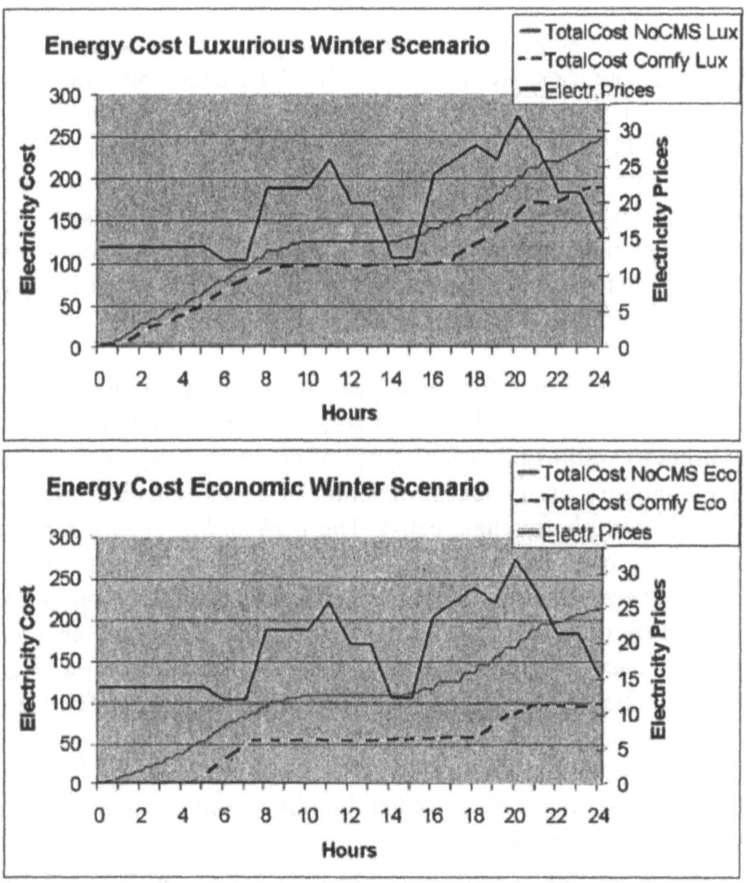

Figure 4. Cumulative costs for a smart building scenarios on a Winter day: savings vary from 20% in the luxurious setting (yuppie Erika) to 45% in the economic setting (student Erik).

There are several general points beyond the specific e-application that are worth noting here in the context of intelligent information processing. First, most current multi-agent applications carry out information and transaction services. This application does that as well but it goes a significant step further: it is an example where agents carry out control tasks through an electronic marketplace that is an alternative to common industrial central controllers [Ygge & Akkermans, 1999].

Second, this e-application is a good example illustrating how much domain knowledge is actually needed to make real-life applications work. *Homebot* agents must for example have knowledge of: building physics, the impact of weather forecasts, the economics of energy purchase and use, etc. All this domain knowledge is actually built into this e-service in a distributed way. It is testimony to the correctness of a major conclusion of knowledge-systems research over many years: generic intelligent techniques are just not strong enough, structuring and processing *domain knowledge* is key to developing successful applications.

Finally, technical and social considerations come together in the notion of comfort. In this application, comfort is the specialization of what counts as "customer satisfaction", an inherently qualitative and perceptual notion for most customers:

- People will typically be able to say whether or not they "like" the climate in a building, but they will find it extremely hard to make this explicit beyond qualitative statements.
- Comfort is a personal concept: users will generally differ in to what extent a given building climate is perceived as comfortable, and what climate they personally prefer.
- Comfort is a sophisticated multi-dimensional concept, as it causally depends on many interacting factors such as air temperature, radiant temperature, humidity, air velocity, clothing, and a person's metabolism (a measure of the person's activity).
- Delivering comfort in buildings is an economic issue: from marketing studies it is known that the financial costs of energy and equipment needed for heating, cooling, air quality, and climate control are key issues for customers and building managers.

Nevertheless, for an automated application we need to turn the central question *"what is customer satisfaction?"* into a causal and quantitative notion of utility. This is a socio-technical issue that is key but known to be hard in many areas (e.g. also in illegal downloading of digital music, cf. [Gordijn, 2002, Ch. 7].)

3. THE SOCIAL CHALLENGE: BUSINESS AND MARKET LOGICS

These illustrations point to the general observation that intelligent information processing and, specifically, the Semantic Web will become a societal success only if it is able to deal with three very different logics of value, that are stated in terms of not necessarily compatible considerations of technology, business models, and market adoption (Figure 5).

To start with the market considerations, the recent rise and fall of many e-commerce initiatives is testimony to the importance of correctly understanding market logics. Extensive customer surveys were done related to the smart building applications discussed in the previous section, with interesting conclusions [Sweet et al., 2000],[Olsson & Kamphuis, 2001],[Jelsma, 2001] such as:

- There actually *is* a strong customer interest in a broad variety of new-e-services, with a variability of this interest across different market segments.
- However, price and cost considerations are primary in this sector, with typically a window for incurring extra costs to the customer for new e-services of no more than 5-10%.
- Design logics of modern buildings (cf. the one of Figure 3) can be such that they run counter the use(r) logics, so that sometimes they prevent their users from doing the right thing, even if both share the same goal of energy efficiency or comfort optimization.

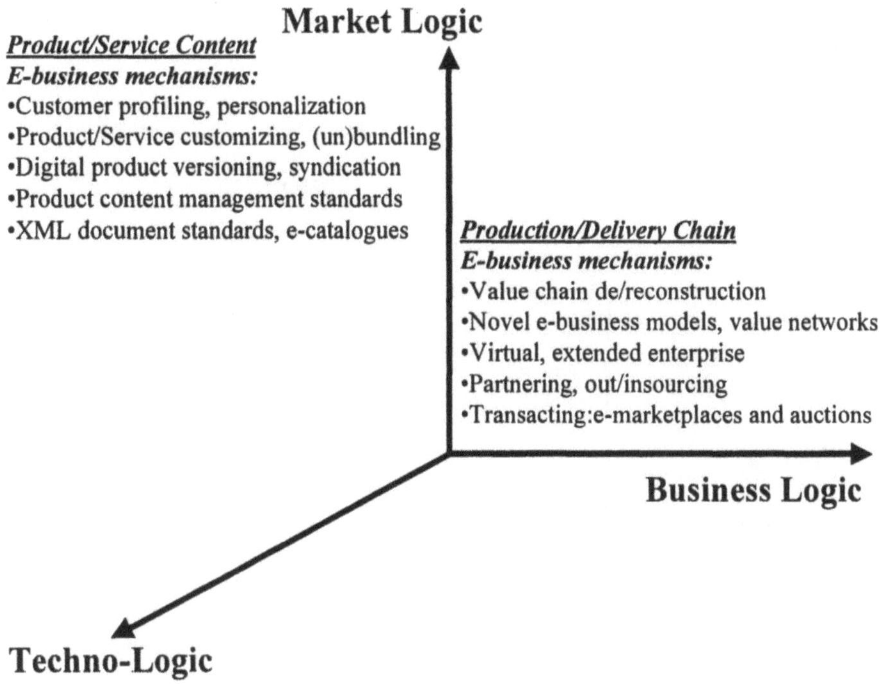

Figure 5. Three different value logics at play in e-applications [Akkermans, 2001].

Market logics refers to the demand side. Business logics refer to the supply side. Due to the developments of the Web, the same (digital) product or service can be created by wholly different value constellations. The degrees of freedom in designing business models have therefore significantly increased. An example of this is depicted in Figure 6. It shows two very different networked e-business models relating to the offering of the same online news service (as considered in a commercial project, see [Gordijn & Akkermans, 2001], [Gordijn, 2002, Ch. 8]). They differ significantly on many different counts, including customer ownership and sensitivity to changes in important financial parameters in the business model. Such considerations similarly apply in the discussed smart building services, because many actors come into play also there and there is quite some freedom in designing the value constellation.

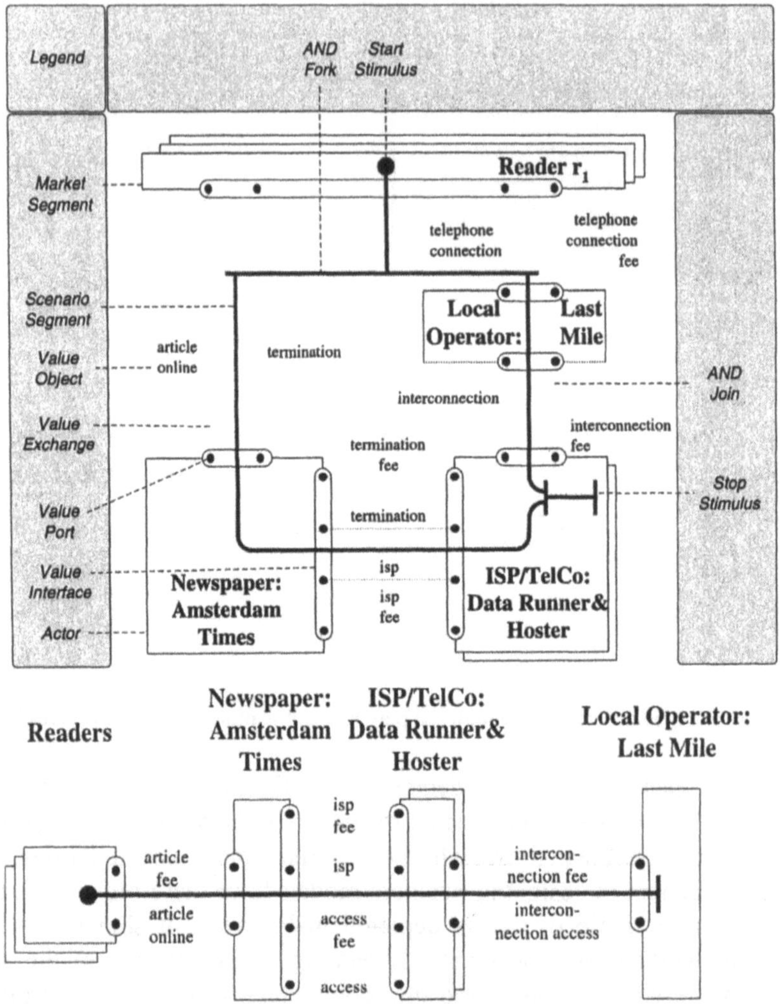

Figure 6. Contrasting e-business models for an online news service.

Generally, the Semantic Web must ultimately enable the creation of *value webs*. Hence, there is a clear need to develop scientifically grounded business analysis tools that help in understanding and designing the intertwined business-technology aspects of the next wave of intelligent information processing applications.

4. CONCLUSION

We are on the eve of a new era of intelligent information processing that centres around the Semantic Web and its applications as a truly promising development. In order to realize its full potential, however, we have to take it for what it is: a great innovation. This implies that we simultaneously have to address the technological, social, and business considerations that play a role in innovations and their adoption by the society at large.

Therefore, a comprehensive research strategy for the next decade of intelligent information processing must be of an integrated socio-technical nature covering all levels indicated in Figure 2:

1. Definition and standardization of the baseline infrastructures, content libraries and languages that make up the Semantic Web.
2. The associated construction of generic smart web services that dynamically bridge the low-level (for the end user) infrastructures and the high-level user applications.
3. Designing and studying innovative e-services, information systems, and business processes at the domain, customer, and business level.
4. Understanding and influencing the business and market logics and critical success factors that will determine the social adoption of smart web-based innovations.

Acknowledgement. This work is partially supported by the European Commission, in the context of the projects OBELIX (project no. EU-IST-2001-33144) and BUSMOD (project no. EU-EESD-NNE5-2001-00256).

REFERENCES

[Akkermans, 2001] J.M. Akkermans: *Intelligent E-Business – From Technology to Value*, IEEE Intelligent Systems, Vol. 16, No. 4 (July-August 2001), pages 8-10. (http://computer.org/intelligent).

[Berners-Lee et al., 2001] T. Berners-Lee, J. Hendler, and O. Lassila: *The Semantic Web*, Scientific American, May 2001.

[Fensel et al., to appear] D. Fensel, J. Hendler, H. Lieberman, and W. Wahlster (Eds.): *Semantic Web Technology*, MIT Press, Cambridge, MA, to appear 2002.

[Gordijn, 2002] J. Gordijn: Value-Based Requirements Engineering: Exploring Innovative E-Commerce Ideas, PhD Thesis Free University Amstewrdam, June 2002. (See also http://www.cs.vu.nl/~gordijn/).

[Gordijn & Akkermans, 2001] J. Gordijn and J.M. Akkermans: *Designing and Evaluating E-Business Models*, IEEE Intelligent Systems Vol. 16, No. 4 (July-August 2001), pages 11-17.

[Gustavsson, 1999] R. Gustavsson: *Agents with Power*, Communications of the ACM, Vol. 42, No. 3 (March 1999) pages 41-47.

[Harmelen & Horrocks, 2000] F. van Harmelen and I. Horrocks: *Questions and answers about OIL*. IEEE Intelligent Systems Vol. 15, No. 6 (November/December 2000), pp. 69–72.

[Kamphuis et al., 2001] R. Kamphuis, C. Warmer, and J.M. Akkermans: *SMART - Innovative services for smart buildings*. In ISPLC-2001, Proceedings of the 5th International symposium on Power-Line Communications and Its Applications, pp. 231-236. Lund University, Sweden, 2001.

[Jelsma, 2001] J.Jelsma: *The SMART System And Its Test Building: Matching Design Logics*, Netherlands Energy Research Foundation ECN, Report ECN-C-02-008, Petten, The Netherlands, December 2001.

[Olsson & Kamphuis, 2001] M. Olsson and R. Kamphuis: *Market Survey of Last-Mile Communication Services Using PLC*, PALAS EU-IST-1999-11379 Project Deliverable D9, Netherlands Energy Research Foundation ECN, Business Unit DEGO, Petten, The Netherlands, June 2001.

[Rogers, 1995] E.M. Rogers: *Diffusion of Innovations*, 4th Ed., The Free Press, New York, 1995.

[Staab et al., 2001] S. Staab, H.-P. Schnurr, R. Studer, and Y. Sure: *Knowledge Processes and Ontologies*, IEEE Intelligent Systems, Vol. 16, No. 1 (January/February 2001), pages 26-34.

[Sweet et al., 2000] P.S. Sweet, M. Olsson, and J.M. Akkermans: "*PLC Service Business Model Development and Market Survey Instrument*", PALAS EU-IST-1999-11379 Project Powerline as an Alternative Local AccesS, Deliverable D7, EnerSearch, Malmö, Sweden, December 2000. (Available from http://palas.regiocom.net and http://www.enersearch.se).

[Ygge & Akkermans, 1999] F. Ygge and J.M. Akkermans: *Decentralized Markets versus Central Control - A Comparative Study*, Journal of Artificial Intelligence Research Vol. 11 (1999), pages 301-333 (http://www.jair.org). (Related work, see: http://www.enersearch.se).

MULTIMODAL REPRESENTATIONS AS BASIS FOR COGNITIVE ARCHITECTURE

Making Perception More Central to Intelligent Behavior

B. Chandrasekaran
Dept.of Computer & Inf. Science
The Ohio State University
Columbus, OH, 43210, USA

Abstract: In this talk, I outline a view of "cognitive state" as fundamentally multi-modal, i.e., as an integrated and interlinked collection of "images" in various modalities: the perceptual ones, and the kinesthetic and conceptual modalities. Thinking, problem solving, reasoning, etc. are best viewed as sequences of such states, in which there is no intrinsically preferred mode. Representational elements in one mode invoke elements in other modes. The external world also at various points contributes elements to one mode or another. Perception and imagination are more continuous in this view than in the traditional views. In recent years, there has been much interest in the notion of "mental images." However, the focus in this stream of research has been on a very special class of mental images, namely visual ones. The proposed view is an extension and generalization of this notion, not only to other perceptual modalities, but also to kinesthetic and conceptual modalities. I think the proposed view of the essential nature of the mental state opens up new ways of thinking about cognitive architecture, and also suggests new ways of building smart machines. I'll outline why I think so.

Key words: Cognitive architecture, multimodal representation, agent architecture.

EXTENDED ABSTRACT

In this talk, I outline a view of "cognitive state" as fundamentally multi-modal, i.e., as an integrated and interlinked collection of "images" in various modalities: the perceptual ones, and the kinesthetic and conceptual modalities. Thinking, problem solving, reasoning, etc. are best viewed as sequences of such states, in which there is no intrinsically preferred mode. Representational elements in one mode invoke elements in other modes. The external world also at various points contributes elements to one mode or another. Perception and imagination are more continuous in this view than in the traditional views. In recent years, there has been much interest in the notion of "mental images." However, the focus in this stream of research has been on a very special class of mental images, namely visual ones. The proposed view is an extension and generalization of this notion, not only to other perceptual modalities, but also to kinesthetic and conceptual modalities. I think the proposed view of the essential nature of the mental state opens up new ways of thinking about cognitive architecture, and also suggests new ways of building smart machines. I'll outline why I think so.

My argument will proceed in a number of steps:

(i) The standard view in both AI and Cognitive Science is that "thought" is essentially like a sentence in natural language, i.e., it is either a proposition or an "attitude" (like want P) towards a proposition. The Language of Thought Hypothesis makes this claim in a formal way. All the AI knowledge representation approaches, whether or not their authors think of them as being in the so-called "logic framework," are essentially symbol structures in which the symbols stand for objects and relations in some world.

(ii) I propose that this view of the cognitive state is too narrow, and that having a thought is typically not merely entertaining a proposition or some attitude to it, but having perceptual experiences as well. This claim is not simply of philosophical interest, but I claim that it opens up ways of thinking about building robots that make use of their experience in interesting new ways.

(iii) Let us start with the simple, but common, example of reasoning with external diagrams. An essential role of diagrams in many cases is that the problem solver "sees" some relationship in the diagram; without the diagram, he would, at best, need to construct a series of inferences to arrive at the same piece of information. The relevant point for me here is that the representation of the problem state is distributed between the external diagram and internal representations inside the head of the problem solver. It is also bi-modal - some of the representation is perceptual and some propositional.

(iv) Now suppose there is no external diagram, but the problem solver has to imagine the situation diagrammatically. Think of the example, "Imagine taking one step forward, one step to the right and one step back. Where are you with respect to the starting point?". Controversy about mental images notwithstanding, the mental image is playing the same functional role in the solution of the problem in this case as the external diagram. The problem state is still bi-modal, but entirely inside the head of the problem solver.

As an aside, a significant aspect of the debate over mental imagery is over the conundrum of how mental images can really be images, since images, in order to be seen, have to be processed by a perception system, and there are no eyes inside the head. I'll briefly outline an earlier proposed of mine as a solution to this paradox.

(v) The next step in the argument is to generalize the representation to multiple modalities. As far as external representations go, in addition to images, we can have three-dimensional models which we can take in visually or by touch. Sound can mark locations and carry specific information. Similarly, there is no reason to restrict the notion of an internal image to the visual modality. In principle, internal images are possible in all modalities of perceptual and kinesthetic experience. In addition to imagining visual situations, we "hear" tunes; we can imagine moving our bodies in various ways, and so on. Clearly some modalities are stronger than others, and people differ in the kinds of modalities their internal images are rich and complex. (Beethoven famously continued to compose music even after he became deaf.) So at this point, we can begin to think of a multi-modal state, spanning all modalities, perceptual, kinesthetic and of course conceptual. The state can be distributed between the inner and outer worlds of the agent.

(vi) I then propose that the cognitive architecture in which the cognitive state is multimodal in the sense above, and describe a number of multi-modal mechanisms that can cause changes of states. When combined with a goal-directed engine such as Soar, we have the basics of a framework for problem solving in which perception is not simply restricted to giving information about the external world, but can support thinking more directly by supporting exploration of multi-modal problem spaces.

(vii) So far it might appear as if the goal is to give a computational account of cognitive states in humans or even animals, but without any particular reason to believe that this is a good architecture for biological agents, or for robots. I will argue for the computational advantages of such an architecture, and propose that it is actually a good idea for natural or artificial agents. I'll conclude with reasons why this way of thinking is a new way of thinking about integrated robots.

(viii) I'll end with an account of technical issues that need to be solved to make progress in realizing this vision. A key challenge is technical solutions to the problem of representing general images in such a way that they are structured so that they can be composed in various ways, and at the same time can support information extraction, much as we get information from external and internal images.

Acknowledgement: Prepared through participation in the Advanced Decision Architectures Collaborative Technology Alliance sponsored by the U.S. Army Research Laboratory under Cooperative Agreement DAAD19-01-2-0009.

AGENT-BASED COMPUTING

Nicholas R. Jennings
Dept. of Electronics and Computer Science,
University of Southampton, Southampton SO17 1BJ, UK.
nrj@ecs.soton.ac.uk

Abstract Agent-based computing represents an exciting new synthesis for both Artificial Intelligence and, more generally, Computer Science. It has the potential to improve the theory and the practice of modelling, designing and implementing complex computer systems. Yet, to date, there has been little systematic analysis of what makes the agent-based approach such an appealing and powerful computational model. To rectify this situation, this paper aims to tackle exactly this issue. The standpoint of this analysis is the role of agent-based software in solving complex, real-world problems. In particular, it will be argued that the development of robust and scalable software systems requires autonomous agents that can complete their objectives while situated in a dynamic and uncertain environment, that can engage in rich, high-level interactions, and that can operate within flexible organisational structures.

Keywords: autonomous agents, agent-oriented software engineering, complex systems

Introduction

Building high quality, industrial-strength software is difficult. Indeed, it has been argued that developing such software in domains like telecommunications, industrial control and business process management represents one of the most complex construction tasks humans undertake (both in terms of the number and the flexibility of the constituent components and in terms of their interconnections). Against this background, a wide range of software engineering paradigms have been devised. Each successive development either claims to make the engineering process easier or to extend the complexity of applications that can feasibly be built. Although evidence is emerging to support these claims, researchers continue to strive for more effective techniques. To this end, this paper will argue that analysing, designing and implementing complex software systems as a collection of interacting, autonomous agents (i.e., as a *multi-agent system*) affords software engineers a number of significant advantages over contemporary methods. This is not to say that *agent-oriented software engineering* [Jennings 2000] represents a silver bullet [Brooks 1995] – there is no evidence to suggest it will represent an order of magnitude improvement in productivity. However, the increasing number of deployed applications [Jennings and Wooldridge 1998, Parunak 1999] bears testament to the potential advantages that accrue from such an approach.

In seeking to demonstrate the efficacy of agent-oriented techniques, the most compelling argument would be to quantitatively show how their adoption had improved the development process in a range of projects. However, such data is simply not available (as it is not for other contemporary software engineering approaches like patterns, application frameworks and component-ware). Given this fact, the best that can be achieved is a qualitative justification of why agent-oriented approaches are well suited to engineering complex, distributed software systems.

1. MANAGING COMPLEXITY IN SOFTWARE SYSTEMS

Industrial-strength software is complex: it has a large number of parts that have many interactions [Simon 1996]. Moreover this complexity is not accidental [Brooks 1995], it is an innate property of such systems. Given this situation, the role of software engineering is to provide structures and techniques that make it easier to handle complexity. Fortunately for designers, this complexity exhibits a number of important regularities [Simon 1996]:

- Complexity frequently takes the form of a hierarchy. That is, a system that is composed of inter-related sub-systems, each of which is in turn hierarchic in structure, until the lowest level of elementary sub-system is reached. The precise nature of these organisational relationships varies between sub-systems, however some generic forms (such as client-server, peer, team, etc.) can be identified. These relationships are not static: they often vary over time.

- The choice of which components in the system are primitive is relatively arbitrary and is defined by the observer's aims and objectives.

- Hierarchic systems evolve more quickly than non-hierarchic ones of comparable size (i.e., complex systems will evolve from simple systems more rapidly if there are clearly identifiable *stable intermediate forms*, than if there are not).

- It is possible to distinguish between the interactions *among* sub-systems and those *within* sub-systems. The latter are both more frequent (typically at least an order of magnitude more) and more predictable than the former. This gives rise to the view that complex systems are *nearly decomposable*: sub-systems can be treated almost as if they are independent, but not quite since there are some interactions between them. Moreover, although many of these interactions can be predicted at design time, some cannot.

Drawing these insights together, it is possible to define a canonical view of a complex system (figure 1). The system's hierarchical nature is expressed through the "related to" links, components within a sub-system are connected through "frequent interaction" links, and interactions between components are expressed through "infrequent interaction" links.

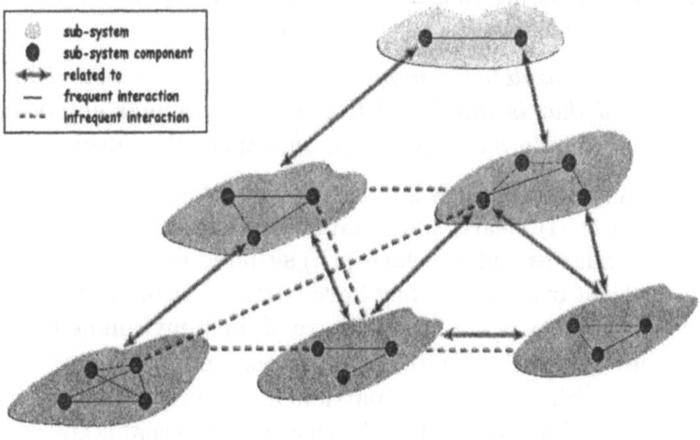

Figure 1. View of a Canonical Complex System

Given these observations, software engineers have devised a number of fundamental tools of the trade for helping to manage complexity [Booch 1994]:

- *Decomposition*: The most basic technique for tackling large problems is to divide them into smaller, more manageable chunks each of which can then be dealt with in relative isolation (note the nearly decomposable sub-systems in figure 1). Decomposition helps tackle complexity because it limits the designer's scope.

- *Abstraction*: The process of defining a simplified model of the system that emphasises some of the details or properties, while suppressing others. Again, this works because it limits the designer's scope of interest at a given time.

- *Organisation*[1]: The process of defining and managing the interrelationships between the various problem solving components (note the sub-system and interaction links of figure 1). The ability to specify and enact organisational relationships helps designers tackle complexity by: (i) enabling a number of basic components to be grouped together and treated as a higher-level unit of analysis and (ii) providing a means of describing the high-level relationships between various units.

2. THE CASE FOR AGENT-ORIENTED SOFTWARE ENGINEERING

The first step in arguing for an agent-oriented approach to software engineering involves identifying the key concepts of agent-based computing. The first such concept is that of an agent:

an agent is an encapsulated computer system that is situated in some environment, and that is capable of flexible, autonomous action in that environment in order to meet its design objectives [Wooldridge 1997]

There are a number of points about this definition that require elaboration. Agents are: (i) clearly identifiable problem solving entities with well-defined boundaries and interfaces; (ii) situated (embedded) in a particular environment over which they have partial control and observability – they receive inputs related to the state of their environment through sensors and they act on the environment through effectors; (iii) designed to fulfil a specific role – they have particular objectives to achieve; (iv) autonomous – they have control both over their internal state and over their own behaviour; (v) capable of exhibiting flexible problem solving behaviour in pursuit of their design objectives – being both reactive (able to respond in a timely fashion to changes that occur in their environment) and proactive (able to opportunistically adopt goals and take the initiative) [Wooldridge and Jennings 1995].

When adopting an agent-oriented view, it soon becomes apparent that most problems require or involve multiple agents: to represent the decentralised nature of the problem, the multiple loci of control, the multiple perspectives or the competing interests. Moreover, the agents will need to interact with one another: either to achieve their individual objectives or to manage the dependencies that ensue from being situated in a common environment. These interactions can vary from simple semantic interoperation (information passing), through traditional client-server type interactions, to rich social interactions (the ability to cooperate, coordinate and negotiate about a course of action). Whatever the nature of the social process, however, there are two points that qualitatively differentiate agent interactions from those that occur in other software engineering paradigms. Firstly, agent-oriented interactions generally occur through a high-level (declarative) agent communication language (often based on speech act theory [Mayfield et al. 1995]). Consequently, interactions are conducted at the *knowledge-level* [Newell 1982]: in terms of which goals should be followed, at what time and by whom (cf. method invocation or function calls that operate at a purely syntactic level). Secondly, as agents are flexible problem solvers, operating in an environment over which they have only partial control and observability, interactions need to be handled in a similarly flexible manner. Thus, agents need the computational apparatus to make context-dependent decisions about the nature and scope of their interactions and to initiate (and respond to) interactions that were not foreseen at design time.

In the majority of cases, agents act either on behalf of individuals/companies or as part of some wider initiative. Thus, there is typically some underpinning organisational context to agents' interactions. This context defines the nature of the relationship between the agents. For example, they may be peers working together in a team or one may be the manager of the others. To capture such links, agent systems have explicit constructs for modelling organisational relationships (e.g. manager, team member). In many cases, these relationships are subject to ongoing change: social interaction means existing relationships evolve (e.g. a team of peers may decide to move to a more hierarchical structure as their numbers grow) and new relations are created (e.g. a number of unrelated agents may decide to form a team to deliver a service that no one individual can offer). The temporal extent of these relationships can also vary enormously: from providing a service as a one-off, to a permanent bond. To cope with this variety and dynamic, agent researchers have devised protocols that enable organisational groupings to be formed and disbanded, specified mechanisms to ensure groupings act together in a coherent fashion and developed structures to characterise the macro behaviour of collectives [Jennings and Wooldridge 1998, Wooldridge and Jennings 1995].

Drawing these points together (figure 2), it can be seen that: (i) adopting an agent-oriented approach to software engineering means decomposing the problem into multiple, autonomous components that can act and interact in flexible ways to achieve their set objectives; (ii) the key abstraction models that define the agent-oriented mindset are agents, interactions and organisations; and (iii) explicit structures and mechanisms are often used to describe and manage the complex and changing web of organisational relationships that exist between the agents.

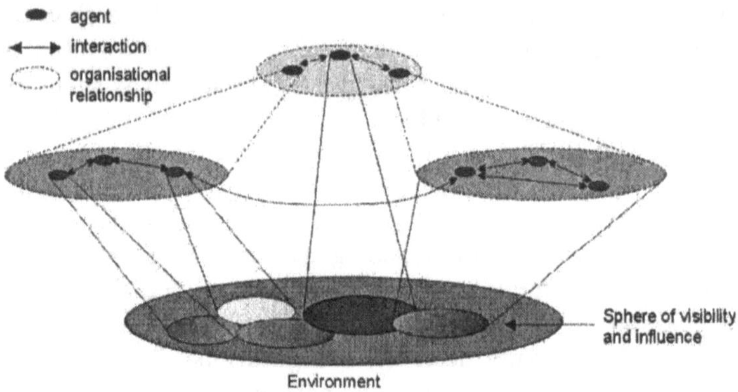

Figure 2. Canonical View of a Multi-agent System

2.1. The Software Engineering Credentials of the Agent-Oriented Approach

Here the argument in favour of an agent-oriented approach to software engineering is composed of the following steps:

- show that agent-oriented decompositions are an effective way of partitioning the problem space of a complex system;
- show that the key abstractions of the agent-oriented mindset are a natural means of modelling complex systems; and
- show that the agent-oriented philosophy for modelling and managing organisational relationships is appropriate for dealing with the dependencies and interactions that exist in complex systems.

When taken together, these steps form a complete mapping between the characteristics of a complex system and the key software engineering abstractions for handling complexity as they apply to agent-based systems.

The Merits of Agent-Oriented Decompositions.
Complex systems consist of a number of related sub-systems organised in a hierarchical fashion (figure 1). At any given level, sub-systems

work together to achieve the functionality of their parent system. Moreover, within a sub-system, the constituent components work together to deliver the overall functionality. Thus, the same basic model of interacting components, working together to achieve particular objectives occurs throughout the system. Given this fact, it is entirely natural to modularise the components in terms of the objectives they achieve[2]. In other words, each component can be thought of as achieving one or more objectives. A second important observation is that complex systems have multiple loci of control: "real systems have no top" [Meyer 1988] pg 43. Applying this philosophy to objective-achieving decompositions means the individual components should localise and encapsulate their own control. Thus, entities should have their own thread of control (i.e. they should be active) and they should have control over their own actions (i.e. they should be autonomous).

For the active and autonomous components to fulfil both their individual and collective objectives, they need to interact (recall complex systems are only nearly decomposable). However the system's inherent complexity means it is impossible to *a priori* know about all potential links: interactions will occur at unpredictable times, for unpredictable reasons, between unpredictable components. For this reason, it is futile to try and predict or analyse all the possibilities at design-time. It is more realistic to endow the components with the ability to make decisions about the nature and scope of their interactions at run-time. From this, it follows that components need the ability to initiate (and respond to) interactions in a flexible manner.

The policy of deferring to run-time decisions about component interactions facilitates the engineering of complex systems in two ways. Firstly, problems associated with the coupling of components are significantly reduced (by dealing with them in a flexible and declarative manner). Components are specifically designed to deal with unanticipated requests and can spontaneously generate requests for assistance if they find themselves in difficulty. Moreover because these interactions are enacted through a high-level agent communication language, coupling becomes a knowledge-level issue. At a stroke this removes syntactic concerns from the types of errors caused by unexpected interactions. Secondly, the problem of managing control relationships between the software components (a task that bedevils traditional objective-based decompositions) is significantly reduced. All agents are continuously active and any coordination or synchronisation that is required is handled bottom-up through inter-agent interaction.

From this discussion, it is apparent that the natural way to modularise a complex system is in terms of multiple autonomous components that can act and interact in flexible ways in order to achieve their set objectives. Given this, the agent-oriented approach is simply the best fit to this ideal.

The Suitability of Agent-Oriented Abstractions.

A significant part of the design process is finding the right models for viewing the problem. In general, there will be multiple candidates and the difficult task is picking the most appropriate one. When designing software, the most powerful abstractions are those that minimise the semantic gap between the units of analysis that are intuitively used to conceptualise the problem and the constructs present in the solution paradigm. In the case of complex systems, the problem to be characterised consists of sub-systems, sub-system components, interactions and organisational relationships. Taking each in turn:

- Sub-systems naturally correspond to agent organisations. They involve a number of constituent components that act and interact according to their role within the larger enterprise.
- The case for viewing sub-system components as agents has been made above.
- The interplay between the sub-systems and between their constituent components is most naturally viewed in terms of high-level social interactions: "in a complex system... at any given level of abstraction, we find meaningful collections of objects that collaborate to achieve some higher level view" [Booch 1994] pg 34. This view accords precisely with the knowledge-level treatment of interaction afforded by the agent-oriented approach. Agent systems are invariably described in terms of "cooperating to achieve common objectives", "coordinating their actions" or "negotiating to resolve conflicts".
- Complex systems involve changing webs of relationships between their various components. They also require collections of components to be treated as a single conceptual unit when viewed from a different level of abstraction. Here again the agent-oriented mindset provides suitable abstractions. A rich set of structures are available for explicitly representing organisational relationships. Interaction protocols exist for forming new groupings and disbanding unwanted ones. Finally, structures are available for modelling collectives. The latter point is especially useful in relation to representing sub-systems since they are nothing more than a team of components working together to achieve a collective goal.

Flexible Organisational Structures.
Organisational constructs are first-class entities in agent systems – explicit representations are made of organisational relationships and structures. Moreover, agent-oriented systems have the concomitant computational mechanisms for flexibly forming, maintaining and disbanding organisations. This representational power enables agent systems to exploit two facets of the nature of complex systems. Firstly, the notion of a primitive component can be varied according to the needs of the observer. Thus at one level, entire sub-systems can be viewed as singletons, alternatively teams or collections of agents can be viewed as primitive components, and so on until the system eventually bottoms out. Secondly, such structures provide the stable intermediate forms that are essential for the rapid development of complex systems. Their availability means that individual agents or organisational groupings can be developed in relative isolation and then added into the system in an incremental manner. This, in turn, ensures there is a smooth growth in functionality.

2.2. Will Agent-Oriented Techniques Be Widely Adopted?

There are two key pragmatic issues that will determine whether agent-oriented approaches catch on as a software engineering paradigm: (i) the degree to which agents represent a radical departure from current software engineering thinking and (ii) the degree to which existing software can be integrated with agents. Each point will now be dealt with in turn.

A number of trends become evident when examining the evolution of programming models. Firstly, there has been an inexorable move from languages that have their conceptual basis determined by the underlying machine architecture, to languages that have their key abstractions rooted in the problem domain. Here the agent-oriented world view is perhaps the most natural way of characterising many types of problem. Just as the real-world is populated with objects that have operations performed on them, so it is equally full of active, purposeful agents that interact to achieve their objectives[3]. Indeed, many object-oriented analyses start from precisely this perspective: "we view the world as a set of autonomous agents that collaborate to perform some higher level function" [Booch 1994] pg. 17. Secondly, the basic building blocks of the programming models exhibit increasing degrees of localisation and encapsulation [Parunak 1999]. Agents follow this trend by localising purpose inside each agent, by giving each agent its own thread of control, and by encapsulating action selection. Thirdly, ever richer mechanisms for promoting re-use are being provided. Here, the agent view also reaches new heights. Rather than stopping at re-use of sub-system components (design patterns and component-ware) and rigidly pre-ordained interactions (application frameworks), agents enable whole sub-systems and flexible interactions to be re-used. In the former case, agent designs and implementations are re-used within and between applications. Consider, for example, the class of agent architectures that have beliefs (what the agent knows), desires (what the agent wants) and intentions (what the agent is doing) at its core. Such architectures have been used in a wide variety of applications including air traffic control, process control, fault diagnosis and transportation [Jennings and Wooldridge 1998, Parunak 1999]. In the latter case, flexible patterns of interaction such as the Contract Net Protocol (an agent with a task to complete advertises this fact to others who it believes are capable of performing it, these agents may submit a bid to perform the task if they are interested, and the originator then delegates the task to the agent that makes the best bid) and various forms of resource-allocation auction (e.g. English, Dutch, First-Price Sealed Bid, Vickrey) have been re-used in significant numbers of applications. In short, agent-oriented techniques represent a natural progression of current software engineering thinking and, for this reason, the main concepts and tenets of the approach should be readily acceptable to software engineering practitioners.

The second factor in favour of a wide-spread take up of agents is that their adoption does not require a revolution in terms of an organisation's software capabilities. Agent-oriented systems are evolutionary and incremental as legacy (non-agent) software can be incorporated in a relatively straightforward manner. The technique used is to place wrapping software around the legacy code. The wrapper presents an agent interface to the other software components. Thus from the outside it looks like any other agent. On the inside, the wrapper performs a two-way translation function: taking external requests from other agents and mapping them into calls in the legacy code, and taking the legacy code's external requests and mapping them into the appropriate set of agent communication commands. This ability to wrap legacy systems means agents may initially be used as an integration technology. However, as new requirements are placed upon the system, so bespoke agents may be developed and added. This feature enables a complex system to grow in an evolutionary fashion (based on stable intermediate forms), while adhering to the important principle that there should always be a working version of the system available.

3. CASE STUDY: PROVISIONING A VIRTUAL PRIVATE NETWORK

As an exemplar of a complex software system consider the task of dynamically provisioning a public communication network (such as the Internet) as a virtual private network for end users. To be concrete, let the task in question be setting up a video-conferencing meeting [Faratin et al. 2000]. This application involves a variety of different individuals and organisations (figure 3). There are the end users that are each represented by their personal communication agent (PCA). The providers of services on the network (such as setting up a video-conference, for example) are each represented by a service provider agent (SPA). Finally, there are the agents that represent the network provider on whose telecommunications infrastructure the services will actually be delivered (each represented by a network provider agent (NPA)). In setting up a video-conference call, the various PCAs negotiate (using one of the techniques described in [Jennings et al. 2001]), on behalf of their user, with one another in order to find a suitable time for the call. When they come to an agreement, one of the PCAs then contacts, and subsequently negotiates with, the various SPAs that offer the video-conference service (not all SPAs will do this). This negotiation revolves around the cost of the conference call and the quality of service that is desired. The SPA that wins the contract then negotiates with the various NPAs to determine which of them can deliver the desired quality and bandwidth at the best price.

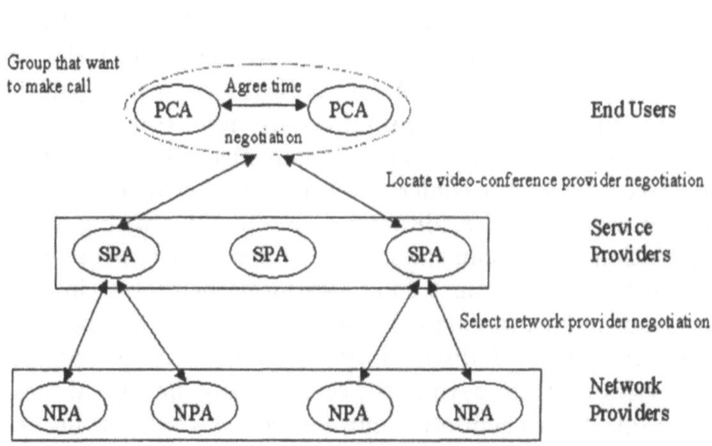

Figure 3. Dynamic Provisioning of Virtual Private Networks by End Users

This application highlights many of the benefits that are claimed above for an agent-oriented approach to software engineering. Firstly, autonomous agents are the most natural means of representing the distinct individuals and organisations that are present in the application. Each such entity is an active problem solver that has its own objectives to achieve and has control over the actions it chooses and the resources that it expends. The agents need to be responsive to changes in their environment (e.g. a NPA may need to buy in additional network capacity from another NPA in order to maintain its agreed upon quality of service if part of its network fails) and they need to be able to opportunistically adopt new goals as they present themselves (e.g. two SPAs may discover they have complementary service capabilities and may decide to act together in order to offer a new service).

Secondly, the agents need to engage in knowledge-level interactions in order to achieve their individual objectives. In this case, agents typically represent self-interested entities and so the main form of interaction is negotiation. Thus, to set the time of the video conference or to select a particular service/network provider the agents make proposals, trade offers, make concessions and, hopefully, come to agreements. This rich form of interaction is necessary because the agents represent autonomous (competitive) stake holders and also to ensure that agents can arrange their activities in a manner that is appropriate to their prevailing circumstances.

Finally, there is a very clear and explicit notion of organisational context. The application involves a number of different real-world organisations: individual end users, companies that provide the different types of services and network providers that control the underlying telecommunications infrastructure. These relationships directly affect the agents' behaviour. For example, if a SPA and a NPA are in fact part of the same organisation, then their negotiations are more cooperative in nature than if they represent two unrelated companies. Similarly, the PCAs that have agreed to hold a conference call, act as a team rather than a collection of individuals. Additionally, during the ongoing operation of the application new organisational groupings can appear and then disband. The PCAs of distinct end users form themselves into collectives when they require a particular service (e.g. all the participants of the video-conference). Individual SPAs combine their capabilities to offer new services that are beyond the scope of any individual provider. Competing NPAs form themselves into temporary coalition in order to respond to particularly large requests for network resources [4].

4. CONCLUSIONS

Agent-oriented techniques are increasingly being used in a range of telecommunication, commercial and industrial applications. However if they are to enter the mainstream of software engineering then it is vital that clear arguments are advanced as to their suitability for solving large classes of problems (as opposed to specific point solutions). To this end, this paper has sought to justify precisely why agent-oriented approaches are well suited to developing complex, distributed software systems. These general points are then made more concrete by showing how they apply in a specific telecommunications application. In making these arguments, it is possible for proponents of other software engineering paradigms to claim that the key concepts of agent-oriented computing can be reproduced using their technique. This is undoubtedly true. Agent-oriented systems are, after all, computer programs and all programs have the same set of computable functions. However, this misses the point. The value of a paradigm is the mindset and the techniques it provides to software engineers. In this respect, agent-oriented concepts and techniques are both well suited to developing complex, distributed systems and an extension of those currently available in other paradigms.

Notes

1. Booch actually uses the term "hierarchy" [Booch 1994]; however, this invariably gives the connotation of control. Hence the more neutral term "organisation" is used here.

2. The view that decompositions based upon functions/actions/processes are more intuitive and easier to produce than those based upon data/objects is even acknowledged within the object-oriented community (see [Meyer 1988] pg 44).

3. Although there are certain similarities between object- and agent- oriented approaches (e.g. both adhere to the principle of information hiding and recognise the importance of interactions), there are also a number of important differences. Firstly, objects are generally passive in nature: they need to be sent a message before they become active. Secondly, although objects encapsulate state and behaviour realisation, they do not encapsulate behaviour activation (action choice). Thus, any object can invoke any publicly accessible method on any other object. Once the method is invoked, the corresponding actions are performed. Thirdly, object-orientation fails to provide an adequate set of concepts and mechanisms for modelling complex systems: for such systems "we find that objects, classes and modules provide an essential yet insufficient means of abstraction" [Booch 1994] pg 34. Individual objects represent too fine a granularity of behaviour and method invocation is too primitive a mechanism for describing the types of interactions that take place. Recognition of these facts, led to the development of more powerful abstraction mechanisms such as design patterns, application frameworks, and component-ware. Whilst these are undoubtedly a step forward, they fall short of the desiderata for complex systems developments. By their very nature, they focus on generic system functions and the mandated patterns of interaction are rigid and pre-determined. Finally, object-oriented approaches provide only minimal support for specifying and managing organisational relationships (basically relationships are defined by static inheritance hierarchies).

4. In contrast, an object-oriented approach is less suitable for this problem because: it cannot naturally represent the autonomous problem solving behaviour of the constituent components (recall objects do not encapsulate action choice), it has nothing to say about the design of flexible problem solvers that balance reactive and proactive problem solving nor about inter-agent negotiation (other than the fact that it involves message exchanges) and it has no innate mechanism for representing and reasoning with the fact that the agents represent different stakeholder organisations (other than the fact that they are different classes).

References

G. Booch (1994). *Object-oriented analysis and design with applications.* Addison Wesley.

F.P. Brooks (1995). *The mythical man-month.* Addison Wesley.

P. Faratin, N.R. Jennings, P. Buckle, and C. Sierra (2000). *Automated negotiation for provisioning virtual private networks using FIPA-compliant agents.* Proc. 5th Int Conf. on Practical Application of Intelligent Agents and Multi-Agent Systems, Manchester, UK, 185-202.

N.R. Jennings (2000). *On Agent-Based Software Engineering* Artificial Intelligence 117(2): 277-296.

N.R. Jennings, P. Faratin, A. R. Lomuscio, S. Parsons, C. Sierra and M. Wooldridge (2001). *Automated negotiation: prospects, methods and challenges* Int. J. of Group Decision and Negotiation 10 (2) 199-215.

N.R. Jennings and M. Wooldridge (eds.) (1998). *Agent technology: foundations, applications and markets.* Springer Verlag.

A. Newell (1982). *The knowledge level.* Artificial Intelligence 18:87-127.

J. Mayfield, Y. Labrou, and T. Finin (1995). *Evaluating KQML as an agent communication language.* In M. Wooldridge, J.P. Muller and M. Tambe, eds., Intelligent Agents II, Springer, 347-360.

B. Meyer (1988). *Object-oriented software construction.* Prentice Hall.

H.V. D. Parunak (1999). *Industrial and practical applications of distributed AI.* In G. Weiss, ed., Multi-agent systems, MIT Press, 377-421.

H.A. Simon (1996). *The sciences of the artificial.* MIT Press.

M. Wooldridge (1997). *Agent-based software engineering.* IEE Proc Software Engineering 144:26-37.

M. Wooldridge and N.R. Jennings (1995). *Intelligent agents: theory and practice.* The Knowledge Engineering Review 10(2): 115-152.

ARCHITECTURES AND SOLUTIONS FOR THE KNOWLEDGE WEB

Enrico Motta
Knowledge Media Institute
The Open University
MiltonKeynes, UK
e.motta@open.ac.uk

1. ABSTRACT

In this presentation I will discuss some of the work currently being carried out at the Knowledge Media Institute (KMi) of The Open University, to support the development of 'semantic' web resources and to enable knowledge sharing and collaboration on the web. I will use the terms 'Semantic Web' and 'Knowledge Web' to refer to the basic semantic infrastructure needed to support interoperability and semantic web services (the Semantic Web), and to the knowledge-intensive services and functionalities that we are developing on top of the Semantic Web, to support knowledge sharing and collaborative work (the Knowledge Web). Work at the semantic web level includes libraries of reusable components for knowledge-intensive systems; ontology editors and servers; next-generation, ontology-based annotation tools; and site and interface ontologies to support knowledge-based generation and filtering of web pages. While the Semantic Web is about semantic infrastructure, tools and resources, the Knowledge Web is by and large about people, processes and organisations and about the integration of 'smart' technology into work-processes. Many of the examples I will present concern technologies in daily use at our lab. For instance, we have an electronic newsletter, Planet, which allows KMi members to quickly inform other KMi members and the external world about important events related to KMi. Planet addresses a basic organisational need: how can knowledge be made available quickly throughout an organisation? This knowledge publishing process is enhanced by a number of smart technologies which support semantic search of the archive, personalised views over the newsletter, and the production of intelligent newspaper layouts based on an automatic analysis of the importance of the submitted stories. News publishing is but one way to share knowledge, which accounts for one-off postings. In other cases we may want to support intensive discussions about some artefact, such as an academic paper. Our D3E toolkit provides the basic technology to associate discussion spaces with web resources. In addition, we can augment D3E-based discussion spaces with semantic web technology, to provide additional support for group discussions, such as allowing participants to access relevant resources, in response to semantic queries. Finally, I will also briefly talk about our work on the next generation of digital libraries. This aims at allowing authors and readers to augment digital libraries resources (e.g., an academic paper) with formal statements about the scholarly contribution made by each resource and the conceptual relation between resources in the library (e.g., this paper proposes a theory which builds on the work by author X, or refutes theory Y proposed by author Z, etc..).

References

Motta E. (2001). The Knowledge Modelling Paradigm in Knowledge Engineering. In S.K. Chang (editor), *Handbook of Software Engineering and Knowledge Engineering*. World Scientific Pub. Co, 2001. ISBN: 981-02-4973-X

Motta E., Buckingham-Shum, S. and Domingue, J. (2000). Ontology-Driven Document Enrichment: Principles, Tools and Applications. *International Journal of Human-Computer Studies, 52(6),* pp. 1071-1109.

Buckingham-Shum, S., Motta E. and Domingue, J. (2000). ScholOnto: An Ontology-Based Web Server for Research Documents and Discourse. *International Journal of Digital Libraries, 3 (3)*, August/Sept. 2000, Springer-Verlag

Domingue, J. B. and Motta, E. (2000). Planet-Onto: From News Publishing to Integrated Knowledge Management Support. *IEEE Intelligent Systems*, 15(3), May-June 2000, pp. 26-32.

Motta E. *Reusable Components for Knowledge Models: Principles and Case Studies in Parametric Design.* IOS Press, 1999.

Domingue, J. B. and Motta, E. (1999). A Knowledge-Based News Server Supporting Ontology-Driven Story Enrichment and Knowledge Retrieval. In Fensel and Studer (eds), *11th European Workshop on Knowledge Acquistion, Modelling, and Management (EKAW '99)*, Springer-Verlag, LNAI 1621.

Stutt, A. and Motta, E. (1998). Knowledge Modelling: An Organic Technology for the Knowledge Age. In Eisenstadt, M. and Vincent, T. (editors), *The Knowledge Web*, Kogan Press.

SEMANTIC WEB AND PEER-TO-PEER TECHNOLOGIES FOR DISTRIBUTED LEARNING REPOSITORIES

Wolfgang Nejdl
*Computer Science Department, Stanford University, nejdl@db.stanford.edu**

Abstract

Metadata for the World Wide Web is important, but metadata for Peer-to-Peer (P2P) networks is absolutely crucial. In this paper we discuss the open source project Edutella and related projects, which combine semantic web and peer-to-peer technologies in order to make distributed learning repositories possible and useful. We describe the main services of the Edutella network infrastructure and its architecture based on the exchange of RDF metadata, starting with the query service as one of the core services of Edutella. We discuss the Edutella Common Data Model (ECDM) as basis for the Edutella query exchange language (RDF-QEL-i) implementing distributed queries over the Edutella network, and discuss as one example an O-Telos-Peer with native Datalog query and inference capabilities. We then sketch a new P2P routing topology which minimizes broadcast traffic and distance between the peers in such a network, as well as a modification language needed for supporting distributed update and annotation. A short section discusses the changing role of adaptation in these distributed repositories (as open corpus hypermedia instead of the closed ones investigated in most research projects so far). Finally, we discuss an application of the Edutella network for digital libraries (OAI-P2P) and the use of Edutella in the ELENA project which aims to create smart spaces for learning.

1. Introduction

While in the server/client-based environment of the World Wide Web metadata are useful and important, for *Peer-to-Peer (P2P)* environments metadata are absolutely crucial. Information Resources in P2P networks are no longer organized in hypertext like structures, which can be navigated, but are stored on numerous peers waiting to be queried for these resources if we know what we want to retrieve and which peer is able to provide that information. Query-

* on leave from the University of Hannover, Germany

ing peers requires metadata describing the resources managed by these peers, which is easy to provide for specialized cases, but non-trivial for general applications.

P2P applications have been successful for special cases like exchanging music files. However, retrieving a song like "Material Girl from Madonna" does not need complex query languages nor complex metadata, so special purpose formats for these P2P applications have been sufficient. In other scenarios, like exchanging educational resources, queries are more complex, and have to build upon standards like IEEE-LOM/IMS [IEEE-LTSC, 2001, IMS, 2001] metadata with up to 100 metadata entries, which might even be complemented by domain specific extensions.

Furthermore, by concentrating on domain specific formats, current P2P implementations appear to be fragmenting into niche markets instead of developing unifying mechanisms for future P2P applications. There is indeed a great danger (as already discussed in [Dornfest and Brickley, 2001]), that unifying interfaces and protocols introduced by the World Wide Web get lost in the forthcoming P2P arena.

Edutella Infrastructure. The Edutella project [Edutella, 2002, Nejdl et al., 2002c, Nejdl et al., 2002b] addresses these shortcomings of current P2P applications by building on the W3C metadata standard RDF [Lassila and Swick, 1999, Brickley and Guha, 2000]. The project is a multi-staged effort to scope, specify, architect and implement an RDF-based metadata infrastructure for P2P-networks based on the recently announced JXTA framework [Gong, 2001]. The initial Edutella services will be *Query Service* (standardized query and retrieval of RDF metadata), *Replication Service* (providing data persistence / availability and workload balancing while maintaining data integrity and consistency), *Mapping Service* (translating between different metadata vocabularies to enable interoperability between different peers), *Mediation Service* (define views that join data from different metadata sources and reconcile conflicting and overlapping information) and *Annotation Service* (annotate materials stored anywhere within the Edutella Network).

The Edutella infrastructure aims to provide the metadata services needed to enable interoperability between heterogeneous JXTA applications. The main application area we discuss within this paper are P2P networks for the exchange of educational resources (using schemas like IEEE LOM, IMS, and ADL SCORM [ADL, 2001] to describe course materials), other application areas are possible as well.

As the query service is one of the core services in Edutella, upon which other services are built, we specify in Section 2 the Edutella Common Data Model (ECDM) as basis for the Edutella query exchange language and format (see [Nejdl et al., 2002c, Nejdl et al., 2002b]). Section 3 discusses as one example an O-Telos-Peer [Wolpers et al., 2002], built upon the ConceptBase system [Jarke et al., 1995], which shares with RDF(S) a very similar data model, and provides native Datalog query and inference capabilities (see also [Nejdl et al., 2001]). In section 4 we sketch a new P2P routing topology, called HyperCuP, which is described in [Schlosser et al., 2002]. The HyperCuP topology minimizes broadcast traffic and distance between the peers in such a network, allowing it to scale to large numbers of peers. Section 5 discusses annotation and modification in the Edutella network, described in [Nejdl et al., 2002c, Nejdl et al., 2002b] and [Nejdl et al., 2002a]. Section 6 discusses the changing role of adaptation in these distributed repositories (as open corpus hypermedia instead of the closed hypermedia systems investigated in most research projects so far), see also [Henze and Nejdl, 2002]. Finally, we discuss an application of the Edutella network for digital libraries (OAI-P2P) [Ahlborn, 2002] and the use of Edutella in the EU/IST project ELENA which aims to create smart spaces for learning.

2. Edutella Query Service

The Edutella Query Service is a standardized query exchange mechanism for RDF metadata stored in distributed RDF repositories and serves both as query interface for individual RDF repositories located at single Edutella peers as well as query interface for distributed queries spanning multiple RDF repositories (storing RDF statements based on arbitrary RDFS schemata).

One of the main purposes is to abstract from various possible RDF storage layer query languages (e.g., SQL) and from different user level query languages (e.g., RQL, TRIPLE): The Edutella Query Exchange Language and the Edutella Common Data Model provide the syntax and semantics for an overall standard query interface across heterogeneous peer repositories for any kind of RDF metadata. The Edutella network uses the query exchange language family RDF-QEL-i (based on Datalog semantics and subsets thereof) as standardized query exchange language format which is transmitted in an RDF/XML-format.

We will start with a simple RDF knowledge base and a simple query with the following RDF XML Serialization:

```
<lib:Book about="http://www.xyz.com/sw.html">
  <dc:title>Software Engineering</dc:title>
</lib:Book>

<lib:Book about="http://www.xyz.com/ai.html">
  <dc:title>Artificial Intelligence</dc:title>
</lib:Book>

<lib:AI-Book about="http://www.xyz.com/pl.html">
  <dc:title>Prolog</dc:title>
</lib:AI-Book>
```

Evaluating the following query (plain English)

> "Return all resources that are a book having the title 'Artificial Intelligence' or that are an AI book."

we get the query results shown in Figure 1, depicted as RDF-graph.

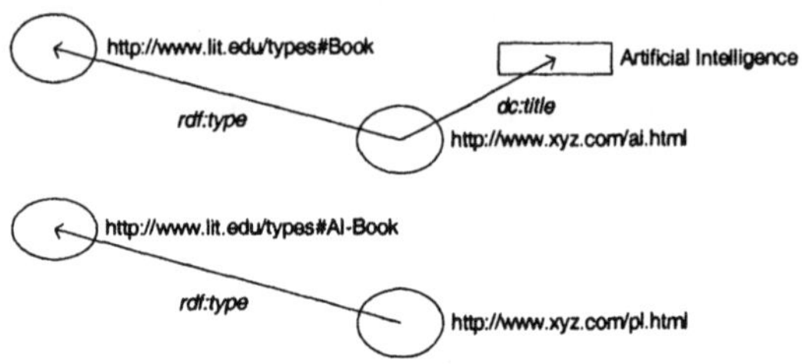

Figure 1. Query Results as RDF Graph

Edutella peers can be highly heterogeneous in terms of the functionality (i.e., services) they offer. A simple peer has RDF storage capability only. The peer has some kind of local storage for RDF triples (e.g., a relational database) as well as some kind of local query language (e.g., SQL). In addition the peer might offer more complex services such as annotation, mediation or mapping.

To enable the peer to participate in the Edutella network, Edutella wrappers are used to translate queries and results from the Edutella query and result exchange format to the local format of the peer and vice versa, and to connect the peer to the Edutella network by a JXTA-based P2P library. To handle queries, the wrapper uses the common Edutella query exchange format and data model for query and result representation. For communication with the Edutella network the wrapper translates the local data model into the Edutella Common Data Model ECDM and vice versa, and connects to the Edutella Network using the JXTA P2P primitives, transmitting the queries based on ECDM in RDF/XML form.

In order to handle different query capabilities, Edutella defines several RDF-QEL-i exchange language levels, describing which kind of queries a peer can handle (conjunctive queries, relational algebra, transitive closure, etc.) The same internal data model is used for all levels.

Edutella Common Data Model (ECDM). The ECDM is based on Datalog, which is a well-known non-procedural query language based on Horn clauses without function symbols. A Datalog program can be expressed as a set of rules/implications (where each rule consists of one positive literal in the consequent of the rule (the head), and one or more negative literals in the antecedent of the rule (the body)), a set of facts (single positive literals) and the actual query literals (a rule without head, i.e., one or more negative literals).

Literals are predicates expressions describing relations between any combination of variables and constants such as title(http://www.xyz.com/book.html, 'Artificial Intelligence'). Disjunction is expressed as a set of rules with identical head. Additionally, we can use negation as failure in the antecedent of a rule, with the semantics that such a literal cannot be proved from the knowledge base. A Datalog query then is a conjunction of query literals plus a possibly empty set of rules [Silberschatz et al., 2001].

Datalog queries easily map to relations and relational query languages like relational algebra or SQL. In terms of relational algebra Datalog is capable of expressing selection, union, join and projection and hence is a relationally complete query language. Additional features include transitive closure and other recursive definitions.

The example knowledge base in Datalog reads

```
title(http://www.xyz.com/ai.html,'Artificial
                                  Intelligence').
type(http://www.xyz.com/ai.html,Book).
title(http://www.xyz.com/sw.html,'Software
                                  Engineering').
type(http://www.xyz.com/sw.html,Book).
title(http://www.xyz.com/pl.html,'Prolog').
type(http://www.xyz.com/pl.html,AI-Book).
```

Each RDF repository can be viewed as a set of ground assertions either using binary predicates as shown above, or as ternary statements "s(S,P,O)", if we include the predicate as an additional argument. In the following examples, we use the binary surface representation.

Example Query in (binary) Datalog notation.

```
aibook(X) :- title(X, 'Artificial Intelligence'),
             type(X, Book).
aibook(X) :- type(X, AI-Book).
?- aibook(X).
```

Since our query is a disjunction of two (purely conjunctive) subqueries, its Datalog representation is composed of two rules with identical heads. The literals in the rules' bodies directly reflect RDF statements with their subjects being the variable X and their objects being bound to constant values such as 'Artificial Intelligence'. Literals used in the head of rules denote derived predicates (not necessarily binary ones). The query expression "aibook(X)" asks for all bindings of X, which conform to the given Datalog rules and our knowledge base, with the results:

```
aibook(http://www.xyz.com/ai.html)
aibook(http://www.xyz.com/pl.html)
```

Internally Edutella Peers use a Datalog based model to represent queries and their results. Figure 2 visualizes this data model as UML class diagram.

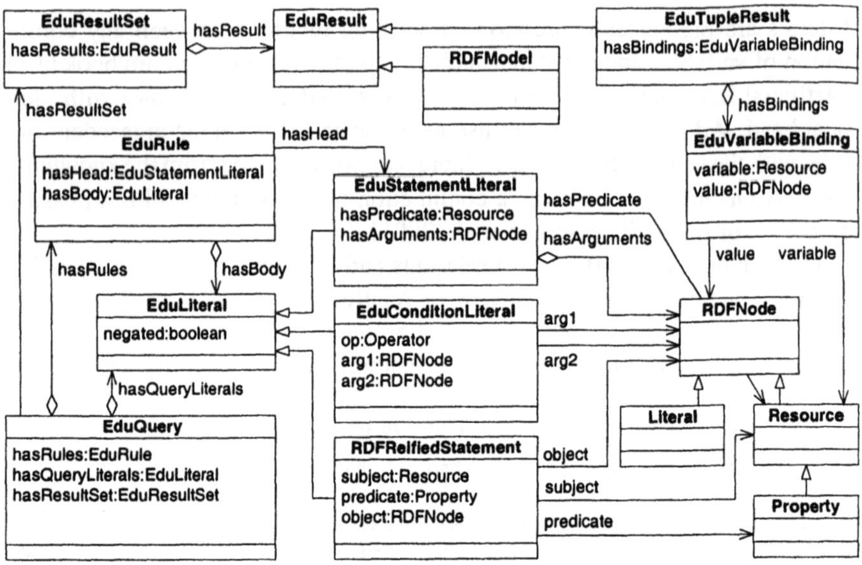

Figure 2. Edutella Common Data Model (ECDM)

The Edutella Wrapper API includes the ECDM as well as wrappers for different query languages, and is available as source code from the Edutella Project Page[1]. We are currently extending the ECDM with two important features from the TRIPLE language [Sintek and Decker, 2002], namely model IDs (to explicitly distinguish between different models/peers) and function symbols (useful to construct new IDs for models, resources and for complex values expressed as terms instead of strings).

Our current prototype environment features a set of different peers to demonstrate various aspects of the translation from ECDM to local query languages. It contains the QEL query exchange mechanism, a simple mediator and the wrapping of different repository peer types, including an OLR (Open Learning Repository) based peer [Dhraief et al., 2001] using a subset of IMS/LOM RDF metadata stored in a relational database, a DbXML-based peer [Qu and Nejdl, 2001] as a prototype for an XML repository using a simple mapping service to translate from RDF-QEL-1 queries (conjunctive queries) to Xpath queries over the appropriate XML-LOM schema, AMOS-II-based peers [Risch and Josifovski, 2001] with local repositories, KAON-based peers [Maedche et al., 2002] allowing remote annotation [Handschuh et al., 2001] using an RDF-based ontology format, and an O-Telos-Peer [Jarke et al., 1995] and [Wolpers et al., 2002], which we describe in section 3.

The environment also supports the design and integration of other tools which make use of RDF metadata. The Ont-O-Mat editor and annotation tool is described shortly in section 5 and more detailed in [Nejdl et al., 2002c], the concept browser Conzilla [Nilsson and Palmér, 1999] allows us to use a graphical query representation for QEL-1 and QEL-2.

3. Advanced Datalog Capabilities in an Edutella-O-Telos-Peer

O-Telos, ConceptBase and RDF. Once we have introduced Datalog as a query language, we can also use it for general inference purposes or to express integrity constraints on RDF data. Basic RDF is very similar to a binary relational model (if we view properties as predicates with two arguments), which is extended by RDF schema into an object oriented model (using classes and class hierarchies, instantiation of classes, as well as domains and ranges for properties). A very similar scheme has been used for the object-oriented meta modeling language O-Telos [Kramer et al., 1991] [Mylopoulos et al., 1990], as we have discussed in a previous paper [Nejdl et al., 2001] in more detail, where we have described an RDF variant called O-Telos-RDF, which extends RDF using statement IDs and explicit instantiation not only of classes but also of properties, and provides better reification capabilities and more powerful meta-modeling functionality compared to RDF(S).

The O-Telos language has been implemented in a system called ConceptBase [Jarke et al., 1995], which is a deductive object-oriented database, very useful as a repository for modeling and storing metadata (e.g. [Jeusfeld et al., 1998]). ConceptBase implements a powerful query and reasoning mechanism (rules and constraints) based on (stratified) Datalog and uses the Lloyd-Topor transformation [Lloyd and Topor, 1984] to allow arbitrary first order logic formulas in the body of rules.

Our O-Telos-Peer provides advanced query capabilities (up to RDF-QEL-5) for RDF data stored in or imported into the ConceptBase subsystem of the O-Telos-Peer. In order to store the RDF metadata in ConceptBase the peer has to translate RDF to O-Telos. We have developed a translation based on the axioms from O-Telos-RDF [Nejdl et al., 2001], which is quite straightforward and stresses the similarity of the two formalisms RDF(S) and O-Telos/O-Telos-RDF, with differences in notation and serialization (triples vs. quadruples and XML vs. frame syntax). Using this translation we can import arbitrary RDF(S) data into ConceptBase and then use the reasoning capabilities of ConceptBase for querying, inferencing, and integrity checking on RDF(S) data.

Query Classes. RDF queries are posed to the O-Telos-Peer using RDF-QEL queries as described in section 2. RDF-QEL queries are translated into O-Telos queries using the interesting feature of O-Telos Query Classes as specified in [Jarke et al., 1995]. O-Telos results are then translated to either a RDF graph result in XML serialization or the RDF triple format. In our book example we stored the RDF description of the resource with the URL `http://www.xyz.com/jv.html` and the title “Just Java”. Now suppose we want to know from the database which books have the title “Just Java”, which is depicted in RDF-QEL-1 and XML as follows:

```
<?xml version='1.0' encoding='ISO-8859-1'?>
<!DOCTYPE rdf:RDF
 [ <!ENTITY a 'http://purl.org/dc/elements/1.1/'>
   <!ENTITY rdf 'http://www.w3.org/1999/02/22-rdf-syntax-ns#'>
   <!ENTITY b 'http://www.edutella.org/edutella#'>
   <!ENTITY c 'http://www.w3.org/2000/01/rdf-schema#'>
 ]>
<rdf:RDF xmlns:a="&a;" xmlns:rdf="&rdf;" xmlns:b="&b;"
         xmlns:c="&c;" >
  <b:QEL1Query rdf:about="#genQuery">
    <b:hasVariable rdf:resource="#X"/>
    <b:hasVariable rdf:resource="#Y"/>
    <b:hasResultType rdf:resource="&b;GraphResult"/>
  </b:QEL1Query>
  <b:Variable rdf:about="X" a:title="Just Java" c:label="X">
    <a:title rdf:resource="#Y"/>
  </b:Variable>
  <b:Variable rdf:about="Y" c:label="Y"/>
</rdf:RDF>
```

The query asks for at least one resource in the database which has a property called dc:title with a value “Just Java”. The resulting resource(s) are returned as RDF graph in XML notation. The peer constructs from the RDF query representation the respective O-Telos Query Class, taking the ECDM representation of the query as input. In our example the corresponding query class defines the attributes title and namespace, the constraint varX declares that all instances of the answer set must have an attribute named title with the value “Just Java”.

```
QueryClass EduQuery isA Individual with
    retrieved_attribute
        title : String;
        namespace : String
    constraint
        varX : $ exists Y/Individual A(this,title,Y)
                      and A(this,title,"Just Java") $
end
```

The answer consists of RDF statements declaring that there is a resource with URL `http://www.xyz.com/jv.html`. This resource is the domain of a property named title which has the range “Just Java”. The title property is defined in the Dublin Core namespace.

```
jv_html in EduQuery with
    title
        titl : "Just Java"
    namespace
        naml : "http://www.xyz.com/"
end
```

4. HyperCuP Peer-to-Peer Routing

Obviously, routing in P2P networks is crucial for scaling up the network. Most P2P networks evolve in an unorganized manner, and are prone to suffer from serious scalability problems, limiting the number of nodes in the network, creating network overload and pushing search times to unacceptable limits. In [Schlosser et al., 2002] we describe the HyperCuP topology for P2P networks, which organizes the peers into a deterministic graph topology featuring symmetry (i.e. every node can equally originate searches and broadcasts), low network diameter, a limited node degree (of logarithmic order to the amount of peers in the network) and load balancing of traffic in the network.

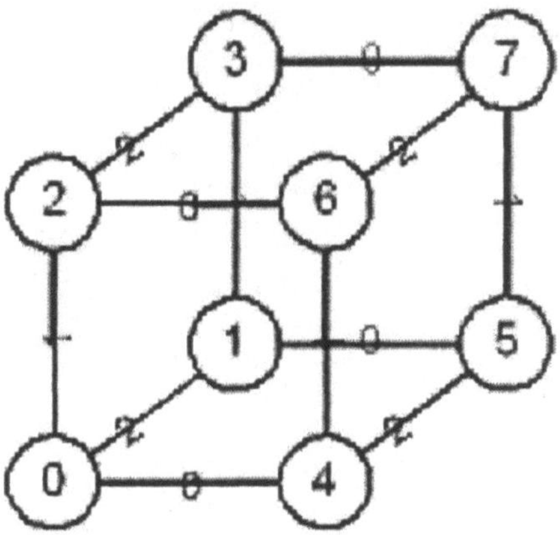

Figure 3. A Hypercube with Dimension 3

We arrive at this by constructing a hypercube with all available peers, as shown in figure 3. To construct a hypercube of base 2 and dimension d, for each dimension the set of nodes is split into two partitions 0 and 1, which are defined by the d-th digit (0 or 1) in the binary encoding of the node number (from 0 to 2^d-1), giving d partitions/dimensions for the hypercube and thus d neighbors for each node. Broadcasting on this topology guarantees that each node receives messages exactly once, featuring a network diameter logarithmic to the amount of nodes. Searching, i.e. broadcast along only a limited number of nodes, is efficient for the same reasons. [Schlosser et al., 2002] also provides a construction and maintenance algorithm which permits nodes to join and leave the network arbitrarily (also for number of nodes not equal to 2^d), with a low message overhead (logarithmic to the amount of nodes in the network), and not requiring any central servers or supernodes.

5. Edutella Annotation and Modification

Annotation Service. In order to easily provide metadata for a particular document, the Edutella annotation service provides a document viewer and a browser for RDF schemata. Using the browser, a corresponding definition, e.g. Dublin Core, is loaded into the annotation tool to be browsed. Fields for annotation are displayed according to the schema definition and may either be filled by typing or by marking and dragging information from the document viewer. The Edutella annotation service is composed of the Edutella peer libraries and the KAON tool-suite[2] [Maedche et al., 2002] incorporating the Ont-O-Mat Plugin Framework[3] and Annotation application [Handschuh et al., 2001] (cf. Figure 4).

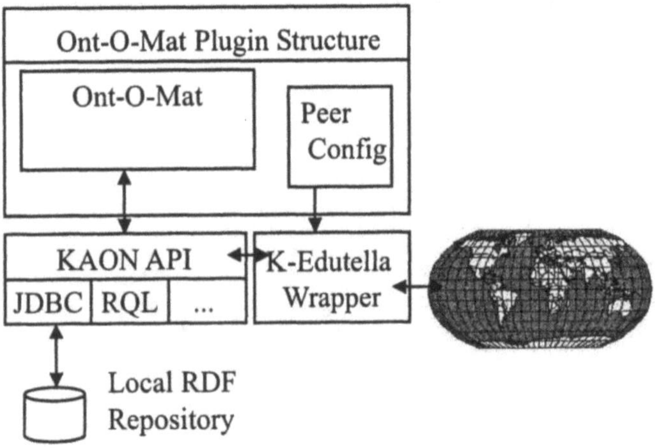

Figure 4. Ont-O-Mat as Edutella Peer

KAON is a Semantic Web tool suite originally created in isolation of Edutella. The Ont-O-Mat Framework is part of this tool suite and provides a java-based plugin structure which allows for loading services dynamically. One such service is the annotation tool Ont-O-Mat which uses the KAON API to query for RDF schema definitions in order to build up its ontology browser. It queries for instances, attributes and relationships in order to let its users explore the current state of the knowledge base.

The Edutella Wrapper for KAON (K-Edutella Wrapper) is again a KAON plugin. The task of the K-Edutella Wrapper is to wrap the KAON-API for QEL and vice versa. The K-Edutella Wrapper calls JXTA lower levels for services like registration, pipes, etc. in order to connect to the Edutella network. Using Ont-O-Mat, a user can directly connect the Edutella network in order to query metadata from other peers or provide metadata from his repository.

Modification and Update Language. For this annotation service and also for additional replication functionality between distributed peers, we need a standardized mechanism to communicate metadata changes. In [Nejdl et al., 2002a] we present a basic language designed for communicating metadata changes between distributed RDF repositories, designed for use cases such as the one depicted in figure 5.

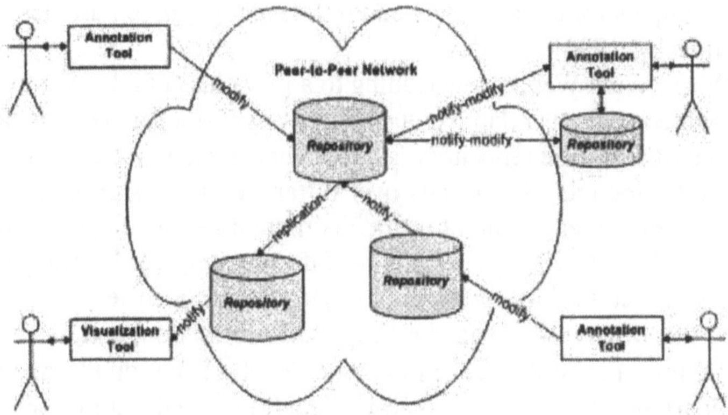

Figure 5. Annotation / Replication Use Case

Our proposal specifies a modification exchange language with subgraph-centered granularity (in contrast to statement- or resource-centered requests), where an RDF query language can deliver the query result as a subgraph of the repository. Therefore we can design modification commands as a combination of a query to specify the affected statements and a specification of the changes to these statements. In this context, an update consists of a query specifying the changed statement(s) and the description of the new statement(s). The repository can then change the selected statements accordingly. This approach can also handle variables in the modification specifications, supports change patterns , enables replacing the object part of a statement without knowing its actual value, and integrates nicely with our query exchange language QEL, which is used to specify the subgraph selection. The language uses modification messages as atomic transaction unit, which may contain multiple commands. The repository can process such a message in one chunk, thereby allowing a stateless modification/update protocol.

6. Adaptation in Open Corpus Hypermedia

Another important topic for learning materials is personalization to different users. Adaptive hypermedia systems have a longer tradition than the World Wide Web, and have been based on general hypermedia systems, which can be described as a set of nodes (containing multiple forms of media such as text, video, audio, graphics, etc.) connected by links [Rada, 1995]). Adaptive hypermedia systems generally include two forms of adaptation: content level and link level adaptation. Using content level adaptation, the document's content is tailored to the needs of a specific user, for example by hiding specialized information or by inserting additional explanations. Using link level adaptation, the user's possibilities to navigate the hypermedia documents are personalized. Techniques for content level and link level adaptation are described e.g. in [Brusilovsky, 1996].

The World Wide Web is now leading to a new class of adaptive hypermedia systems which we call "adaptive open corpus hypermedia" [Henze and Nejdl, 2002]. The hypermedia repository is no longer a closed system managing only local data, but potentially extends over different sites, using metadata to describe the structure and content of the distributed resources (see also [Henze, 2000, Dhraief et al., 2001]). This is useful especially for learning resources, as authors can add arbitrary learning objects to an open learning repository. However, this often leads to an oversupply of information, and link level adaptation becomes a central issue. For content level adaptation the metadata of a specific learning object must deliver information to redesign the presentation of the learning object itself.

Standardization. Even though personalization is treated in several standardization working groups, metadata standardization efforts for user-oriented data are still in early stages, compared to standardization efforts for learning object metadata (LOM) and course structure metadata (IMS CP) incorporated in the current SCORM 1.2 standard. Interesting in this context is the IEEE LTSC Learner Model Working group P1484.2, which works on standards for exchanging learner profiles, covering the information dimensions "personal, "relations", "security", "preference", "performance" and "portfolio". Important extensions to the current status of these metadata proposals are in the area of learning processes of individual users or learning styles, which are crucial parts of a learner model and will probably play a role for the development of a standard for course sequencing (IEEE P1484.6 Course Sequencing, no proposed standard so far).

Knowledge Models. User knowledge is the main source of information for adaptation in educational hypermedia. Based on the user's actual knowledge state, information is selected, examples are proposed, reading sequences are generated and appropriate learning steps are presented to the user.

A knowledge model for OAHS has to be *universally valid* (throughout the different corpora of the learning repository), *expandable* (learning objects on new topics may be added to one of the corpora) and *expressive* (the knowledge contained in one single corpus must be describable as a valid model on its own). Ontologies as formal explicit specifications of shared conceptualizations [Gruber, 1993] meet these requirements and can therefore be used within a knowledge model to describe the domain to be learned by the student. Concepts in the knowledge model then define a *controlled vocabulary* for describing the knowledge of the application domain and can be used for metadata annotation of the learning objects (LOM category General, data element 1.6 Keywords). The learning objects themselves are described and identified by a set of keywords describing their content.

Adaptive Functionality as Queries. Furthermore, once the metadata in an OAHS describe distributed learning resources and are represented in RDF, most adaptive functionalities in an OAHS can be represented as RDF-QEL queries, which can be distributed through the Edutella P2P network.

7. OAI-P2P: P2P Solutions for Digital Libraries

In the digital library community, the Open Archive Initiative (OAI) has defined a metadata harvesting protocol (OAI-PMH) to achieve interoperability among distributed archives, based on HTTP and XML as well as the Dublin Core metadata scheme [Lagoze and de Sompel, 2001]. To keep the instruction set simple, OAI-PMH calls for a separation between data and service providers. Data providers establish an OAI-PMH-based interface to local digital resources, while service providers (like ARC [Liu et al., 2001] and SCIRIUS[4] provide facilities for searching across multiple archives plus value-added features like ranking and unified access to other sources.

This separation exposes the simplicity of the protocol as the source of its' strength (low barrier to adoption) and its' weakness. OAI-PMH is designed as simple as possible for data providers at the expense of service providers, creating and maintaining an OAI-PMH service provider requires much more resources than setting up a data provider. On the other hand, OAI-PMH offers no front-end services. Data providers offer an interface for metadata harvesting to outsiders but do not have any immediate advantages (like a query service for outside repositories) from their efforts, unless a service provider provides an interface to their data.

OAI-P2P. In essence, the OAI-PMH defines client-server-relationships, with the data provider and the service provider responding to client requests.

However, digital libraries in most cases act both as a client and as a server, at the same time trying to obtain outside material for inside users and offering inside resources to outside users. Similar initial situations have spawned the emergence of services like Napster and Gnutella, which offer resource sharing by means of peer-to-peer structures. [Ahlborn, 2002] describes an organizational and technical framework which merges the OAI-PMH concept with a true peer-to-peer approach (OAI-P2P). It thus takes the OAI-PMH one step further by extending query services to data providers and by avoiding the dependencies of centralized server-based systems.

In an OAI-P2P system, there is no separation between service provider and data provider (each peer maintains separate subsystems for data storage and query handling). Each query is routed to appropriate peers by the network, no administration is necessary to introduce new peers. Of course such a network still benefits from additional service providers which replicate metadata, thereby enhancing the reliability and performance of the net. However, although performance may suffer if such a peer is discontinued, overall communication and services will stay alive even if a single node dies.

Individual digital libraries may want to decide which other repositories they share their data with and which repositories they want to access. In the OAI framework, choosing the scope of the community is the prerogative of the service provider, who may arbitrarily decide which data providers to include. Using the OAI-P2P approach peers can devise community specific access policies using the peer group concept.

Queries. Merging data provider and service provider functionality means that an OAI-based peer-to-peer digital library network has to address issues outside the OAI-PMH scope. OAI-PMH does not state how data providers should set up source metadata. Although very small archives can use flat files to store XML-metadata, most institutional data providers use a dedicated relational database from which OAI output is created. On the other hand, current OAI service providers replicate the metadata they have harvested in relational databases to provide for clients' queries. In order to give service provider functionality to each data provider in a P2P context, repositories must be able to pose, process and accept advanced queries, an ability which they used already to build an OAI-compliant infrastructure in the first place. Using Edutella's support for a range of query exchange languages (RDF-QEL-i), OAI-P2P is able to adapt to heterogeneous peers as well as changing demand on metadata scope and query complexity.

8. ELENA: Smart Spaces for Learning

Which steps are coming next? We are currently starting up the EU/IST funded research project ELENA (under the general topic "ambient intelligence"), aimed at creating a smart space for learning. Smart learning spaces in this context are defined as educational service mediators, which allow the consumption of heterogeneous learning services via assessment tools, learning management systems, educational (meta) repositories and live delivery systems such as video conferencing systems or interactive TV (see figure 6). Central design element of the ELENA smart learning space is a dynamic learner profile, which includes learning history, learner specific information and learning goals. Interconnecting learning services in a smart learning space leads to an empowerment of learners since they become capable of choosing among a variety of knowledge sources in order to achieve their personal learning goals.

Figure 6. ELENA Architecture

Acknowledgments. This paper discusses and sketches the Edutella infrastructure and necessary technologies for this network in more detail as well as two application areas (digital libraries and smart learning spaces), developed in several projects. As an overview paper, it contains a lot of material from other, more detailed, papers, which are referenced and included in the bibliography. The author gratefully acknowledges the numerous and invaluable contributions of his co-workers, which appear as co-authors on these papers, and the many discussions we have had on these issues.

Specifically, I want to thank Rudi Studer, Steffen Staab, Julien Tane and Raphael Volz from AIFB/Karlsruhe and L3S, Wolf Siberski, Martin Wolpers, Changtao Qu, Nicola Henze, Boris Wolf, Ingo Brunkhorst and Hadhami Dhraief from KBS/Hannover and L3S, Benjamin Ahlborn, TIB Hannover, Manfred Jeusfeld from Tilburg, Stefan Decker from Stanford, Michael Sintek (Stanford and DFKI), Mario Schlosser (Hannover and Stanford), Ambjörn Naeve, Mikael Nilsson and Matthias Palmér from CID/Stockholm, Tore Risch from Uppsala and Gustav Neumann and Bernd Simon from Vienna.

References

[ADL, 2001] ADL, T. T. (2001). SCORM Specification v1.2. http://www.adlnet.org/Scorm/scorm.cfm.

[Ahlborn, 2002] Ahlborn, B. (2002). Oai-p2p: A peer-to-peer network for open archives. Technical report, University of Hannover. submitted for publication.

[Brickley and Guha, 2000] Brickley, D. and Guha, R. V. (2000). W3C Resource Description Framework (RDF) Schema Specification. http://www.w3.org/TR/1998/WD-rdf-schema/. W3C Candidate Recommendation.

[Brusilovsky, 1996] Brusilovsky, P. (1996). Methods and techniques of adaptive hypermedia. *User Modeling and User Adapted Interaction*, 6(2-3):87–129.

[Dhraief et al., 2001] Dhraief, H., Nejdl, W., Wolf, B., and Wolpers, M. (2001). Open learning repositories and metadata modeling. In *International Semantic Web Working Symposium (SWWS)*, Stanford, CA.

[Dornfest and Brickley, 2001] Dornfest, R. and Brickley, D. (2001). The power of metadata. http://www.openp2p.com/pub/a/p2p/2001/01/18/metadata.html. excerpted from the book "Peer-to-Peer: Harnessing the Power of Disruptive Technologies.

[Edutella, 2002] Edutella (2002). The Edutella Project. http://edutella.jxta.org/.

[Gong, 2001] Gong, L. (2001). Project JXTA: A technology overview. Technical report, SUN Microsystems. http://www.jxta.org/project/www/docs/TechOverview.pdf.

[Gruber, 1993] Gruber, T. R. (1993). A translation approach to portable ontology specifications. *Knowledge Acquisition*, 5:199–220.

[Handschuh et al., 2001] Handschuh, S., Staab, S., and Maedche, A. (2001). CREAM - creating relational metadata with a component-based, ontology-driven annotation framework. In *Workshop on Knowledge Markup and Semantic Annotation at the First International Conference on Knowledge Capture (K-CAP'2001)*, Victoria, BC, Canada.

[Henze, 2000] Henze, N. (2000). *Adaptive Hyperbooks: Adpatation for Project-Based Learning Resources*. PhD thesis, University of Hannover.

[Henze and Nejdl, 2002] Henze, N. and Nejdl, W. (2002). Knowledge modeling for open adaptive hypermedia. In *Proceedings of the 2nd International Conference on Adaptive Hypermedia and Adaptive Web Based Systems*, Malaga, Spain.

[IEEE-LTSC, 2001] IEEE-LTSC (2001). IEEE LOM Working Draft 6.1. http://ltsc.ieee.org/wg12/index.html.

[IMS, 2001] IMS (2001). IMS Learning Resource Metadata Specification v1.2.1. http://www.imsproject.org/metadata/index.html.

[Jarke et al., 1995] Jarke, M., Gallersdörfer, R., Jeusfeld, M., Staudt, M., and Eherer, S. (1995). ConceptBase - a deductive object base for meta data management. *Journal on Intelligent Information Systems*, 4(2):167 – 192.

[Jeusfeld et al., 1998] Jeusfeld, M. A., Jarke, M., Nissen, H. W., and Staudt, M. (1998). ConceptBase - Managing Conceptual Models about Information Systems. In Bernus, P., Mertins,

K., and Schmidt, G., editors, *Handbook on Architectures of Informations Systems*. Springer Verlag.

[Kramer et al., 1991] Kramer, B. M., Chandhri, V. K., Koubarakis, M., Topaloglon, T., Wang, H., and Mylopoulos, J. (1991). Implementing Telos. *SIGART Bulletin*, 2(3).

[Lagoze and de Sompel, 2001] Lagoze, C. and de Sompel, H. V. (2001). The open archives initiative: Building a low-barrier interoperability framework. In *Proceedings of the ACM/IEEE Joint Conference on Digital Libraries*.

[Lassila and Swick, 1999] Lassila, O. and Swick, R. R. (1999). W3C Resource Description framework (RDF) Model and Syntax Specification. http://www.w3.org/TR/REC-rdf-syntax/. W3C Recommendation.

[Liu et al., 2001] Liu, X., Maly, K., Zubair, M., and Nelson, M. L. (2001). Arc: an oai service provider for cross-archive searching. In *Proceedings of the ACM/IEEE Joint Conference on Digital Libraries*.

[Lloyd and Topor, 1984] Lloyd, J. W. and Topor, R. W. (1984). Making prolog more expressive. *Journal of Logic Programming*, 3:225–240.

[Maedche et al., 2002] Maedche, A., Staab, S., Studer, R., Sure, Y., and Volz, R. (2002). Seal — Tying up information integration and Web site management by ontologies. *IEEE Data Engineering Bulletin*. http://www.research.microsoft.com/research/db/debull/.

[Mylopoulos et al., 1990] Mylopoulos, J., Borgida, A., Jarke, M., and Koubarakis, M. (1990). Telos: A language for representing knowledge about information systems. *ACM Transactions on Information Systems*, 8(4).

[Nejdl et al., 2001] Nejdl, W., Dhraief, H., and Wolpers, M. (2001). O-Telos-RDF: A resource description format with enhanced meta-modeling functionalities based on O-Telos. In *Workshop on Knowledge Markup and Semantic Annotation at the First International Conference on Knowledge Capture (K-CAP'2001)*, Victoria, BC, Canada.

[Nejdl et al., 2002a] Nejdl, W., Siberski, W., Simon, B., and Tane, J. (2002a). Towards a modification exchange language for distributed rdf repositories. In *Proceedings of the 1st International Semantic Web Conference*. Springer LNCS.

[Nejdl et al., 2002b] Nejdl, W., Wolf, B., Qu, C., Decker, S., Sintek, M., Naeve, A., Nilsson, M., Palmér, M., and Risch, T. (2002b). EDUTELLA: a P2P Networking Infrastructure based on RDF. In *Proceedings of the 11th International World Wide Web Conference*, Hawaii, USA. http://edutella.jxta.org/reports/edutella-whitepaper.pdf.

[Nejdl et al., 2002c] Nejdl, W., Wolf, B., Staab, S., and Tane, J. (2002c). Edutella: Searching and annotating resources within an rdf-based p2p network. In *Proceedings of the Semantic Web Workshop, 11th International World Wide Web Conference*, Honolulu, Hawaii, USA.

[Nilsson and Palmér, 1999] Nilsson, M. and Palmér, M. (1999). Conzilla - towards a concept browser. Technical Report CID-53, TRITA-NA-D9911, Department of Numerical Analysis and Computing Science, KTH, Stockholm. http://kmr.nada.kth.se/papers/ConceptualBrowsing/cid_53.pdf.

[Qu and Nejdl, 2001] Qu, C. and Nejdl, W. (2001). Towards interoperability and reusability of learning resources: A SCORM-conformant courseware for computer science education.

Technical report, Learning Lab Lower Saxony, University of Hannover. submitted for publication.

[Rada, 1995] Rada, R. (1995). *Interactive Media*. Springer.

[Risch and Josifovski, 2001] Risch, T. and Josifovski, V. (2001). Distributed data integration by object-oriented mediator servers. *Concurrency and Computation: Practice and Experience*, 13(11):933 – 953.

[Schlosser et al., 2002] Schlosser, M., Sintek, M., Decker, S., and Nejdl, W. (2002). HyperCuP – shaping up peer-to-peer networks. submitted for publication.

[Silberschatz et al., 2001] Silberschatz, A., Korth, H. F., and Sudarshan, S. (2001). *Database Systems Concepts*. McGraw-Hill Higher Education, 4 edition.

[Sintek and Decker, 2002] Sintek, M. and Decker, S. (2002). TRIPLE—An query, inference, and transformation language for the semantic web. In *Proceedings of the 1st International Semantic Web Conference*. Springer LNCS.

[Wolpers et al., 2002] Wolpers, M., Nejdl, W., and Brunkhorst, I. (2002). O-Telos provider peers in RDF-based P2P environments. Technical report, University of Hannover. submitted for publication.

MANAGING MULTIPLE ONTOLOGIES AND ONTOLOGY EVOLUTION IN ONTOLOGGING

A. Maedche, B. Motik, L. Stojanovic, R. Studer, R. Volz

FZI Research Center for Information Technologies at the Univ.of Karlsruhe,Germany
email: {maedche, motik, stojanov, studer, volz}@fzi.edu

Abstract: Ontologging is an ontology-driven environment to enable next generation knowledge management applications building on Semantic Web technology. In this paper we first present the conceptual architecture underlying Ontologging. Second, we focus on two important challenges for ontology-based knowledge management, namely the supporting multiple ontologies and managing ontology evolution. We will provide a general approach for handling these two essential issues within the Ontologging architecture.

Key words: Knowledge management, ontology mapping, ontology evolution.

3. INTRODUCTION

"People can't share knowledge if they do not speak a common language" [6]. This simple insight accurately characterizes what makes knowledge management a challenging task. Its goal to reach global knowledge access within different departments of an enterprise is usually difficult due to the fact that different departments usually encompass different vocabularies, which hinders commu-nication. Consider the case of a large company consisting of different departments, e.g. Human Resources, Production, Sales, etc. Under optimal circumstances we can assume that the first problem of collecting, organizing, and distributing the knowledge within one department has been solved. Ontologies have shown to be the right answer to these structuring and modelling problems by providing a basis for the definition of meaning. They can be used to provide the conceptual basis for communication among humans and machines [2].

However, we have been confronted with several problems when using ontologies in real-world applications. In this paper we consider the following two important problems: First, the traditional approach to design one large-scale ontology, which covers all departments, has shown to be difficult due to effort, scale and maintainability. To facilitate communication between multiple communities one approach is to rely on multiple ontologies, where individual ontologies are defined, e.g. for each department, and mappings between ontologies establish the linkage between the individual domains. Second, knowledge management systems typically operate in changeable environments. Business dynamics result in several necessary changes within the applications. Consequently, the underlying ontology changes and evolves over time [2]. Clearly, the ontological changes have to be propagated to the depending artefacts in order to keep an overall consistency. This question of managing the necessary evolution of ontologies has not yet sufficiently been approached in literature and practice.

In this paper we introduce a novel approach that tackles these difficulties by allowing the management of multiple ontologies and introducing means for ontology evolution. Ontologging, an ontology-based environment targets beside other research questions these two core problems introduced above. It builds on Semantic Web standards to enable the next generation of knowledge management applications. Based on a short introduction of the comprehensive Ontologging architecture we will present an approach for handling the two essential issues of managing multiple ontologies and supporting ontology evolution.

4. ARCHITECTURE

To enable the described enhanced of existing ontology-based knowledge management approaches a comprehensive architecture is required. We pursue a clearly separated three layered architecture within our Ontologging system. On the top layer, the presentation layer, relevant information is accessed, browsed, queried and edited. We distinguish between the two different users, namely the knowledge manager and the normal end user. In this paper we mainly focus on the knowledge manager and the corresponding methods and tools supporting him in his work with respect to dealing with multiple ontologies and managing ontology evolution. Normal end users access the system via different clients, e.g. a MS Office-based connector and a Web-based browsing and querying interface.

Presentation clients access the different the systems backend via an integrated SOAP-based Web service interface[1] hiding the complexity of the

[1] http://www.w3.org/2002/ws/

different APIs to application programmers. There exist dedicated interfaces for multiple ontology and metadata management, user management and documents management. Additionally, services in the middleware layer provide value adding functionality on top of the core data, e.g. we provide intelligent services for user personalization and different kinds of agents. Finally, on the lowest layer, the data layer, data relevant for the overall system is stored. There, we mainly rely on relational database technology.

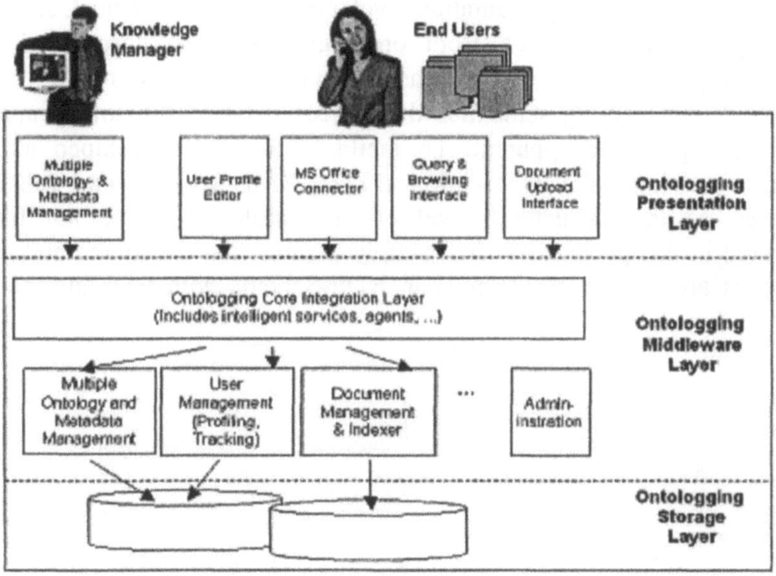

Figure 1. Overall Ontologging Architecture

In the following we will mainly focus on the multiple ontology and metadata management parts within Ontologging. First, we will discuss the underlying modules enabling multiple ontologies. Second, we will discuss the internal support and strategies we provide for the overall ontology evolution process. It is important to mention that both methods and components are driven by meta-ontologies, a so-called semantic bridging and an evolution ontology that capture the relevant information to support multiple ontologies and evolving ontologies.

5. MULTIPLE ONTOLOGIES

An ontology mapping process is the set of activities required to transform instances of a source ontology into instances of a target ontology. By studying the process and analysing different approaches from the literature

[9] we observed a set of commonalities and assembled them into the our MAFRA mapping conceptual framework, outlined in Figure 2. The framework consists of five horizontal modules describing the phases that we consider fundamental and distinct in a mapping process. Four vertical components run along the entire mapping process, interacting with horizontal modules.

Within the horizontal dimension, we identified following five modules:

Lift & Normalization. This module focuses on raising all data to be mapped onto the same representation level, coping with syntactical, structural and language heterogeneity. Both ontologies must be normalized to a uniform representation, in our case RDF(S), thus eliminating syntax differences and making semantics differences between the source and the target ontology more apparent. To facilitate that, we developed a LIFT approach providing means to bring DTDs, XML-Schema, and relational databases[2] to the structural level of the ontology. Lift is not further elaborated in this paper - we shall simply assume that the source and target ontologies are already represented in RDF-Schema with their instances in RDF.

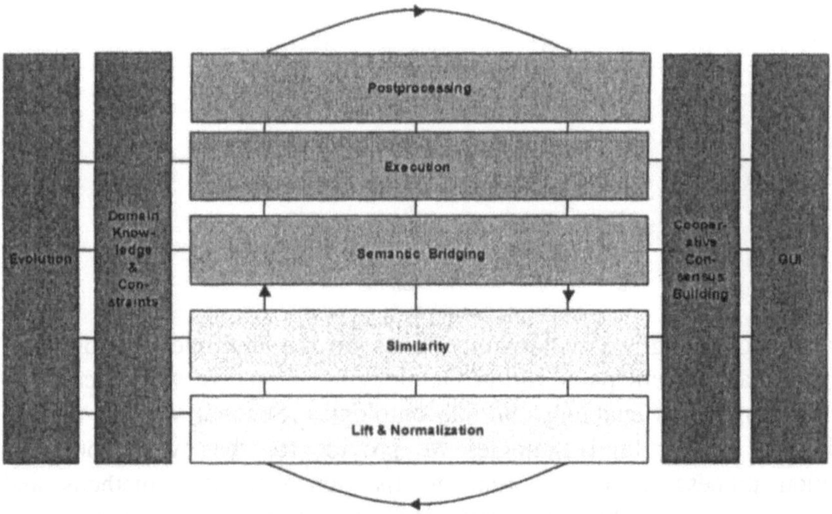

Figure 2. Conceptual Mapping Architecture

Similarity. This module establishes similarities between entities from the source and target ontology. Similarity between conceptual models is hard to measure and often establishing a suitable similarity measure is a very subjective task. Several different similarity measures have been proposed in

[2] http:// kaon.semanticweb.org/REVERSE

literature [1, 9, 11] focusing on different aspects of ontology entities. We don't further elaborate on this issue, as it is not in scope of this paper.

Semantic Bridging. Based on the similarities computed in the previously described phase, the semantic bridging module is responsible for establishing correspondence between entities from the source and target ontology. Technically, this is accomplished by establishing semantic bridges[3] - entities reflecting correspondence between two ontology entities [8]. Apart from the semantic correspondence, additional "procedural" information is needed to further specify the transformation to be performed, e.g. translation of measures like currencies.

Execution. This module actually transforms instances from the source ontology into target ontology by evaluating the semantic bridges defined earlier. In general two distinct modes of operation are possible, namely offline (static, one-time transformation) and online (dynamic, continuous mapping between source and the target) execution.

Post-processing. The post-processing module takes the results of the execution module to check and improve the quality of the transformation results. The most challenging task of post-processing is establishing object identity - recognizing that two instances represent the same real-world object. Furthermore, by computing statistical properties of transformed instances, it is possible to check whether semantic bridges were under specified.

The vertical dimension of MAFRA contains modules that interact with horizontal modules during the overall process. Following four modules have been identified and will be only shortly mentioned in this paper:

Evolution. This modules focuses on keeping semantic bridges obtained by the "Semantic Bridge" module, which must be kept in synchrony with the changes in the source and target ontologies. Evolving ontologies on the Semantic Web result in an update requirement of the corresponding semantic bridges. Although this may be achieved by reapplying the mapping process, this is probably not the most efficient or accurate way. Thus, the mapping process must have an evolution component that will reuse the existing semantic bridges in adapting them to new requirements.

Cooperative Consensus Building. The cooperative Consensus Building module is responsible for establishing a consensus on semantic bridges between two communities participating in the mapping process. This is a requirement as one has to choose frequently from multiple, alternatively possible mappings .The amount of human involvement required to achieve consensus may be reduced by automating the mapping process as much as possible.

[3] http://www.fzi.de/wim/staff/Nuno/bridges

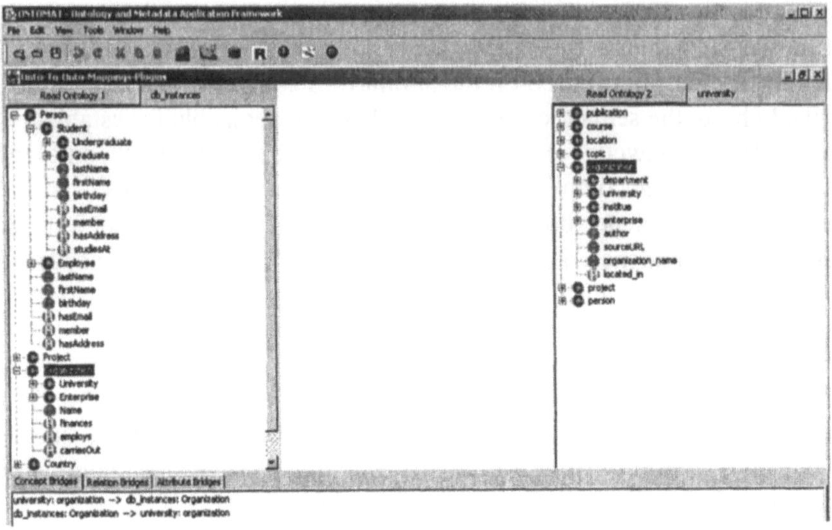

Figure 3. Interface for instantiating the semantic bridging ontology

Graphical User Interface. Mapping is a difficult and time consuming process, which is not less difficult than building an ontology itself, i.e. deep understanding of both conceptualisations required on human side, thus extensive graphical support must be given and it is a separate issue how this can be achieved in an optimal way. The graphical user interfaces modules (Figure 3) allows the users drive the mapping process, provide domain constraint and background knowledge, create semantic bridges, refine bridges according to the results of the execution module, etc.

6. EVOLVING ONTOLOGIES

Ontology evolution (OE) is the timely adaptation of an ontology to changed business requirements, to trends in ontology instances and patterns of usage of the ontology-based applications, as well as the consistent management/propagation of these changes to dependent elements. A modification in one part of the ontology may generate subtle inconsistencies in other parts of the same ontology, in the ontology-based instances as well as in depending ontologies and applications [5]. This variety of causes and consequences of the ontology changes makes OE a very complex operation that should be considered as both, an organizational and a technical process [12]. It requires a careful analysis of the types of the ontology changes that can trigger evolution as well as the environment in which the whole OE process is realized.

The overall OE process is presented in Figure 4. It has a cyclic structure, since validation of realized changes may induce new changes in order to obtain model consistency or to satisfy users' expectations. In the following we will shortly elaborate on each of the phases.

Change Representation. To resolve changes, they have to be identified and represented in a suitable format. Elementary changes in the ontology shown in Table 1 are derived from our ontology definition [6] given in specifying fine-grained changes that can be performed in the course of OE. However, this granularity of OE changes is not always appropriate. Often, intent of the changes may be expressed on a higher level. For example, the may need to generate a common superconcept of two concepts. He may bring the ontology into desired state through successive application of a list of elementary evolution changes. However, there is an impedance mismatch between the intent of the request and the way the intent is achieved. Moreover, a lot of unnecessary changes may be performed if each change is applied alone. To avoid these drawbacks, it should be possible to express changes on a more coarse level, with the intent of change directly visible. We introduce the composite changes (e.g. Merge_concepts, Extract_subconcepts, Extract_related_concept) representing a group of elementary changes applied together.

Semantics of Change. Application of an elementary change in the ontology can induce inconsistencies in other parts of the ontology. We distinguish syntax and semantic inconsistency. Syntax inconsistency arises when undefined entities at the ontology or instance level are used or ontology model constraints are invalidated. Semantic inconsistency arises when meaning of an ontology entity is changed [16]. For example, removal of a concept which is the only element of domain set for some property results in syntax inconsistency [4]. Resolving that problem is treated as a request for a new change in the ontology, which can induce new problems that cause new changes and so on. If an ontology is large, it may be difficult to fully comprehend the extent and meaning of each induced change. The task of 'semantics of change' phase is to enable resolution of induced changes in a systematic manner, ensuring consistency of the whole ontology. To help in better understanding of effects of each change, this phase should contribute maximum transparency providing detailed insight into each change being performed.

However, for each change in the ontology, it is possible to generate different sets of additional changes, leading to different final consistent states. Most of existing systems for the ontology development provide only one possibility for realizing a change and this is usually the simplest one. For example, the deletion of a concept always causes the deletion of all its subconcepts.

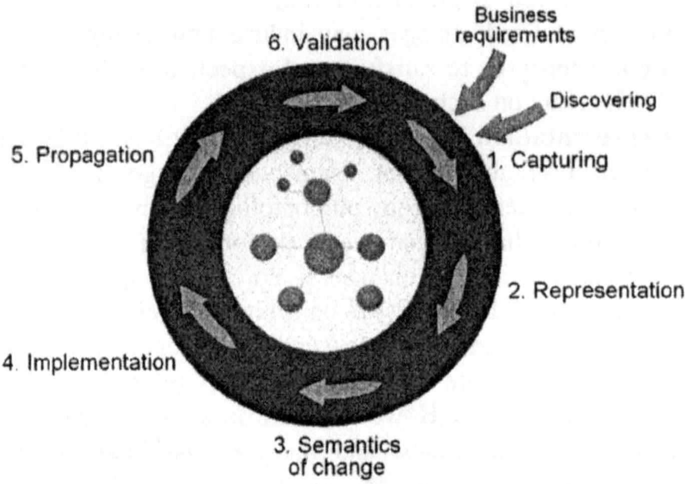

Figure 4. Cycle Ontology Evolution Process

Table 1. Elementary changes in the ontology and associated metadata

Change	Elementary change
Add	Add_Concept; Add_SubConceptOf Add_Property; Add_SubPropertyOf; Add_Domain; Add_Axiom; Add_InstanceOf; Add_PropertyInstanceOf
Delete	Delete_Concepl; Delete_SubConceptOf; Delete_Property; Delete_SubPropertyOf; Delete_Domain; Delete_Axiom; Delete_InstanceOf; Delete_PropertyInstanceOf
Modify	Set_Property_Range

Thus, to resolve a change, the evolution process needs to determine answers at many *resolution points* – branch points during change resolution where taking a different path will produce different results. Each possible answer at each resolution point is an *elementary evolution strategy*. Common policy consisting of a set of elementary evolution strategies, each giving an answer for one resolution point, is an *evolution strategy* and is used to customize the OE process. Thus, an evolution strategy unambiguously defines the way how elementary changes will be resolved. Typically a particular evolution strategy is chosen by the user at the start of the OE process (the left part of Figure 5).

Change Implementation. In order to avoid performing undesired changes, before applying a change to the ontology, a list of all implications to the ontology should be generated and presented to the user [15]. He should be able to comprehend the list and approve or cancel the change (the right part of Fig. 5). When the changes are approved, they are performed by successively resolving changes from the list. If changes are cancelled, the ontology should remain intact.

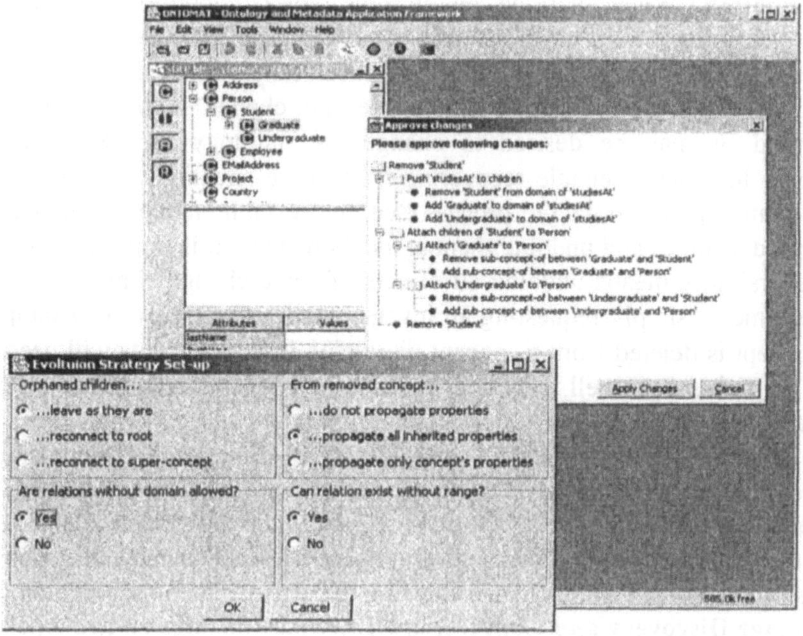

Figure 5. Ontology Evolution in KAON[4] framework: Evolution Strategy Set-up and Ontology Evolution User Interface in OntoMat-SOEP

Change Propagation. First, when the ontology is modified, ontology instances need to be changed to preserve consistency with the ontology [5]. This can be performed in three steps. If the instances are on the Web, they are collected in the knowledge base[5]. In the second step, modification of instances is performed according to the changes in the ontology [14]. In the last step "out-of-date" instances on the Web are replaced with corresponding "up-to-date" instances. Second, ontologies often reuse and extend other ontologies. Therefore, an ontology update might also corrupt ontologies that depend on the modified ontology and consequently, all artefacts that are based on these ontologies. This problem can be solved by recursive applying the OE process on these ontologies. However, besides of the syntax inconsistency, the semantic inconsistency can also arise when, for example, the dependent ontology already contains a concept that is added in the original ontology. Third, when an ontology is changed, applications based on the changed ontology may not work correctly. An OE approach has to recognize which change in the ontology can affect the functionality of dependent applications [10] and to react correspondingly [13].

[4] http://kaon.semanticweb.org/SOEP
[5] http://kaon.sematicweb.org/CRAWL

Validation. When working on an ontology collaboratively, different ontology engineers may have different ideas about how the ontology should be changed. Moreover, the ontology engineer may fail to understand the actual effect of the change and approve the change that shouldn't be performed. It may be desired to change the ontology for experimental purposes. In order to enable recovering from these situations, we introduce the validation phase in the OE process (see Figure 4). It enables validation of performed changes and undoing them at user's request. It is important to note that reversibility means undoing all effects of some change, which may not be the same as simply requesting an inverse change manually. For example, if a concept is deleted from a concept hierarchy, its subconcepts will need to be either deleted as well, attached to the root concept, or attached to the parent of the deleted concept. Reversing such a change is not equal to recreating the deleted concept – one needs, also, to revert the concept hierarchy into original state. The problem of reversibility is typically solved by creating evolution logs. An evolution log, based on the evolution ontology described in the following, tracks information about each change, allowing to reconstruct the sequence of changes leading to current state of the ontology.

Change Discovery and Capture. In OE we may distinguish two types of changes: top-down and bottom-up, whose generation is part of the "capturing phase" in the OE process. Top-down changes are explicit changes, driven, for example, by top-manager who want to adapt the system to new requirements and can be easily realized by an OE system. However, some changes in the domain are implicit, reflected in the behaviour of the system and can be discovered only through analysis of its behaviour. For example, if a customer group doesn't contain members for a longer period of time, it may mean that it can be removed. This second type of change mined from the set of ontology instances are called bottom-up changes. Another source of bottom-up changes is the structure of the ontology itself. Indeed, the previously described "validation phase" results in an ontology which may be in a consistent state, but contains some redundant entities or can be better structured with respect to the domain. For example, multiple users may be working on different parts of an ontology without enough communication. They may be deleting subconcepts of a common concepts at different points in time to fulfil their immediate needs. As a result, it may happen that only one subconcept is left. Since classification with only one subclass beats the original purpose of classification, we consider such ontology to have a suboptimal structure. To aid users in detecting such situations, we investigated the possibilities of applying the self-adaptive systems principles and proactively make suggestions for *ontology refinements* – changes to the ontology with the goal of improving ontology structure, making the ontology easier to understand and cheaper to modify. As known to authors, none of existing systems for ontology development and maintenance offer support for (semi-) automatic ontology improvement.

6.1 Evolution Ontology

The backbone of the whole evolution process is a meta-ontology for evolution that enables representation, analysis, realization and sharing ontological changes in a more systematic and consistent way. It is a specific ontology that is designed to support all phases in the evolution process of an ontology.

The evolution ontology consists of three parts. First part is about mechanisms to represent changes (see Table 1). Ontological changes [6] are represented using the top level concept "*Change*" and its relations. For every change, it is also useful to know who is *author* of the change and when it is happened (*date*). The *cause* of the change is used to represent the source of the change (business requirements or the learning process) and the *relevance* of the change describes whether and how it can fulfil the requirements. Also, OE is a managerial process and it needs some properties to support decision-making like *cost*, *priority*, etc. The order of changes is also very important as it enables recovery of implemented changes (if the result of the validation phase is unsatisfied) and/or mining trends (patterns) to improve the OE process. To solve semantics of change problem, the evolution ontology contains axioms that derive additional changes. The derived change and the required change are connected using *parentChange* relation.

The second part of the evolution ontology containing relations like *prototypical*, *primary_key*, etc. represents semantic information about the domain ontology explicitly [16], because the conceptual structure of the evolution ontology aims to provide enough mechanisms to deal with problems of syntax as well as semantic inconsistencies. The third part of the evolution ontology aims to support data-driven self-improvement of the domain ontology. We enforce formal discovering of changes by representing some heuristics as axioms in the evolution ontology. For example, if all subconcepts have the same property, the property may be moved to the parent concept.

7. RELATED WORK AND CONCLUSION

In the last decade, there has been much active research in the area of ontology-based systems. However, there are very few approaches investigating the problems of changing in the ontologies.

Heflin [4] points out that ontologies on the Web will need to evolve and he presents SHOE, a web-based knowledge representation language that supports multiple versions of ontologies. Although good design may prevent many ontological errors, some errors will not be realized until the ontology is put to use. However, this problem as well as the problem of the change propagation are not treated. Moreover, the user cannot customize the way of performing the change and the problem of the identification of the change is not analysed. In contrast to the OE that allows access to all data (to ontology itself and to dependent artefacts) only through the newest ontology, ontology versioning allows access to data through different version of the ontology. Thus, OE can be treated as a part of the ontology versioning. Ontology versioning is analysed in [5]. Authors provide an overview of causes and consequences of the changes in the ontology. However, the most important flaw is the lack of a detailed analysis of the effect of specific changes on the interpretation of data which is a constituent part of our work.

Other research communities also have influences our work. The problem of schema evolution and schema versioning support has been extensively studied in relational and database papers [10]. However, there are several differences that steam from different knowledge models and different usage paradigms. Research in OE can also benefit from the many years of research in knowledge-based system evolution. The script-based knowledge evolution [15] that identifies typical sequences of changes to knowledge base and represents them in a form of scripts, is similar to our approach. In contrast to the knowledge-scripts that allow the tool to understand the consequences of each change, we go step further by allowing the user to control how to complete the overall modification and by suggesting the changes that could improve the ontology.

There is only little work concerning the support of using multiple ontologies. Again, our approach is motivated by classical work on federated database and mediators done by the database community [17]. Nevertheless, our approach goes beyond classical techniques, as it provides an integrated view on the overall multi-ontology scenario, from discovering mappings, representing mappings [1] to processing mappings.

In this paper we have presented Ontologging, the corporate ontology modeling and management system. Ontologging is an ontology-based environment to enable next generation knowledge management applications building on Semantic Web standards. In this paper we have mainly focused on two important challenges for ontology-based knowledge management: First, the management of multiple ontologies and, second, the handling of ontology evolution in dynamic environments. Both approaches rely on heavily using meta-primitives, also represented in the form of ontologies.

ACKNOWLEDGEMENTS

The research presented in this paper was profited from fruitful discussion with our Ontologging project partners from Insead (France), Meta4 (Spain), Deltatec (Belgium), Archetypon (Greece) and Indra (Spain). Research for this paper was financed by European Commission, IST project "Ontologging" (IST-2000-28293).

REFERENCES

1. Doan A., Madhavan J., Domingos P., Halevy A., Learning to map between ontologies on the Semantic Web, In *Proc. of the World-Wide Web Conference 2002.*
2. Fensel D., Ontologies: Dynamics Networks of Meaning, In *Proc. of the 1st Semantic web working symposium*, Stanford, CA, USA, July 30th-August 1st, 2001.
3. Franconi E., Grandi F., Mandreoli F., A semantic approach for schema evolution and versioning in object-oriented databases, In *Proc. of the 1st International Conf. on Computational Logic (CL'2000)*, Springer-Verlag, 2000.
4. Heflin J., Towards the Semantic Web: Knowledge Representation in a Dynamic, Distributed Environment, Ph.D. Thesis, University of Maryland, College Park. 2001.
5. Klein M., Fensel D., Ontology versioning for the Semantic Web, In *Proc. International Semantic Web Working Symposium (SWWS)*, USA, 2001.
6. Maedche A., Staab S., Stojanovic N., Studer R., Sure Y., SEmantic PortAL - The SEAL approach. to appear: In *Creating the Semantic Web*, D. Fensel, J. Hendler, H. Lieberman, W. Wahlster (eds.) MIT Press, MA, Cambridge, 2001.
7. Maedche A., Staab S., On Comparing Ontologies, Internal Report 403, Institute AIFB, University of Karlsruhe, 2001.
8. Maedche A., Motik B., Silva N., Volz R., MAFRA – An Ontology Mapping FRAmework in the Context of the Semantic Web, Internal Report, FZI, 2002.
9. Rahm N., Bernstein P., A survey of approaches to automatic schema matching. *VLDB Journal*, 10(4):334–350, 2001.
10. Roddick J.F., A Survey of Schema Versioning Issues for Database Systems, *Information and Software Technology*, 37(7): 383-393, 1996.
11. Staab S., Maedche A., Comparing Ontologies - Similarity Measures and a Comparison, Internal Report 408, Institute AIFB, Karlsruhe University.
12. Staab S., Schnurr H.-P., Studer R., Sure Y., Knowledge Processes and Ontologies, *IEEE Intelligent Systems*, 16(1), 2001. Special Issue on Knowledge Management
13. Stojanovic L., Stojanovic N., Handschuh S., Evolution of the Metadata in the Ontology-based Knowledge Management Systems, In *Proc. of Experience Management 2002*, Berlin, March 7-8, 2002.
14. Stojanovic L., Stojanovic N., Volz R., Migrating data-intensive Web Sites into the Semantic Web, *ACM Symposium on Applied Computing SAC*, pp. 1100-1108, 2002.
15. Tallis M., Gil Y., Designing Scripts to Guide Users in Modifying Knowledge-based Systems, In *Proc. of the Sixteenth National Conference on Artificial Intelligence (AAAI-99)*, Orlando, FL, 1999.
16. Tamma V.A.M., Bench-Capon T.J.M, A conceptual model to facilitate knowledge sharing in multi-agent systems, *In Proc. of the OAS 2001*, Montreal, pp. 69-76., 2001
17. Wiederhold G., Genesereth M., Basis for Mediation, In *Proc. COOPIS'95 Conference*, Vienna Austria, available from US West, Boulder CO, May 1995.

IKAT: A TOOL FOR INCREMENTAL DEVELOPMENT OF ONTOLOGIES THROUGH VERSIONS

Mikel Larrañaga, Jon A. Elorriaga
University of the Basque Country

Abstract: In this paper an ontology-based knowledge acquisition tool is presented. This work is focused on the incremental development of ontologies and aims to help with the creation and maintenance of knowledge-based systems. The tool uses the version concept to implement the evolution of the ontologies. IKAT facilitates the development of ontologies through versions propagating automatically changes to the knowledge bases built based on them. An analysis of the possible operations upon ontologies has been carried out, and as a result a set of plausible operations has been chosen and their treatment implemented.

Key words: Knowledge acquisition, ontologies, knowledge engineering, reusability.

1. INTRODUCTION

Ontologies, which had been used in other areas such as philosophy, were adopted to represent the knowledge in order to minimize the communication difficulties in KBS development teams. In knowledge engineering area, ontologies are defined as " an explicit specification of a conceptualization" [3]. They provide a formalism for the representation of a concrete domain that can be understood without any ambiguity either by different people or by a computer. Obviously, a broadly accepted representation of the domain is hardly reached immediately, so the process of building ontology must be gradual and requires several refinements.

Many ontology-based tools appeared with the aim of relieving the mentioned bottleneck by minimizing the knowledge engineers role as they allow domain experts to transfer their knowledge to a computer system even though they are not familiar with computers. Some of these tools are Protégé-

2000 [1], Ontolingua [2] and Kads22 [5]. However, most of these tools lack of facilities to incrementally enhance ontologies. SHOE language [4] allows versioning of ontologies but it does not automate the updating of KBs built based on them. The work here presented focuses on the incremental development of ontologies and presents IKAT. The aim of this tool is to allow the refinement and modification of ontologies and to automatically propagate changes to concrete KBs.

The paper starts presenting IKAT design issues. Next the architecture of IKAT is detailed and the last section focus on how IKAT helps with the incremental ontology development by using versions. Finally we present some conclusions and future research lines.

2. DESIGN AND IMPLEMENTATION

IKAT is a general propose knowledge acquisition tool that aids to constructing knowledge-based systems; in order to allow the gradual ontology definition in an intuitive way, IKAT uses the **version** concept. A version of an ontology includes the ontology itself and the KBs built based on it. New versions of an ontology can be created by experts on the following circumstances:

- **While the ontology is being developed:** An ontology will go through several phases until a consensus is reached. Each of these phases can be a version.
- **As an improvement of the original ontology:** When the domain changes, the ontology that describes it also must change, e.g., a production system describing ontology must update itself if a new product or a production way appears.
- **As an adaptation of the ontology to a particular application:** An ontology that describes completely a domain may have too much information for a simple application, e.g., a car domain describing ontology can include even the car production process, but there are a lot of entities and relations that an expert diagnose tool of the electrical system does not need.
- **As an enhancement of existing KBSs:** User can extend the ontology a KBS is based on in order to exchange information with others KBS.

IKAT distinguishes two different phases in the ontology building process in the way Protégé does: the definition of the abstract objects of the domain (classes) and the definition of the concrete objects (instances). IKAT allows building several knowledge bases of an ontology for particular applications.

3. ARCHITECTURE OF IKAT

Figure 1 shows the architecture of IKAT. The kernel of IKAT is composed by two functional modules (Ontology Acquisition Module and Knowledge-Base Acquisition Module), which exchange information with the *Knowledge-Base Library* information repository. Each of the components of the IKAT architecture will be described below. The architecture of IKAT has been designed in three layers in order to enhance its changeability. The Ontology Acquisition Module, the Knowledge Acquisition Module and the KB Library are part of the kernel layer. Communication Interface is on the middle layer and it communicates the top layer (graphic interface) with the kernel layer. Communication Interface allows IKAT to be used in the two different modes: as an autonomous tool through the graphic interface or used by another application through the communication interface.

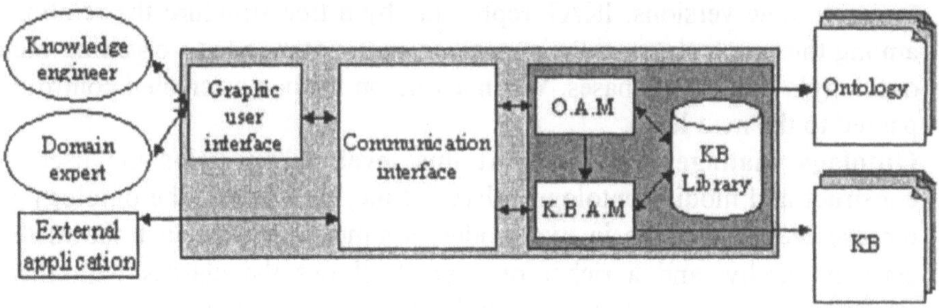

Figure 1. Architecture of IKAT

3.1 Ontology Acquisition Module (OAM)

On this module, the user creates the classes, attributes and relations among classes that describe the domain are created. This module is the responsible of building and managing the ontologies. Once the ontology has been completely defined, it generates the executable code that will be used in knowledge based system, and stores the internal representation so that it can be used to create new version or even to update the current ontology.

3.2 Knowledge Base Acquisition Module (KBAM)

On this module, the user defines the instances of each of the KBs based on the ontology that has been built on the OAM. This module is the responsible of building the KBs based on the ontology. As Figure 1 illustrates, this module communicates with the Ontology Acquisition module.

This message interchange is because some of the operations applied to the ontology imply some updates in its knowledge bases.

3.3 Communication Interface

It contains the complete set of high-level functions defined for IKAT. These functions can be used either by the graphic interface or by any external application.

3.4 Graphic Interface

IKAT defines three working levels:

- **General management level:** IKAT has a set of windows that allows the user to create, refine and delete ontologies and knowledge bases as well as to create new versions. IKAT represents by a tree structure the relations among the ontologies and their versions and another one to organize each ontology's knowledge bases. When a version is open or created control is passed to the next level.
- **Ontology management level:** At this level, IKAT helps the user to construct and modify ontologies. Every time, the state of the ontology is represented by a graph in two modes, a simple one that just shows the class hierarchy, and a richer one which shows the classes with their attributes. Once the ontology is defined, the user can go through to the next level and define the knowledge bases. Figure 2 shows the interface for this level.
- **Knowledge base management level:** Another tree structure is used in this level to show the defined instances and classes.

3.5 Knowledge-Base Library

This is the responsible of storing and retrieving the created ontologies and knowledge bases together with their versions for future use. As it is shown on Figure 1, both functional modules (OAM and KBAM) generate an output file. OAM generates a file containing the code implementing the abstract objects of the domain; KBAM produces a file with the defined instances of each KB. Joining these files, we get the skeleton of the desired knowledge based system. IKAT uses an internal object-oriented representation language for the ontologies and KBs.

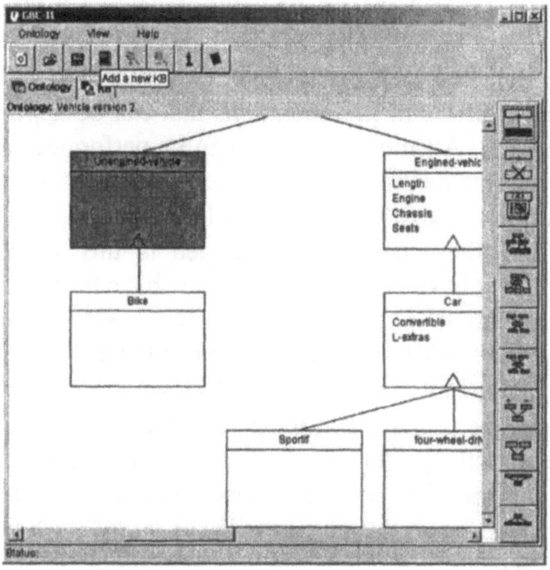

Figure 2. Ontology Management Level

4. INCREMENTAL DESIGN IN IKAT

In order to promote the incremental design of ontologies and KBs, IKAT provides versioning facilities and automatic propagation of changes in complex operations on ontologies.

4.1 Ontology versioning

As it has been mentioned above, building an ontology is not a simple process, but it requires successive improvements. This ontology refining is facilitated in IKAT by generating successive versions of it, and thus, reusing the represented knowledge. A version is generated by making a copy of the whole ontology and all the KBs based on it. Besides, the reference to the original copy to the original ontology is stored. Therefore, IKAT stores all the versions of the ontology in a structured way. As it will be mentioned in next section, any operation is propagated to KBs by IKAT adapting them to the changes that happen on the ontology. Therefore, IKAT quickens the process of building knowledge based systems by facilitating the updating of the ontologies they use to represent the domain. Propagations of operations through versions could be performed that way.

4.2 Automatic propagation of operations to KBs

In order to enhance IKAT with operation that will facilitate ontology development, an analysis of the operations that can be applied to ontologies has been carried out. All this operations can be performed on ontologies, so the changes they provoke must be propagated to the KBs built based on them. Therefore, complex operations that hardly could be performed on KBs without rebuilding them have been included in this analysis. Once most important operations have been identified, they have been analysed obtaining the effects they entail on the ontology and its KBs In addition, several treatments have been proposed and among them the appropriate treatment has been chosen taking into account the following criteria: (1) automatic propagations must be promoted in order to lighten the work, (2) constructive operations are directly performed, and (3) the destructive operations will demand user confirmation. In some cases and in order to maximize the automatic propagation of the changes, IKAT proposes a different way to make the operation.

Besides the basic operations such as creating a new class or instance, IKAT provides the following complex operations with the aim of facilitating the incremental development of ontologies/KBs by automating the propagation of changes. These propagations can happen in two different levels: (1) on the ontology due to the inheritance, such as propagating an attribute or removing from descendants an inherited attribute, or (2) on KBs so as to keep the consistency among the ontology and the KBs built based on it.

Table 1 and Table 2 summarize the most relevant operations that have been analysed. These tables present the operations and their effects on the ontology and the proposed treatments. In addition, the effects on KBs are detailed taking into account each treatment. The selected treatment of the operation is shown shadowed. Reasons for choosing a particular treatment are also specified in these tables by its criteria number.

4.2.1 Operations on Ontologies

- **Class Specialization**: Specialization can be defined as the creation of a set of disjoint subclasses according to one or several attributes. The individual objects of the specialized class will be relocated into the subclasses according to the values of the attributes that compose the disjunction criteria. To perform this operation, a leaf class, i.e., a class without any subclasses, must be selected.
- **Generalization of a set of classes that have at least a common ancestor:** This operation needs that the classes share at least a common

ancestor. IKAT allows two generalization modes:

- A type generalization: In this type of generalization, a new class will replace the set of classes. The new class contains only the common attributes of all the classes that are included in the operation and will be subclass of all their common ancestors. Their subclasses will descend from the new class. Due to this operation, the descendants of the selected classes will not inherit non-common attributes anymore. Therefore, those attributes will be also removed from instances of the selected classes and their descendants.
- B type Generalization: IKAT generates a new ancestor for the set of selected classes that includes their common attributes. These attributes will be inherited from the selected classes, so it is not necessary to represent them in the subclasses. In this case, instances are not really affected because there are neither new attributes nor redefinitions

- **Modifying the defined class-superclass relations**: IKAT allows creating new class-superclass relations (New class superclass relation), removing defined relations (Remove class superclass relation) and even replacing any superclass (Change superclass) by another one. Precedence order, i.e. the priority among classes, that determines from which superclass an attribute is inherited if it is defined in more than one, can also be modified (Change Precedence order). Adding a new class-superclass relation may cause some attributes to appear in the class and its subclasses and also another ones to be redefined. Changing class-superclass relation may also cause some attributes to be modified, new attributes to appear and other ones to be deleted. Removing a class-superclass relation may cause some attributes redefinitions and some others to be removed. When an attribute is removed from a class it is also removed from any of its instances or any descendant that inherited it. When an attribute is redefined, the value it has on instances is replaced by its new default value. When a new attribute is propagated it is initialized on instances with its default value.
- **Class removing operations:** IKAT provides three different operations for removing classes.
  - A type Class Removal: The subclasses of the removed class will be related directly to the ancestors of the removed class. Instances of the descendants of the removed class will not inherit its attributes anymore. Besides, as classes have changed their ancestors, some of the attributes may be redefined and, thus, they will change their value. IKAT will look for the new value/s on the class that propagates the attribute.
  - B type Class Removal: The subclasses of the removed class will be from now on descendants of the brother class (i.e., a class with a common ancestor) the user has chosen as new parent. Instances will suffer several changes on their attributes, i.e., some attributes will be

removed, new ones propagated and some others will change their value. IKAT will use the default values that are defined on the new parent to initialize the new attributes and to modify the ones that will be redefined.

Table 1. Operations and their effects on the ontology

Operation	Effects on the ontology	Effects on the KBs	Treatments	Criteria
Class Specialization	Class becomes abstract	Instances are relocated	Deny User must relocate each instance	(1),(2)
	New subclasses		Relocate instances according to the values of their attributes	
A type generalization	Selected classes will be replaced by the new one	If all attributes are added to the new class, conflicts on attribute definitions.	Deny All attributes of the selected class Only common attributes	(1),(3)
		Otherwise, redefined attributes change their value	Ask for confirmation. New class will define only common attributes.	
B type generalization	Selected classes will be subclasses of the new one. (based on the previous operation)		Deny Change directly	(1), (2)
New class superclass relation	New attributes inherited	New attributes initializized	Deny Change directly Ask for confirmation	(1), (3)
	Some attributes redefined	Redefined attributeds change their value		
Remove class superclass relation	Some attributes removed	Attributes removed	Deny Change directly	(1), (3)
	Some attributes redefined	Redefined attributes change their value	Ask for confirmation	

- C type Class Removal: IKAT allows removing classes in a recursive way. This operation is propagated through the hierarchy by deleting the descendants of the removed class if it is their only ancestor or deleting the class-superclass relation in other case. As a result of this operation, instances of removed classes will be deleted. Instances of the modified descendant classes will suffer attribute removals and modifications; thus, the modified attributes will take their value/s from the next priority parent.

Table 2. Operations on ontologies and their effects

Operation	Effects on the ontology	Effects on the KBs	Treatments	Criteria
Class Specialization	Class becomes abstract New subclasses	Instances are relocated	Deny User must relocate each instance Relocate instances according to the values of their attributes	(1),(2)
A type generalization	Selected classes will be replaced by the new one	If all attributes are added to the new class, conflicts on attribute definitions. Otherwise, redefined attributes change their value	Deny All attributes of the selected class Only common attributes Ask for confirmation. New class will define only common attributes.	(1),(3)
B type generalization	Selected classes will be subclasses of the new one. (based on the previous operation)		Deny Change directly	(1), (2)
New class superclass relation	New attributes inherited Some attributes redefined	New attributes initializied Redefined attributeds change their value	Deny Change directly Ask for confirmation	(1), (3)
Remove class superclass relation	Some attributes removed Some attributes redefined	Attributes removed Redefined attributes change their value	Deny Change directly Ask for confirmation	(1), (3)

- **Modifying class properties**: IKAT permits modification of the properties of the class. For example, the user can determine if instances of the class can be defined or not. If the user establishes that a class can not have any instance, IKAT will delete all its instances

- **Modifying attribute properties**: As well as class properties can be modified, IKAT allows redefining the properties of attributes that were specified while creating it. For example, the type of value and the cardinality of the attribute can be modified. If the type of value is changed, the value of the instances will be replaced by its new default value. If cardinality of the attributes is reduced to a single value, the instances will only keep the first value they had on the attribute.
- **Removing attributes:** Also attributes can be removed. As a result of this operation, the attribute will be removed from every instance that mentions any of the affected classes.

All the operations that have been described in this section involve the instances that are defined on each of the KB built based on the modified ontology. IKAT takes into account the modifications the ontology has suffered and automatically updates its knowledge bases.

4.2.2 Operations on KBs

As classic operations on KBs, such as defining new instances, do not entail any problem, they will not be mentioned in this section:

- **Relocating instances in other classes:** IKAT allows relocating instances in other classes and it automatically removes all the no more needed slots, adds the new ones and updates the ones that are redefined giving them default values.
- **Removing instances:** IKAT allows the removal of instances from the knowledge bases too. IKAT maintains the relations between instances, which is updated as an instance is removed.

5. BENEFITS OF USING IKAT

In order to show the advantages IKAT provides to the user, the amount of operation it saves to the user will be quantified. The major benefits of using IKAT are obtained with complex operations on ontologies where slots removals and redefinitions are propagated through the ontology and the KBs. Constructive ontology operations and knowledge base operations are already supported by other similar systems so they are not taken into account. However, in those systems, side effects like slot removals and redefinitions due to complex destructive operations on ontologies are not automatically performed. This can cause problems when trying to load a knowledge base after modifying the ontology it is based on, so the user should perform this changes on instances manually before using the KB. As it has been explained above, IKAT's complex operations are refined into a sequence of basic operations such as slot redefinitions and slot removals. Therefore, the number of updates the user should perform manually in other systems can be calculated with the following formula:

$$Updates = AffInst * BO$$

Where *Updates* represents the number of modifications the user should perform, *AffInst* is the number of affected instances and *BO* is the number of basic operations that must be performed. *BO* is quite easy to obtain (see Table 1 and Table 2), but in order to get the number of modified instances the ontology should be carefully analysed because slot redefinitions can be found in any descendant class. Therefore, the formula here presented calculates the number of instance updates in the worst case:

$$AffInst = Inst(c) + InstDesc(c)$$

$$InstDesc(c) = \sum_{i=1}^{SCN(C)} \left(Inst(sc_i(c)) + InstDesc(sc_i(c)) \right)$$

$$Inst(c) = \sum_{j=1}^{KBN} I(KB_j, c)$$

Inst(C): Number of instances of C class

InstDesc (C): Number of instances of the descendants of C class

SCN(C): Number of subclasses of C class

SCi(C): i-th Subclass of C class

KBN: Number of knowledge bases based on the ontology

It is impossible to specify with a general formula the number of instance updates that can happen on an ontology because there is no way to describe on it when a class redefines a slot. Therefore, this recursive formula will be illustrated with a sample ontology so as to get an idea of how much work IKAT could save to the user. The class hierarchy of this ontology has a binary tree structure in order to ease the calculation of the number of affected classes and instances. Let's suppose that *X* KBs have been defined based on this sample ontology and *K* instances have been defined for each class on each knowledge base; if there are *P* levels from the modified class to the bottom of the hierarchy then the number of instances can be represented by the following formula:

$$Inst = \left(1 + \sum_{i=1}^{P} 2^i \right) * K * X$$

6. CONCLUSIONS

In this paper, IKAT, a tool that supports the full life cycle of an ontology, has been described. IKAT graphic interface allows the knowledge engineer or domain expert both to define an ontology by specifying its abstract objects, and to construct the Knowledge Base (KB) creating and relating instances. The interface releases the user from knowing the language implementation details.

Several tools for editing ontologies have been developed. IKAT contributes in this area providing a means for incremental ontology development through versions. An ontology is constructed in a gradual process involving a team of experts. However, during this process KBs can be developed based on the ontology or a fragment of it. Therefore, a knowledge acquisition tool should support the management of different versions of an ontology. Also, in order to lighten the workload of updating the ontologies and the Knowledge Bases (KBs) based on them, such a tool should maximize the automatic propagations of the changes in the ontologies and knowledge bases. IKAT was designed with these aims.

7. ACKNOWLEDGMENTS

The works presented in this paper are supported by the University of the Basque Country (UPV/EHU) (1/UPV 00141.226-T-13946/2001), the Economy Department of the Gipuzkoa Council (IRIS-D(II); RF 949/2001), the Basque Government (UE1999/36) and the CICYT (TIC99-0252).

8. REFERENCES

[1] Eriksson, H., Fergerson, R. W., Shahar, Y. and Musen, M. A. Automatic Generation of Ontology Editors. *Twelfth Banff Knowledge Acquisition for Knowledge-based systems Workshop,* Banff, Alberta, Canada. 1999.

[2] Farquhar, A., Fikes, R. and Rice, J. The ontolingua server: Tool for collaborative ontology construction. *IJHCS*, 46(6): 707--728. 1997.

[3] Gruber, T. R. A translation approach to portable ontology specifications. *Knowledge Acquisition* 5, 199--220. 1993.

[4] Heflin, J. and Hendler, J. Dynamic ontologies on the Web. Proceedings of the Seventh National Conference on Artificial Intelligence (AAAI-2000). AAAI/MIT Press, Menlo Park, CA, pp. 443-449. 2000.

[5] Kabel, S. and Anjewierden, A. An introduction to KADS22 functionality. http://www.swi.psy.uva.nl/projects/kads22/help/intro/intro.htm. 1999

A TEMPLATE-BASED APPROACH TOWARD ACQUISITION OF LOGICAL SENTENCES

Chih-Sheng Johnson Hou, Natalya F. Noy and Mark A. Musen
Stanford University, Stanford, CA 94305
{johnsonh, noy, musen} @ smi.stanford.edu

Abstract: Ontology-development languages may allow users to supplement frame-based representations with arbitrary logical sentences. In the case of the Ontolingua ontology library, only 10% of the ontologies have any user-defined axioms. We believe the phrase "writing axioms is difficult" accounts for this phenomenon; domain experts often cannot translate their thoughts into symbolic representation. We attempt to reduce this chasm in communication by identifying groups of axioms that manifest common patterns creating 'templates' that allow users to compose axioms by 'filling-in-the-blanks.' We studied axioms in two public ontology libraries, and derived 20 templates that cover 85% of all the user-defined axioms. We describe our methodology for collecting the templates and present sample templates. We also define several properties of templates that will allow users to find an appropriate template quickly. Thus, our research entails a significant simplification in the process for acquiring axioms from domain experts. We believe that this simplification will foster the introduction of axioms and constraints that are currently missing in the ontologies.

Key words: frame-based system, knowledge acquisition, knowledge representation

1. AXIOMS IN FRAME-BASED SYSTEMS

Frame-based representation systems (FRS) are a popular choice for knowledge representation [6]; their taxonomic categorization of canonical concepts often bears close resemblance to the way humans describe knowledge and is easy to understand. Because of this cognitive simplicity, FRSs serve as efficient tools for knowledge representation and acquisition.

Even though knowledge-representation constraints inherent in FRSs guarantee many advantages, they also foster several limitations across virtually all systems. A frame-based system alone has limited expressivity: it cannot naturally represent negations, disjunctions, and existential quantification. One cannot restrict a value of one property based on another property. To overcome these limitations, some FRSs employ more expressive compensatory axiom languages, which are based on first-order logic, to encode these relationships.

With the proliferation of approachable user interfaces such as the Protégé-2000 ontology-editing environment [8] for frame-based knowledge acquisition, many domain experts participate in knowledge acquisition, often without the collaboration of knowledge engineers. Domain experts enter information about classes and properties of concepts through a convenient interface. Unfortunately, to specify additional relational information, they encounter an axiom-editing environment that has remained free-text based. The act of conceptualizing a thought in a symbolic representation is often extremely difficult for a domain expert. For example, one may not understand why representing the simple constraint "every employee has a unique ID" in an axiom in first-order logic requires the equivalent English translation of "for every two employees both of whom have IDs, if the two employees are not the same, their IDs cannot be identical." Figure 1 shows this axiom in Protégé Axiom Language (PAL), which is an axiom language for the Protégé-2000 ontology-editing environment based on Knowledge Interchange Format (KIF) [5]. Even if a domain expert understood the formulation of the axiom, he would still have to struggle with the foreign syntax (Figure 1). These factors can lead to a failure to encode critical knowledge realizable only through axioms. For example, in Ontolingua [7], only about 10% of the ontologies include manually generated axioms.

To achieve truly meaningful transfer of knowledge we must attempt to reduce the barrier between a user and a knowledge acquisition system introduced in the axiom-acquisition phase. We identified a limited number of axiom templates, which would enable domain experts to specify most of the axioms by simply filling in the blanks in sentences describing the templates. This user-interface paradigm strongly parallels the task of acquiring instances of classes in traditional frame-based systems.

We examined axioms in ontologies in the Ontolingua ontology library [7] and several private Protégé ontologies [8] and discovered that most axioms that developers have chosen to encode have repetitive meanings and structures across different domains. In fact, we discovered that 20 templates accounted for 85% of the user-defined axioms. We acknowledge that this approach will not encompass the modeling of every axiom possible, but may be sufficient for common requirements.

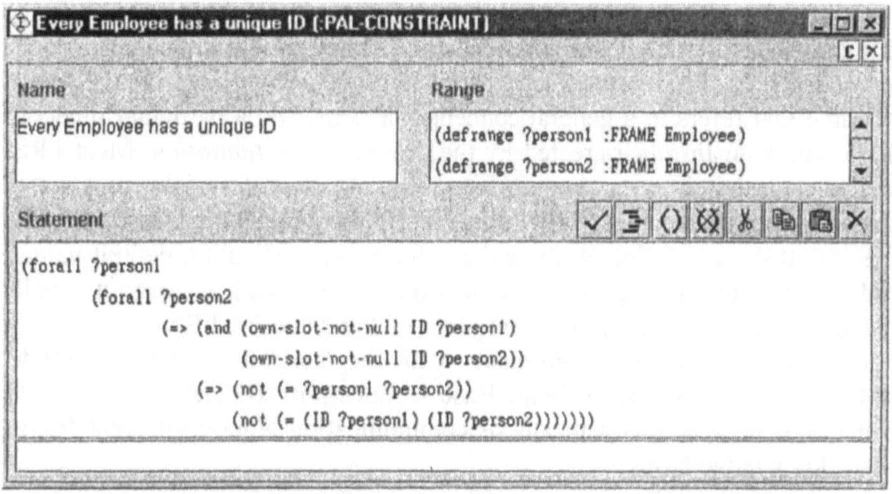

Figure 1. A Text-Based Axiom-Editing Environment in Protégé-2000. The axiom in the Protégé Axiom Language (PAL) says that every employee must have a unique ID.

2. METHODS FOR COLLECTING TEMPLATES

In order to identify axiom templates that would cover a large fraction of axioms that users have put in knowledge bases, we selected two ontology libraries that contained ontologies contributed by developers in many domains. We looked at axioms in ontologies from the Ontolingua ontology library [7] and from several Protégé ontologies [8]. These sources contain knowledge bases from diverse fields and have ample axioms. Ontolingua and Protégé have very similar knowledge models. The two systems introduce their own axiom languages, which are very similar. The axiom language of Ontolingua is KIF, a declarative language for expressing logical statements, and the Protégé Axiom Language (PAL) is a subset of KIF.

We examined 18 ontologies and 592 axioms. This set included ontologies for chemical elements, enterprise, bibliographic data, and malaria. Most have 10 to 30 axioms. We did not examine those axioms associated with upper level ontologies. These axioms seldom produce context-independent reusable patterns due to their complexity and specificity. We also did not examine computer-generated axioms, which contain information encodable in the native frame-based representation.

2.1 Knowledge Model

We chose the general frame-based knowledge model of Protégé[8]. A frame is a data structure that represents objects, abstract categorizations of objects, or concepts. Each frame has slots that contain values that describe the frame. A frame that refers to a general concept is a *class*, and a particular object of that class is an *instance* created by the process of *instantiation*. Most FRSs organize classes in a taxonomic hierarchy. A *superclass* is a superset of instances in its subclasses. Subclasses inherit slots from superclasses. We can specify attributes of slots such as the value type, cardinality, default values, and a data range. However, as we previously mentioned, we cannot usually specify relations between different slots of the same or different instances. These assumptions are consistent with the general knowledge model underlying the Open Knowledge-Base Connectivity (OKBC) protocol [3], which was designed as a means of communication among different frame-based knowledge bases.

2.2 From patterns to templates

Our process for generating generic axiom templates from the actual axioms in the ontologies consisted of the following steps:

1. We identified axioms that followed exactly the same **pattern**. They were identical except for the names of specific variables and frames.
2. We generalized similar patterns into **templates**. A template accounted for minor variations among patterns. For example, two patterns "A contains B" and "A does not contain B" give rise to one template "A contains/does not contain B."
3. We derived generic properties for categorizing the templates.

Consider the following two axioms in Athena_Client, a private Protégé ontology by Samson Tu:

```
(forall ?process
    (=> (slot-not-null inhibited_by_object ?process)
        (/= "cytochalazin" (name (inhibited_by_object ?process)))))

(forall ?process
    (=> (slot-not-null inhibited_by_object ?process)
        (/= "neuraminadase" (name (inhibited_by_object ?process)))))
```

These axioms vary only in referred slot value "cytochalazin" and "neuraminadase." Thus, these two axioms give rise to the following pattern:

All instances of class ___ do not contain the value ___ in slot ___.

We then generalize these patterns further, trying to satisfy two constraints: (1) have a small number of templates in the final collection, simplifying the search for the appropriate template for the domain expert; (2) ensure that the templates do not become too general as to be incomprehensible because of the many variations that they have. Section 3 will explore the methodologies for deriving templates from similar patterns and generic properties from the templates.

Every instance of class ___ whose (slot ___ has value ___)(*N) must have (slot ___ has value ___)(*M).

Example: A student who has fewer than 180 units or who has not completed the distribution requirement cannot graduate. ⇔ Every instance of **Class Student** whose **Slot units-completed : Class Student** has value **< 180 OR Slot distribution-completed : Class Student** has value **false** must have **Slot is-graduating : Class Student** has value **false.**

Every instance of class ___ appears at least once in slot ___ of any instance of class ___.

Example: Every student has at least one advisor. ⇔ Every instance of **Class Student** appears at least once as a value of **Slot advisee : Class Professor** of any instance of **Class Professor.**

Every instance (A) of class ___ that is a value of slot ___ of instance (B) of class ___ must have the same value in its slot ___ as in slot ___ of B.

Example: Every student project that is a continuation of a previous project has the same starting data available as the final data available of the previous project. ⇔ Every instance (A) of **Class Project** that is a value of **Slot continuation-of : Class Project** of instance (B) of **Class Project** must have the same value in its **Slot starting-data : Class Project** as in **Slot final-data : Class Project** of B.

For every instance of class ___, slots ___ and ___ cannot have the same value.

Example: A student does not have an activity he both likes an dislikes. ⇔ For every instance of **Class Student, Slot favorite-activities : Class Student** and **Slot disliked-activities : Class Student** cannot have the same value.

Table 1. A partial list showing templates as "fill-in-the-blanks" sentences and sample usages.

3. AXIOM TEMPLATES AND THEIR PROPERTIES

The most simplistic form of a template consists of a fill-in-the-blanks sentence and an example of usage. By coupling these features, we ensure that a specific example will clarify its generalized template when the user does not immediately understand the latter. Table 1 represents a partial list of the 20 templates we identified in this reduced form.

The expanded form of a template incorporates additional details about its usage. For example, many templates allow for variations: different number of conditions or resulting statements of the same type, different modifiers, and so on (Section 3.1). Thus, as mentioned before, a template gives rise to several patterns (Section 3.2) where all the possible alternatives have been specified. Therefore, in addition to its English-language representation, each template requires the relevant information from which one can extract a single pattern and instantiate an axiom. The complete definition of a template consists of the following elements, as shown in Figure 2 (the numbers in the list correspond to the numbers in the figure):

1. The English-language representation or the "name" of the template as a "fill-in-the-blanks" sentence. For the template in Figure 2, this representation is:

   Every instance of class ___ appears at least once in slot ___ of any instance of class___

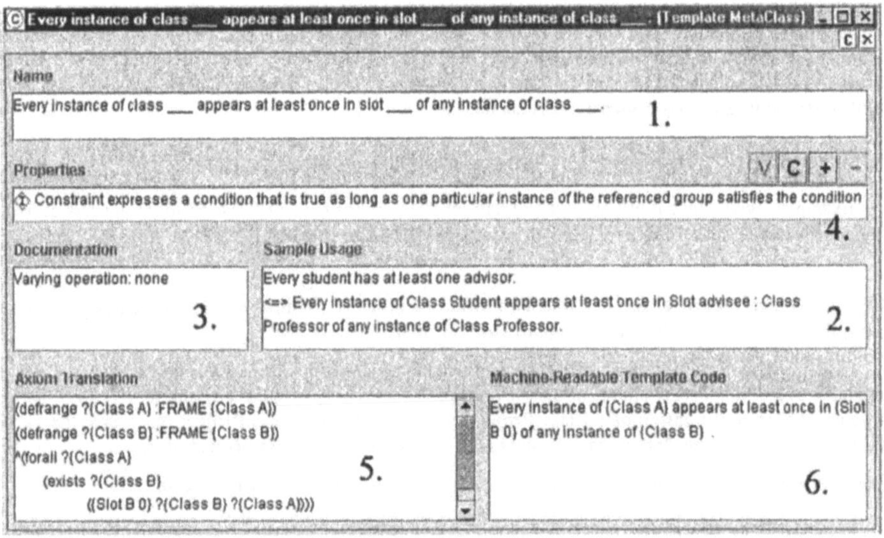

Figure 2. Elements of a complete template definition. Numbers on the figure correspond to elements in the list in Section 3. Each template definition includes a sentence with blanks to fill in, a sample usage, documentation, a list of properties, a prototypical axiom translation and a machine-interpretable expression of the template.

2. A sample usage sentence that includes a possible interpretation of the template with the blanks already filled in:

   Every student has at least one advisor ⇔ Every instance of **Class Student** appears at least once in **Slot advisee : Class Professor** of any instance of **Class Professor.**

3. Documentation: A short description of the varying operations one may perform on the templates. This field for the sample template is left blank because the template represents a single pattern rather than a group of patterns. We consider this issue in Section 3.1.
4. A set of properties describing the template. We discuss properties in Section 3.2.
5. A 'generalized' pattern that derives from the source axioms of a template. We replace specific frame and/or value references by variables and

indicate where variations (Section 3.2) are possible. Below is a translation of the example template into Protégé Axiom Language (PAL):

(defrange ?{Class A} :FRAME {Class A})

(defrange ?{Class B} :FRAME {Class B})

^(forall ?{Class A} (exists ?{Class B} ({Slot B 0} ?{Class B} ?{Class A})))

6. Machine-interpretable expression of the template: The expression contains information that enables the automatic generation of a template as an English sentence in the user interface. It also dictates what type of frame can fill in the blank or specifies additional modifiers (see section 3.1). This feature allows us to set additional user-interface controls on the types of the allowed frames that users can fill in a particular blank. Furthermore, we can use this structured internal representation to generate axioms by substituting specific values to the 'generalized' pattern.

   Every instance of {Class A} appear at least once in {Slot B 0} of any instance of class {Class B}

   The above example limits user's choice of a slot to those slots of the second class B, thus effectively preventing users from composing potentially inappropriate axioms.

3.1 Variations in Templates

Each template can have several variations. Variations can result from using multiple conditions or resulting statements, or from applying different operations to slot values.

3.1.1 Generating multiple conditions

A template can be a generalization of many patterns or a single pattern. Consider this template:

Slot ___ of instances of class ___ must contain elements that are instances of the class specified by slot ___

The sample usage of this template is:

A student (Instance of Class Students) can only enroll in the courses offered by the Business School (slot Allowed-Course-Group)

A user may only fill in the values to generate axioms but may not alter the template in any way to produce an axiom with a slightly different pattern. However, among the axioms that we examined, we found patterns with multiple conditions or multiple resulting statements. For example, consider the following axiom:

```
(exists ?current_med
    (and(drug_name ?current_med "hydrochlorothiazide")
        (> (daily_dose ?current_med) 25))
```

It states, “There exists a medication named “hydrocholorothiazide” with a daily dose greater than 25ml.” Notice that there are two statements in this axiom: “medication is named “hydrocholorothiazide” and “dose is greater than 25ml.” Consider another example:

```
(exists ?drug_usage
    (Drug_Class_Name ?drug_usage Beta-Blockers-Cardioselective))
```

It states “There exists a drug of the type ‘cardioselective beta-blocker.’” Here we have only one statement: “drug class name is Beta-Bloker-Cardioselective.” To account for this type of variation, we generalize the templates to allow an arbitrary number of conditions and resulting statements. For example, we can generalize the above pattern to:

There exists an instance of class ___ that contains (value ___ in slot ___.) (*N) (1)

The “N” modifier indicates that there can be more than one condition or statement. Therefore, this template generalizes patterns such as:

There exists an instance of class ___ that contains value ___ in slot ___ .

There exists an instance of class ___ that contains value ___ in slot ___ and value ___ in slot ___.

This convenient notation allows template designers to store structurally similar patterns into one template. This notation therefore prevents users from enumerating every variation to ensure coverage of the library as if there was a one-to-one mapping from patterns to templates. We will explain the use of varying operations such as those represented inside the round brackets to generate additional patterns.

3.1.2 Varying operations

Another way to customize a template is to specify an explicit operation or to use the built-in varying operations. Consider the following further generalization of pattern (1):

There must be (at least one/exactly one/at most one) instance of class ___ that contains/does not contain value ___ in slot ___

This example provides choices of operations among “only one/ at least one/ at most one,” and between “contains value ___ / does not contain value ___.” Thus, the template can lead to equally valid fill-in-the-blank patterns such as:

1) Only one slot ___ of instances of class ___ contains value ___.

2) At most one slot ___ of instances of class ___ does not contain value ___.

3) At least one of the instances of class ___ contains ___ in its slot ___.

Each slot type entails a specific set of operations on the slot. For example, for a numeric slot, operations are comparison functions such as <, <=, =, >=, >, =, not =; for a slot that has other instances as its value, operations are "contains/does not contain"; for a string-valued slot, operations are about substrings, such as "present/not present/begins with/ends with". These variations are implicit in the template because we can derive them directly from the slot value type.

3.2 Properties of templates

A process that is equally important to identifying templates is devising a strategy to organize them. We believe that organizing the templates into an inheritance hierarchy is not feasible: The templates are usually so abstract that even more general "super-templates" will be very vague and incomprehensible. A template may also fall into multiple categories. However, the latter situation contributes to an alternate solution for organizing templates. First, consider the following example that shows how a template can belong to multiple categories. We identified a group of templates that is concerned with expressing a condition that is true as long as one particular instance of the referenced group satisfies the condition:

1. All instances of class ___ appear at least once in slot ___ of any instance of class ___.
2. Every instance (A) of class ___ that is a value of slot ___ of instance (B) of class ___ must have the same value in its slot ___ as in slot ___ of B.

Similarly, there is another group represented by the following characteristic: the value of an instance's slot is determined by the slots of other instances in the former instance's slots.

1. Every value (B) of slot ___ of an instance (A) of class ___ must contain the same value in slot ___ of A and the value in slot ___ of B.
2. Every instance (A) of class ___ that is a value of slot ___ of instance (B) of class ___ must have the same value in its slot ___ as in slot ___ of B.

Note that the second templates from both examples are identical. We identified several properties of templates, which are not mutually exclusive:

1. Constraint involves direct comparisons between every instance of a class.
2. Constraint expresses a condition that is true as long as one particular instance of the referenced group satisfies the condition
3. Constraint involves value(s) of a slot determined by another own slot(s)

4. Constraint involves value(s) of a slot determined by the slots of other instances(in/not in former instance's) slots
5. Constraint involves multiple constraining/constrained slots.

We distinguish these high-level descriptions of templates from the previously discussed "super-template," because the former is not an attempt to find a more structurally general representation of template groups. Rather, this type of categorization describes the templates at a very high level that assumes no knowledge about the templates' structure, but only the common "thoughts" that they express.

We believe that these characterizations of templates can serve as the basis of implicit organization through descriptions rather than through a hierarchical organizational scheme; hence we call them "properties" of templates. We create a flat hierarchy of templates in which all templates have the superclass *template*, but each contains a section describing the properties that it satisfies. This strategy also permits much flexibility; the user can customize the templates by creating new properties. This feature also enables searching for templates by filtering out the ones that do not satisfy user's particular characterization, rather than searching through a predetermined sequence of classifications/tree-traversals unfamiliar to the intended users.

4. DISCUSSION

After examining axioms in existing ontology libraries we identified two important facts: (1) Many ontologies simply lack axioms, likely because axioms are very hard for domain experts to write. (2) Most of the axioms that do exist in the ontologies can be described by a small set of templates. We can use these templates to allow users to specify axioms by selecting an appropriate template and filling in the blanks rather than by having to conceptualise and express a complex axiom in first-order logic.

Tu and Musen [11] observe in a clinical domain that most of the axioms that domain experts need to write follow a limited set of patterns. They created a Protégé-based knowledge-acquisition tool for medical guidelines. In their approach, instead of writing an axiom in PAL, a domain expert fills in a form that looks exactly as a form for any regular instance in the knowledge base. For example, there is a check box to mark whether actions are predicated on the presence or the absence of a particular criterion; there is a box to select from the list of time periods; there is a box to select a value from the list of conditions, and so on. Once the user fills in the form, the system automatically generates an axiom in PAL. In this approach, the user can specify a large fraction of axioms simply by performing a fairly intuitive task—filling in blanks in a form. However, the templates are specific to defining medical guideline criteria. It would be impossible to use them verbatim in another application area.

Research in classifying and representing axioms in a user-friendly way has been relatively sparse in the knowledge base community. Staab and Mädche [9] recommend an approach similar to ours: They note that many axioms that they encountered in ontology-engineering projects follow similar patterns. They abstract several classes of axioms, such as algebraic axioms (e.g., reflexivity and symmetry of properties), axioms dealing with composition of relations, axioms describing part–whole relations and so on. The representation of an axiom (the one that the user sees) is then a predicate for which a user needs only to specify arguments. The user does not need to worry about the symbolic representation of the axiom in a specific language. For the types of axioms that the authors discuss, the predicate approach works well. However, it is unclear how the same approach would work for slightly different variations of axioms and axioms with varying number of conditions. In addition, for many users a look at the predicate name does not immediately clarify what the underlying axioms are about (e.g., consider a predicate "PartonomicRolePropagation"). In the ontology libraries that we considered, most axioms did not fall in the categories identified by Staab and Mädche. However, we affirm the approach of representing axioms as objects in a knowledge base and allowing users to represent axioms at a conceptually high level of abstraction.

Researchers have applied this idea not only to specifying single axioms but also to specifying sets of axioms. In some cases, a set of axioms represents a complex knowledge-base component, such as the description of a physical process [1,2]. In other cases, a set of parameterised axioms represents a new constraint that cannot be directly expressed in the corresponding language [10]. As a result, the task of the knowledge-base designer is greatly simplified, since all he needs to do is to instantiate a particular pattern rather than to write a set of axioms from scratch. In addition, the user creates the definition in an intuitive syntax and the system can translate it into several specific languages if necessary. We not only identify a set of these recurring patterns, but we do so as a result of analysing a large set of real-world axioms that users have created in their ontologies.

The use of design patterns in object-oriented programming [4] is another approach to adopting recurring representation patterns as the building blocks of design. A design pattern records, explains, and evaluates patterns of code in object-oriented systems. Similar to our templates, design patterns encode information for structuring, creating, and managing the 'design idioms.'

Our primary goal in designing the set of axiom templates is to facilitate the task of specifying axioms for domain experts. Naturally, the primary

application of this research is to design an easy-to-use interface, which would enable domain experts to specify axioms quickly and easily.
In the interface, we may present a set of available templates and a list of their properties. If a user finds the size of initial list of template unwieldy for browsing, he can examine the list of properties (Section 3.2), and check the ones that are likely to be compatible with his thought to filter out unlikely candidates from the template list. A user can browse the remaining templates, each of which is accompanied by a sample usage in both English and fill-in-the-blanks representations. Once ready, the user can simply select appropriate variations, fill in the blanks, and 'instantiate' an axiom without encountering the obscure syntax of the axiom language. Note that such an interface will work for many underlying axiom languages because the selection and instantiation of a template is the same regardless of the underlying language. We envision that advanced users will be able to extend the set of templates which we also model as an ontology in Protégé; the templates are simply classes in the knowledge base. Thus, the advanced users can create new template classes and a processing engine can incorporate them into the interface. Similarly, they may create new instances of the class *Property* to introduce additional categorization of templates.
We are currently implementing such a system to perform empirical evaluation on coverage, usability, and readability of the templates. To evaluate coverage, we will examine axioms in an ontology library that we have not yet considered and determine what fraction of axioms in that library our templates represent. To evaluate usability, we will perform user studies where we will first ask domain experts to express constraints in English that they hope to incorporate in their knowledge base but cannot encode in an axiom language. We can then measure the ratio of axioms they actually are able to encode with our template-based system compared to the number of constraints that we deem expressible in that language. The result will attest the practicality of our strategy in promoting the composition of more axioms. Finally, we will experiment with several alternatives for the English representations of the templates to derive the most intuitive statements.

ACKNOWLEDGMENTS

We are very grateful to Samson Tu, Mor Peleg and Iwei Yeh for sharing their Protégé ontologies. We would also like to thank Monica Crubézy for suggestions about template designs. This work was supported in part by a contract from the U.S. National Cancer Institute. Johnson Hou was supported by the Stanford President's Scholar Intellectual Exploration Grant for lower-division undergraduate students.

REFERENCES

1. Barker, K., Clark, P. and Porter, B. A Library of Generic Concepts for Composing Knowledge Bases. In: *1st Int Conf on Knowledge Capture (K-Cap'01)*. Victoria, BC, 2001.
2. Clark P., Thompson, J., and Porter, B. Knowledge Patterns. In *KR'2000 (Proc 7th Int Conf)*, pages 591-600, Eds: A. Cohn, F. Giunchiglia, B. Selman, CA:Kaufmann, 2000.
3. Chaudhri, V.K., Farquhar, A., Fikes, R., Karp, P.D. and Rice, J.P. OKBC: A programmatic foundation for knowledge base interoperability. In: *Fifteenth National Conference on Artificial Intelligence (AAAI-98)*. Madison, Wisconsin: AAAI Press/The MIT Press, 1998.
4. Gamma, E., Helm, R., Johnson, R. and Vlissides, J., *Design Patterns: Elements of Reusable Object Oriented Software*. Reading, MA: Addison-Wesley, 1999.
5. Genesereth, M.R. and Fikes, R.E., *Knowledge Interchange Format, Version 0.3, Reference Manual*, Knowledge Systems Laboratory, Stanford University, 1992.
6. Karp, P.D., *The design space of frame knowledge representation systems*, SRI AI Center: Menlo Park, CA, 1993.
7. Ontolingua, *Ontolingua System Reference Manual*, Knowledge Systems Lab, Stanford University, http://www-ksl-svc.stanford.edu:5915/doc/frame-editor/index.html
8. Protégé, *The Protege Project*, Stanford Medical Informatics, Stanford University, http://protege.stanford.edu, 2000.
9. Staab, S. and Mädche, A. Axioms are objects, too - Ontology Engineering Beyond the Modeling of Concepts and Relations. In: *ECAI 2000 Workshop on Ontologies and Problem-Solving Methods*. Berlin, 2000.
10. Staab, M. Erdmann, A. Maedche. Engineering ontologies using semantic patterns. In A. Preece & D. O'Leary (eds.), *Proceedings of the IJCAI-01 Workshop on E-Business & the Intelligent Web*. Seattle, 2001.
11. Tu, S.W. and Musen, M.A. Modeling Data and Knowledge in the EON Guideline Architecture. In: *MedInfo 2001*. London, 2001.

CONFIGURING ONLINE PROBLEM-SOLVING RESOURCES WITH THE INTERNET REASONING SERVICE

Monica Crubézy,[1] Wenjin Lu,[2] Enrico Motta,[2] and Mark A. Musen[1]
[1]*Stanford Medical Informatics, 251 Campus Drive, Stanford CA 94305-5479, USA.*
email: {crubezy, musen}@smi.stanford.edu
[2]*Knowledge Media Institute, The Open University, Milton Keynes, MK7 6AA, UK.*
email: {e.motta, w.lu}@open.ac.uk

Abstract: Existing services on the World-Wide Web tend to be "integral." For instance, online services for data analysis are available, but usually it is neither possible to modify the underlying reasoning system, nor to configure it for a different domain, nor to integrate different services to produce new functionalities. Our research goal is to develop the technological framework needed to provide sophisticated online problem-solving resources, configurable for different applications. We describe the design and initial implementation of the Internet Reasoning Service—a Web-based front-end enabling developers to prototype knowledge-based applications quickly out of reusable components in distributed libraries. Our aim is to make reliable problem-solving technology available to a wider audience and to provide the level of intelligent support needed to allow rapid generation of Web-based reasoning services.

Key words: Problem-solving methods, ontologies, reusable components, knowledge-based systems, knowledge acquisition, adapters, Web services.

1. INTRODUCTION

Many resources on the Web are now dynamic services that provide some functionality for end users, such as booking a plane, and analyzing gene data. These services, however, tend to be "integral:" usually, it is neither possible to modify the underlying reasoning system of these services, nor to configure it for a different domain, nor to integrate different services to produce new functionalities. The necessary technologies and frameworks for service identification, configuration and interoperability on the Web still remain to be developed. To foster this objective, the competence of each Web service must be specified, so that brokering agents can locate services, match them to user needs and configure them to realize specific user tasks. This approach is central to the IBROW project[6] [2]. In this context, we focus on configurable reasoning services: our goal is to develop the methodology and tool support needed to provide sophisticated problem-solving facilities (e.g., a heuristic-classification technology) on the Web, which different users (e.g., archeologists, biologists) can configure for specific applications. Note that our approach differs from the recently appeared "Web services," that tend to offer only predefined, limited reasoning functionalities, very specific to a given domain context (see Section 4).

Our approach stems from research on knowledge-based system (KBS) development by reuse [1, 3, 4, 6, 7, 11]. This area has identified domain-independent problem-solving strategies, or *problem-solving methods (PSMs)* [1, 6, 7, 11, 12], that provide standard ways of addressing stereotypical knowledge-intensive problems, or *generic tasks* [4], such as diagnosis, design, and classification. To foster the reuse of PSMs, structured *libraries* have been developed, in which the methods are indexed and retrieved for different domains and purposes [1, 3, 6, 11-13]. Furthermore, comprehensive frameworks take a PSM-centered view to support KBS development from reusable components [7, 11, 14, 17]. This process involves modeling a user problem as a generic task, and configuring an appropriate PSM, by integrating the generic components with domain-specific information.

This reuse-centered approach is now the most established and robust paradigm in knowledge engineering. However, the level of actual component reuse is still quite low, due to several pragmatic barriers: libraries of problem-solving components are few and far between, often they are not available online, and different libraries are not interoperable, neither at the knowledge level nor at the symbol level. Furthermore, existing frameworks for KBS development do not offer sufficient guidance for users to select and configure the reasoning component of their system.

We describe here the *Internet Reasoning Service (IRS)*, a Web-based front-end that enables developers to prototype knowledge-based applications quickly out of reusable components in distributed libraries. Based on a well-defined process model, the IRS overcomes the limitations of KBS-development frameworks by providing semi-automated support for each step of this application-configuration process. We have implemented the IRS as a Web-based server, integrated with the OCML reasoning platform [11] and the generic Protégé-2000 knowledge-modeling environment [14]. In this paper

[6] http://www.swi.psy.uva.nl/projects/ibrow/home.html

we provide an overview of the IRS and we show how it was used to produce a classification problem solver for the domain of Roman pottery archeology.

2. THE INTERNET REASONING SERVICE

Problem-solving libraries contain reusable software components, which can be configured into a running application to solve users' problems. These components are primarily tasks and PSMs, which model the reasoning building blocks of a KBS. For example, we have developed a library of reusable components for heuristic classification problem-solving [12]—the task of matching an unknown object, denoted by a set of 'observables,' to a 'solution space' of classes of similar objects. The IRS supports users in operating a set of distributed libraries of problem-solving resources to achieve tasks in their domain. The IRS provides different levels of support, from interactive browsing facilities for the manual selection and configuration of reasoning resources, to intelligent, semi-automated assistance in building an executable application.

The IRS relies on the knowledge-level descriptions of the problem-solving components in the libraries. The *Unified Problem-solving Method-development Language* (UPML)[7] is a Web-compatible framework that we have designed in IBROW for modeling the reusable components of a knowledge system [15]. UPML distinguishes three kinds of components: (1) *tasks*, which are functions that a KBS can achieve (e.g., classification), (2) *PSMs*, which are methods that implement the reasoning process of a KBS to realize a task (e.g., an optimal heuristic classifier), and (3) *domain models*, which are views on domain knowledge, as used by tasks and PSMs (e.g., archeology). Each component (e.g., a domain model) defines a particular *ontology*—a specification of the important concepts involved in the component model (e.g., the notion of 'solution space' for the classification task). PSMs and tasks specify a set of *input* and *output roles*. Each PSM also defines a functional *competence* in the form of a set of logical *preconditions* and *postconditions*. For instance, the competence of an optimal heuristic classifier states that the output solutions are optimal with respect to the input solution space. Each task is further characterized with a logical *goal expression* and a set of *assumptions* on domain knowledge. These components of a KBS can be configured and combined together in different running systems through the creation of explicit architectural elements—*adapters* [7]. In particular, *bridge* adapters connect two kinds of components, such as a PSM and a domain model, by way of *mapping relations* between

[7] http://www.cs.vu.nl/~upml/

the ontologies of both components. This way, a bridge between the optimal heuristic classifier PSM and the archeology domain maps the notion of 'abstractor' introduced by the PSM and a data-abstraction function for archeology observables.

The process of configuring the reasoning component of a KBS involves several activities: mapping generic tasks and PSMs to a domain model (e.g., mapping the generic classification task to a database of archeological artifacts to produce an artifact-classification application), mapping PSMs to tasks (e.g., selecting a particular abstraction method for performing the data-abstraction subtask of classification), or, in general, adapting existing components (e.g., specializing the data-to-solutions matching component of the classification process by introducing fuzziness in the matching process). More precisely, we have identified a clear process model for the IRS, that involves eight steps, from task selection to application execution (*Figure 1*). The manual completion of each step requires significant skills from users: the goal of the IRS is to guide users through the entire configuration process.

In the following, we detail each step of the IRS process model. Although our approach is agnostic of any specific problem-solving library, we illustrate the use of the IRS with examples taken from our experiment in configuring components of a classification problem-solving library [12] for the archeology domain. In this domain, the user is an archeologist who wishes to develop automated support for classifying Roman-pottery artifacts, based on information collected about the artifacts.

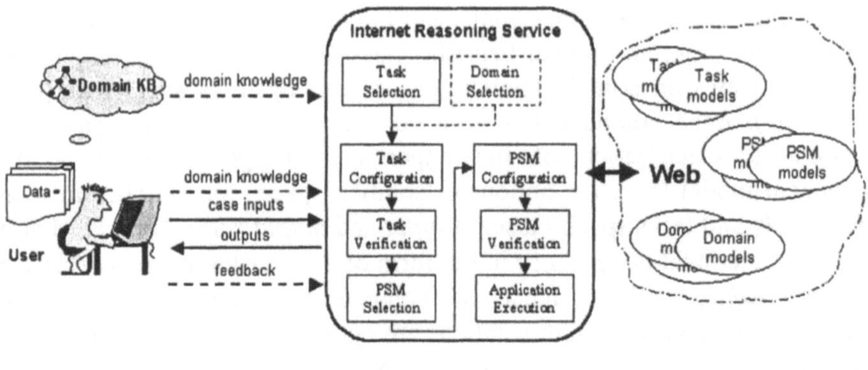

Figure 1. The IRS: use scenario and process model.

Task selection. IRS users first need to characterize the goal of their application in terms of one of the tasks known to the IRS, e.g., *classification*. Task selection is hard: it means adopting a particular viewpoint to impose over an application. For instance, the solutions to the benchmark Sisyphus-I office-allocation problem [9] included both i) approaches that modeled the problem as a design problem and ii) approaches that modeled it as a classification problem. In other words, a specific application does not necessarily fall into a particular task model. Rather, it is a task model that provides a conceptual viewpoint for characterizing an application and for focusing the knowledge-acquisition process. The IRS supports users in browsing and navigating UPML-based descriptions of the various tasks in the available libraries, along with examples of the ways tasks have been applied previously. Users select a task by choosing a refinement of a high-level task (e.g., *optimal-solution classification*).

Task configuration. In this crucial step, users configure the selected task (e.g., *single-solution classification*) for their particular domain (e.g., archeology) by providing relevant domain knowledge to fill the input–output roles defined by the task. The IRS provides support adapted to the understanding that users have of the configuration process, allowing for a direct reuse of pre-existing configurations or more advanced experimentation. First, the IRS supports the direct acquisition of the value of an input role, according to the task ontology. For example, users can define a new *match criterion* (a mechanism to assess the degree-of-fit between data and solutions) in terms of the task ontology. Alternatively, users simply can select a default value for the input role from the library. Finally, if domain knowledge does not conform to the task ontology, the IRS supports users in constructing a *mapping relation* between the task role and domain knowledge. A domain-task mapping relation defines the transformation of a piece of domain knowledge into an instantiated role for the task [16]. In our experiment, we mapped the role *solution-space* to a hierarchy of archeological artifact types, and the notion of *observables* to attributes of artifacts, such as 'provenance,' 'material,' etc. In the application-execution step, these attributes are instantiated by case-data values. Output roles clearly are not instantiated with actual knowledge structures at this stage; however, mappings also may be required for outputs to conform to the domain ontology. Creating explicit architectural elements that isolate the configuration knowledge for a set of components maximizes the reusability of these components. However, this activity requires that users understand the connections and adaptations needed on the knowledge components to be assembled into a working system. The IRS reduces the complexity of the configuration process by providing structured mapping templates that users instantiate for their particular case. Nevertheless, more research is needed to ease the configuration process further.

The IRS generates a *task-domain bridge* for the relevant task and domain ontologies, to store the set of mapping relations created during the task-configuration step. The IRS allows users to backtrack to the task-selection step if their domain does not match the expectations of the task (e.g., the task expects single-valued observables when domain observables are multi-valued), and to select another refinement of the high-level task.

Domain selection. In this phase, users specify the domain knowledge that they intend to use in their application. The IRS provides a range of pre-existing domain models stored in available UPML-compliant libraries, from which users simply can make a selection. The advantage of selecting an available domain model is that, in many cases, no configuration effort will be needed, given that mappings themselves are often reusable. In our archeological experiment we can see that the mappings discussed earlier tend to be generic (observables ⇒ artifact features; solution space ⇒ hierarchy of artifact types). Alternatively, the IRS enables users to provide domain knowledge directly by filling-in knowledge-acquisition forms. Another possibility is that users provide their own knowledge base. In this case, users need to solve the related interoperability problems, both at the knowledge and at the symbol level (see Section 4).

Task verification This step consists in checking the assumptions that the selected task defines on domain knowledge. The IRS performs this step automatically by running an assumption-checking engine on the task input roles—possibly obtained from domain inputs through mapping relations—and the assumptions of the task. The IRS notifies users about the inputs that do not satisfy the assumptions of the task. In this case, the IRS guides users back to the task-configuration step, so that they can re-specify the erroneous inputs. However, it is important to note that not all assumptions are necessarily verifiable. For instance, our task model for *single-solution classification* includes the assumption that only one solution exists in the target domain. Clearly this assumption cannot be verified in the general case.

PSM selection. This step focuses on selecting a PSM that can realize the configured task. Similarly to the task-selection step, the IRS provides users with the list of PSMs that match the configured task and supports users in browsing the description of each PSM. The IRS uses different means to compute the list of PSM candidates for realizing the task. First, the UPML description of the library may include a set of *PSM–task bridges*. Each bridge encodes a connection between a task and a PSM that can realize that task, together with a set of mapping relations between the task and PSM ontologies. Such a bridge connects the *single-solution classification* task and the *heuristic-admissible-solution classifier* PSM in our classification library. Alternatively, the IRS carries out a competence-matching process, by reasoning about the competence of PSMs and the goal of the current task. In general, such reasoning requires full first-order logic theorem-proving support, which is not part of the current implementation of the IRS. Finally, users themselves can choose among all available PSMs in the library.

PSM configuration. This step is similar to the task-configuration step, at the level of the selected PSM: the IRS guides users in specifying the domain entities that fill-in the input–output roles of the PSM. Some of the roles for the PSM are "inherited" from the configured task, through a corresponding *PSM–task bridge*. If not already provided in the library, the IRS supports the creation of such a bridge to map the inputs and outputs of the configured task to the ones of the selected PSM. In addition, the selected PSM may define supplemental roles. For example, the *heuristic-admissible-solution classifier* PSM defines the notion of an *abstractor*—a function that computes abstract observables from raw data. In our archeology domain, we defined such a function to abstract from the specific geographical site in which the artifact was found (i.e., the 'provenance' feature) to a more coarse-grained area, more useful to classify the artifact. The IRS supports the acquisition of domain-method mapping knowledge in a way similar to the domain-task mapping during task configuration. The IRS finally stores the result of the PSM configuration as a *PSM-domain bridge* created for the user's domain.

PSM verification. This step focuses on verifying that the selected PSM can be applied to the task and the domain in accordance with the assumptions of the PSM and the results of the configuration process. This step is essentially the same as the task-verification step. For instance, in the case of our chosen heuristic classifier, the assumption-checking engine will verify that the solution hierarchy (i.e., the hierarchy of artifact types) contains no cycles. As a result, the IRS notifies users about the domain inputs that do not satisfy the assumptions or preconditions of the PSM. In this case, the IRS guides users back either to the task-configuration step or to the PSM-configuration step, to re-specify the inputs that are not satisfied.

Application execution. This final step consists in running the configured PSM to realize the specified task, with domain case data entered by the user. The IRS first acquires case data from the user and instantiates the case inputs of the PSM by interpreting the domain–task, task–PSM and domain–PSM mapping relations. The IRS also checks the preconditions of the PSM and task on the mapped case data. The IRS then invokes the PSM code with the mapped inputs, by running a code interpreter either locally or remotely. Knowledge about the location and type of PSM code is stored in *pragmatics* fields of the UPML description of the PSM. Finally, the IRS fills-in the domain outputs with the results of PSM execution, possibly transformed with domain–PSM mapping relations defined at PSM-configuration time.

3. INITIAL IMPLEMENTATION OF THE IRS

We have implemented the IRS design as a prototype tool, which exploits knowledge, Web and HCI technologies already available to our two groups. We first have implemented the IRS generic design in Java, as a Web front-end based on the OCML modeling language [11]. We also have implemented the IRS design as a service integrated to the widely-used Protégé-2000 knowledge modeling environment [14].

The IRS Web-based front-end. Our first implementation of the IRS capitalizes on knowledge and Web technologies available at the Knowledge Media Institute, mainly the OCML modeling and execution language [11] and a large library of problem-solving components, compliant with the UPML framework, and accessible online through a knowledge-level API. We use OCML to describe both the UPML properties of knowledge components and their actual contents. The IRS is directly connected to the LispWeb server, an online interpreter that processes OCML requests.

We have developed an initial implementation of the IRS, which supports all activities in the process model described in Section 2. Browsing support and ontology-driven knowledge-acquisition facilities enable users to instantiate role values directly, or to select pre-existing ones from a library. The IRS supports mapping through pre-defined OCML constructs, as well as 'free-form' constructs for expressing arbitrary mappings [11]. The IRS also provides library-specific high-level mapping templates, such as a 'Map to Hierarchy' template for the classification library, which allows the user to simply state that a particular domain hierarchy instantiates the role 'solution space'. The IRS also supports assumption-checking and a limited form of competence matching, which relies on pre-existing relations between tasks and PSMs. Finally, the IRS supports the application-execution step by invoking the OCML environment to interpret the PSM code on the case data inputs that the user enters in special-purpose forms.

Integration of the IRS design with Protégé-2000. We also have implemented the IRS design as an extension to Protégé-2000[8], a tool developed at Stanford for ontology development and ontology-driven knowledge-base construction [14]. Our IRS extension interfaces domain knowledge bases to libraries of tasks and PSMs, specified in UPML with a Protégé-based UPML editor [15]. This extension implements the user interface of the IRS with the ontology-driven, graphical knowledge-acquisition support of Protégé, to enable users to select and configure application components.

[8] http://protégé.stanford.edu

Most importantly, Protégé brings additional support to the IRS for the two configuration steps, by providing a structured methodology for mapping roles of reasoning components to corresponding domain entities. Our methodology provides a typology of mapping-relation templates—a *mapping ontology* [16], which covers a wide range of mapping relations, from simple renaming mappings, to complex numerical or lexical expressions of entities. Protégé guides users in the configuration steps based on this mapping ontology and the input–output definition of the task or PSM. In addition, Protégé incorporates a *mapping interpreter* [16], which runs the mapping relations with the domain entities to create PSM-level entities.

The IRS extension of Protégé is connected to the IRS Web-based server, to which it delegates the steps of task and PSM-verification, as well as the execution of the configured PSM with case data that users enter in knowledge-acquisition forms.

4. DISCUSSION

Our research is related to existing work in the area of Web and knowledge technologies. Our comparison highlights the strengths of our approach together with the main issues still to be addressed.

Configurable Web services. Recent industrial efforts aim to provide online, configurable services on the Web. They address the syntactic-level interoperability of Web services with standardized protocols for component-functionality description and communication (e.g., UDDI[9], WSDL[10], .Net[11], Jini[12]). Software components can thus be discovered, usually by a centralized look-up service. Although these distributed Web services can cooperate to achieve a certain goal, they typically provide only predefined functionalities.

Semantic approaches stem from research in earlier agent technology. Web services declare their capabilities and requirements, and special-purpose agents mediate those services to users by locating, matching and connecting them [18]. Shared ontologies of Web services and plan-like procedures, described in the recently-designed DAML-S[13] language, further enable agents to perform tasks for users, by dynamically chaining primitive steps realized by Web sites [10]. These services, however, implement relatively fine-grained, ad-hoc procedures that solve limited problems. Furthermore, such approaches assume that users and services share the same domain of

[9] http://www.uddi.org/

[10] http://msdn.microsoft.com/xml/general/wsdl.asp

[11] http://www.microsoft.com/net/

[12] http://www.sun.com/jini/

[13] http://www.daml.org/services/

discourse, ignoring the issue of mapping domain, task and method ontologies. Thus, such Web services are less reusable in different domains.

Our goal also is to provide configurable services on the Web. However, the services that we provide are complete, robust, and reusable methods for achieving common knowledge-intensive tasks in various domains. Our user-centered, ontology-driven approach to component configuration provides a full framework to model problem solvers, that the IRS then uses for constructing knowledge-based applications for different contexts.

Competence matching. Currently we do not address adequately the issue of retrieving PSMs that can realize the user-specified task. The list of possible candidate PSMs can be computed by a competence-matching process. This process involves reasoning over the competence of both the configured task and the available PSMs: candidate PSMs are selected if their postcondition statement fulfills the goal of the task, and if their preconditions do not contradict the assumptions of the task. Agent-based approaches such as RETSINA include an efficient competence-matching process, which retrieves agents, based on the services that they advertize in the LARKS language [18]. However, LARKS provides relatively weak representational machinery to express the formal competence of agents. A similar approach is under investigation by other members of the IBROW consortium. An important issue is to design contents-specification formalisms, which strike the right balance between expressiveness and efficiency in support of competence matching. The IRS must also address the possible mismatch between the ontologies of the task and of the available PSMs. Although usually not as different as the ontologies of domains and tasks, the ontologies of tasks and PSMs sometimes need to be mapped through explicit relations, which in turn need to be interpreted as part of a competence-matching process.

Interoperability. Component interoperability is at the center of the IRS—and, more generally, the IBROW—approach. Typically, each problem-solving library uses a specific knowledge-modeling language to express properties of its components, and includes pieces of code in a particular programming language. The federated UPML framework alleviates this difficulty only at the modeling level. Knowledge-level interoperability requires shared ontologies and either common modelling languages or the use of standard knowledge-level APIs, such as OKBC [5]. Protégé brings to the IRS its support for OKBC-compliant languages. At the execution level, configured components—including possible domain knowledge provided by users in a proprietary format—need to be assembled in an interoperable system. The use of distributed-computing standards, such as CORBA,[14] has

[14] http://www.corba.org/

proven to be a successful means for encapsulating problem-solving components and combining them into platform-independent, operational systems [8]. Indeed our initial IBROW broker prototype used a CORBA-based architecture to operate heterogeneous components [2] and we have also implemented a generic CORBA-based interface to the IRS, that enables library providers to make their components available to the IRS.

5. CONCLUSION

Our IRS approach strongly builds on proven knowledge-engineering techniques. The key asset that the IRS adds to these techniques is a principled methodology and user-centered tool support for prototyping knowledge systems by configuring reusable components from structured libraries. Although some symbol-level and knowledge-level interoperability issues remain to be addressed, we believe that the IRS approach will foster a wider diffusion of knowledge-engineering paradigms, by lowering the current conceptual and engineering barriers to applying them.

The Web vehicle will allow us to perform a large evaluation experiment of our IRS approach, that promises to simplify system construction by component reuse. We plan to evaluate aspects such as speed up in system construction and exploitation, efficacy and utility of built systems and straightforwardness of the application-building process for domain users. At the same time, the heterogeneous, distributed and versatile nature of the Web will challenge us to incorporate more automated support in the IRS, with simplified procedures and customized interactions, so that less-experienced users also can benefit from advanced distributed problem-solving services.

Current users of the IRS are reasonably skilled developers, who wish to prototype a KBS application, or simply explore KBS technology. Over time, we aim to broaden the target audience of the IRS, by making it possible for less-experienced developers to create applications with the IRS. Finally, although the current focus of our research is on facilitating user access to sophisticated reasoning services, which involve heterogeneous ontologies, we expect to harness the technologies produced in this research in support of more 'mundane' levels of service provision on the Web. In these cases we can take advantage of scenarios in which ontology mapping and service interoperability issues are greatly simplified.

ACKNOWLEDGEMENTS

This work is part of the IBROW Project, funded by the IST program of the European Community. We thank our IBROW collaborators for the many stimulating discussions on the topics discussed in this paper. Finally, we thank our two anonymous reviewers for their helpful comments.

REFERENCES

1. Benjamins, V.R. Problem Solving Methods for Diagnosis, University of Amsterdam, 1993.
2. Benjamins, V.R., Plaza, E., Motta, E., Fensel, D., Studer, R., Wielinga, R., Schreiber, G., Zdrahal, Z. and Decker, S., An intelligent brokering service for knowledge-component reuse on the World-Wide Web. in *KAW'1998*, (1998).
3. Breuker, J.A., and van de Velde, W. (ed.), *The CommonKADS Library for Expertise Modeling*. IOS Press, Amsterdam, 1994.
4. Chandrasekaran, B. Generic tasks for knowledge-based reasoning: High-level building blocks for expert system design. *IEEE Expert, 1* (3). 23-30.
5. Chaudhri, V.K., Farquhar, A., Fikes, R., Karp, P.D. and Rice, J.P., OKBC: A programmatic foundation for knowledge base interoperability. in *AAAI'1998*, (Madison, Wisconsin, 1998), AAAI Press/The MIT Press, 600-607.
6. Eriksson, H., Shahar, Y., Tu, S.W., Puerta, A.R. and Musen, M.A. Task modeling with reusable problem-solving methods. *Artificial Intelligence, 79*. 293-326.
7. Fensel, D. and Motta, E. Structured Development of Problem Solving Methods. *IEEE Transactions on Knowledge and Data Engineering, 13* (6). 913-932.
8. Gennari, J.H., Cheng, H., Altman, R. B., Musen, M.A. Reuse, CORBA, and Knowledge-Based Systems. *International Journal of Human-Computer Studies, 49* (4). 523-546.
9. Linster, M. Problem Statement for Sisyphus: Models of Problem Solving. *International Journal of Human-Computer Studies, 40* (2). 187-192.
10. McIlraith, S.A., Son, T.C. and Zeng, H. Semantic Web Services. *IEEE Intelligent Systems, 16* (2). 46-53.
11. Motta, E. *Reusable Components for Knowledge Modelling: Principles and Case Studies in Parametric Design.* IOS Press, Amsterdam, 1999.
12. Motta, E. and Lu, W., A Library of Components for Classification Problem Solving. in *PKAW'2000*, (Sydney, Australia, 2000).
13. Musen, M.A., Modern Architectures for Intelligent Systems: Reusable Ontologies and Problem-Solving Methods. in *AMIA Annual Symposium*, (Orlando, FL, 1998), 46-52.
14. Musen, M.A., Fergerson, R.W., Grosso, W.E., Noy, N.F., Crubézy, M. and Gennari, J.H., Component-Based Support for Building Knowledge-Acquisition Systems. in *Conference on Intelligent Information Processing (IIP 2000) of the International Federation for Information Processing World Computer Congress (WCC 2000)*, (Beijing, China, 2000).
15. Omelayenko, B., Crubézy, M., Fensel, D., Benjamins, V.R., Wielinga, B.J., Motta, E., Musen, M.A. and Ding, Y. UPML: The Language and Tool Support for Making the Semantic Web Alive. in Fensel, D., Hendler, J., Liebermann, H. and Wahlster, W. eds. *To appear in: Creating the Semantic Web*, MIT Press, In press.
16. Park, J.Y., Gennari, J.H. and Musen, M.A., Mappings for Reuse in Knowledge-Based Systems. in *Eleventh Banff Knowledge Acquisition for Knowledge-Based Systems Workshop*, (Banff, Alberta., 1998).
17. Schreiber, A.T., Akkermans, J.M., Anjewierden, A.A., de Hoog, R., Shadbolt, N.R., van de Velde, W., and Wielinga, B.J. *Knowledge Engineering and Management: The CommonKADS Methodology*. MIT Press, Cambridge, 2000.
18. Sycara, K., Lu, J., Klusch, M. and Widoff, S., Matchmaking among Heterogeneous Agents on the Internet. in *AAAI Spring Symposium on Intelligent Agents in Cyberspace*, (Stanford, CA, 1999).

SEMANTIC WEB AND MULTI-AGENTS APPROACH TO CORPORATE MEMORY MANAGEMENT

Fabien Gandon, Rose Dieng-Kuntz, Olivier Corby, Alain Giboin
ACACIA project, INRIA Sophia Antipolis, <Firstname>.<Name>@sophia.inria.fr

Abstract: Organisations have increasingly large amount of heterogeneous documents to manage and organise in order to turn them into active and helpful corporate memories. We present an approach based on semantic Web and multi-agents systems to implement a framework for corporate semantic Web management.

Key words: semantic web, multi-agents system, corporate memory, knowledge management, ontologies, information retrieval.

1. INTRODUCTION

Increasingly rapid staff turnover, swiftly changing environments, ever growing size and spreading of infrastructures lead organisations to look for tools and methodologies to manage a persistent active memory of their experience. This memory is more and more often taking the form of an intraweb *i.e.* an intranet based on the Web technologies. It leads to amounts of semi-structured information internally available on-line but buried and dormant in their mass. In the CoMMA [1] IST project, we developed a system in charge of managing an intraweb for two knowledge management scenarios: (1) assistance to the integration of newcomers in an organisation and (2) support to the technology monitoring processes. This prototype exploits the semantic Web technologies and it relies on the O'CoMMA ontology used to semantically annotate the intraweb resources. To manage these annotations, information agents were developed to constitute a multi-agent system (MAS) *i.e.* a loosely coupled network of agents that work together as a society. A MAS is heterogeneous when it includes agents of at least two types. A Multi-Agents Information System (MAIS) is a MAS aiming at providing some or full range of functionalities for managing and exploiting information resources. The application of MAIS to corporate memories means that the co-operation of agents aims at enhancing information capitalisation in the company. The MAIS projects CASMIR [4] and Ricochet [5] focus on the gathering of information and adapting interaction to the user's preferences, learning interest to build communities and collaborative filtering inside an organisation. KnowWeb [13] relies on mobile agents to support dynamically changing networked environment and exploits a domain model to extract concepts describing a documents in order to use them to answer queries. RICA [1] maintains a shared taxonomy in which nodes are attached to documents and uses it to push suggestions to interface agents according to user profiles. Finally FRODO [20] is dedicated to building and maintaining distributed organisational memories with an emphasis on the management of domain ontologies.

The CoMMA software architecture is an heterogeneous MAIS that focuses on providing retrieval, pull and push functionalities to support the exploitation of the intraweb during the two application scenarios. The different tasks involved in the exploitation process were allocated to different agent types, the instances of which are distributed over the intranet.

This paper details our approach in three sections: first we present the notion of a *corporate semantic Web* relying on an *ontology*; then we explain the role of *models and the global architecture of the memory*; last, we portray the *multi-agents architecture* for managing the memory. In our conclusion we discuss the evaluation of the prototype.

2. TOWARDS A CORPORATE SEMANTIC WEB

A corporate memory is, by nature, an heterogeneous and distributed information landscape. Corporate memories are facing the same problem of information retrieval and information overload as the Web. Therefore semantic Web technologies can be helpful as emphasised in this section.

2.1 The concept of a corporate semantic Web

XML is becoming an industry standard for exchanging data or documents. In CoMMA, we are especially interested in RDF, the Resource Description Framework [17], and its XML syntax. RDF is the foundation of the semantic Web [3], a promising approach where the semantics of documents is made explicit through annotations to guide later exploitation. RDF allows us to annotate the resources of the memory semantically. It uses a simple data model as the basis for a language for representing properties of resources (anything that can be pointed by an URI such as Web pages or images) and the relationships between them. The corporate memory is thus studied as a *corporate semantic Web*: we describe the semantic content of corporate documents through semantic annotations then used to search the mass of information of the corporate memory.

Just as an important feature of new software systems is the ability to integrate legacy systems, an important feature of a corporate memory management framework is the ability to integrate the legacy archives. Since RDF annotations can be either internal or external to the document, existing documents may be kept intact and annotated externally. This is complementary to the MAS ability to include legacy systems by wrapping them into an agent. Even if wrappers are not addressed in CoMMA, a new agent could be added to wrap, for instance, the access to a database using a mapping between the DB schema and the O'CoMMA ontology.

RDF makes no assumption about a particular application domain, nor defines *a priori* the semantics of any application domain; the annotations are based on an ontology which is described and shared thanks to the primitives provided by RDF Schema [6] (RDFS). The idea is (a) to specify the corporate memory concepts and their relationships in an ontology formalised in a schema in RDFS, (b) to annotate the documents of the memory in RDF using the schema (c) to exploit the annotations to search the memory.

2.2 Ontology engineering and its result: O'CoMMA

We proposed a method to build ontologies and applied it to obtain O'CoMMA (see [15] for more details). The method relies on three stages:

1. Scenario analysis and Data collection: Scenarios are textual descriptions of the organisational activities and interactions concerning the intended application. They were used for data-collection together with semi-structured interviews, work-place observation and document analysis. This last technique can be coupled with natural language processing tools for scaling-up the approach. Whenever possible, existing ontologies were partially reused (mainly TOVE[15] and Cyc[16]): we manually revisited the parts that were interesting for our scenarios ; if the informal definition of a notion had the meaning we were looking for, the terms denoting this notion and the definition were added to the lexicon from which we built the ontology. Other non company-specific sources or standards helped us structure upper parts of the ontology or list the leaves of some precise specialised area (e.g. MIME).

[15] www.eil.utoronto.ca/tove/ontoTOC.html

[16] www.cyc.com/cyc-2-1/cover.html

2. Terms collection, analysis and organisation: The terms denoting notions appearing relevant for the application scenarios are collected, analysed and organised in a set of informal tables forming a lexicon on which the ontology will be built. The synonyms and ambiguous terms are spotted and marked as such. Definitions in natural language are proposed, discussed and refined especially to eliminate fuzziness, circular definitions and incoherence.

3. Structuring the ontology: Combining bottom-up, top-down and middle-out approaches as three complementary perspectives of a complete methodology, the obtained concepts are iteratively structured in a taxonomy. The initial tables evolve from a semi-informal representation (terminological tables of terms & notions) towards semi-formal representation (subsumption links, signatures of relations) until each notion has a unique formal identifier (usually one of its terms) and a position in the hierarchy of concepts or relations. Tables are then translated in RDFS using scripts.

O'CoMMA contains: 470 concepts organised in a taxonomy with a depth of 13 subsumption links; 79 relations organised in a taxonomy with a depth of 2 subsumption links; 715 terms in English and 699 in French to label these primitives; 547 definitions in French and 550 in English to explain the meaning of these notions. In the ontology three layers appear: (1) a general top that roughly looks like other top-ontologies, (2) a large and ever growing middle layer divided in two main branches: one generic to corporate memory domain (document, organisation, people...) and one dedicated to the application domain (e.g. telecom: wireless, network, etc.), (3) an extension layer, specific to the scenario and to the company, with complex concepts (Trend analysis report, New Employee Route Card, etc.). The upper part, which is quite abstract, and the first part of the middle layer, which describes concepts common to corporate memory applications, are reusable in other corporate memory application. The second part of the middle layer, which deals with the application domain, is reusable only for scenarios in the same domain. The last layer containing specific concepts is not reusable as soon as the organisation, the scenario or the application domain changes. However, this last layer is by far the closest to day-to-day users' interest.

Concepts are formalised as RDFS classes. Relations and attributes are formalised as RDFS properties. Instances of these classes and properties are created to formulate annotations. Terms are formalised as RDFS labels of classes and properties and are independent from the internal unique system identifier of the class or property. Likewise the natural language definitions are captured as RDFS comments. The ability to specify the natural language used enables us to have multilingual ontologies. A notion (concept or property) with several terms linked to it is characteristic from the synonymy of these terms. A term associated to several notions is ambiguous.

Using XSLT style sheets, we reproduce the intermediate documents that were used to build the ontology and we propose different views of the ontology: (a) initial terminological table representing a lexicon of the memory; (b) tables of concepts and properties; (c) pages for browsing and searching at the conceptual or terminological levels: they allow search for concepts or relations linked to a term, navigation in the taxonomy, search for relations having a signature compatible with a given concept; (d) list of instances of a notion: a sample of instances plays the role of examples to ease understanding of a notion; (e) filtered view of the ontology using a user's profile so as to propose preferred entrance points in the ontology; (f) indented tree of concepts or relations.

The choice of RDF(S) enables us to base our system on a standard that benefits from the web-based technologies for networking, display and browsing, and this is an asset for the integration to a corporate intranet.

2.3 CORESE: Conceptual Resource Search Engine

As CoMMA aims at offering information retrieval from the corporate memory, we needed to rely on a search engine. Keyword-based search engines works at the term level. Ontologies are a means to enable software to reason at the semantic level. To manipulate the ontology, the annotations, and infer from them, we developed CORESE [8] a prototype of search engine enabling inferences on RDF annotations and information retrieval from them. CORESE combines the advantages of using (a) the RDF(S) framework for expressing and exchanging metadata, and (b) the query and inference mechanisms available for Conceptual Graph (CG) formalism [18]. CORESE is an alternative to SiLRi [10] which uses frame logic. There is an adequacy between RDF(S) and CG: RDF annotations are mapped to factual CGs; the class hierarchy and the property hierarchy of an RDF schema are mapped to a concept type hierarchy and a relation type hierarchy in CGs.

CORESE queries are RDF statements with wildcard characters to describe the pattern to be found, the values to be returned and the co-references. Regular expressions are used to constrain literal values and additional operators are used to express disjunction and negation. The RDF query is translated into a CG which is projected on the CG base in order to find matching graphs and to extract the requested values. The answers are then translated back into RDF. The CG projection mechanism takes into account the specialisation links described in the hierarchies translated from the RDF schema. Both precision and recall are thus improved.

As a lesson of CoMMA, a limitation of RDFS appeared when formalising implicit information and background knowledge. For instance, when we declare that someone manages a group, it is implicit that this person is a manager. Thus the 'manager' concept should be a 'defined concept', *i.e.* a concept having an explicit definition enabling this concept to be derived from other existing concepts whenever possible. However the notion of defined concept does not exist in RDFS, even thought the ability to factorise knowledge in an ontology requires the ability to express formal definitions. In the current version of the CoMMA system, the formal definitions are coded in rules written in an RDF/XML rule language specially created for RDF(S) and CORESE. As explained in [9], an inference engine exploits these rules to complete the annotation base with deducible implicit facts. Instead, one could extend the RDFS model to add the missing expressiveness as in DRDF(S) [11], OIL [14], or DAML+OIL [21]. For instance, symmetry, transitivity and reflexivity characteristics of properties required CORESE-specific extensions of RDFS.

Although CORESE can be used in a client-server fashion, it also offers an API; thus, in CoMMA, modules of CORESE are integrated in the agents handling the ontology or the annotations, so as to provide them with the abilities needed for their roles.

3. MODEL-BASED MEMORY

Users of the corporate memory are, by nature, heterogeneous and distributed in the corporation. In order to give the CoMMA system an insight of its environment and of the users it is interacting with, the memory is based on models of the organisational structure and on user profiles enabling customisation, learning of preferences and push technologies.

To materialise the user profiles, we *annotate people* using primitives defined in the ontology. A user's profile captures aspects of the user that we identified as relevant for the system behaviour. It contains administrative information and explicit preferences (e.g. topic interests). It also positions the user in the organisation: role, location and potential acquaintance network, enabling the system to target push actions. In addition, the system derives information from the usage made by the user. It collects the history of visited documents and user's feedback and from this it learns some of the user's interests [16]. These derived criteria are then used for result presentation or push technology enabling the emergence of communities of interest. The user's profile also records preferred entrance points into the ontology in order to hide the ontology upper level and to propose middle concepts (e.g. person, document, domain topics) from which the user can start browsing the ontology in a MyYahoo fashion.

	The memory is composed of the **D**ocuments, their **A**nnotations, the **S**tate of Affairs (user profiles and organisation model) and the **O**ntology. The whole follows a prototypical life-cycle, evolving and interacting with each other.
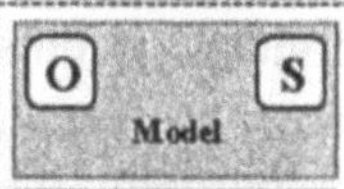	The **O**ntology and the **S**tate of Affairs form the model on which is based the structuring of the memory.
	The archive structure relies on the **A**nnotations of the **D**ocumentary resources.
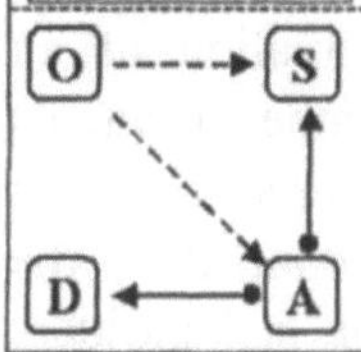	The **A**nnotations and the **S**tate of Affairs are formalised using the conceptual vocabulary provided by the **O**ntology. The **A**nnotations refer to the **D**ocuments (ex: report http://www...) and to the objects of the **S**tate of Affair (ex: written by Mr. X for the division ABCD)

Figure 1. The Architecture of the Memory

An enterprise model is an oriented, focused and somewhat simplified explicit representation of the organisation. So far, the enterprise modelling field has been mainly concerned with simulation and optimisation of the production system design. It provides benchmark for business processes and are used for re-engineering them. But the shift in the market rules led organisations to become aware of the value of their memory and the fact that organisation models have a role to play in this application too [19]. In CoMMA, the model aims at supporting corporate memory activities involved in the application scenario. The system exploits the aspects described in the model for the interaction between agents and above all between agents and users. We used RDF to implement our organisational description, annotating the organisational entities (departments, activities, laboratories, etc.) with their relations (manages, employs, includes, etc.).

Annotated environments containing explanations of the purpose and the uses of spaces and activities allow agents to quickly become intelligent actors in those spaces [12]. In CoMMA, the corporate memory is an annotated world: with RDF(S), we describe the semantic content of documents and the organisational state of affair through semantic annotations (Figure 1); then agents use and infer from these annotations in order to search the mass of information of the corporate memory.

4. MULTI-AGENTS SOFTWARE ARCHITECTURE

The tasks to be performed on the corporate memory, the corporate memory itself and the population of users are distributed and heterogeneous.

Therefore, it is interesting to have a heterogeneous and distributed software architecture. Multi-agents systems have been acknowledged as an excellent candidate to provide a software architecture supporting the semantic Web framework [3]. The MAS paradigm appeared very well suited for the deployment of a software architecture above the distributed information landscape of the corporate memory: on the one hand, individual agents locally adapt to users and resources they are dedicated to; on the other hand, thanks to co-operating software agents distributed over the intranet, the system capitalises an integrated and global view of the corporate memory.

A MAS architecture is a structure that portrays the different families of agents and their relationships. A configuration is an instantiation of an architecture with a chosen arrangement and an appropriate number of agents of each type. One given architecture can lead to several configurations and a given configuration is tightly linked to the topography and context of the place where it is deployed (organisational and intranet layout, stakeholders location). Thus, the architecture must be designed so that the set of possible configurations covers the different corporate organisational layouts foreseeable. The configuration is studied and documented at deployment time whereas the architectural description is studied and fixed at design time. The architectural analysis starts from the highest level of abstraction (i.e. the society) and by successive refinements (i.e. nested sub-societies) it goes down to the point where agent roles and interactions can be identified.

4.1 From the Macro level to the Micro level

We adopted an organisational approach: the MAS architecture is tackled, as in a human society, in terms of roles and relationships. The functional requirements of the system do not simply map to some agent functionality but influence and are finally diluted in the dynamic social interactions of individual agents and in the set of abilities, roles and behaviours attached to them. Considering the system functionalities, we identified three sub-societies of agents dedicated to resources (ontology and model; annotations; yellow pages needed for managing interconnection) and one dedicated to users (*Figure 2*). Analysing the resource-dedicated sub-societies, we found that there was a recurrent set of possible organisations for these sub-societies: hierarchical, peer-to-peer or replication. Depending on the type of tasks to be performed, the size and complexity of the resources manipulated, a sub-society organisation is preferred to another.

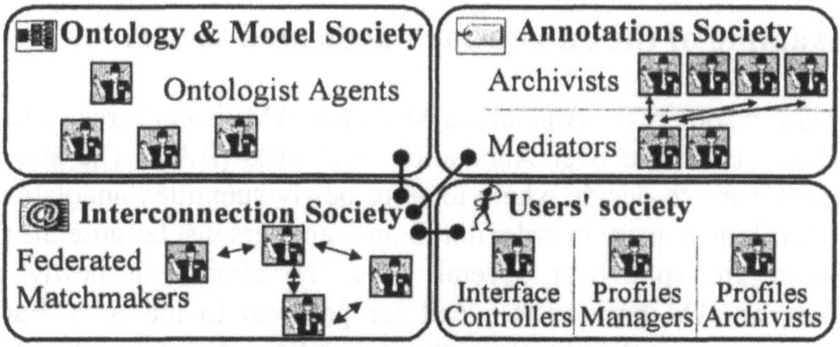

Figure 2. Multi-Agents Architecture of CoMMA

The sub-society dedicated to the ontology and model is currently organised as a replication sub-society (*i.e.* an ontologist agent has a complete copy of the ontology). The annotation-dedicated sub-society is a hierarchical organisation as described in the last section. The yellow pages agents are in a peer-to-peer organisation and are provided by the JADE platform [2] used in CoMMA. Agents from the user-dedicated sub-society are concerned with interface, monitoring, assistance and adaptation to the user. Because they are not related to a resource type like the previous ones, they cannot be studied using our typology. We can distinguish at least two recurrent roles in this type of sub-society: (1) user interface management: to dialogue with the users for enabling them to express their request and refine them, and to present results in an adequate format; (2) management of user profiles: to store the profiles and make them available for interface purposes, learning techniques and pro-active searches.

From the architecture analysis, we identified agent roles and we studied their characteristics and interactions in order to implement the corresponding behaviours in a set of agent types. Roles represent the position of an agent in a society and the responsibilities and activities assigned to this position and expected by others to be fulfilled. Then comes the specification of role interactions specified with protocols that the agents must follow for the MAS to work properly. The definition of a protocol starts with an acquaintance graph at role level, that is a directed graph identifying communication pathways between agents playing the considered roles. Then we specified the possible sequences of messages. Both the acquaintance network and the protocols derived from the organisational analysis and the use cases dictated by the application scenarios.

From the role and interaction descriptions, the different partners of CoMMA proposed and implemented agent types that fulfil one or more roles. Behaviours come from the implementation choices determining the responses, actions and reactions of the agent. The implementation of a behaviour is constrained by the associated role and is subject to the toolbox of technical abilities available to the designers.

4.2 Example of the annotations-dedicated society

In this sub-society the Annotation Mediator (AM) is in charge of handling annotations distributed over Annotation Archivists (AAs). The stake is to find mechanisms to decide where to store newly submitted annotations and how to distribute a query in order not to miss answers just because the needed information are split over several AAs. To allocate a newly posted annotation, an AM broadcasts a call for proposal to the AAs. Each AA measures how semantically close the annotation is, , from the types of concepts and relations present in its archive. The closest AA wins the bid. We defined a pseudo-distance based on the ontology hierarchy and AM uses it to compare the bids of the different AAs following a contract-net protocol. The solving of a query may involve several annotation bases distributed over several AAs; the result is a merging of partial results. To determine if and when an AA should participate to the solving of a query, the AAs calculate the overlap between the list of types present in their base and the list of types of notions used in the query. With these descriptions, the AM is able to identify at each step of the query decomposition the AAs to be consulted. Once the AA and AM roles had been specified properly together with their interactions, we integrated modules of CORESE [8] in the agent types implementing these roles to provide the needed technical abilities.

5. EVALUATION & CONCLUSION

The prototype was evaluated by end-users from a telecom company (T-Nova System) and a construction research centre (CSTB) through two trials at the 8th month and the 22nd month. The very last prototype was presented and discussed during an open day at the end of the project.

During the first trial we performed: (a) an evaluation of the *architecture*, (b) an evaluation of the design *methodology*, and (c) an evaluation from the *user*'s point of view of *usefulness* and *usability*. Four T-Nova employees participated for the new employee insertion (NEI) scenario. Three CSTB librarians participated for the technology monitoring (TM) scenario. As a result, the system meet the needs (usefulness) but its interfaces were not user-friendly (usability). The reason was that the first interfaces were built for designers and knowledge engineers to test the integration, and not for end-users. Thus users could not have a clear view of the system functionalities. Interface were reengineered for the second trial.

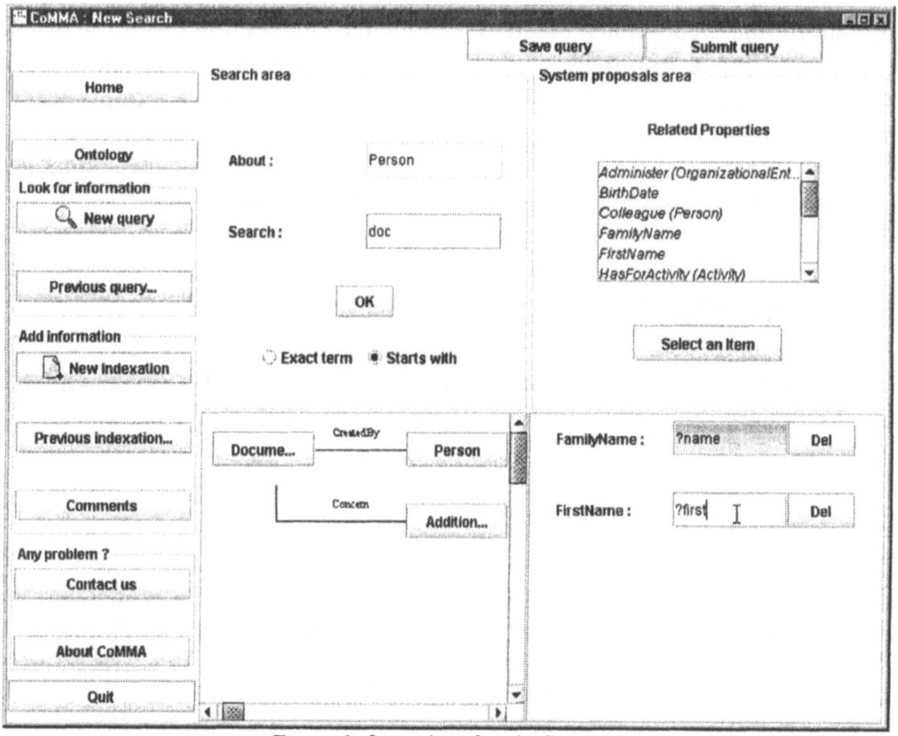

Figure 3. Query interface in CoMMA

The second trial was prepared by a series of iterative evaluations with end-users participating directly to the re-design of the interfaces. Then we made a final evaluation in two steps: (a) users (6 for TM scenario and 4 for NEI) used the system to perform scenario-related tasks ; their comments were classified in terms of positive and negative usability aspects and spontaneous recommendations. (b) 4 TM users and 1 NEI user were rated the severity of the negative usability aspects that had been identified. Then we asked a GUI designer to assess the design effort necessary to implement the proposed recommendations. Both ratings were used to determine the importance of the critics made. Results showed that the CoMMA system was still *useful*, but also *usable*: the GUIs being less complex (*Figure 3*), users accepted them, and were not reluctant to manipulate them.

Both evaluations were "small-scale" evaluations: small number of users, small number of annotations (about 1000), and small duration of use. This short-period of use did not allow us to observe searching, indexing, and learning phenomena. However, a middle-scale test was successfully performed in our organisation with 10000 annotations about 850 documents.

From the developer point of view, we appreciated the ontology-oriented and agent-oriented approach because it supported specification and distribution of implementation while smoothing the integration phase. We are convinced that an approach based on knowledge engineering (*i.e.* formalising knowledge about resources of an intraweb through semantic annotations based on an ontology) and distributed artificial intelligence (*i.e.* multi-agents information system loosely coupled by a cooperation based on semantic message exchanges) can provide a powerful paradigm to solve complex distributed problems such as organisational memory management.

6. ACKNOWLEDGEMENTS

We thank our colleagues of ACACIA and CoMMA (IST-1999-12217) for our discussions, and the European Commission that funded the project.

7. REFERENCES

[1] Aguirre, Brena, Cantu-Ortiz, Multiagent-based Knowledge Networks. To appear in the special issue on Knowledge Management of the journal Expert Systems with Applications.

[2] Bellifemine, Poggi, Rimassa, Developing multi agent systems with a FIPA-compliant agent framework. Software Practice & Experience, (2001) 31:103-128

[3] Berners-Lee, Hendler, Lassila, The Semantic Web, *Scientific American*, May 2001:35-43

[4] Berney, Ferneley, CASMIR: Information Retrieval Based on Collaborative User Profiling, Proc. of PAAM'99, pp. 41-56. www.casmir.net

[5] Bothorel, Thomas, A Distributed Agent Based-Platform for Internet User Communities, In Proc. of PAAM'99, Lancashire, pp. 23-40.

[6] Brickley, Guha, Resource Description Framework Schema Specification 1.0, W3C Candidate Recommendation 27 March 2000

[7] CoMMA http://www.si.fr.atosorigin.com/sophia/comma/Htm/HomePage.htm

[8] Corby, Dieng, Hébert, A Conceptual Graph Model for W3C Resource Description Framework. In Proc. ICCS'2000 Darmstadt Germany

[9] Corby, Faron, CORESE: a corporate semantic web engine, Proc. of WWW02 Workshop on Real World RDF & Semantic Web, Hawai 2002.

[10] Decker, Brickley, Saarela, Angele. A Query Service for RDF. *Query Languages* 98, W3C Workshop.

[11] Delteil, Faron, Dieng, Extension of RDFS based on the CG formalism, *Proc. ICCS'01*

[12] Doyle, Hayes-Roth, Agents in Annotated Worlds, In Proc. Autonomous Agents, ACM Press / ACM SIGART, Minneapolis, MN USA (1998) p173-180

[13] Dzbor, Paralic, Paralic, Knowledge Management in a Distributed Organisation, In Proc. of the BASYS'2000 - 4th IEEE/IFIP International Conference on Information Technology for Balanced Automation Systems in Manufacturing, Kluwer Academic Pub-lishers, London, September 2000, ISBN 0-7923-7958-6, pp. 339-348

[14] Fensel, Van Harmelen, Horrocks, McGuinness, Patel-Schneider. OIL: An ontology infrastructure for the semantic web. IEEE Intelligent Systems, 16(2):38-45, 2001.

[15] Gandon, Engineering an Ontology for a Multi-Agents Corporate Memory System, In Proc. ISMICK'01, Université de Technologie de Compiègne, p209-228.

[16] Kiss, Quinqueton, Multiagent Cooperative Learning of User Preferences, Proc. of European CMLP & PKDD, 2001.

[17] Lassila, Swick, Resource Description Framework (RDF) Model and Syntax Specification, W3C Recommendation 22 February 1999

[18] Sowa, *Conceptual Structures: Information Processing in Mind and Machine*, Addison-Wesley, 1984.

[19] Rolstadås, Development trends to support Enterprise Modeling, in Rolstadås and Andersen *Enterprise Modeling: Improving Global Industrial Competitiveness*, Kluwer Academic Publisher, p3-16, 2000

[20] Van Elst, Abecker, Domain Ontology Agents in Distributed Organizational Memories. To appear in Dieng & Matta eds, Knowledge Management and Organizational Memories, Kluwer, 2002 .

[21] Van Harmelen, Patel-schneider, Horrocks , Reference description of the DAML+OIL ontology markup language. http://pride.daml.org/2000/12/reference.html. March 2001.

MOBILE CONSTRAINTS FOR SEMANTIC WEB APPLICATIONS

Peter Gray, Kit Hui, and Alun Preece
University of Aberdeen, Computing Science Department, Aberdeen, Scotland
pgray,khui,apreece@csd.abdn.ac.uk

Abstract We present a framework for semantic web applications based on constraint interchange and processing. At the core of the framework is a well-established semantic data model (P/FDM) with an associated expressive constraint language (Colan). To allow data instances to be transported across a network, we map our data model to the RDF Schema specification. To allow constraints to be transported, we define a Constraint Interchange Format (CIF) in the form of an RDF Schema for Colan, allowing each constraint to be defined as a resource in its own right. We show that, because Colan is essentially a syntactically-sugared form of first-order logic, and P/FDM is based on the widely-used extended ER model, our CIF is actually very widely applicable and reusable. Finally, we outline a set of services for constraint fusion and solving, which are particularly applicable to business-to-business e-commerce applications. These services are accessible using the CIF.

1. Introduction and Motivation

The *semantic web* vision is to enable rich machine-processing of web information sources [2]. Most of the work done to date in realising this vision has focussed upon developing "web friendly" representations for structured data. Building on the XML standard, a number of proposals for expressing data schemas have appeared, including RDF, RDFS, and XML Schema [4]. These approaches support the representation and communication of entity-relational information in web applications, for example, allowing a set of instances of some entity type to be gathered from several structured web pages, and transported for storage in a web-connected database.

The next significant stage in the realisation of the semantic web lies in extending the basic data schema representations with information on how the data can and should be used. This information can take various forms, including logical axioms, rules, constraints, or even functional and procedural representations. This work will create the ***reasoning services*** for the semantic web. Berners-Lee's vision for these reasoning services is that they are built on top of the data schema representations. Early work in this direction included inference engines for large-scale ontologies [4, 8], mechanisms for representing and reasoning with business rules [11], and mobile constraint languages and constraint-solving frameworks [13, 7].

In this paper, we present a Constraint Interchange Format (CIF) aimed specifically at business-to-business e-commerce applications on the semantic web. The constraint language is well-established, having been used successfully in diverse and challenging application domains such as representing and reasoning about protein structures in biomedical applications [6], and configuring telecommunications network services [5]. Earlier versions of the CIF were based on Prolog term structures; this paper presents a new XML encoding of the CIF, designed to be more open and less platform-dependent than its predecessor. The new XML-CIF has been modelled using the RDF Schema specification, so that constraints become web resources about which statements can be made (for example, statements about the authorship and context of a constraint). In addition, the CIF has been designed to refer to RDF Schema definitions so that the terms referred to in a constraint can have corresponding RDF Schema descriptions. The motivation here is to allow applications of RDF Schema to use our CIF and constraint-solving services, in keeping with Berners-Lee's vision of reasoning services atop the data representation layer.

The paper is organised as follows: the next section introduces our constraint language, Colan, and the semantic data model upon which it operates; the following section describes the design of the XML-CIF encoding of Colan expressions; the penultimate section gives an overview of the constraint-solving services already available for semantic web applications using the CIF; the final section concludes.

2. The Colan Constraint Language

An entity-relationship (ER) diagram (or UML class diagram) is commonly thought of as being useful chiefly as a diagrammatic guide or visualisation of the types of entities and relationships in a database (or an object-oriented application); it is less commonly seen as an operational basis for forming queries or specifications. In our previous work [1, 6] we showed how quantified constraints can be expressed in our Colan language, in a very readable form of first order logic, including evalu-

```
constrain each t in tutor such that astatus(t)="research"
  so that each s in advisee(t) has grade(s) > 60;
```

First-order logic version:

$(\forall t,s,g)\ tutor(t) \wedge astatus(t,\text{'research'}) \wedge advisee(t,s) \wedge grade(s,g) \Rightarrow g>60$

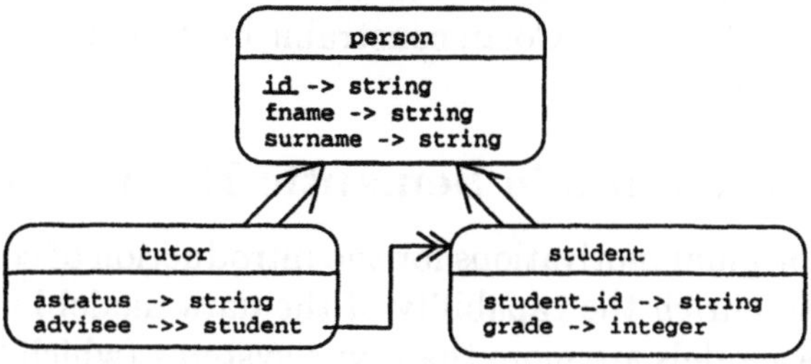

Figure 1. Example Colan constraint and ER diagram for corresponding schema.

able functions which can be computed over data values represented in the ER diagram. Hence, the underlying data model is called the Functional Data Model (FDM). The semantics of the objects referred to in Colan constraints are described in terms of this extended ER data model, which is of the kind in widespread use in UML and in database schemas. Our FDM, P/FDM (Prolog/Functional Data Model) is a Semantic Data Model based on Shipman's original data model [12]. (For full details of P/FDM, Colan [1], and related work, see: www.csd.abdn.ac.uk/~pfdm)

An example Colan constraint is shown in Figure 1, which expresses a constraint on a university database containing student records. A variable `t` ranges over an entity type `tutor` which is populated with stored object instances. Each of these instances may be related to instances of student entities through the relationship `advisee`, which delivers a set of related entities as in an object-oriented language. Thus functions may also represent a derived relationship, or method. The entity classes can form part of a subtype hierarchy, in which case all properties and methods on the superclass are inherited by each subclass. Method definitions may be overridden, but not constraints.

This is significant for semantic web applications, since it means that information represented in this way is not restricted to human inspection — it can be proof-checked mechanically, transformed by symbol manipulation, or sent to a remote constraint solver. Moreover, given a standardised interchange format, data and attached constraints from multiple sources can be gathered together, checked for compatibility, and used to derive new information. Because the P/FDM data model is an extended ER model, it maps very easily onto the RDF Schema specification, as we shall show in the following section.

Colan is as expressive as the subset of first-order logic that is useful for expressing integrity constraints: namely, *range-restricted* constraints [1, 6]. This class of constraints includes those first-order logic expressions in which each variable is constrained to be a member of some finite set of values. Figure 1 shows the Colan constraint in the equivalent first-order logic representation.

2.1. Constraints in Semantic Data Models

One of our original motivations for the introduction of constraints into P/FDM was to enrich the capability of the data model in capturing semantics. Data models are more than type systems (which they resemble syntactically) because they also represent constraints on the data. Thus a powerful constraint language has enabled us to capture the semantic information that others have endeavoured to express by extending the diagrammatic notation of the ER model. Thus, although the original FDM was somewhat lacking in semantics, we have been able to more than make up for that by introducing constraints.

In doing this, we have capitalised on a cardinal virtue of the FDM, that it enables one to make well-formed mathematically precise computations over data stored as instances of entities related by an ER diagram. Thus we based the Colan formalism for constraints on just these well-formed computations, revising and extending it to use the full expression syntax of P/FDM's Daplex query language. Crucially, because the expressions are fully quantified and referentially transparent, it is straightforward to move them into other contexts and transform them in ways which preserve their semantics. This would not be so if our expression of data semantics had been confined to a diagrammatic notation.

In summary, we have introduced our constraint language, Colan, and the semantic data model upon which it operates, and we have argued for the applicability of this language and data model to semantic web applications. The following section describes our new XML encoding of Colan in the form of a Constraint Interchange Format (CIF) based on the RDF Schema specification.

3. XML Constraint Interchange Format

In defining our Constraint Interchange Format, we were guided by the following design principles:

- the CIF would need to be serialisable into XML, to make it maximally portable and open;
- constraints should be represented as resources in RDF, to exploit RDF's widely-used data model and ease of parsing, and so that RDF statements can be made about the constraints themselves;
- there must be no modification to the existing RDF and RDF Schema specifications, so that the CIF would be layered cleanly on top of RDF;
- it must be possible for constraints to refer to terms defined in any RDF Schema, with such references made explicit.

As we showed in the previous section, the entity-relational basis of both our P/FDM data model and RDF made it relatively straightforward to map from the former to the latter. In building the RDF Schema for our CIF we were guided by the existing grammar for Colan [6] which relates constraints to entities, attributes and relationships present in the ER model. This grammar serves as a *metaschema* for the Colan constraints (such metaschemas are very common in relational and object database systems). A number of issues arose in developing the RDF Schema for CIF, discussed in the following subsections.

3.1. Metaclasses for Entities and Relations

Our implementation of the P/FDM semantic data model makes use of an `entmet` class that holds information on all *entity* classes, and a `propmet` class that holds information on relationships (functions), both stored and derived. The metaschema is fully queryable, and for this purpose the property values of members of these metaclasses are all held as strings (as is common in data dictionaries), so that the answer to a query on them returns the name of an entity or relation and not the contents of the entity or relation. The P/FDM Daplex definitions of the `entmet` and `propmet` classes are shown in Figure 2, together with their superclass, `objmet`.

The property `rdfname` on the `entmet` and `propmet` classes holds the unique URI for an RDF resource, and thus provides an explicit link to the RDF Schema definition for the corresponding RDF Schema class or property. Thus, constraints carry explicit relationships to the domain ontology (as represented by an RDF Schema) for the terminology to which they refer. We chose to employ our own `entmet` and `propmet` classes rather than use the RDF `Class` and `Property` classes directly, in order to maintain close compatibility with our original Colan metaschema,

```
% objmet - superclass of entity and property metaclasses
declare objmet ->> entity
declare oname(objmet) -> string

% entmet - the metaclass of all entity classes
declare entmet ->> objmet
declare super(entmet) -> entmet
declare rdfname(entmet) -> string % link to RDF Schema

% propmet - the metaclass of all properties (functions)
declare propmet ->> objmet
declare fname(propmet) -> string
declare firstargtype(propmet) -> entmet
declare resulttype(propmet) -> entmet
declare has_inv(propmet) -> boolean
declare rdfname(propmet) -> string % link to RDF Schema
```

Figure 2. P/FDM Daplex definitions for entity and property metaclasses.

and support extensibility in the CIF (for example, Figure 2 shows that `propmet` has additional properties not required by RDF `Property`).

In the RDF Schema we introduce the corresponding metaclasses, `entmet` and `propmet`, which will record the graph of classes and properties. Thus there will be one instance of the `entmet` class for each actual class representing a real-world entity in the instance level RDF Schema for a given application domain. These metaclasses then provide the natural result types for properties used in constraints. Thus, for example, we can use them to say that an atomic boolean value in a predicate in a constraint can be derived by comparing the property value of a variable which holds an entity identifier with another value given by an expression. This entity and property must be known. We could even write a metalevel constraint to require their consistency, as checked by a type checker.

Figure 3 shows the RDF Schema definitions corresponding to the Daplex definitions of the `objmet` and `entmet` classes from Figure 2. It is worth noting that, because properties in RDF are global, some of the original local P/FDM property names must be renamed (for example, `entmet_rdfname` in Figure 3, renamed from `rdfname` in Figure 2).

The basic rules we used when mapping the P/FDM declarations to RDF Schema are as follows:

- a P/FDM class *c* defined as an `entity` (declared as *c* `->> entity`) maps to an RDF resource of type `rdfs:Class` (where `rdfs` is the namespace prefix for the RDF Schema descriptions);

```
<rdf:RDF
  xmlns:rdf="http://www.w3.org/1999
   /02/22-rdf-syntax-ns#"
  xmlns:rdfs="http://www.w3.org/
   2000/01/rdf-schema#">

<rdfs:Class rdf:ID="objmet">
  <rdfs:subClassOf rdf:resource=
   "http://www.w3.org/2000/01/
    rdf-schema#Resource"/>
</rdfs:Class>

<rdf:Property rdf:ID="oname">
  <rdfs:domain rdf:resource=
   "#objmet"/>
  <rdfs:range rdf:resource=
   "http://www.w3.org/2000/01/
    rdf-schema#Literal"/>
</rdf:Property>

<rdfs:Class rdf:ID="entmet">
  <rdfs:subClassOf
   rdf:resource="#objmet"/>
</rdfs:Class>

<rdf:Property rdf:ID="super">
  <rdfs:domain
   rdf:resource="#entmet"/>
  <rdfs:range
   rdf:resource="#entmet"/>
</rdf:Property>

<rdf:Property
 rdf:ID="entmet_rdfname">
  <rdfs:domain
   rdf:resource="#entmet"/>
  <rdfs:range rdf:resource=
   "http://www.w3.org/2000/
    01/rdf-schema#Literal"/>
</rdf:Property>
...
</rdf:RDF>
```

Figure 3. RDF Schema definitions for the `objmet` and `entmet` classes.

- a P/FDM class c declared to be a subtype of another class s (declared as c `->>` s) maps to an RDF resource of type `rdfs:Class`, with an `rdfs:subClassOf` property the value of which is the class named s;
- a P/FDM function f declared on entities of class c, with result type r (declared as $f(c)$ `->` r) maps to an RDF resource of type `rdf:Property` with an `rdfs:domain` of c and an `rdfs:range` of r.

3.2. Representation of Variables in Constraints

A fundamental notion in Colan is that a variable is always introduced in conjunction with a set that it ranges over. Thus terms such as `(p in pc)` and `(e in employee)` are common, as in the example expressions:

```
(p in pc) such that name (p) = "xxx"
(e in employee) such that salary (e) > 5000 and age (e) < 50
```

This is represented in the syntax by the `setmem` metaclass, while variables themselves are described by the `variable` class, both defined as shown in Figure 4. An instance of the `variable` class is a legal instance of an `expr` class (representing an expression) by virtue of a series of subclass relationships. There is also a semantic constraint that such an instance must already have been introduced with a quantifier; this is not

```
<rdfs:Class rdf:ID="variable">
  <rdfs:subClassOf
   rdf:resource="#operand"/>
</rdfs:Class>

<rdf:Property rdf:ID="varname">
  <rdfs:domain
   rdf:resource="#variable"/>
  <rdfs:range rdf:resource=
   "http://www.w3.org/2000/01/
    rdf-schema#Literal"/>
</rdf:Property>

<rdfs:Class rdf:ID="setmem">
  <rdfs:subClassOf
   rdf:resource="#boolprim"/>
</rdfs:Class>
```

```
<rdf:Property rdf:ID="var">
  <rdfs:domain
   rdf:resource="#setmem"/>
  <rdfs:range
   rdf:resource="#variable"/>
</rdf:Property>

<rdf:Property rdf:ID="set">
  <rdfs:domain
   rdf:resource="#setmem"/>
  <rdfs:range
   rdf:resource="#setexpr"/>
</rdf:Property>
```

Figure 4. RDF Schema definitions relating to the `setmem` metaclass.

currently captured in the RDF Schema but could possibly be represented using the RDF Schema `ConstraintResource` extension mechanism. An example XML-CIF fragment corresponding to the Colan fragment (`p in pc`) is shown in Figure 5.

Space prohibits us from including the full CIF RDF Schema here, but both it and the full P/FDM schema are available at: www.csd.abdn.ac.uk /research/akt/cif/ together with example constraints. In summary, our CIF RDF Schema serves the purpose of describing what are valid constraints, themselves expressed at an instance level in RDF. It combines the information in a grammar, which is normally used by a syntax checker or a parser, with information normally held in a database schema and used to validate database queries. The interesting thing is that the P/FDM data description language is expressive enough to capture this, especially cardinality constraints. RDF is not so expressive, although it does provide for schema constraints such as cardinality through the `ConstraintResource` extension mechanism.

It should be noted that the metaschema makes a clean separation between the description of *constraints* (both universal and existential) and *expressions*. Constraints and their boolean components are a representation of first-order logic, with the usual connectives. Any knowledge source that uses FOL should be able to understand this. Expressions refer to facts about entities, their subtypes, attributes and relationships, and is based on the widely-used concepts of an ER model. The corresponding data could be held in XML or a variety of storage schemas.

The following section describes our existing framework for using CIF constraints, as used in KRAFT [10] and for which communication and

```
<cif:setmem>
  <cif:var>
    <cif:variable ID="#p">
      <cif:varname>p</cif:varname>
    </cif:variable>
  </cif:var>
  <cif:set>
    <cif:entset>
      <cif:entclass>
        <cif:entmet>
          <cif:entmet_rdfname>
            http://www.aktors.org/
             domain/pc_config#pc
          </cif:entmet_rdfname>
        </cif:entmet>
      </cif:entclass>
    </cif:entset>
  </cif:set>
</cif:setmem>
```

Figure 5. XML-CIF fragment corresponding to the Colan fragment `(p in pc)`.

coordination are achieved by the exchange and fusion of constraint knowledge.

4. Fusion of Constraints from Different Sources

Having a semantic data model (P/FDM) extended with constraints (Colan) and mapped into an open interchange format (RDF Schema and XML-CIF) supports a range of applications in which information needs to be moved across a network with rich metalevel information describing how the information can be used. An example application common in *business-to-business e-commerce* involves the composition of a package product from components selected from multiple vendors' catalogues (for example, consumer electronic equipment, package holidays, fitted kitchens, or financial products). In each case, there are various kinds of constraints which must be aggregated and solved over the available component instances: constraints representing customer requirements ("I want a PC with a colour printer"), constraints representing rules for what constitutes an acceptable package ("any printer must have a driver that is compatible with the PC OS"), and constraints representing restrictions on the use of particular components ("this printer has drivers only for Windows OSes").

In this last case, the ability to store constraints together with data in P/FDM allows instructions to be attached to the class descriptor for data objects in a product catalogue database. When a data object is retrieved, these attached instructions must also be extracted to ensure that the data is properly used. Thus the attached constraint becomes mobile knowledge which is transported, transformed and processed in a distributed environment. An advantage of this approach is that we can use constraint logic solving techniques to see if a complex set of constraints, whose form is not known until runtime, does have a solution.

4.1. A Constraint Fusion Example

To demonstrate constraint fusion from different sources, consider a configuration problem where a PC is built by combining components from vendors. All of the constraints below are expressed in Colan and so would be exchanged using the XML-CIF representation described in the previous section.

The user specifies his requirement in the form of constraint through the user-agent. In this example, he specifies that the PC must use a "pentium2" processor but not the "win95" OS:

```
constrain each p in pc
  to have cpu(p)="pentium2" and name(has_os(p)) <> "win95"
```

For the components to fit together, they must satisfy certain constraints imposed by the solution database. For example, the size of the OS must be smaller or equal to the hard disk space for a proper installation:

```
constrain each p in pc
    to have size(has_os(p)) =< size(has_disk(p))
```

Now the candidate components from different vendors may have instructions attached to them as constraints. In the vendor database of operating systems, "winNT" requires a memory of at least 32 megabytes:

```
constrain each p in pc such that
    manufacturer(p) = "HAL" and name(has_os(p))="winNT"
        to have memory(p) >= 32
```

When we fuse all constraints together so that they apply to the solution database, we get the description of an equivalent constraint satisfaction problem (note the *conditional constraint* in the last line):

```
constrain each p in pc
    to have cpu(p)="pentium2"
    and name(has_os(p)) <> "win95"
    and size(has_os(p)) =< size(has_disk(p))
    and if manufacturer(p) = "HAL" and name(has_os(p))="winNT"
        then memory(p)) >= 32 else true
```

The process of solving the application problem, therefore, is to retrieve data from other databases and populate the solution database while satisfying (i) all the integrity constraints attached to the solution database, (ii) constraints on data objects and (iii) user requirement constraints. This process corresponds to a generate-and-test approach where invalid candidates are rejected by database integrity constraints. A more efficient prune-and-search approach can be achieved by exporting constraint fragments to a constraint fusing mediator which composes the overall description as a constraint satisfaction problem (CSP) for a configuration task so that it may plan the solution. The CSP is then analysed and decomposed into database queries and constraint logic programs which are fed across to distributed databases and constraint solvers, under the control of a mediator [9].

5. Discussion and Conclusion

In this paper, we have presented a framework for semantic web applications based on constraint interchange and processing. At the core of the framework is a well-established semantic data model (P/FDM) with an associated expressive constraint language (Colan). To allow data instances to be transported across a network, we have mapped our data model to the less expressive (but adequate) RDF Schema. To allow constraints to be transported, we have provided a Constraint Interchange Format (CIF) in the form of an RDF Schema for Colan, allowing each constraint to be defined as a resource in its own right.

Because Colan is essentially a syntactically-sugared form of first-order logic, and P/FDM is based on the widely-used extended ER model, our CIF is actually very widely applicable and reusable. Through the KRAFT project, we have available a set of services for constraint fusion and solving, which are particularly applicable to business-to-business e-commerce applications. All of these services can be accessed using the CIF.

We targeted our approach for use with RDF Schema, and in particular the XML encoding of RDF Schema, in an effort to maximise the applicability of our work. RDF Schema is the simplest and most universal of the semantic web data representations, while still being adequately expressive for our purposes. In linking Colan to RDF Schema, we also allow its usage with more expressive data modelling languages built on top of RDF Schema, including DAML+OIL [4], and the anticipated recommendations of the W3C WebOnt initative (www.w3c.org). However, a basic requirement of our approach in defining the RDF Schema for Colan expressions was that it should in no way require modification to the underlying RDF definitions (this is in contrast to the OIL approach, which requires modification at the RDF layer in order to capture certain kinds of expression [3]).

Our constraint interchange and solving services are being incorporated into the AKT infrastructure, as one of the basic knowledge reuse mechanisms in the AKT service layer. Further information on this work can be found at: www.aktors.org

Acknowledgements. This work is funded by the UK Engineering and Physical Sciences Research Council (EPSRC) under the Advanced Knowledge Technologies (AKT) Interdisciplinary Research Collaboration (IRC). The AKT IRC comprises the Universities of Aberdeen, Edinburgh, Sheffield, Southampton and the Open University. The constraint fusion services were developed in the context of the KRAFT project, funded by the EPSRC and British Telecom. An earlier version of this paper was presented at the IJCAI-01 workshop *E-Business and the Intelligent Web.*

References

[1] N. Bassiliades and P.M.D Gray. CoLan: a Functional Constraint Language and Its Implementation. *Data and Knowledge Engineering*, 14:203–249, 1994.

[2] Tim Berners-Lee, editor. *Weaving the Web.* Orion, 1999.

[3] Stefan Decker, Sergey Melnik, Frank van Harmelen, Dieter Fensel, Michel Klein, Jeen Broekstra, Michael Erdmann, and Ian Horrocks. The semantic web: The roles of XML and RDF. *IEEE Internet Computing*, Sept–Oct:63–74, 2000.

[4] Dieter Fensel, Ora Lassila, Frank van Harmelen, Ian Horrocks, James Hendler, and Deborah L. McGuinness. The semantic web and its languages. *IEEE Intelligent Systems*, November/December 2000.

[5] N. J. Fiddian, P. Marti, J-C. Pazzaglia, K. Hui, A. Preece, D. M. Jones, and Z. Cui. A knowledge processing system for data service network design. *BT Technical Journal*, 17(4):117–130, October 1999.

[6] P. M. D. Gray, S. M. Embury, K. Hui, and G. J. L. Kemp. The evolving role of constraints in the functional data model. *Journal of Intelligent Information Systems*, 12:113–137, 1999.

[7] P. M. D. Gray, K. Hui, and A. D. Preece. Finding and moving constraints in cyberspace. In *Intelligent Agents in Cyberspace*, pages 121–127. AAAI Press, 1999. Papers from the 1999 AAAI Pring Symposium Technical Report SS-99-03.

[8] Jeff Heflin and James Hendler. Dynamic ontologies on the web. In *Proceedings of the Seventeenth National Conference on Artificial Intelligence (AAAI-2000)*, pages 443–449, Menlo Park, CA, 2000. AAAI Press.

[9] Kit-ying Hui and Peter M. D. Gray. Developing finite domain constraints – a data model approach. In *Proceedings of the 1st Internatinal Conference on Computational Logic (CL2000)*, pages 448–462. Springer-Verlag, 2000.

[10] A. Preece, K. Hui, A. Gray, P. Marti, T. Bench-Capon, Z. Cui, and D. Jones. KRAFT: An agent architecture for knowledge fusion. *Inernational Journal of Cooperative Information Systems*, 10(1 & 2):171–195, 2001.

[11] D. Reeves, B. Grosof, M. Wellman, and H. Chan. Toward a declarative language for negotiating executable contracts. In *Artificial Intelligence for Electronic Commerce: Papers from the AAAI-99 Workshop*, Menlo Park, CA, 1999. AAAI Press.

[12] D.W. Shipman. The Functional Data Model and the Data Language DAPLEX. *ACM Transactions on Database Systems*, 6(1):140–173, March 1981.

[13] M. Torrens and B. Faltings. Smart clients: constraint satisfaction as a paradigm for scaleable intelligent information systems. In *Artificial Intelligence for Electronic Commerce: Papers from the AAAI-99 Workshop*, Menlo Park, CA, 1999. AAAI Press.

A KNOWLEDGE BASED FRAMEWORK FOR THE DESIGN OF SOFT-COMPUTING SYSTEMS

Satheesh Ramachandran Madhav Erraguntla Perakath Benjamin
Knowledge Based Systems, Inc. *KBSI.* *KBSI.*

Abstract: This paper presents a systematic framework for the design of intelligent decision support systems based upon soft computing paradigms like *neural networks*, *genetic algorithms*, *simulated annealing* and *fuzzy logic*. The approach applies knowledge based systems techniques to support development and application of models in these computing paradigms. The long-term goal of this research is to automate the design of soft-computing systems from a domain expert's description of the problem situation and a set of input data.

Key words: word processing

1. INTRODUCTION

This paper presents a systematic framework for the design of intelligent decision support systems based upon soft computing paradigms like *neural networks*, *genetic algorithms*, *simulated annealing* and *fuzzy logic*. The approach applies knowledge based systems techniques to support development and application of models in these computing paradigms. The long-term goal of this research is to automate the design of soft-computing systems from a domain expert's description of the problem situation and a set of input data. The research results that are presented in this paper address a near term goal in providing intelligent assistance and model design principles to decision makers regarding the use evolving computation paradigms in decision-making. The main product of this research effort is a demonstration version of a ***Generalized Modeling and Analysis Toolkit (GMAT)***. GMAT is being developed under a DoD funded research contract (KBSI, 98). Currently GMAT supports the knowledge-based application of neural network and fuzzy logic models (Surkan, 89; Zimmerman, 91; Zadeh, 93;

Wu, 94). This focus of this paper is the knowledge-based assistance provided in GMAT in the development of neural network and fuzzy logic models.

Soft computing paradigms such as artificial neural nets (ANN) and fuzzy set theoretic modeling techniques have been used with increasing success in recent years for a variety of different *commercial* and *military* applications (Martinez, 89). The realm of current application domains extend from pattern recognition with reconnaissance images for military intelligence to inventory forecasting for retail warehousing to fraud detection in the financial sector. Two key factors responsible for the recent increases in neural network and fuzzy logic applications are (i) advances in information technology (increased efficiency in the collection, storage and control of information) and (ii) significant progress in analytical and computational techniques (because of increased availability of tractable algorithms and software). These new generation information processing systems exhibit capabilities like adaptability, robustness, generalization, and the ability to work amidst the imprecision and uncertainty of the real world, making them attractive solution technologies for complex problems (Guiasa, 93). Nevertheless, the full potential offered by these powerful techniques have remained largely unharnessed because of the inherent difficulties in designing, calibrating and applying these models.

2. RESEARCH MOTIVATIONS AND CHALLENGES

Specifically, the effective use of soft computing techniques is greatly hindered because of the following reasons:

1) Technology inaccessibility: Soft computing techniques such as neural networks and fuzzy logic technology are still relatively inaccessible to the industry. Despite progress in more versatile algorithms (such as Radial Basis Functions, Wavenets, Fuzzy Associate Memories) and their applications to forecasting, consumer behavior models, pattern recognition, signal processing and control, etc., neural networks and fuzzy logic remains a highly academic subject with applications in a few progressive domains. In spite of the power and flexibility of these techniques and their potential applicability to numerous, common problems in the industry, the proliferation of these technologies into the industry remains limited. This is mainly because of the complexity in the theory of these techniques and the high degree of expertise required to model and apply them properly. Existing tools attempt to provide assistance to users that are experts in neural network and fuzzy logic by automating the low-level calculations involved in using these techniques. However, these tools provide little assistance to a non-expert user of these technologies. A user of the currently available tools is expected to possess a fair amount of expertise before he can start using these powerful techniques to solve his problems. There is a need for knowledge based tools that provide assistance to novice users, in each and every step involved in using these technologies – right from problem identification, to development of appropriate models, to model calibration, usage, and eventually in documenting and re-use of models and expertise. Unless such assistance is provided, neural networks, fuzzy logic, genetic algorithms and simulated annealing will remain mere interesting academic concepts, and used exclusively by a "privileged few" high technology users.

2) Absence of soft computing modeling methodologies: Currently, no structured methodologies are available for developing and using soft computing models. Even though the theory of neural networks and fuzzy logic are well grounded in sound scientific principles, their application remains an art. The process of developing neural network and fuzzy logic models is a highly skilled process. There is no single, unique model corresponding to a problem situation – very often developing appropriate neural network and fuzzy logic models involves intuition and guesses based on experience in order to arrive at the correct calibration (for example, formulating the best neural network model architecture often involves iterative determination of appropriate model structure, transfer functions, leaning algorithms, parameters, etc). The initial model is then refined based on experiments. Skill is required not only in developing sound models, but also in ensuring adequate levels of model calibration (for example, over-fitting in a neural network might result in blind replication of patterns), and specifying appropriate values for the calibration parameters (such as neural network learning and momentum rates). This expertise in neural network and fuzzy logic can only be obtained through years of hands-on experience in applying these techniques to solve practical problems. The long learning curves associated with them render these powerful technologies unattractive for solving the real world, immediate problems of the industry. Availability of a structured methodology to support the process of designing, training, interpreting, and reusing neural network and fuzzy logic models would decrease the reliance of neural network and fuzzy logic experts, resulting in an increase in the use and popularity of these technologies. The timing appears right for the design and insertion of such methods; a method that is an encapsulation of "best practice".

3) Lack of design rationale capture and re-use mechanisms: As stated previously, developing and using soft computing models is a knowledge intensive, iterative process. Developing the suitable calibrated system for a given problem situation involves a significant amount of experimentation. This process involves conducting a set of experiments by making experience-based guesses about the architecture features that will be appropriate to the focus problem situation. Most often, the performance of these initial experiments will not be satisfactory. However, this experimentation process serves a very important function – the insights gained, observations made regarding the design concepts that seem to work and (often more importantly) those design concepts that do not seem to work – help in designing better neural networks in the next stage. This process of experimentation, deduction and incremental refinement is repeated until a model with acceptable performance characteristics is obtained. The experimentation process, the design *rationale*, and the knowledge gained during the entire design process are important knowledge assets that must be captured, organized, and maintained. For example, the expertise gained by neural network design and experimentation expertise is an important source of information for ideal architectures (type and number of neurons, number of hidden layers, etc.), network parameters (learning rate, momentum rates and their step sizes, etc.), training conditions (number of epochs, extent of cross-validation, etc.), input factors and variables, metrics (mean square error, absolute error, maximum error, etc.), and learning algorithms. It is important to capture such design rationale and experimentation information in a form that is re-usable. Contemporary soft computing modeling tools provide adequate support for representing and browsing the final design of the models. However, no support is provided by existing tools for capturing and organizing the vast knowledge involved in the development, incremental refinement, and introspection phases of modeling. Lack of proper methodologies to capture and re-use the knowledge involved in the design and development of soft computing models makes it difficult to exploit the results of developing one model in other subsequent design endeavors. Every model development becomes a new, unfamiliar activity to be explored and performed from scratch, without the assistance of the previous model design rationales and insights.

The GMAT research initiative targets these technological and pragmatic barriers directly. The research establishes the technical viability of a knowledge-based approach for the effective application of neural nets and fuzzy logic (these two techniques are the focus of our research) to a variety of decision problems. The following sections outline the technical approach adopted in GMAT.

3. FRAMEWORK FOR INTELLIGENT SYSTEM DESIGN

The overall solution is an end-to-end support environment that captures and delivers knowledge and experience to allow domain experts and synthetic algorithm engineers to produce workable first time applications. GMAT is designed to leverage and compliment existing COTS tools for fuzzy logic and neural networks. GMAT distinguishes itself from COTS packages by automating the entire life cycle of design and development for rapidly applying fuzzy logic and neural networks to real world problem situations. This section presents an example application to illustrate GMAT concept of operation. This commercial endeavor involves application of neural network and genetic algorithms technology to cash management solutions in the commercial banking sector. The results are currently being deployed to forecast the movement of money in over 2000 branches and 6000 ATMs nationwide.

3.1 Bank Cash Management Application:

We employed the GMAT system to develop a cash management application for the banking industry. The Department of Treasury prescribes norms for the cash level that must be maintained by each bank to support reserve requirements. As a result of recent regulation changes, banks currently have more leeway as to the levels of cash reserves they must maintain. Banks are attempting to minimize the cash they carry to the new reserve levels and yet meet the customer requirements. The less cash they carry for day-to-day operations, the more they will have for long term investments, resulting in more profits without increased fees. A critical piece of information required for solving this optimization problem is an accurate forecast of customers' daily withdrawals and deposits, so that banks can keep a minimal amount of cash required to support the forecasted level of activity. We used GMAT to develop neural network based predictive (causal and time-series based) models to forecast withdrawals and deposits for branches and ATMs. Although the application seemingly falls under the purview of a traditional MRP-type forecasting (followed by optimization) problem, many pitfalls were encountered. The data in many cases were insufficient, often spurious, and most critically, the amount of time that was required for building forecasting models for each of the over 2000 branches/ATM's were prohibitive in terms of time and effort. Firstly, the GMAT data management functions for data verification, repair and transformation were useful in reducing the upfront data preparatory time, and the consistency and quality of the prepared data had an impact on the ultimate performance of the forecasting models. The support provided by GMAT in integrating the various soft-computing paradigms led to significant reduction in the 2000+ model calibrations. One such innovation involved the application of cluster analysis to identify groupings in ATM's and branches. The idea here is that ATM's and branches that exhibited statistically similar cash withdrawal and deposit patterns could be served by the same forecasting models. This enabled us to reduce the number of forecasting models that were built. Once the cash requirements are forecasted, the GMAT tool also provided the capability to develop optimal cash delivering schedules (ordering policies) based upon a genetic algorithm based optimizing capability. The forecasts that are supplied by the neural network models are ultimately used by a genetic algorithm based optimizer to determine the optimal cash ordering and transportation policies.

3.2 Structured Methodology

The GMAT methodology provides guidelines for the development process of intelligent information processing models. The supporting GMAT toolkit is intended to support the domain user in every step of the problem-solving life cycle. The systematic model development process that is supported by GMAT is described in Sections 4.1 through 4.7:

4. GMAT FUNCTIONAL DESCRIPTION

In this section, we describe the functional description of the GMAT toolkit.

4.1 Problem Domain and Goal Specification

In GMAT, the highest-level definition is a *project*, which corresponds to a subset of an enterprise that has one or more problem situations and a set of enterprise variables that are used in generating models to solve the problem situations. The GMAT tool helps with the definition of decision-making goals that are associated with each of the problem situations. The goals are used to focus and direct the knowledge discovery process. In its current implementation, the GMAT goal modeler allows for the (a) selection goals from the Goal Template Library, (b) addition of new goals, (c) goal editing, and (d) organization of goals in a hierarchy. The rationale for goal capture is the observation that decision-making endeavors are goal-directed. The goal definition capability thus provides the preliminary context needed for decision-making using knowledge discovery.

4.2 Data Acquisition, Assessment, Verification and Validation

An early step in the GMAT methodology involves capturing domain knowledge in terms of the variables in the domain and their data sources. Data source refers to the location in a database or text file where the values for that variable are present. GMAT supports data retrieval from relational databases and comma-delimited text files. There are three types of basic variable categorization that is supported by GMAT. A variable can be either crisp or fuzzy. Crisp variables have numeric or text values. Fuzzy variables can be specified in terms of their fuzzy classes, and membership functions can be specified for these classes. Variables are also classified as basic or derived, based on whether the data is directly available or some transformation needs to be performed. Finally variables can be defined as either independent or dependent. Independent variables are analogous to key fields in databases. Once identified, raw data must next be verified, validated, repaired, and transformed before it can be applied to solve domain problems. By supporting these data management functions independent of the problem goals, GMAT allows for reuse of validated and cleansed data across different modeling goals.

Among the vexing problems in data intensive applications like neural networks and fuzzy logic based systems is the error in input data. Errors in the input data could result from mis-specification, omission, corruption, approximation, etc. In the calibration of soft-computing systems, even a few incorrect data points could drastically change the intended pattern that these systems are expected to learn, resulting in poor model performance. In other situations, the data point might be correct, but the value it represents might be an extremely rare phenomenon that skews the underlying pattern. In such situations, it might be necessary to remove that data point or modify it appropriately so that the model learns the desired pattern and not some isolated deviation in the input data. GMAT provides automated as well as user-assisted support for detection of possible errors or anomalies in the data. GMAT supports the following methods for detecting errors in the input data:

- Visual Inspection—in this method the data points associated with variable are displayed in different ways as a graph or plot (2D or 3D visualizations). GMAT has a built-in data browser that retrieves data from the data source and displays it for the user. As a result of this feature, the user requires minimal knowledge in database management systems
- Detection of standard anomalies—Users can specify standard anomalies such as negative values, zero values, or null values where

such conditions are not expected. Also, the user can get a list of data points that are outside the 2σ and 3σ limits.

- User-defined Anomalies—In addition to standard anomalies, users can specify mathematical relationships/constraints that need to be maintained between different variables. For example, in the banking application, the user can check for inconsistencies to the following constraint: *End Cash* = *Begin cash* – *Withdrawals* + *Deposits*. GMAT provides an SQL builder to aid the user in defining and validating such relationships.

4.2.1 Data Repair

GMAT allows for automatically fixing suspected anomalous data points. The repair strategies supported in GMAT include the replacement of data points with different approximation strategies such as average within a range, average based on a condition, median, interpolation, etc.

4.2.2 Data Transformation

In most industrial and military applications, there is a large mismatch between the available data and data that is required as input to a neural network. For example, temporal data may be clustered better if the clustering algorithm was done on the frequency series rather than the time series. As another example, consider an image processing application, where the input is a pixel grid representing a reconnaissance satellite picture. Before this input can be analyzed using neural networks for patterns or classification, data reduction transformations are needed to reduce the huge input matrix (on the order of 600x800) to a more manageable size. Existing COTS packages for soft computing methods require the input data to be externally pre-processed and converted to the appropriate input format. Such pre-processing and conversion is supported by GMAT in the form of a repository of data transformation utilities. GMAT supports the following transformations: 1) Fuzzy Transformations, and Qualitative Encoding, 2) Frequency Transformations (Fourier Transformations), and 3) Mathematical Transformations.

More recent hybridized neuro-fuzzy models have the ability to include qualitative factors in the analysis in addition to quantitative data. For pure mathematical and statistical analysis of input data, there are numerous analytical methods that perform the job as efficiently as neural networks. However, these neuro-fuzzy hybrid modeling paradigms excel in comparison to traditional techniques in their ability to include highly subjective, qualitative factors in the analysis. These qualitative factors represent experience-based, empirical associations developed by human experts gained during years of working in the domain. These associations are often too fuzzy and qualitative to be accounted for in an analytical model. At the same time, they are an important part of the domain knowledge and have to be captured and exploited in order to obtain sound analysis results. For example, in the banking application, it was known that cash demand is "low" on Mondays, "high" on Fridays, and "medium" on other days of the week. GMAT provides support for incorporation of such qualitative, human inputs into the analysis. During training, GMAT provides assistance to refine these qualitative associations based on the patterns observed in the input data.

4.3 Model Selection

Once domain knowledge for a project has been captured in terms of project variables that are valid, verified, transformed, and scrubbed, they can be used across different problem situations. In GMAT, the problem situation definition includes specification of the problem focus name and the problem focus type. Currently, users can select the following problem focus types: clustering, discrimination, forecasting, qualitative analysis (fuzzy operators, fuzzy neural networks, fuzzy associative memories) and causal models (neural networks based curve-fitting). Once a problem situation type has been specified, GMAT provides knowledge-based support for selection of appropriate solution technology type. For example, if the user specifies the problem situation as being of the *clustering* type, she can choose either the *k-mean* algorithm or the unsupervised Kohonen Neural Network as the technology solution. Additionally, GMAT has built-in templates for standard technology solution types. The knowledge of pairing a problem situation type to a solution technology type is implemented as a knowledge base. Users can specify alternative solution designs for a given problem situation. Each solution design uses a specific technology type.

4.4 Model Design and Configuration

In this section, we describe the assistance that GMAT provides for neural network model design (the support for other paradigms follow similar principles). For neural network based technology, generating the best neural network is by no means a simple task. This is because there are various choices of neural network architecture design, input and output variable combinations, and exemplar constraints. As a result, it is possible to create a large number of alternative neural network designs (NND) and training sets (TS). The final neural network model must be selected from among the various NND-TS pairs. However, for *each* NND-TS pair, a substantial amount of time and effort must be spent on experimentation and simulation (Section 4.5). Unless automated support is provided, neural network model generation is an extremely tedious and time-consuming task. GMAT supports this activity by automatically generating neural network models from the design specifications, and by preparing the input and desired output training sets. The following four design criteria give rise to different NND-TS pairs.

1. **Neural Network Architecture:** A typical neural network architecture design involves parameters such as (i) Number of processing elements at the input/output level, (ii) Input level transformation functions, (iii) Output level transformation functions, (iv) Number of Hidden layers, (iv) Number of axons for each hidden layer, (v) Hidden layer transformation functions, (vi) Number of axons for each hidden layer, (vii) Learning Algorithm and type.
2. **Input combination.** This is the list and order of project-level variables that form inputs to the neural network. The number of processing elements in the input layer is determined by the input combination.
3. **Output combination.** This is the list and order of project-level variables that form output to the neural network. The number of processing elements in the output layer is determined by the output combination.
4. **Exemplar constraint.** This is a set of restrictions for deriving a training set. For example, the user may want to avoid all training sets that have negative values.

While the combinations of the former three design criteria give rise to the different NNDs, the combinations of the latter three design criteria give rise to the different TSs.

4.5 Neural Network Calibration (or Training) Management

Developing a good neural network model for a given NND-TS pair is itself an iterative, experiment-based, incremental refinement process. After training and analyzing the performance of a neural network model, improvements are made. This process of training and incremental refinement is continued until a neural network with acceptable performance is obtained. Existing neural network tools provide little support for this iterative training and refinement process. Factors that determine the result of training of a NND with a TS include the (i) learning rate, (ii) momentum rate, (iii) the step size, (iv) maximum number of epochs, (v) type and extent of cross validation, and the (vi) termination criterion for training (number of epochs versus desired error level).

GMAT supports various experimental designs based on combinations of the above variables. For each experiment, GMAT invokes the neural network simulator to train each NND-TS pair, calculate the mean percent error, and save it to the GMAT database. As an alternative, the user can specify an experiment to be under the control of the *Neural Network Controller* that can monitor the performance of a neural network in real-time while the neural network is being trained. In order to optimize the performance of the neural network, the controller modifies the learning rate and the momentum rate in real-time. This controller itself is implemented using fuzzy logic and neural network technologies.

4.6 Training Result Browser and Execution Control

GMAT displays the results of the neural network training for each experiment. The user can browse through the various executions and determine the performance of the training of each NND with any training set. The user can also execute the best neural network or any given neural network with new data that is different from the training set. Each new execution is stored in the GMAT database to facilitate reuse of results.

4.7 Design Rationale Capture

GMAT provides extensive support for capture of design rationale for each experiment and a visual trace of all experiments relating to a problem situation. All aspects of a problem situation, problem solution, experiment design, neural network training, and execution are stored in the GMAT database for future reference. Using the design rationale capture mechanism and the trace, the user can quickly understand the experiments that were conducted. Description fields provide for the capture of notes for a given problem situation, experiment or training, where as name of experimenter/modeler and date created/executed provide for configuration management.

5. GMAT ARCHITECTURE

Due to page limitation GMAT architecture is not included in the final version. Please contact the authors for the complete version of the paper.

Acknowledgements

GMAT application was designed and developed under funding from Army SBIR Phase I and Phase II funding (KBSI, 98). We acknowledge the support of Army SBIR program and Mr. Kachesh Pathak in particular in our endeavors.

References

1. Davis, L. (Editor). (1991). *Handbook of Genetic Algorithms*, Van Nostrand Reinhold, New York, NY.
2. Dubois, Didier and Prade, H. (1980). *Fuzzy Sets and Systems: Theory and Applications*, Academic Press, New York.
3. Goldberg, D. E. (1989). *Genetic Algorithms in Search, Optimization, and Machine Learning*, Addison-Wesley.
4. Graham, A. (1997). Seed Money Available to Develop and Prototype National Space Reconnaissance Data Capabilities – How MERIT Can Help Your Program. *PM*, May-June.
5. Guiasa, S. (1993). A Unitary Treatment of Several Known Measures of Uncertainty Induced by Probability, Possibility, Fuzziness, Plausibility, and Belief, *Uncertainty in Intelligent Systems*. Amsterdam: North Holland Press, 355-366.
6. Knowledge Based Systems, Inc. (1998). *"Generalized Event Representation Modeling and Analysis Tool (GERMAT)*, Army Phase II SBIR Contract No. DASG60-98-C-0051.
7. Kosko, B. (1992). *Neural Networks and Fuzzy Systems: A Dynamical Systems Approach for Machine Intelligence*. New York: Prentice Hall.
8. Lin, C.T. & George, C.S. (1991). Neural Network Based Fuzzy Logic Control System. *IEEE Transactions on Computers*, 1320-1325.
9. Martinez, Tony. (1989). Neural Networks Applicability: Classifying the Input Space. *Proceeding of the Fifth IASTED International Symposium*.
10. Rumelhart D. E., et al. (1987). *Parallel Distributed Processing*, MIT Press, Cambridge, MA, 1987.
11. Surkan, A. & Cao, H. (1989). Models of Artificial Neural Networks: An Emerging Learning Technology. *Proceeding of the Fifth IASTED International Symposium*.
12. Wu, J.K. (1994). *Neural Networks and Simulation Methods*.
13. Zadeh, L. (1993). Soft Computing and Fuzzy Logic. *IEEE Software*, 48-56.
14. Zimmerman, H. J. (1991). *Fuzzy Set Theory*, Kluwer, Boston, MA.

A REVERSE ENGINEERING APPROACH FOR MIGRATING DATA-INTENSIVE WEB SITES TO THE SEMANTIC WEB

Nenad Stojanovic[1], Ljiljana Stojanovic[2], Raphael Volz[1]

[1] *AIFB Institute, Univ. of Karlsruhe, Germany, {nst,rvo}@aifb.uni-karslruhe.de*

[2] *FZI Research Center for Information Technologies at the Univ. of Karlsruhe, Germany stojanov@fzi.edu*

Abstract: The Semantic Web is intended to enable machine understandable web content and seems to be a solution for many drawbacks of the current Web. It is based on metadata that formally describe the semantics of Web contents. In this paper we present an integrated and semi-automatic approach for generating shared-understandable metadata for data-intensive Web applications. This approach is based on mapping a given relational schema into an already existing ontology structure using a reverse engineering process. As a case study we present this style of a schema- and data-migration for our Institute web portal. The presented approach can be applied to a broad range of today's data-intensive Web sites.

Key words: Database reverse engineering, ontology

1. INTRODUCTION

The Semantic Web is one of today's hot keywords. It is about bringing "[...] structure to the meaningful content of Web pages, creating an environment where software agents, roaming from page to page, can readily carry out sophisticated tasks for users." [2]. In order to enable this, web sites are enhanced with metadata that provide formal semantics for Web content. The key technology involved here are ontologies. Ontologies provide consensual domain models, which are understandable to both human beings and machines as a shared conceptualisation of a specific domain that is given. Using ontologies, web content is made suitable for machine consumption, opposing to the content found today, which is primarily intended for human consumption.

Currently people are slowly starting to build the Semantic Web, thus ontology-based metadata is being provided. This process of generating such metadata - also called semantic annotation - is mostly done by hand and therefore cumbersome and expensive. Visual annotation tools [9] make this task much easier, but even with sophisticated tools it is laborious to provide semantic annotations. Additionally, a maintenance problem arises; annotations must be consistent, must make proper reference, redundancy must be avoided and of course be maintained which results in a need for constant synchronization with their corresponding web content. However, because ontologies aim at consensual community (domain) knowledge, it is not enough to provide only *formal* semantics for information, but also *real-world semantics* allowing to link a machine processable content with the meaning for humans, based on *consensual* terminologies [7].

In this paper we address these problems and give a solution for an important class of those data-intensive web sites that draw their data from relational databases. These sites have moved away from static, fixed web pages to those that are dynamically generated at the time of user requests from data in relational databases. In order to migrate these web sites into the Semantic Web we have developed an approach which is based on mapping the given relational schema into an existing ontologic structure, using a reverse engineering process. Using this mapping the database content can be directly used to provide the intended semantic annotations. We also present a tool that supports this mapping in a semi-automatic manner.

The benefits of the proposed approach are manifold: The process of providing metadata is automated and thus inexpensive and fast. Consequently, the content of dynamic web pages is machine-understandable and therefore visible for specialized search engines. Moreover, the problem of dynamic updating metadata according to changes in corresponding web pages is also resolved. The most important benefit is that information from various community members could be exchanged on the semantic basis.

Our approach can be applied to a broad range of today's data-intensive Web sites. One of the most common applications for such data-intensive web sites are most e-commerce applications, many kinds of directories and "reporting sites"[17]. Such data-intensive web sites have numerous benefits, i.e. a simplified maintenance of the web design (due to complete separation between data and layout), the automated updating of web content, etc. Moreover, the using of ontologies as a mediation level for product data exchange is already proposed [15]. Our approach could be a mechanism for resolving semantic problems that arise in this integration process.

[17] providing for example information about stock-quotes or the current weather

The paper is organized as follows: Section 2 details the mapping architecture, mapping process and rules used in it. In Section 3 we present our case study by concluding with some lessons we learned. Before we conclude we contrast our contribution with related work.

2. THE MAPPING ARCHITECTURE AND PROCESS

2.1 Design rationale

Source data: Our mapping architecture is grounded on the logical database model found in running database systems [1]. The reader may note that the logical database model does not specify formal semantics of the contained information and thus is not sufficient per se as a conceptual backbone for the Semantic Web.

The reason for basing our approach on the logical data model is that most often no conceptual model (like an ER model) was created during the conception of the database or this information is lost by now. Naturally a mapping from ER models to ontologies preserves more information (like cardinalities).

The target data model for our mapping approach is F-Logic. F-Logic was developed to combine the rich data-modelling primitives of object-oriented databases with logical languages as developed for deductive databases [8].

Implementation constraints: The architecture should require only minor changes on the existing web application. Therefore the initial data is not converted. The newly implemented "Semantic Web" part of the web application should reference this source data and create the required information (in form of RDF data) on demand and dynamically by applying mapping rules specified in this paper. Another reason not to convert the data is that permanent synchronization would be needed.

Information preservation: We reinstate that the goal of this mapping is to preserve a maximum of information under the ontology framework. It is important to say that this process of the schema transformation cannot be lossless. Due to the static nature of ontologies no dynamical aspects in SQL-DDLs can be converted, thus triggers, referential actions (like ON UPDATE etc.) and assertions cannot be mapped.

2.2 Migration architecture

The general migration architecture is depicted in figure 1. The input of the migration is a relational model that is derived from the SQL DDL. The database schema is mapped into the given ontology using the mapping process described bellow, which applies the rules specified in the following sections. The same holds for database instances that are transformed into a knowledge base, which is based on the domain ontology.

The actual mapping is computed once (under the supervision and revision of the designer) and must be recomputed only if the database schema or ontology is changed. The knowledge base is computed on demand. The ontology, into which the database is mapped, is given in F-Logic. In order to publish data on the Web, F-Logic files have to be translated into RDF. This translation is straightforward. Servlets are used to create the RDF output files from the ontology and the database data. The legacy HTML files must be changed minimally to contain a reference to their metadata descriptions[18]. This provides the semantic annotations for the legacy content.

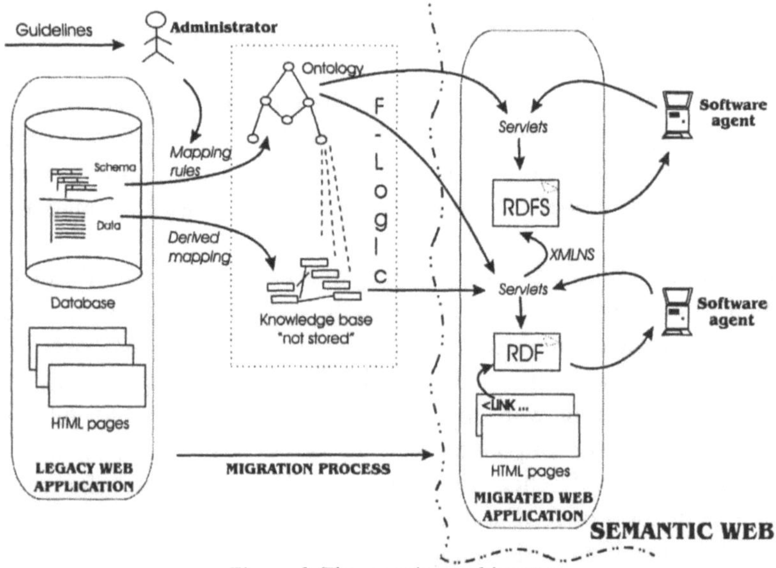

Figure 1. The mapping architecture

2.3 Mapping Process

The mapping process enhances the semantics of the database by providing additional ontological entities. For example, for some database entities some explicit axioms, which formally describe some properties of those entities, are added in the destination ontology (see examples given subsequently).

Our proposed mapping method consists of four steps:

1. Capture information from a relational schema through reverse engineering (consider relations, attributes, attributes types, primary keys, foreign keys / inclusion dependencies);

[18] HTML handles this situation with the following tag: `<LINK rel="meta" href="mydocMetadata.DC.RDF">`

2. Analyse the obtained information to map database entities into ontological entities, by considering a set of mapping rules which are briefly sketched in section 2.4 and fully described in [14]. These rules are originally made in order to enable the derivation of a new ontology from a given database schema. In this approach they are reused and adapted in order to guideline the mapping of a database schema into the given ontology (some of the remarks are given in the section 3.1). This phase is split into:

2a. alignment of the top-level terms (decision on which relation identifier corresponds to which concept identifier);

2b. using existing concept creation rules to determine the relations in the relational schema that are related to a concept;

2c. using attribute creation rules to assign relation's attributes to the attributes of a concept;

Note: Since the ontology is already given, the usage of the mentioned rules does not impose changes in the definition of the ontology. These rules help in the alignment between relational entities and ontological entities.

3. Evaluate, validate and refine the mapping. Check whether all relational entities are mapped into corresponding ontological entities, i.e. whether the existing ontology is conceptually rich enough to completely represent the relational schema. Also, the implicit semantic of the relational model must be mapped into explicit ontological structures (e.g. for each n:m relation in the relational model a rule specifies that the corresponding ontological relations are inverse).

4. Form a knowledge base ("data migration").

The implemented system, presented in next section, provides assistance in all phases. Actually, the reverse engineering process cannot be completely automated as some situations can arise where several rules could be applied. User interaction is then necessary if such ambiguities occur and domain semantics cannot be inferred.

2.4 Mapping rules

In [14] we have defined a set of mapping rules, which enable incremental creation of a new ontology. In this section we briefly reinterpret these rules. We refer to an example schema that models some aspects of a university. The example is depicted in figure 2. Table 1 shows the translated schema in F-Logic.

Rules for concepts: The mapping from relations to concepts is not a trivial process. We can neither assume that every concept is derived from exactly one relation nor vice versa.

Table 1. Created ontology

Concept	Relation	Predicate & Axiom
Object[].	Student[	Key(Student, studID).
Student::Object.	studID=>>Number;	NotNull(Student, familyname).
PhDStudent::Student.	givenname=>>String;	Inverse(Course, studID, Student,
School::Object.	familyname=>>String;	courseID).
Staff::Object.	schoolID->>School;	MustExists(Offering, lecturerID).
Course::Object.	courseID=>>Course].	...
CourseTermin::Object.	PhDStudent[	Forall C1,R1,C2,R2 Inverse(C1,R1,C2,R2)
CourseMaterial::Object.	year=>>String].	<-
Quarter::Object.	School[	Forall IR1, IR2 EXISTS IC1 IC2 IR1:C1
Offering::Object.	faculty=>>String;	and IR2:C2 and IC1:C1 and IC2:C2 and
	studID=>>Student	(Forall IC1[R1->>IR2]<-IC2[R2->>IR1])
	...	and
	].	(Forall IC1[R2->>IR1]<-IC1[R1->>IR2]).
	...	

The simplest way to create a concept is a direct mapping a relation from the source schema to a target concept in the ontology. However, there are two exceptions defined in two additional rules. The first of them treats relations which only exist to express (n:m) relationships between some other relations. This kind of relations contains only a pair of foreign-key attributes (e.g. the relation **ENROL** in figure 2) and it is not converted into a concept. A second exception are those relations whose primary key is also a foreign key (e.g. the relation **STAFF-DETAIL** in figure 2). Most likely this relation provides additional information to the relation, which is refered to by the foreign key. Thus, this relation is not mapped into the concept, because the distributed information can be integrated into one concept.

Relational schema

STUDENT (studID, givenname, familyname, schoolID)
PhDSTUDENT (studID, year)
SCHOOL (schoolID; faculty)
STAFF (lecturerID, room)
STAFF-DETAIL (lecturerID, address)
COURSE (courseID, subject, equip)
COURSE-TERMIN (courseID, tnumberID, date)
COURSE-MATERIAL (courseID, mnumberID, version)
ENROL (courseID, studID)
QUARTR (quarterID, year)
OFFERING (lecturerID, courseID, quarterID)

Figure 2. Relational example schema

In our example, the **ENROL** relation does not have a corresponding concept, as its definition contains only primary keys (***courseID*** and ***studID***) which are also foreign keys to the relations **COURSE** and **STUDENT**. This information is expressed by ontological relations between the concepts **Course** and **Staff**.

Moreover, no concept was derived from the relation **STAFF-DETAILS**, since information about a particular entity (**Staff**) can be collected from multiple relations (**STAFF** and **STAFF-DETAILS**). All other relations in example schema are converted into corresponding concepts, e.g. the relation **STUDENT** is mapped into a single concept **Student**.

Rules for inheritance: Extracting inheritance relationship from a relation schema usually requires behavioural information. It can be created when an inclusion dependency between keys of two relations exists. If for each tuple in relation r1 exists a tuple with the same primary key in another relation r2, then this can be regarded as a specialisation because attributes of both r1 and r2 belong to the primary key in a tuple r1. For example, an inheritance relation between concept **Student** and concept **PhDStudent** is detected, based on the inclusion dependency defined on key attributes of the corresponding relations (**STUDENT** and **PhDSTUDENT**).

This rule is a specialization of the second exception for concept creation. In general the user has to decide which rule is to be applied.

Rules for ontological relations: There are several possibilities to create ontological relations from a relational schema. Again we have a default rule that is applied if no other relation rules can be applied. In this case all source attributes are converted to ontological relations. For example, the attribute ***givenname*** in the relation **STUDENT** is mapped to the ontological relation ***givenname*** , that applies to the concept **Student**.

A second relation creation rule treats many-to-many relationship. It applies if a source relation contains exactly two foreign keys and has no other attributes. This relation is then converted to multi-valued concept references. For example, the relation **ENROL** contains only foreign keys, referencing the **STUDENT** and **COURSE** relations. The rule leads to the creation of two multi-valued relations ***studID*** and ***courseID,*** which are attached to the corresponding concepts. These two ontological relations are mutually inverse which is additionally represented with a corresponding ontology axiom (**Inverse(Course, *studID*, Student, *courseID*)**).

A third rule treats one to many relationships. Again key references are converted to concept references. In distinction to previous rule on the "one" side only an ontological relation with a single-valued concept reference is created. For example, the relation **STUDENT** has a foreign key ***schoolID*** which refers to the primary key of the relation **SCHOOL**. A single-valued relation ***schoolID*** of type **School**, is attached to the **Student** concept. A multi-valued relation ***studID*** is attached to the concept **School**. We assume that ontological relations are multi-valued. If one ontological relation has to be single-value, the corresponding axiom (**SingleValue(Student, *schoolID*)**) is used to provide support for this type of constraints.A fifth rule groups the attributes which are distributed in several relations. All attributes (except primary keys) of the relation **STAFF-DETAILS** (***address***) are mapped into ontological relations with the domain **Staff**, because the relation **STAFF-**

DETAILS represents additional information about the same person, which is represented by a tuple in the **STAFF** relation.

An inclusion dependency between the keys of two relations in both directions leads to a one-to-one relationship. We also introduce a rule that handles this kind of relationships. In this case both foreign keys are converted to single-valued ontological relations that are mutually inverse. In our example, a relation **COURSE-TERMIN** has the keys ***courseID*** and ***tnumberID*** referencing the keys ***courseID*** and ***mnumberID*** of the relation **COURSE-MATERIAL** and vice versa. The corresponding single-valued relations are attached to the created concepts. The reader may note that these relations are mutually inverse (**Inverse(Course-Termin, *mnumberID*, Course-Material, *tnumberID*)**).

Non-binary relationships representing relationships of higher degrees must be transformed into further concepts and a set of the binary relations. RDF does not provide means for n-ary relations, therefore complex relations are decomposed into a group of several binary relations. For example, the relation **OFFERING** denotes a relationship between staff, courses, and quarters. For each involved database relation a new relation is added to the concept **Offering** connecting the corresponding concepts (**Staff, Course** and **Quarter**), which are also connect with the concept **Offering**. These relations are mutually inverse and single-valued. We need further semantics for this kind of relations, which ensures that the group of binary relations only exists as a whole. For example, one of the staff S has offered course C in quarter Q **if and only if there exists** a course-offering O, such that this course-offering O has relations with staff S, course C and quarter Q. In order to define this, we introduce a new axiom **MustExist**.

2.5 Data Migration

Once the ontology is created, the process of *data migration* can start. The objective of this task is the creation of ontologicy instances (that form a knowledge base) based on the tuples of the relation database.

The data migration process has to be performed in two phases:

1. In the first phase the instances are created. A unique identifier to each instance is assigned. This translates all attributes, except for foreign-key attributes, which are not needed in the metadata.
2. In the second phase, relations between instances are established using the information contained in the foreign keys in the database tuples. This is accomplished using a mapping function, that maps keys to ontological identifiers.

In our particular implementation the Ontobroker F-Logic inference engine [5] is used. Ontobroker's API function *dbaccess* enables the generation of the instances from the given relational database on the fly. In the next section we describe a tool-support for the (semi-)automation of the presented mapping process and its application in a real-world case-study.

3. THE AIFBNET CASE STUDY

Our case study concerns the Web site of our Institute AIFB[19], which in the first version was a database application. In order to enable the processing of the site content by machine agents we decided to describe the content explicitly and formally. However, to make the new application more sharable (for the research community) we decided to create a domain ontology – the benefits of a such approach for information integration are obvious [18].

This ontology is developed independently from the relational model of our database application, as it should sublimate community demands and not only our particular instantiation.

The ontology is developed using the OTK methodology, the process and accumulated experiences in its creation are described in [18].

Our DB-based application contains real data about researchers, projects and the institute. In order to avoid redundant work we need to map the content of the database into the knowledge base of the ontology-based Web-site. To do the mapping extensive tool support has to be given t to give the required user interaction for the resolution of the mentioned ambiguities in the applicability of rules.

For the automation of the mapping process we used ONTOMAT-REVERSE, a tool for semi-automatically connecting relational databases to ontologies, implemented as a plug-in for the KAON[20] ontology environment. ONTOMAT–REVERSE supports some phases in the adapted mapping process, particularly capturing information from the relational schema, validation of the mapping process and data migration. For step 2 of the mapping process ONTOMAT-REVERSE generates some recommendations based on the mapping rules [14], as will be presented in the following text.

The alignment of the top level terms is very difficult and can not be completely automated. Some guidelines could be proposed comparing entities names on the syntax level [12]. In this case that the ontology definition contains a lexical layer [13] (labels, synonyms, stems) to support a more efficient string matching performance. ONTOMAT-REVERSE supports the alignment of top level terms using the lexical layer of the AIFB ontology. For example, the source relation "Projekt" is mapped into the concept "Project", since the edit distance between "Project" is "Projekt" is

[19] www.aifb.uni-karlsruhe.de

[20] http://kaon.semanticweb.org

very small. The output of this phase is a set of the mapping pairs in the form {(name_of_relation, name_of_concept)}.

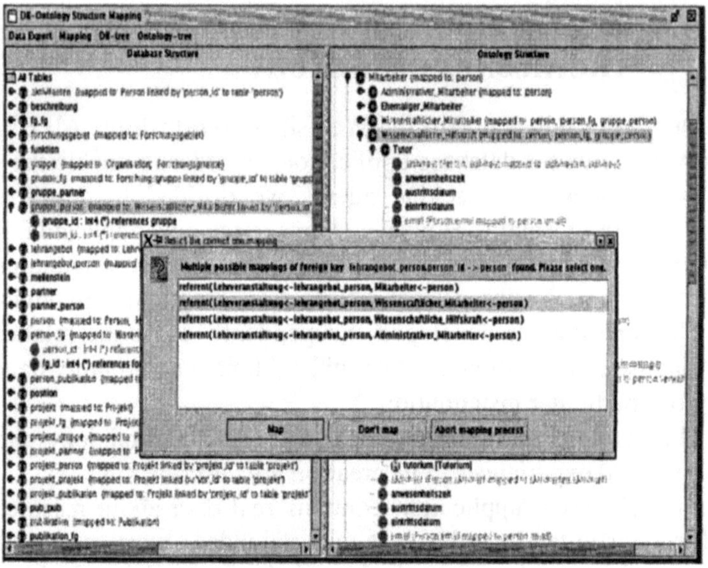

Figure 3. A screenshot of ONTOMAT-REVERSE

As already mentioned, ONTOMAT-REVERSE supports the validation step: for example, it is discovered that the relation "Beschreibung" is not mapped into any concept. After the analysis of the structure and the content of this relation, it is determined that this relation has neither foreign keys nor that other relations have a foreign key to this relation. However, the relations to the other relations are hard-coded and can be discovered only by an analysis of the content of this relation. Therefore additional heuristic rules for concept and attribute creation are implemented, which operate on the identifiers of source relations. Thereby the set of mapping pairs can be extended. For example, we can discover that the relations "Projekt_FG", "Projekt_Person", "Projekt_Gruppe" all correspond to the concept "Projekt".

Figure 3 shows how ONTOMAT-REVERSE makes recommendations for assigning attributes of the source relation to ontological relations between concepts in the ontology. The left side of figure 3 depicts the structure of the source schema. The right side shows the target ontology. Highlighted entities are mapped to each other. Recommendations for mapping attributes are listed in the dialog.

The data migration process is performed according to the guidelines described in the section 2. First object identifiers for instances are created using functions that map tuple identifiers from the source database to instance identifiers in the knowledge base. Afterwards relations between instances are instantiated. An illustration of the data migration process and the mentioned phases is presented in the Figure 4.

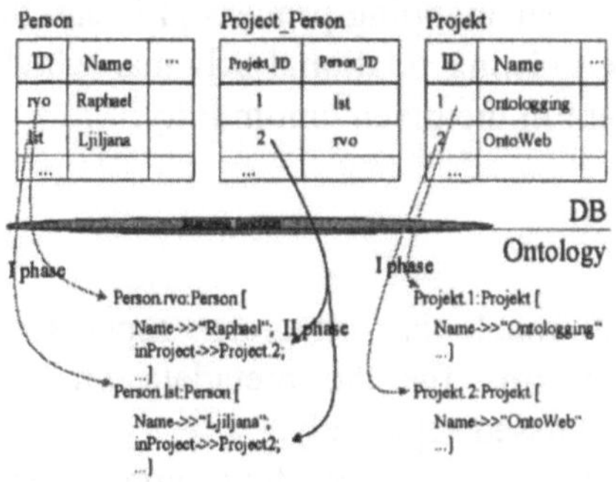

Figure 4. The data migration process – An example

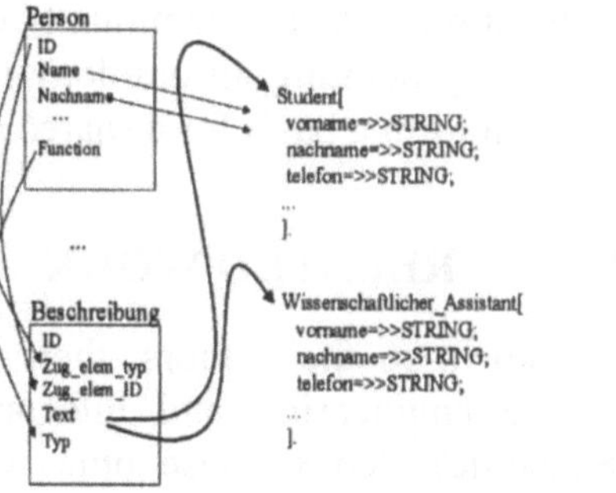

Figure 5. Type of the concept Person is codified in the attribute Function in the relation Person, but in the ontology there exists is-a hierarchy of concept Person and therefore another mapping is possible

3.1 Lessons learned

The result of applying our mapping process in real-world case studies suggest the formation of heuristic-mapping rules, which will be implemented in the next version of ONTOMAT-REVERSE.

- The order of applying the mapping rules is very important. Our experience suggests to create concepts first, establish the concept hierarchy afterwards and do the creation of ontological relations as a last step.

- As already emphasised is the section 2, the reverse engineering process cannot be completely automated. User interaction is necessary to resolve ambiguities and to infer domain semantics.

- - One exception for the creation of an ontological relation can be the existence of a local key in the relation schema that is used to maintain internal consistency of the data across various tables. The user might choose not to represent such local keys, which were created for implementation purposes only, in the domain ontology.

- In the case of NULL values the mapping procedure should not assign any value to the corresponding ontological relation.

- Various "irregular situations" might occur in the structure of the relational schema. For example, a relation might not have primary key. Thus IDs must be generated and the consistency of data is very hard to achieve. An example is depicted in the Figure 5. Such kind of the problems is not treated in the presented mapping approach and must be resolved per hand presenting a challenge for our future work.

The presented user scenario could be generalized for each community. The only prerequisite is that a commonly shared community ontology exists. In the absence of the community ontology, our mapping process [17] can be used for generating an ontology from the existing relational schema, which can then form a basis for a shared agreement in the given community.

4. RELATED WORK

As known to the authors, there is no approach that integrates aspects of reverse engineering and integration platforms for the metadata on the (Semantic) Web, so those topics will be discussed separately.

Database reverse engineering: There are very few approaches investigating the transformation of a relational model into an ontological model. The most similar approach to our approach is the project Infosleuth [11]. In this project an ontology is built based on the database schemas of the sources that should be accessed. The ontology is refined based on user queries. However, there are no techniques for creating axioms, which are a very important part of an ontology. Our approach is heavily based on the mapping of some database constraints into ontological axioms. Moreover, the semantic characteristics of the database schema are not always analysed.

More work has been addressed on the issue of explicitly defining semantics in database schemas [4], [16], extracting semantics out of database schema [4], [10] and transforming a relational model into an object-oriented model [3], which is close to an ontological theory. Rishe [16] introduces semantics of the database as a "means" to closely capture the meaning of user information and to provide a concise, high-level description of that information. In [4] an interactive schema migration environment that provides a set of alternative schema mapping rules is proposed. In this approach, which is similar to our approach on the conceptual level, the re-engineer repeatedly chooses an adequate mapping rule for each schema artefact. However, this stepwise process creates an object-oriented schema, therefore axioms are not discussed.

Information integration: In the broader sense our approach could be treated as an information integration approach [14], [19], while we provide a platform for resolving semantic problems that arise in this integration process. The information mediation architecture contains intermediate layer that mediates between human user and information sources. That layer has a dual structure: the mediator deals with the human user and the wrappers deal with the information sources [7]. In our approach information sources have a uniform structure, so that the role of wrapping is dedicated to the mapping process. In [6] an approach for reconciling XML data is presented, based on intermediate conceptual models. In this case, a human expert is needed to reverse-engineer the underlying conceptual model for an XML schema, and to specify formally how the original schema maps onto the corresponding conceptual model. Our approach provides the guidelines how to make such kind of reverse engineering, so that some phases can be automated and user intervention is avoided.

5. CONCLUSION

In this paper we proposed a novel, integrated and semi-automated approach for migrating data-intensive Web applications into the Semantic Web which can be applied to a broad range of today's business Web sites.

The approach starts with transforming the relational database model into corresponding ontological structures, which are then used for mapping the content of the database into an ontology-based knowledge base. The knowledge base can then be published on the web using RDF.

Publishing such statements on the web makes content of the web pages (in the last instance also the content of a given database) public and machine understandable, which is the prerequisite to achieve the Semantic Web. As a side effect, the issue of making the semantics of a database more explicit is also addressed and our approach leads to more formal semantics that could be used, for example, for the maintenance of data-driven applications and also in the simplified migration to other databases.

Moreover, the presented scenario can be very popular in the e-commerce domain, where the usage of ontologies as mediation level for product data exchange is already proposed [15] and our approach could be a mechanism for resolving the semantic problems that arise in this integration process.

The benefits of the proposed approach are manifold: The process of providing metadata is automated and thus inexpensive and fast. The problem of dynamic updating metadata according to changes in corresponding web pages is also resolved. The most important benefit is that information from various community members could be exchanged on the semantic bases. This paves the way to unleash the full-power of the Semantic Web.

ACKNOWLEDGEMENTS

The research presented in this paper would not have been possible without our colleagues and students at the Institute AIFB, University of Karlsruhe, and FZI, Karlsruhe. We thank out student Gert Pache who implemented ONTOMAT-REVERSE. Research for this paper was partially financed by EU in the IST-funded projects "OntoLogging" and "WonderWeb".

REFERENCES

1. Abiteboul S., Hull R., Vianu V. *Foundation of databases*, Addison-Wesley Publishing Company, 1995.

2. Berners-Lee T., *XML 2000 – Semantic Web talk*, http://www.w3.org/2000/Talks/1206-xml2k-tbl/slide10-0.html, 2000
3. Behm A., Geppert A., Dittrich, K., *On the Migration of Relational Schemas and Data to Object-Oriented Database Systems*, Proc. of the 5th Int. Conference on Re-Technologies for Information Systems, pp. 13-33, 1997.
4. Chiang R., Barron T., Storey V., *Reverse engineering of relational databases: Extraction of an EER model from a relational database*, Journ. of Data and Knowledge Engineering, Vol. 12, No. 2, March 1994, pp. 107–142., 1994.
5. Decker S., Erdmann M., Fensel D., Studer R., *Ontobroker: Ontology Based Access to Distributed and Semi-Structured Information*, In R. Meersman et al., editors, Database Semantics: Semantic Issues in Multimedia Systems, pps 351–369. Kluwer Academic Publisher, 1999.
6. Decker S., van Harmelen F., Broekstra J., Erdmann M., Fensel D., Horrocks I., Klein M., Melnik S., *The Semantic Web - on the Roles of XML and RDF*, IEEE Internet Computing. September/October, 2000.
7. Fensel D., *Ontologies: Dynamic Networks of Meaning*, International Semantic Web Working Symposium (SWWS), Stanford, July 2001.
8. Kifer M., Lausen G., Wu J., *Logical Foundations of Object-Oriented and Frame-Based Languages*, Journal ACM, 42:741–843, 1995.
9. Handschuh, S., Staab, S., Maedche, *A. CREAM — Creating relational metadata with a component-based, ontology-driven annotation framework*, ACM K-CAP 2001. October, Vancouver.
10. Hainaut J.L., *Database Reverse Engineering, Models, Techniques and Strategies. 10th Conf. on ER Approach*, San Mateo (CA), 1991.
11. Kashyap V., *Design and creation of ontologies for environmental information retrieval*, 12th Workshop on Knowledge Acquisition, Modelling and Management (KAW'99), Banff, Canada, October 1999.
12. Levenshtein I. V., *Binary Codes capable of correcting deletions, insertions, and reversals*, Cybernetics and Control Theory, 10(8):707–710, 1966.
13. Maedche A., *Ontology Learning Supporting Emergent Semantics*, IEEE Intelligent Systems - Trends & Controversies, 2002.
14. Melnik S., Decker S., *A Layered Approach to Information Modeling and Interoperability on the Web*, In Proceedings of the Workshop "ECDL 2000 Workshop on the Semantic Web", 2000.
15. Omelayenko B. Fensel D., *An Analysis of B2B Catalogue Integration problems: Content and Document Integration*, In Proceedings of the International Conference on Enterprise Information Systems (ICEIS-2001), 2001.
16. Rishe N., *Database Design: The Semantic Modeling Approach*, McGraw-Hill, 1992.
17. Stojanovic L., Stojanovic N., Volz R., *Migrating data-intensive Web Sites into the Semantic Web*, ACM Symposium on Applied Computing SAC, Madrid, 2002.
18. Stojanovic N., Maedche A., Staab S., Studer S., Sure Y., *SEAL — A Framework for Developing SEmantic PortALs*. ACM K-CAP-2001, 2001.
19. Wache H., Vögele T., Visser U., Stuckenschmidt H., Schuster G., Neumann H., Hübner C., *Ontology-Based Integration of Information - A Survey of Existing Approaches*, In Proceedings of the IJCAI-01 Workshop on Ontologies and Information Sharing, pp 108-118, Seattle, USA, August 4-5, 2001.

SYSTEMATIC GENERATION OF BAYESIAN NETWORKS FROM SYSTEMS SPECIFICATIONS

Michael Borth, Hermann von Hasseln
DaimlerChrysler Research and Technology
Michael.Borth@DaimlerChrysler.com, Hermann.v.Hasseln@DaimlerChrysler.com

Abstract: The usefulness of Bayesian network technology for expert-systems for diagnosis, prediction, and analysis of complex technical systems has been shown by several examples in the past. Yet, diagnosis systems using Bayesian networks are still not being deployed on an industrial scale. One reason for this is that it is seldom feasible to generate networks for thousands of systems either by manual construction or by learning from data.
In this paper, we present a systematic approach for the generation of Bayesian networks for technical systems which addresses this issue. We use existing system specifications as input for a domain-dependent translation process that results in networks which fulfil our requirements for model-based diagnosis and system analysis. Theoretical considerations and experiments show that the quality of the networks in terms of correctness and consistency depends solely on the specifications and translation rules and not on learning parameters or human factors. We can significantly reduce time and effort required for the generation of Bayesian networks by employing a rules-based expert system for generation, assembly and reuse of components. The resulting semi-automatic process meets the major requirements for industrial employment and helps to open up additional application scenarios for expert systems based on Bayesian networks.

Key words: knowledge-based design methodologies, Bayesian networks, knowledge acquisition, component reuse, expert-systems for diagnosis

1. INTRODUCTION

Given the well-known advantages of Bayesian networks for diagnosis systems, we at DaimlerChrysler Research and Technology are naturally considering their use for next-generation systems with predictive diagnosis and system analysis functionality. Recently, we have seen extensive work on modelling techniques that allow the construction of Bayesian networks for complex systems and their application in several domains, including ours: dynamic technical systems of high complexity. We can safely assume that it is possible to construct a useful Bayesian network for a given system, but this is immaterial as long as the resources needed to do so for all required systems are unreasonable high. This is clearly the case for the existing procedures, considering the thousands of (sub-) systems and their interworking as prevalent at DaimlerChrysler.

This determines the starting point for our paper. After we describe the requirements for the Bayesian networks and the processes for their generation, which result from our application scenario, we briefly review the existing procedures for the generation of networks. This defines the need for a new process with improved efficiency. We introduce our solution and propose a system architecture for its realisation. Finally, experiments and theoretical considerations illustrate the advantages of our approach and point to open research questions.

2. BAYESIAN NETWORKS FOR ADVANCED DIAGNOSIS SYSTEMS

Diagnosis has the purpose to infer the state of a system and often to provide the information needed to repair it. Thus, diagnosis is part of a more general process that determines the requirements for the diagnosis system. The process of building a diagnosis system is for the most part independent of this and has its own requirements. In this chapter, we introduce requirements of both types relevant to our work and cite their consequences.

2.1 Advanced Diagnosis Systems

DaimlerChrysler uses diagnostics for highly complex systems in the performance of a variety of tasks. These include the monitoring of systems in operation in order to detect failures, predictive diagnosis to enable maintenance prior to the failure or diagnosis and decision support during repair. These tasks result in several requirements for a diagnosis system [1]:

- Accomplishment of the diagnostic task.
- Efficiency: minimal computational costs.
- Reasonable diagnostic process.
- Utilisation of different sources of information.

Additionally, we expect an expert system to help us analyse the technical system itself. The identification of critical components or possible compensational behaviour is necessary to enhance product quality.

2.2 Bayesian Networks for Diagnosis

Even though no diagnostic technique is best geared to solve all diagnosis tasks with respect to all criteria [2], we will focus solely on Bayesian networks in this paper. Their general suitability as core technology for expert systems for diagnosis is well documented (see e.g. [3], [4], [5]) and needs no further illustration. However, there are several approaches on how to use Bayesian networks in the best possible way, and our design decisions must reflect the requirements of our application scenario.

First, we have to decide between model-based or symptom-based diagnosis systems. This determines what we have to model: which variables, states, etc. We use model-based systems, because they account for combinations of faults and compensational behaviour and allow predictive diagnosis and system analysis. Secondly, we have to decide how to build the Bayesian networks. The complexity of our technical systems and their modular, component-based assembly strongly suggests the use of object-oriented (OO) Bayesian networks [6].

2.3 Network Generation

We have a number of additional requirements for the network generation. Most importantly, this process must be highly efficient, since the use of Bayesian networks on an industrial scale requires networks for thousands of systems and their individual components.

This requirement alone proscribes the manual construction of the networks using knowledge engineering, since this approach requires a combined effort of knowledge engineers, diagnosis experts, and system experts. There are several methodologies that reduce the manual effort, e.g. by supporting the construction of models from a knowledge base [7] or by assisting the experts with a standardized process. Yet, we found that it is simply not feasible to depend on human experts in our scenario, especially since the interactions between different components of a technical system can be so complex that an expert is unable to understand and use all the available information. This loss of information will detract from the quality of the diagnosis, as will any mistake made during the construction of a network. Since we cannot rely on humans to work without errors, we have to test the constructed networks with respect to all the sensible system states and modes of operation. This process is extremely expensive and may even not be feasible. Learning the networks from data is also impractical. The necessary data simply does not exist for most systems, especially not prior to the real-life application. Even if we assume the existence of adequate data, we cannot rely on models generated by machine learning without extensive testing (see above). This adds to the overall effort for data preparation and optimisation of learning parameters. The resulting amount of necessary time and manpower is not acceptable.

To summarize, we need a new approach for network generation that results in object-oriented Bayesian networks which fulfil our requirements for model-based diagnosis and system analysis. The new process has to be largely independent of manual work to guarantee efficiency and faultlessness. Thus, it must be semi-automatic at the least and has to use inputs other than those of human experts.

3. SYSTEMANTIC GENERATION FROM SYSTEM SPECIFICATIONS

The specifications of the systems are a natural choice for such an input. Embedded in the process of system design and construction, they provide the necessary information in high quality. This chapter describes how we turn this information into Bayesian networks suitable for diagnosis systems.

3.1 Technical Specifications

Specifications come in many forms and typically consist of several documents, including diagrams, simulation models, formula, data, etc. They describe at least the following aspects:

- Design information: components and their composition.
- Functional information: functional effects, operation of the system.

Most likely, additional data is available about the quality of the components (e.g. the mean time between failures) or can be obtained from domain experts. Since Bayesian networks are insensitive to imprecision in the probabilities [8], small quantitative errors in this process pose no real problems. Experience shows that a suitable question strategy prevents qualitative errors [9]. Knowledge about the domains of the technical systems complements the specifications. For example, a specification of an electric system will not specify that a faulty component breaks the electric circuit, since this is a fundamental fact based on the laws of physics.

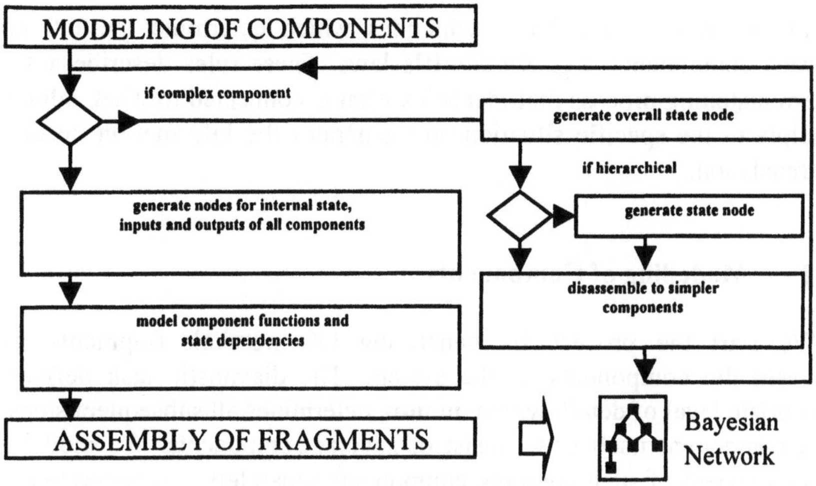

Figure 1: Systematic generation

3.2 Systematic Generation

Whenever a system specification conforms to the requirement that it comprises the information set out above, we can build a Bayesian network using the process outlined in figure 1.

The process results in a Bayesian network that is a valid description of the system. We neither omit any relevant information, nor add anything that is not in the specification. Thus, the entirety of the components, their functionalities, and interactions are represented.

3.2.1 Translation Rules

The translation of the relevant elements of the specification into network fragments and the subsequent assembly of the fragments follow rules which determine how the available information must be used. The generation of such sets of domain-dependent rules is a fundamental part of our approach. Their use must ensure the consistent and correct translation of the specifications. Our approach to guarantee this is to use only rules which represent principles of object-oriented design as well as physical laws and facts to model component functionality, interaction and assembly.

Every domain has (surprisingly few) different types of components, like, for the electric domain, conductor, capacitors, transistors, ground, etc. Each has a specific functionality. We establish rules for the translation of each component type and its functionality into a fragment of a Bayesian network according to the process laid out in the next section. Additionally, we formulate rules for the basic principles which determine the interaction between components, e.g. Kirchhoff's laws. These rules describe a simple pattern matching process that identifies what is connected to what, adopts the principle to the specific situation and generates the information needed for the translation.

3.2.2 Modelling of Components

We start the process by generating OO network fragments which represent the components of the system. The diagnostic task defines the appropriate level of detail, which, in turn, determines all subsequent steps.

A component itself can consist of several components. We model each sub-component of such complex components separately and generate a node representing the overall state of the complex component which is determined by the sub-components. A complex component is called a hierarchical component, if it has an additional state variable, which determines the states of all sub-components. We generate the node for such a state variable, too and follow this process recursively until we have broken down all complex components to simple components.

We determine the possible internal states of the components and their inputs and outputs. Inputs and outputs are interfaces between components or components and the environment. They transfer either physical quantities or information. The range of possible values of an interface defines the state-space of the according network nodes which we now construct. We generate nodes for the internal states and enter the apriori probabilities for all state variables, except for the overall sates.

Next, we model the state dependent functionality of the components, which are deterministic unless the specification is not detailed enough or the system includes random elements. The conditional probability distribution defined by $P(O{=}o|I_1{=}i_1,\dots,I_n{=}i_n) = 1$ for $F(i_1,\dots i_n) = \mathrm{o}$, else $P = 0$ describes the function $F = F(I_1,\dots, I_n) \rightarrow O$ for the input variables $I_1,\dots, I_n$ and the output variable O [10]. Consequently, we insert connections from all the input nodes and from the state node to the output node and quantify the connections with the appropriate distribution.

Overall state variables of complex components and variables in functional groups directly depend on other state variables. We connect these nodes in accordance with existing causalities.

3.2.3 Assembly of Fragments

The design information in the specification describes how the components are connected to each other. These connections between outputs and inputs simply transfer physical effects or information. Accordingly, we generate 1:1 connections from output nodes to the appropriate input nodes. These connections guarantee that the nodes are in the same state.

We use the same method to connect the input and output nodes which represent the system environment with the components. This step completes the generation of the Bayesian network.

3.3 Modelling of Time

Whenever a specification does not rely solely on static information but describes dynamic effects, we have to model the flow of time. The modeling steps described above already account for this. They do not require that all the modeled entities belong to the same time-frame or that only static values are modeled and not the change of values. Thus, we can use either method to model the dynamics of the system. Depending on the specification we describe the dynamics in time-frames with conventional dynamic Bayesian networks (see [11], [12]) or changes over time, for which we use Arroyo's approach [5].

3.4 Properties of the Process

During the development of the process, we had to analyze several theoretical issues. The most important aspect, for the purpose of this paper, is that we can guarantee that the process always results in a valid Bayesian network. For example, we can show that the process never generates circles (which are not allowed in Bayesian networks) given that the flow of time was modelled in a cored way. Another important aspect is the determinism of the process. Once the required level of detail and the appropriate translation rules are selected, we face no additional design decisions. The tasks in every single step result directly from the information available, the rules, and the results of the preceding steps. The formal proof for these properties is outside the scope of this paper.

4. GENERATION OF NETWORKS BY AN AUTOMATED SYSTEM

The main purpose of the new process is that it be used in an automated system. We propose the system architecture set out below (figure 2).

4.1 Components as Basic Elements

Given the specifications and the required level of detail, the system starts by extracting all components and the information available about them. We use these components as basic elements for all successive steps. To avoid duplicated work, we store all the components in a library, realized as a database. If a component has already been modelled, the component library provides the respective network fragment.

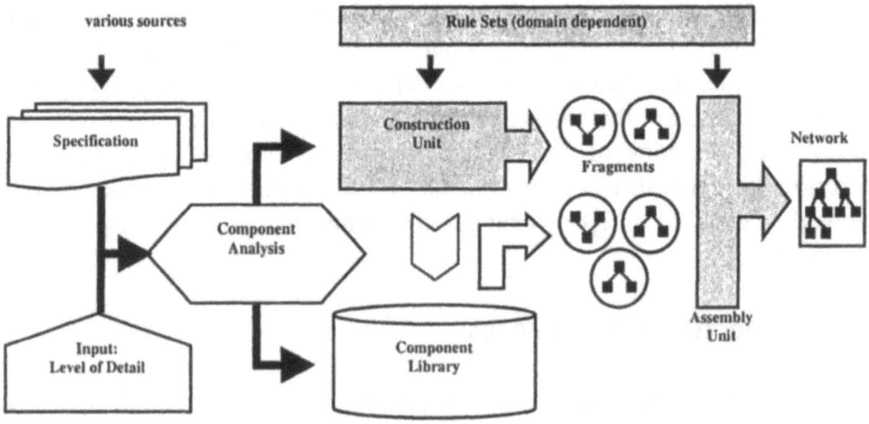

Figure 2: System for network generation (overview)

4.2 Rule-based System for Modelling and Assembly

A rule-based expert system is the heart of the system. It consists of a rule base, the construction unit, and the assembly unit. The rule base holds all translation rule sets and provides the other units with the rules for their tasks.

The construction unit builds the network fragments for new components. It can adapt fragments of known components, use templates for typical ones or construct solely on the basis of rules. The construction unit stores new fragments in the library, together with the component information and details about the construction process (useful for the adaptation mentioned above).

The assembly unit connects all the fragments in accordance to the specification. It constructs both the necessary connections between input and output nodes and the direct dependencies between state variables. The result is an operational network, which maps all information available to the construction system.

4.3 Optimisation and Deployment

It is likely that the resulting network will benefit from optimisation, e.g. by a reduction of the number of nodes or simplifications. We can do this without any loss of functionality by eliminating redundant information and the use of common modeling tricks, as noisy-or gates. For example, we can merge nodes with 1:1 connections, which only transfer information. The basic optimisation procedures follow a small set of simple rules. This enables us to implement the optimization as a rule-based expert system, too.

Finally, we transcribe the generated network into a form suitable for the intended application, e.g. diagnosis software or a hardware realization. This is a standardized process which needs no additional input. We can generate data files for network modelling tools, precompiled networks for an inference engine, or code for a hardware realization [13].

5. EXPERIMENTAL EVALUATION

We tested the systematic generation of Bayesian networks from specifications to evaluate both the process and the resulting networks.

The experiments were representative for a wide range of both digital and analog technical systems and covered different types of diagnostic problems. We decided on the smallest replaceable units as an appropriate level of detail for modelling and translated the system specifications accordingly with domain dependent rules, which we formulated in advance. We tested the Bayesian networks on a predefined set of diagnostic tasks.

5.1 Examples

We will now present some details of our experiments. A complete description of even a single experiment is outside the scope of this paper.

We chose an electrical systems composed of several circuits with common ground as an example for digital systems. The system accepts user input at the power amplifiers, where it also provides diagnostic information. We had to derive the state of all components from the combination of the error codes and the user input. Thus, we had to deal with hidden mistakes, compensational behaviour and feedback circles. To solve this challenge, we had to exploit that effects in electrical circuits are non-directional. Our translation rules for digital electronics account for this by constructing a bi-directional flow of information between the power amplifiers and ground. The electric system also demonstrated that it is indeed possible to work on different aspects of components separately and independently, which negates the need to anticipate every possible combination of functionality. For example, we built a plug as a hierarchical component, where one of the pins is also part of a functional group. These two aspects of the pin correspond to different types of effects, which we model in different nodes.

Our second example, a suspension system (an analogous damped oscillating system where the components interwork) demonstrates another issue: cyclical influences. They require the modelling of time, since the information available at a single moment is insufficient for a diagnosis. In the system specifications, differential equations describe changes over time, so we model the state changes, as set out in section 3. However, we found that both approaches break the cycle where the components influence each other, since any effect occurs later than the cause.

5.2 Results

Our experiments show that systematic generation of Bayesian networks works extremely well given suitable specifications and translation rules, which are the main influence factors for the quality of the results. The modelling of both components and the interactions between them can be done in an automated process by a rule-based expert system.

Our experiments verify that specifications are the ideal input for constructing a representation suitable for system analysis and model-based diagnosis. The resulting diagnosis systems outperformed alternative systems, especially for complex problems, such as multiple faults with compensational behavior. The system analysis works equally well, e.g. the identification of critical components or dependency analysis as described in [14]. The value of different pieces of information for the diagnosis process can be inferred using sensitivity analysis [15], but we have not looked into this in detail thus far.

These positive results show that the translation rules used performed well. Our experiments confirm that the rules must be adequate for both the domain and the level of detail. Hence, we have to construct a set of rules for every combination that we anticipate (a small number). Currently, we select the correct rule set for a given system manually, but we aim at achieving an automatic selection via classification or case-based reasoning.

The correctness of the rules is not self-evident, since they were manually constructed and thus prone to error. As the rules represent basic principles, such as physical laws, the generation of an incorrect rule is unlikely. Far more problematic are incomplete rule sets, which fail to cover existing situations. Such mistakes crop up during the translation process and force a revision of the rule set. A related problem is that the rules are not unequivocal. Often, there are several approaches for the construction of a rule set. Each approach leads to consistent rules, but the resulting networks may differ. It is essential to realize the impact of these modelling decisions on the diagnostic system. The problem is that we cannot deduce them from the system specification. We need additional information on how to interpret the system behaviour. This best illustrates the importance of the rule set. We can anticipate and eliminate such problems if we involve experts for diagnosis during the rule generation.

6. DISCUSSION AND DIRECTIONS FOR FUTURE RESEARCH

Theoretical considerations, exemplary implementation, and experimental evaluation show that our approach for a systematic generation of Bayesian networks from specifications of technical systems works. The resulting networks fulfil the requirements for both diagnosis and system analysis and outperform most alternative diagnosis systems. The process for network generation can be used manually or realized within a semi-automatic system. Such systems meet our requirements for generating Bayesian networks on an industrial scale. In this context, we have to consider the effort needed to build such a system. Even though we see no alternative within our application scenario, others may decide that the advantages of an extensive automation do not prevail over the costs of the necessary components.

We hope that future research will help to reduce these costs. For example, it should be possible to simplify the rule generation and, thus, the building of the expert system by exploiting the hierarchical dependencies between different levels of detail. Another open research question is network optimisation. Currently, we use only elementary mechanisms to simplify the networks. We expect better results from more complex approaches, e.g. pattern-based search-and-replace operations.

7. CONCLUSION

The main contribution of this work is the introduction of a systematic method for the efficient and accurate generation of Bayesian networks for complex technical systems. An implementation of this process in a semi-automatic system allows the generation of networks even for high numbers of systems. This, in turn, allows the industrial employment of the process, since only minimal efforts are required from human experts. We are confident that this will help to open up additional application scenarios for knowledge-based expert systems using Bayesian networks.

REFERENCES

1. A. Heinzelmann: Produktintegrierte Diagnose komplexer mobiler Systeme, Ph.D. Thesis, University of Paderborn, 1998.
2. S. Iwanowski: Technical Diagnosis - Chances and Limitations. DaimlerChrysler Technical Report, 1997.
3. D. Heckerman, M. Wellman: Real World Applications of Bayesian Networks. In *Communications of the ACM*, 38(3), 25-26, 1995.
4. C. Skaaning, F.V. Jensen, U. Kjaerulff: Printing System Diagnosis - A Bayesian Network Application, In *Proceedings of the 9th International Workshop on Principles of Diagnosis*, 1998.
5. G. Arroyo-Figueroa, L. Sucar: A Temporal Bayesian Network for Diagnosis and Prediction. In *Proceedings of the 15th Conference on Uncertainty in Artificial Intelligence*, 1999.
6. D. Koller, A. Pfeffer: Object-oriented Bayesian Networks. In *Proceedings of the 13th Conference on Uncertainty in Artificial Intelligence*, 1997.
7. K. Laskey, S. Mahoney: Network Fragments: Representing Knowledge for Construction Probabilistic Models Networks. In *Proceedings of the 13th Conference on Uncertainty in Artificial Intelligence*, 1997.
8. M. Henrion: Why is diagnosis using belief networks insensitive to imprecision in probabilities?. In *Proceedings of the 12th Conference on Uncertainty in Artificial Intelligence*, 1996.
9. C. Skaaning: Knowledge Acquisition for Bayesian Networks in Diagnosis, Hewlett-Packard Research Report, 1998.
10. S. Srinivas: Building diagnostic models from functional schematics, Stanford University Report No. KSL 94-15, 1994.
11. U. Kjaerulff: A computational scheme for reasoning in dynamic probabilistic networks. In *Proceedings of the 8th Conference on Uncertainty in Artificial Intelligence*, 1992.
12. U. Lerner, R. Parr, D. Koller, G. Biswas: Bayesian Fault Detection and Diagnosis in Dynamic Systems. In *Proceedings of the 16th National Conference on Artificial Intelligence*, 1997.
13. A. Darwiche, G. Provan: Query DAGs. In *Proceedings of the 12th Conference on Uncertainty in Artificial Intelligence*, 1996.
14. L. Portinale, A. Bobbio: Bayesian Networks for Dependency Analysis. In *Proceedings of the 15th Conference on Uncertainty in Artificial Intelligence*, 1999.
15. K. Laskey: Sensitivity Analysis for Probability Assessments in Bayesian Networks. In *Proceedings of the 7th Conference on Uncertainty in Artificial Intelligence*, 1991.

DYNAMIC CHOICE OF AGENT INTERACTION PROTOCOLS

Jean-Luc Koning
Inpg-CoSy
50, rue Laffemas, BP 54
26902 Valence cedex 9, France
Jean-Luc.Koning@esisar.inpg.fr

Abstract One issue that is never tackled when dealing with conversation policies handled by agents is the way they get to choose the right interaction protocol one in order to answer the problem at hand. This paper is a first attempt to automate such a procedure.

This raises a number of questions when trying to find a suited framework that allows to dynamically gather the various agents into "conversation groups". Several groups should be able to coexist at the same time, each solving a specific problem. A single agent should also be able to be part of several groups, i.e., carry several conversations at the same time.

Such a mechanism can be handled via a POS protocol, in exactly the same way as the other regular interaction protocols, except for the fact that this one will be triggered from the beginning and will keep on running the whole time.This paper is a first attempt to automate such a procedure.

Keywords: Autonomous software agents, conversation policies

Introduction

Multiagent systems are based on the notion that if one gathers simple autonomous systems (agents) within a society and that they are endowed with interaction skills, then such a society may show complex behaviors (compared to each of the agent's skills) that are not implemented in any particular individual. The society's intelligence is distributed among its constituents. Besides, one fundamental characteristic of such systems is its ability of interaction between its constituents, i.e., its agents.

In the multiagent system community Cammarata et al., 1988 the communication issue is typically addressed by means of interaction protocols that give more or less flexible guidelines to cognitive agents in their communication with each other. Given its knowledge bases, what it perceives from its outside world and the possible messages it gets from other agents, a cognitive agent communicates with the others both through message passing (direct communication) and modification of the world (indirect communication). More precisely, interaction protocols should enable cognitive agents to know which types of message they may receive, which types they may send and at what time, and they should clarify to a certain extent the agents' side effects on the outside world.

The design of protocols Burmeister et al., 1995 classically relies on building a graph, where vertices represent the system's conversational states, i.e., the current state of the conversation the agents are participating in, and where edges correspond to conversational events, i.e., the sending or receiving of a message. Such protocol graphs describe the possible conversation courses. Yet several inherent weaknesses are attached to this approach.

This kind of representation only offers a syntactic description of the protocol. No semantic information can be taken into consideration. Moreover, the particular family of protocols that are thus addressed falls in the class of regular languages. This means multiagent systems with such protocols deny themselves any chance of a larger interaction expression power.

Making such agent interaction protocols operational requires each agent to possess a general and quite flexible protocol execution algorithm, i.e., primitives for reading, processing, and sending messages. This piece of code is totally independent of any specific protocol. Modifying a multiagent system strategy comes down to substituting a state transition graph description for a new one. A protocol is not actually hard-coded within the agents. Even though schemes have been devised to automate the translation of a graphical representation to an equivalent computable piece of code, such a solution is not fully satisfying. Among other things, they do not lead to a modular enough way of implementing strategies. For instance, adding or removing conversational states to a protocol forces a complete change of protocol.

Note, that when implementing a limited number of heterogeneous roles in a team of few cognitive agents, the standard approach is, though being tedious, still more or less feasible. But for larger teams, based on additional heterogeneity, this is obviously not the way to go. Therefore, we propose here a Protocol Operational Semantics (POS) Koning and Oudeyer, 2000, inspired by the structural operational semantics Plotkin, 1981 of programming languages Hennessy, 1990.

1. Modeling Cognitive Agent Interaction Protocols

1.1. The POS Formalism

POS (Protocol Operational Semantics) is a formalism Oudeyer and Koning, 2000 based on algebraic data types and pattern-matching which enables to easily describe interaction protocols at an agent level. Such a model is not only a theoretical framework, but also to a computational one due to the existence of adequate programming languages, like Pizza/Java Odersky and Wadler, 1997 and other ML languages Milner, 1987.

A protocol is specified by rules of operational semantics Plotkin, 1981. Let us give a brief definition of a simplified version of POS.

A rule is of the following type:

$$\langle R, \phi \rangle \xrightarrow{msg} \langle S, \mathcal{A} \rangle$$

where *msg* is a possibly empty finite list of messages of either type "`Send [destination] text`", or "`Received [origin] text`". R and S are some agent's states. The type of a state is free as long as an equality relation is being defined.

ϕ is a test function on the world which helps determine whether the rule is applicable when a rule is to be chosen. Such a test is not necessarily true during the whole time the rule is applicable. Otherwise one would have to impose that the mappings $\mathcal{A}$ be atomic.

$\mathcal{A}$ is the mapping related to the rule, i.e., the consequences upon the world of the rule that has been chosen by the agent. Particularly, the actions of an agent are modeled through $\mathcal{A}$.

The parameters have been removed since the shape of the awaited messages may in fact be specified in *msg*. It is thus not necessary to over-specify an agent's state anymore.

Here the mappings ϕ and $\mathcal{A}$ are respectively of the following type:

$$\begin{aligned} \phi : &\quad World \rightarrow boolean \\ \mathcal{A} : &\quad World \rightarrow World \end{aligned}$$

World is the type of the world perceived by an agent. This type is more fully described through its implementation at the end of this section.

All the examples that follow to illustrate POS have been implemented using an object-oriented dialect of ML Leroy, 2000. For instance, here is the types' definition for the rules:

```
type rule = {init:     state;
```

```
phi:       test;
messages:  (msg list);
final:     state;
action:    action}
```

We shall see later what are the types defined in order to implement actions and tests.

One imposes that mapping ϕ be without side effects in order to insure that a test made to see whether a rule is applicable does not directly change the world, i.e., without control. Indeed, for example, it would be absurd to break an egg to know whether it is full or empty.

In order to master this test's innocuousness constraint one could bring into play the uniqueness typing developed with the *clean* language Plasmeijer and van Eekelen, 1998 Barendsen and Smetsers, 1996. Such typing enables to guaranty the absence of side effects when needed while allowing some if necessary.

An expression is identified as unique if there is only one reference to that expression. One may then destructively change its value without modifying anything though. On the other hand, if that expression is not identified as unique, there cannot be any modification in it.

Therefore, if this kind of type is forced on function ϕ with no uniqueness identification, then this function's argument is the external world and returns a boolean without modifying the world since it may be referenced somewhere else.

Function $\mathcal{A}$ may use the following type:

$$\mathcal{A}: \quad *\,World \rightarrow *\,World$$

where $*$ is the uniqueness identification. This function's argument is thus a unique world et returns it once it has been modified.

The implemented version of ϕ's and $\mathcal{A}$'s types[1] is thus:

```
type
 int_world_actions = agent * (ext_world ref)
 and int_world_tests = agent * ext_world
 and test   = int_world_tests   -> bool
 and action = int_world_actions -> unit
```

However some problems are left unsolved. Indeed, if a test is a random drawing (tails: the rule is fireable, heads: it is not), the value of an

[1] One notices here that the type given back by the actions is the type `unit` which has the only value `()`. Indeed a call by reference implies that the world is itself modified and it is not necessary to give its value back after an action has been performed.

obtained drawing is not necessarily the same during the sorting of the possible rules and during the firing of a chosen rule. This is why a test is performed again when a rule is fired. One thus validates that a test is correct whenever a rule is being chosen.

1.2. Power of expression

The POS formalism is at least as powerful as formalisms such as finite state automata or colored Petri nets. Indeed, one can transform an automaton or a Petri net into a set of POS rules. Such formalism embodies the necessary power to accept regular languages. Furthermore, it has been shown that the POS formalism exhibits the Turing power, i.e., one may describe a Turing complete language by means of POS rules.

Now the question is, do communication protocols in multiagent systems have to be more expressive than what finite state automata allow them to be. An easy answer would be to be as much expressive as possible because expressiveness cannot harm. Unfortunately such a gain in power of expression is compensated by an increase in complexity regarding the definition of protocols. Because of the simplicity of its rules, POS affords to concentrate on the core of a protocol as opposed to what specification languages can do while avoiding the pitfalls of specification languages.

Therefore POS is a tool which enables to better study protocols that necessitate a Turing power. We have worked in developing and improving it according to this perspective.

2. Dynamic Choice of Protocols by an Agent

2.1. The Issue

One issue that is never tackled when dealing with conversation policies handled by agents is the way they get to choose the right interaction protocol in order to answer the problem at hand. This paper is a first attempt to automate such a procedure.

Let us suppose that a set of agents have at their disposal a number of protocols which can potentially be used in any conversation about a given problem submitted to them. In other words, one steps aside the standard setting where one problem is being solved via interaction protocols within the context of a unique conversation. One is faced here with a set of problems that may be given to a society of agents in any order, or even at the same time.

This raises a number of questions when trying to find a suited framework that allows to dynamically gather the various agents into "conversation groups". Several groups should be able to coexist at the same time, each solving a specific problem. A single agent should also be able to be part of several groups, i.e., carry several conversations at the same time.

2.2. A Solution Based on Recursive Use of Protocols

Such a mechanism can be handled via a POS protocol, in exactly the same way as the other regular interaction protocols, except for the fact that this one will be triggered from the beginning and will keep on running the whole time. Let us call it the *Init Protocol* (whose name stems from the "init" process in a Unix operating system). All the agents of the system will then always be in contact through the related conversation.

Its role will be to manage the requests received any agent for participating in a given conversation, as well as the spontaneous need for an agent to start a new or enter an ongoing conversation. This *Init Protocol* will enable to fork new protocols in order for agents to enter a conversation.

Another important element is the table that is associated to every conversation. It will list all the participating agents along with the conversation's description. In case of a standard conversation (not operated by the *Init Protocol*), a table holds the following information :

- t_i denotes the table's address. This characterizes any table and allows the agents to access it.
- the description of the corresponding conversation, which amounts to the name/number of the protocol P_i used. One supposes here that one protocol is being used for any given conversation.
- the list of identities/addresses of the agents involved in the conversation.

The *Init Protocol* will also possess such a corresponding table with the following information.

- its address denoted by t_{init}.
- the list of addresses of the tables associated to the running conversations, as well as their related description.
- the list of all the agents of the society that can participate in the conversations. Such a list may be dynamic.

3. The Init Protocol

3.1. Its POS definition

Here is a POS definition of the *Init Protocol*:

(1) $\langle Wait, True\rangle \xrightarrow{[Received(SomeOne, Enter(P_i,t_i))]} \langle Ponder(P_i, t_i), NOP\rangle$

(2) $\langle Ponder(P_i, t_i), InterestedIn(P_i, t_i)\rangle \xrightarrow{[]} \langle Wait, Start(P_i, t_i)\rangle$

(3) $\langle Ponder(P_i, t_i), !InterestedIn(P_i, t_i)\rangle \xrightarrow{[]} \langle Wait, NOP\rangle$

(4) $\langle Wait, CurrentlyInterestedIn() = P_j$ *and*

$ExistsConversation(P_j) = t_j\rangle \xrightarrow{[]} \langle Wait, Start(P_i, t_i)\rangle$

(5) $\langle Wait, CurrentlyInterestedIn() = P_j$ *and*

$ExistsConversation(P_j) = null\rangle \xrightarrow{[]} \langle Wait, CreateConversation(P_j)\rangle$

3.2. Its side effects

Three specific side effects need to be introduced depending whether a conversation is being created, entered or left. Such side effects apply to the protocols themselves.

Almost all messages exchanged among the agents belong to a given conversation. However there is one exception where a message is sent from a standard protocol to the *init* conversation, i.e., $Enter(P_i, t_i)$. Such a message is sent by an agent participating in conversation P_i whose table is at address t_i and who would like to call on a receiving agent whose identity/address has been found in table t_{init}.

In order to make up its mind the receiving agent evaluates predicate $InterestedIn(P_i, t_i)$. The first side effect $Start(P_i, t_i)$ is triggered and consists for the calling agents in first adding its name into the table at address t_i, and second "fork"[2] a protocol P_i.

Besides, evaluating *CurrentlyInterestedIn*() looks up the set of protocols at disposal and returns one (its identity/address) at random among the ones the agent considers interesting, or returns *null* if none are available. The expression $ExistsConversation(P_j)$ evaluates to the address of the corresponding table if a conversation that uses P_j already exists. Such a piece of information is available in table t_{init}. The expression otherwise returns *null.*

The second side effect $CreateConversation(P_j)$ amounts for the calling agents to create a new table t_j, add this table's address into table t_{init}, and register its own address into table t_j. Let us note that the first agent to launch a conversation is the one to create the related table. Since this

[2]The word "fork" is used here in the same way as it applies to processes in a Unix system.

table is an independent entity, the creating agent may well leave the conversation while other agents keep on interacting.

This raises the issue of the end of a conversation. Let us first introduce the third side effect that deals with leaving a conversation. $Exit(P_j, t_j)$ consists for the calling agent to unsubscribe from table t_j and "kill"[3] protocol P_j. One therefore needs to endow each table the ability to check whether there still remains any agents which subscribed to the conversation. If such is not the case a table would get rid of itself once it has unsubscribed from table t_{init}.[4]

Regarding the implementation issue, a suggestion would be to have each agent handle one message box per conversation it is involved in. It creates it whenever a protocol is forked and discards it when it leaves the conversation. In order to broadcast the messages into the various message boxes, one may label each message with the table's address t_i related to the conversation at hand.

4. Discussion

The system's architecture described in this paper does not mention any constraint regarding whether the operations should be atomic. In any case this seems difficult to bring into play. This means that when designing protocols, one needs to take into account the possibility that by the time an agent receives a messages (sent by another agent) it has unsubscribed from the conversation.

This is the general problem of interactions in open systems where agents dynamically enter or leave the system. One way to address this is to design protocols that are not sensitive to such dynamic behavior. This for example is the case for the second POS protocol in the RoboCup application detailed in Oudeyer and Koning, 2000.

Another way would consist in explicitly implementing the synchronization within the protocol. A message would inform of its intent to leave a conversation and then would pause until some acknowledgment is sent back to it.

So far, one implicitly forced the conversations to be based on different protocols (P_i) at any time. One could nonetheless contemplate the use of several conversations based on a single protocol. This raises the problem of how two simultaneous conversations run by an agent get mutually influenced. Such a problem seriously needs to be tackled when considering the building of an actual multiagent system. One could imagine

[3]The word "kill" is an analogy to the killing of processes in Unix systems.
[4]Such tables could almost be considered as agents.

that a designer provide constraints such as "*P_3 and P_5 cannot be run at the same time*". An agent would then be able to use such constraints in order to decide among *InterestedIn*(...) and *CurrentlyInterestedIn*(...).

5. Summary and Perspectives

This paper dealt with the issue for an agent to dynamically choose among interaction protocols.

From a practical standpoint, one is left here with the question of making such a paradigm operational. Several implementation examples have been suggested so far, with typed functional languages (ML/Haskel), or object oriented languages (Java/Pizza). The next stage consists in defining a means to implement POS protocols without assuming the use of any particular programming languages for the agent's internal architecture.

One suited solution to implement this is through the XML technology, in the same way and possibly as a complement to SOAP, which is an XML language that allows to accomplish some remote procedure call in an easy and light approach.

Acknowledgments

I would like to thank Pierre-Yves Oudeyer and Pierre-François Dutot for their help in preparing this paper.

References

Barendsen, E. and Smetsers, S. (1996). Uniqueness typing for functional languages with graph rewriting semantics. *Math. Struct. in Computer Science*, pages 1–36. Cambridge University Press.

Burmeister, B., Haddadi, A., and Sundermeyer, K. (1995). Generic, configurable, cooperation protocols for multi-agent systems. In Castelfranchi, C. and Muller, J.-P., editors, *From Reaction to Cognition*, volume 957 of *Lecture notes in AI*, pages 157–171, Berlin, Germany. Springer Verlag. Appeared also in MAAMAW-93, Neuchatel.

Cammarata, S., Arthur, D. M., and Steeb, R. (1988). Strategies of cooperation in distributed problem solving. In Bond, A. and Gasser, L., editors, *Readings in Distributed Artificial Intelligence*, pages 102–105. Morgan Kaufmann Publishers, Inc., San Mateo, CA.

Hennessy, M. (1990). *The Semantics of Programming Languages: An Introduction Using Structured Operational Semantics*. Wiley.

Koning, J.-L. and Oudeyer, P.-Y. (2000). Modeling and implementing conversation policies using POS. In d'Auriol, B., editor, *International Conference on Communications in Computing (CIC-00)*, Las Vegas, NV. CSREA Press.

Leroy, X. (2000). *The Objective Caml system, release 3.00.* http://caml.inria.fr/ocaml/htmlman.

Milner, R. (1987). A proposal for standard ML. In *ACM Conference on Lisp and Functional Programming.*

Odersky, M. and Wadler, P. (1997). Pizza into Java: Translating theory into practice. In *4th ACM Symposium on Principles of Programming Languages*, Paris, France.

Oudeyer, P.-Y. and Koning, J.-L. (2000). Modeling soccer-robots strategies through conversation policies. In Mattern, F. and Kotz, D., editors, *2nd IEEE International Symposium on Agent Systems and Application (ASA/MA-00)*, Zürich, Switzerland. Springer Verlag.

Plasmeijer, R. and van Eekelen, M. (1998). *Concurrent Clean Language Report.* HILT - High Level Software Tools B.V. and University of Nijm egen. http://www.cs.kun.nl/~clean.

Plotkin, G. (1981). A structural approach to operationnal semantics. Technical Report DAIMI FN-19, Aarhus university, Computer Science Department, Denmark.

AN ALGEBRAIC CHARACTERIZATION OF EQUIVALENT BAYESIAN NETWORKS

S. K. M. Wong
Department of Computer Science
University of Regina
Regina, Saskatchewan, Canada, S4S 0A2
wong@cs.uregina.ca

D. Wu
Department of Computer Science
University of Regina
Regina, Saskatchewan, Canada, S4S 0A2
danwu@cs.uregina.ca

Abstract In this paper, we propose an *algebraic* characterization for equivalent classes of Bayesian networks. Unlike the other characterizations which are based on the graphical structure of the Bayesian network, our algebraic characterization is derived from its intrinsic algebraic structure, i.e., the factorization of its joint probability distribution. The new proposed algebraic characterization not only provides us with a new perspective to look into equivalent Bayesian networks, but also suggests simple and efficient methods for determining equivalence of Bayesian networks and identifying compelled edges in Bayesian networks.

1. Introduction

Bayesian networks [3, 6] have been well established as a knowledge based system for uncertainty information processing. Based on incomplete or uncertain information from a problem domain, Bayesian networks can help people make decision under uncertain situation using probability.

Being considered a knowledge based system, Bayesian networks have a set of conditional probability distributions, whose product yields a *joint probability distribution*, as its knowledge base; and an efficient inference engine [4, 5], for computing posterior probability based on observed evidence.

The success of Bayesian networks relies on its capability of acquiring and representing conditional independency [2] information in a problem domain. Informally, a Bayesian network consists of a graphical structure, i.e., a directed acyclic graph (DAG) representing conditional indenpendencies; and a set of conditional probability distributions, whose product yields a joint probability distribution. The set of conditional probability distributions, being considered the knowledge base, together with efficient inference engines [4, 5] for computing posterior probability based on observed evidence, composes a knowledge based system for managing uncertain information.

It has been noted that different Bayesian networks may be equivalent in the sense that they represent the same joint probability distribution (and thus conditional independency information as well) [7], even though they have different graphical structures. Research has been done to determine whether two given Bayesian networks are equivalent or not and to find out invariant portions in the DAGs [1, 7] of equivalent Bayesian networks. Graphical criterion has been proposed to determine if two different Bayesian networks are equivalent or not [7]. More recently, Chickering [1] reported a transformational characterization of equivalent Bayesian networks based on the notion of covered edges in a DAG. An algorithm was also designed to find out all edges in a DAG that maintain their directionality in equivalent Bayesian networks.

In this paper, instead of providing another graphical criterion, we propose an *algebraic* characterization for describing equivalent Bayesian networks. This algebraic characterization was inspired by our understanding that the joint probability distribution defined by the set of conditional probability distributions is the essence of a Bayesian network, while the DAG is only an *auxiliary* graphical structure which helps represent conditional independency information inferred from the joint probability distribution. Therefore, we believe that joint probability distribution of a Bayesian network itself alone should possess the capability to describe and characterize equivalent Bayesian networks. By studying different forms of the factorization of a joint probability distribution defined by a Bayesian network, it is discovered that one can use a particular form of the factorization to describe and characterize equivalent Bayesian networks. This discovery further confirms our understanding that the joint probability distribution alone is sufficient to capture the characteristic of equivalent Bayesian networks. Moreover, this algebraic characterization suggests that the problem of identifying compelled edges in a Bayesian network can be viewed from a different perspective such that a simple and efficient algorithm can be easily designed.

The paper is organized as follows. We review pertinent background knowledge in Section 2. The proposed algebraic characterization for equivalent Bayesian networks will be presented in Section 3. Section 4 discusses several applications of the new algebraic characterization, in particular, we propose a method for identifying all compelled edges in a DAG. We conclude our paper in Section 5.

2. Background

We assume readers have familiarities with Bayesian networks to the extent in [6]. We thus will quickly go through the notions that will be used in the paper.

Let U be a finite set of variables, we use $p(U)$ to denote a *joint probability distribution* (jpd) over U. We call $p(V), V \subset U$, *marginal* (distribution) of $p(U)$ and $p(X|Y)$ *conditional probability distribution* (CPD), or simply *conditional*. By XY, where $X \subseteq U, Y \subseteq U$, we mean $X \cup Y$. According to the definition of conditional probability,

$$p(X|Y) = \frac{p(XY)}{p(Y)}, \text{whenever } p(Y) > 0,$$

we thus say in the above expression, the denominator $p(Y)$ is *absorbed* by the numerator $p(XY)$ to yield conditional $p(X|Y)$. It is noted that $p(W)$ can be absorbed by $p(V)$ to yield $p(V - W|W)$ if and only if $W \subset V$. The concept of "absorbed" is very important in our discussion in this paper.

A *Bayesian network* (BN) is a tuple $(\mathcal{D}, P)$, where (a) $\mathcal{D} =< U, E >$ is a *directed acyclic graph* (DAG), as the qualitative part, with $U = \{X_1, \ldots, X_n\}$ as the nodes (variables) of DAG and $E = \{(X_i, X_j) \mid X_i, X_j \in \mathcal{D}\}$ as the set of directed edges (from X_i to X_j) of $\mathcal{D}$; and (b) $P = \{p(X_i|pa(X_i)) \mid X_i \in U\}$ is a set of *conditionals* as the quantitative part, where $pa(X_i)$ denotes the parents of node X_i in DAG $\mathcal{D}$, such that,

$$p(U) = \prod_{i=1}^{n} p(X_i|pa(X_i)). \quad (1)$$

We will use the terms BN and DAG interchangeably if no confusion arises.

Definition 1 [1] Two Bayesian networks are *equivalent* if they define the same probability distribution.

We use $BN1 \approx BN2$ (or $\mathcal{D}_1 \approx \mathcal{D}_2$) to denote that $BN1$ and $BN2$ are equivalent. The relation $\approx$ induces a set of equivalence classes over Bayesian networks.

An edge (X, Y) in a DAG $\mathcal{D}$ is *compelled* if for any DAG $\mathcal{D}' \approx \mathcal{D}$, (X, Y) is also in $\mathcal{D}'$. Otherwise, it is *reversible*. The notion of *covered* edge is important for the study in [1]. An edge (X, Y) is *covered* in a DAG if $pa(Y) = pa(X) \cup X$. A $v - structure$ in a DAG $\mathcal{D}$ is an ordered triple of nodes (X, Y, Z) such that (1) $\mathcal{D}$ contains edges (X, Y) and (Z, Y), and (2) X and Z are not directly connected in $\mathcal{D}$. The *skeleton* of a DAG is the undirected graph obtained by dropping the directionality of every edge in a DAG.

Verma and Pearl characterizes equivalent DAGs using the notions of skeleton and v-structure in DAGs.

Theorem 1 [7] Two DAGs are equivalent if and only if they have the same skeleton and the same v-structures.

Chickering characterizes equivalent DAGs using the notion of covered edges in a DAG.

Theorem 2 [1] Let $\mathcal{D}$ be a DAG containing an edge (X, Y) and $\mathcal{D}'$ be a DAG identical to $\mathcal{D}$ except that the edge (X, Y) in $\mathcal{D}$ is oriented as (Y, X) in $\mathcal{D}'$, $\mathcal{D} \approx \mathcal{D}'$ if and only if (X, Y) is a covered edge in $\mathcal{D}$.

Because of the symmetry between $\mathcal{D}$ and $\mathcal{D}'$, we immediately have:

Corollary 1 (Y, X) is also a covered edge in $\mathcal{D}'$.

Chickering further shows that a property holds for all pairs of equivalent Bayesian networks that differ by a single covered edge orientation if and only if that property holds for all the Bayesian networks in the equivalent class. In other words, a given property is invariant over all equivalent Bayesian networks if and only if we can show that the property is invariant to a pair of DAGs that differ in a single reversal of covered edge.

3. The Algebraic Characterization

In this section, we will present an algebraic characterization that describes the equivalent class of Bayesian networks. We begin with an illustrative example.

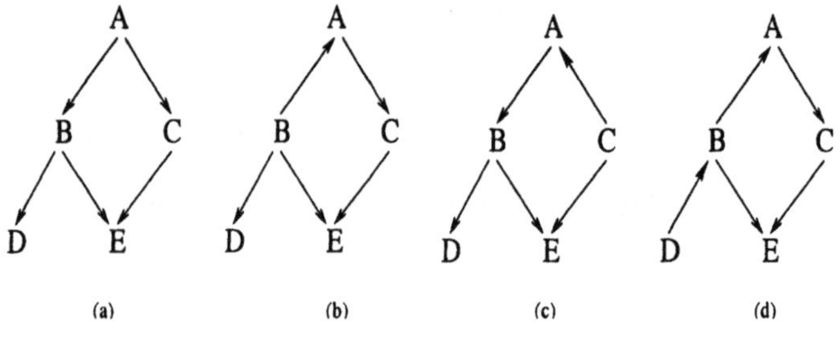

Figure 1. Equivalent Bayesian networks.

Example 1 Consider the BN shown in Figure 1 (a), whose corresponding jpd is written as:

$$p(ABCDE) = p(A) \cdot p(B|A) \cdot p(C|A) \cdot p(D|B) \cdot p(E|BC), \quad (2)$$

$$= p(A) \cdot \frac{p(BA)}{p(A)} \cdot \frac{p(CA)}{p(A)} \cdot \frac{p(DB)}{p(B)} \cdot \frac{p(EBC)}{p(BC)}, \quad (3)$$

$$= \frac{p(BA) \cdot p(CA) \cdot p(DB) \cdot p(EBC)}{p(A) \cdot p(B) \cdot p(BC)}. \quad (4)$$

It is noticed that equation (3) was obtained by rewriting equation (2) according to the definition of conditional probability; equation (4) was obtained by canceling numerator $p(A)$ and denominator $p(A)$ in equation (3). It perhaps should be emphasized here that equation (4) and equation (2) are identities.

For Bayesian networks, we are interested in the jpd being factorized as a product of CPDs according to the topological structure of DAG. The fact that equation (4) and equation (2) are identities imposes the following question: *if we are given equation (4), can we derive any other CPD product factorization other than the one in equation (2)?*

In order to turn equation (4) into CPD factorization, it is obvious that we need to absorb each denominator in equation (4), i.e., $p(A)$, $p(B)$, $p(BC)$. The question imposed above can thus be easily answered by the following demonstrations:

$$p(ABCDEF) = \frac{p(BA) \cdot p(CA) \cdot p(DB) \cdot p(EBC)}{p(A) \cdot p(B) \cdot p(BC)}, \quad (5)$$

$$= p(BA) \cdot \frac{p(CA)}{p(A)} \cdot \frac{p(DB)}{p(B)} \cdot \frac{p(EBC)}{p(BC)}, \quad (6)$$

$$= p(A) \cdot p(B|A) \cdot p(C|A) \cdot p(D|B) \cdot p(E|BC), \quad (7)$$

$$= p(B) \cdot p(A|B) \cdot p(C|A) \cdot p(D|B) \cdot p(E|BC). \quad (8)$$

It is noted that in equation (5), denominator $p(A)$ was absorbed by numerator $p(CA)$; denominator $p(B)$ was absorbed by numerator $p(DB)$; denominator $p(BC)$ was absorbed by numerator $p(EBC)$; this scheme for denominator absorption yields equation (6), which further yields equation (7) and (8). Both equation (7) and (8) represents BN as shown in Figure 1 (a), (b), respectively.

It perhaps should be mentioned that the reason we obtained the equations (7) and (8) was due to the scheme for denominator absorption. It is also noted that for equation (4) we have another 2 schemes for denominator absorption. One scheme for denominator absorption is shown below:

$$p(ABCDEF) = \frac{p(BA) \cdot p(CA) \cdot p(DB) \cdot p(EBC)}{p(A) \cdot p(B) \cdot p(BC)}, \quad (9)$$

$$= \frac{p(BA)}{p(A)} \cdot p(CA) \cdot \frac{p(DB)}{p(B)} \cdot \frac{p(EBC)}{p(BC)}, \quad (10)$$

$$= p(B|A) \cdot p(C) \cdot p(A|C) \cdot p(D|B) \cdot p(E|BC), \quad (11)$$

$$= p(B|A) \cdot p(A) \cdot p(C|A) \cdot p(D|B) \cdot p(E|BC). \quad (12)$$

The BNs corresponding to equation (11) and (12) are shown in Figure 1 (c), (a).

The other scheme for denominator absorption is:

$$
\begin{aligned}
p(ABCDEF) &= \frac{p(BA)\cdot p(CA)\cdot p(DB)\cdot p(EBC)}{p(A)\cdot p(B)\cdot p(BC)}, && (13)\\
&= \frac{p(BA)}{p(B)}\cdot\frac{p(CA)}{p(A)}\cdot p(DB)\cdot\frac{p(EBC)}{p(BC)} && (14)\\
&= p(A|B)\cdot p(C|A)\cdot p(B)\cdot p(D|B)\cdot p(E|BC), && (15)\\
&= p(A|B)\cdot p(C|A)\cdot p(D)\cdot p(B|D)\cdot p(E|BC). && (16)
\end{aligned}
$$

The BNs corresponding to equation (15) and (16) are shown in Figure 1 (b), (d).

So far We have tried all different schemes for denominator absorption and it results in four different BNs shown in Figure 1. Obviously, all these 4 BNs are equivalent and form an equivalent class of BNs.

The above example actually demonstrates that the fraction factorization of a jpd defined by a BN characterizes the equivalent class of BNs and all equivalent BNs in the same class can be obtained from the fraction factorization by absorbing all the denominators. We are now to show that this observation is generally true.

Definition 2 Consider a BN with its jpd as follows:

$$
\begin{aligned}
p(X_1X_2\ldots X_n) &= p(X_1)\cdot p(X_2|pa(X_2))\cdot\ldots\cdot p(X_n|pa(X_n)), && (17)\\
&= \frac{p(X_1)}{1}\cdot\frac{p(X_2,\,pa(X_2))}{p(pa(X_2))}\cdots\frac{p(X_n,\,pa(X_n))}{p(pa(X_n))}, && (18)\\
&= \prod_{i,\,j}\frac{p(X_i,\,pa(X_i))}{p(pa(X_j))}, && (19)
\end{aligned}
$$

where $\{X_i,\, pa(X_i)\} \neq \{pa(X_j)\}$ for any $1 \leq i,\, j \leq n$. Equation (17) is called *Bayesian factorization.* Each $p(X_i|pa(X_i))$ in equation (17) is called a *factor.* We call the equation in (18) *fraction factorization* of the BN. The jpd obtained in equation (19) (by canceling any applicable numerator and denominator in equation (18)) is called the *intrinsic factorization* of the BN.

For instance, the factorization in equation (4) is the *intrinsic* factorization of the BN shown in Figure 1 (a).

It is worth mentioning that the number of denominators in intrinsic factorization is always less than the number of numerators.

Before we present the main result of this paper, consider the following lemma.

Lemma 1 If $\mathcal{D}$ is a DAG containing a covered edge (X, Y) and $\mathcal{D}'$ is a DAG identical to $\mathcal{D}$ except that the edge (X, Y) in $\mathcal{D}$ is now oriented as (Y, X) in $\mathcal{D}'$, then

(a). $pa'(Y) = pa(X)$,

(b). $\{X\} \cup pa'(X) = \{Y\} \cup pa(Y)$,

where $pa'(Y)$ is the parent set for node Y in $\mathcal{D}'$, $pa(X)$ is the parent set for node X in $\mathcal{D}$.

Proof: Since (X, Y) is a covered edge in $\mathcal{D}$, it follows $pa(Y) = \{X\} \cup pa(X)$. Similarly, since (Y, X) is a covered edge in $\mathcal{D}'$, it follows $pa'(X) = \{Y\} \cup pa'(Y)$. Because (X, Y) is the only edge that differs in $\mathcal{D}$ and $\mathcal{D}'$, it then follows $pa'(X) = pa(X) \cup \{Y\}$, $pa'(Y) = pa(Y) - \{X\}$. Moreover, $pa'(Y) = pa(Y) - \{X\} = (\{X\} \cup pa(X)) - \{X\} = pa(X)$; $\{X\} \cup pa'(X) = \{X\} \cup \{Y\} \cup pa'(Y) = \{X\} \cup \{Y\} \cup pa(X) = \{Y\} \cup pa(Y)$.

We now present the algebraic characterization that describes an equivalent class of Bayesian networks.

Theorem 3 Two BNs are equivalent if and only if they have the same intrinsic factorization.

Proof: The proof for the "if" part is trivial. If two BNs have the same intrinsic factorization, they must define the same jpd. We thus only need to prove the "only if" part.

According to [1], we only need to show our claim holds for two equivalent BNs, say $BN1$ and $BN2$, that differ by a single covered edge orientation. We further assume that in $BN1$, we have a covered edge (X, Y), while in $BN2$, we have the edge (Y, X). Consider the fraction factorizations for both $BN1$ and $BN2$. For any node Z of $BN1$ and $BN2$ such that $Z \neq X \neq Y$, we have the factor $p(Z|pa(Z))$, i.e., $\frac{p(Z, pa(Z))}{p(pa(Z))}$, in the fraction factorization of both $BN1$ and $BN2$. We thus focus on the factors for nodes X and Y in $BN1$ and $BN2$. First consider the edge (X, Y) in $BN1$, since (X, Y) is a covered edge in $BN1$, it follows that $pa(Y) = pa(X) \cup \{X\}$. In the fraction factorization of $BN1$, we must have $\frac{p(Y, pa(Y))}{p(pa(Y))} \cdot \frac{p(X, pa(X))}{p(pa(X))}$ (i.e., $p(Y|pa(Y)) \cdot p(X|pa(X))$), which can be simplified as $\frac{p(Y, pa(Y))}{p(pa(X))}$. Similarly, consider the edge (Y, X) in $BN2$, since (Y, X) is also a covered edge in $BN2$ by Corollary 1, it follows that $pa'(X) = pa'(Y) \cup \{Y\}$. In the fraction factorization of $BN2$, we must have $\frac{p(X, pa'(X))}{p(pa'(X))} \cdot \frac{p(Y, pa'(Y))}{p(pa'(Y))}$ (i.e., $p(X|pa'(X)) \cdot p(Y|pa'(Y))$), which can be simplified as $\frac{p(X, pa'(X))}{p(pa'(Y))}$. By lemma (1), it follows immediately that $\frac{p(Y, pa(Y))}{p(pa(X))}$

is identical to $\frac{p(X, pa'(X))}{p(pa'(Y))}$. This indicates that the fraction factorization for $BN1$ and $BN2$ are identical which further results in the fact that $BN1$ and $BN2$ have the same intrinsic factorization.

Corollary 2 All the BNs in the same equivalent class have the same intrinsic factorization.

Theorem (3) and corollary (2) indicate that the intrinsic factorization for an equivalent class of Bayesian networks is *unique* and it characterizes and describes the equivalent class of Bayesian networks algebraically.

4. Applications of the Algebraic Characterization

In this section, we describe some applications of the algebraic characterization proposed.

4.1. Checking Equivalence of Two Bayesian Networks

Both [7] and [1] proposed graphical criterions for determining whether two given Bayesian networks are equivalent or not. In [7], in order to determine whether two Bayesian networks are equivalent or not, a graphical structure, called *rudimentary pattern* of the DAG, is constructed for each of the DAG to be determined, two Bayesian networks are equivalent if and only if they have the same rudimentary pattern.

Under our algebraic characterization, given two Bayesian networks $BN1$ and $BN2$, according to theorem 3 and Corollary 2, we can first compute their intrinsic factorizations respectively. If their intrinsic factorizations are identical, then $BN1$ and $BN2$ are equivalent. This checking procedure is a pure algebraic one and does not involve the construction of a secondary graphical structure, i.e., rudimentary pattern.

4.2. Identifying Compelled Edge in a DAG

Compelled edge identification is very important for learning Bayesian networks as discussed in [1]. An algorithm for identifying all compelled edges in a given DAG was given in [1]. This algorithm consists of two sub-algorithms, one for ordering all the edges in a DAG, the other then labels all the edges in the DAG as either *compelled* or *reversible*. In this section, we propose a much simple method for the same purpose but using the algebraic characterization. The idea is very simple. Recall in example (1), we have demonstrated that from the intrinsic factorization in equation (4), we could derive all Bayesian networks that are equivalent to the one shown in Figure 1 (a) by absorbing all the denominators in equation (4) differently. We now formalize this method of denominator absorption and the notion of denominator absorption scheme.

Considering a Bayesian network $BN = (\mathcal{D},\ P)$, there is no difficulty at all to obtain its intrinsic factorization as shown below:

$$p(X_1X_2\ldots X_n) \;=\; \prod_{i,\,j} \frac{p(X_i,\ pa(X_i))}{p(pa(X_j))}, \tag{20}$$

where $\{X_i,\ pa(X_i)\} \neq \{pa(X_j)\}$, for any $1 \leq i,\ j \leq n$. The equation above describes the class of equivalent Bayesian networks according to Corollary 2. In order to obtain each Bayesian network in the equivalent class, we only need to turn the intrinsic factorization in equation (20) into different Bayesian factorizations each of which corresponds to a Bayesian network in the equivalent class. It is important to note that turning the intrinsic factorization in equation (20) into a Bayesian factorization actually means absorbing all denominators in equation (20). More precisely, let

$$N \;=\; \{p(X_{i_1},\ pa(X_{i_1})),\ p(X_{i_2},\ pa(X_{i_2})),\ \ldots,\ p(X_{i_m},\ pa(X_{i_m}))\},$$

where each element of the set N is a numerator in equation (20). Similarly, let

$$D \;=\; \{p(pa(X_{j_1})),\ p(pa(X_{j_2})),\ \ldots,\ p(pa(X_{j_n}))\},$$

where each element of the set D is a denominator in equation (20). Absorbing denominators in D can be considered as a mapping such that each element $p(pa(X_{j_k}))$, $1 \leq k \leq n$, of D is being mapped to a *distinct* element $p(X_{i_{k'}},\ pa(X_{i_{k'}}))$, $1 \leq k' \leq m$, of N, where $pa(X_{j_k}) \subset \{X_{i_{k'}},\ pa(X_{i_{k'}})\}$. We call such a mapping a *denominator absorption scheme*. Since the number of numerators and the number of denominators in the intrinsic factorization (20) is finite, we can enumerate all possible denominator absorption schemes. If a denominator $d = p(pa(X_{j_k})) \in D$ is always mapped (absorbed) to a numerator $c = p(X_{i_{k'}},\ pa(X_{i_{k'}}))$ in all possible denominator absorption schemes, it then follows immediately that regardless of which denominator absorption scheme one choose to yield Bayesian factorization, this d will always be absorbed by c to yield the conditional $p(\{X_{i_{k'}},\ pa(X_{i_{k'}})\} - pa(X_{j_k}) \mid pa(X_{j_k}))$ in every resulting Bayesian factorization obtained by following any denominator absorption scheme. This indicates that the edges $(X_i,\ X_j)$, where $X_i \in pa(X_{j_k})$, $X_j \in \{X_{i_{k'}},\ pa(X_{i_{k'}})\} - pa(X_{j_k})$ appears in every Bayesian network in the equivalent class, i.e., they are compelled edges.

Example 2 Consider the Bayesian network shown in Figure 2. Its intrinsic factorization is as follows in equation (21):

$$\begin{aligned} p(ABCDEFH) \;=&\; p(A)\cdot p(B)\cdot p(C|A)\cdot p(D|AB)\cdot p(E) \\ &\cdot p(F|D)\cdot p(H|DE), \end{aligned}$$

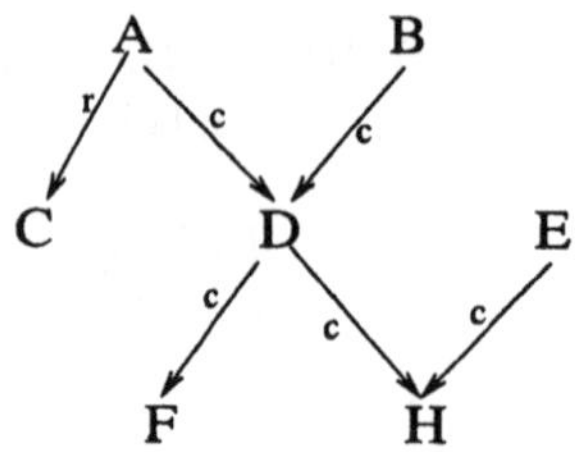

Figure 2. Equivalent Bayesian networks. The edge labeled with 'r' is reversible. The edge labeled with 'c' is compelled.

$$= p(B) \cdot p(CA) \cdot \frac{p(DAB)}{p(AB)} \cdot p(E) \cdot \frac{p(FD)}{p(D)} \cdot \frac{p(HDE)}{p(DE)}. \qquad (21)$$

Let $N = \{p(B),\ p(CA),\ p(DAB),\ p(E),\ p(FD),\ p(FDE)\}$ be the set of numerators and $D = \{p(AB),\ p(D),\ p(DE)\}$ be the set of denominators in equation (21), respectively. In order to turn equation (21) into a Bayesian factorization, it is easy to verify that in all possible denominator absorption schemes, denominator $p(AB)$ must be absorbed by $p(DAB)$, denominator $p(D)$ must be absorbed by $p(FD)$, and denominator $p(DE)$ must be absorbed by $p(HDE)$. This means that the edges $(A,\ D)$, $(B,\ D)$, $(D,\ F)$, $(D,\ H)$, and $(E,\ H)$ are compelled edges.

An algorithm can easily be designed to find out all compelled edges in a DAG, due to the space limit, the complete algorithm will appear in an forthcoming separate paper [8].

5. Conclusion

In this paper, we have proposed an algebraic characterization for describing and characterizing an equivalent class of Bayesian networks. It has been demonstrated that this new characterization really captures the essence of equivalent Bayesian networks algebraically without resorting to any other secondary graphical structures and criterion. Based on this characterization, we also proposed a method for identifying all compelled edges in a DAG. This method can be easily understood and implemented, compared with previously developed graphical algorithm.

References

[1] D.M. Chickering. A transformational characterization of equivalent bayesian network structures. In *Eleventh Conference on Uncertainty in Artificial Intelligence*, pages 87–98. Morgan Kaufmann Publishers, 1995.

[2] A.P. Dawid. Conditional independence in statistical theory. *Journal of the Royal Statistical Society*, 41B:1–31, 1979.

[3] F.V. Jensen. *An Introduction to Bayesian Networks.* UCL Press, 1996.

[4] F.V. Jensen, S.L. Lauritzen, and K.G. Olesen. Bayesian updating in causal probabilistic networks by local computation. *Computational Statistics Quarterly*, 4:269–282, 1990.

[5] S.L. Lauritzen and D.J. Spiegelhalter. Local computation with probabilities on graphical structures and their application to expert systems. *Journal of the Royal Statistical Society*, 50:157–244, 1988.

[6] J. Pearl. *Probabilistic Reasoning in Intelligent Systems: Networks of Plausible Inference.* Morgan Kaufmann Publishers, San Francisco, California, 1988.

[7] T. Verma and J. Pearl. Equivalence and synthesis of causal models. In *Sixth Conference on Uncertainty in Artificial Intelligence*, pages 220–227. GE Corporate Research and Development, 1990.

[8] S.K.M. Wong and Dan Wu. Identifying compelled edges in a dag - a constraint satisfaction problem. In *The 2002 International Conference on Artificial Intelligence (IC-AI'02: Las Vegas, USA, June 24-27, 2002).* Accepted, 2002.

ESTIMATING KNOWLEDGE DECAY

John Debenham
University of Technology, Sydney

Abstract Knowledge 'decay' is a measure of the degradation of knowledge integrity. In a unified knowledge representation, data, information and knowledge are all represented in a single formalism as "items". A unified knowledge representation is extended here to include two measures of knowledge integrity. A rule of inference is defined on the unified knowledge representation that preserves the validity of these two measures. This rule of inference is used to define a normalised knowledge base. The use of a unified knowledge representation and the application of knowledge base normalisation simplify the estimation of knowledge decay.

Keywords integrity management, knowledge-base design

1. INTRODUCTION

Knowledge 'decay' is a measure of the degradation of knowledge integrity. In a *unified* knowledge representation, data, information and knowledge are all represented in a single formalism as "items". A unified model is expressed in terms of "items" and "objects" [1]; objects are item-building operators. A rule of inference, called item (and object) "join" is defined [2]. That rule is extended here so that it accommodates the two measures of knowledge integrity. A single rule for" knowledge decomposition" is defined in terms of that rule. Knowledge decomposition is applied to normalise the knowledge in a knowledge base. Classical database normalisation [3] is a special case of knowledge base normalisation. The use of a unifiedknowledge representation and the application of knowledge base normalisation simplifies the estimation of knowledge decay.

2. UNIFIED KNOWLEDGE REPRESENTATION

The terms 'data', 'information' and 'knowledge' are used here in a rather idiosyncratic sense [1]. The *data* in an application are those things that can be represented as simple constants or variables. The *information* is those things that can be represented as tuples or relations. The *knowledge* is those things that can be represented either as programs in an imperative language or as rules in a declarative language. Items are a unified knowledge representation; they have a uniform format no matter whether they represent 'data', 'information' or 'knowledge' things.

The key to the unified representation is the way that the meaning of an item, the item 'semantics' is specified. The *semantics* of an item is a function that *recognises* the members of the "value set" of that item. The *value set* of an information item is the set of tuples that are associated with a relational implementation of that item. Knowledge items, including complex, recursive knowledge items, have value sets too [1]. For example, the item, which represents the rule "the sale price of parts is the cost price marked up by a universal mark-up factor", could have a value set of quintuples associated with *[part/sale-price, part/cost-price, mark-up]*.

The notion of an item is extended here to incorporate two integrity measures. The *item tuple integrity measure* for an item is a measure of the likelihood that a given tuple should *not* belong to the value set of that item. The *item set integrity measure* for an item is a measure of the likelihood that a given set is an invalid value set of that item. Items are *either* represented informally as "i-schema" *or* formally as λ-calculus expressions. The i-schema notation is used in applications. Formally, given a unique name A, an n-tuple $(m_1, m_2, \ldots, m_n)$, $M = \Sigma_i m_i$, if:

- S_A is an M-argument expression of the form:

  $$\lambda y_1^1 \ldots y_{m_1}^1 \ldots y_{m_n}^n \bullet [S_{A_1}(y_1^1, \ldots, y_{m_1}^1) \wedge \ldots \wedge S_{A_n}(y_1^n, \ldots, y_{m_n}^n) \wedge J(y_1^1, \ldots, y_{m_1}^1, \ldots, y_{m_n}^n)] \bullet$$

  where $\{A_1, \ldots, A_n\}$ is an ordered set of not necessarily distinct items, each item in this set is called a *component* of item A.
- V_A is an M-argument fuzzy expression of the form:

  $$\lambda y_1^1 \ldots y_{m_1}^1 \ldots y_{m_n}^n \bullet [V_{A_1}(y_1^1, \ldots, y_{m_1}^1) \wedge \ldots \wedge V_{A_n}(y_1^n, \ldots, y_{m_n}^n) \wedge K(y_1^1, \ldots, y_{m_1}^1, \ldots, y_{m_n}^n)] \bullet$$

  where $\{A_1, \ldots, A_n\}$ are the components of item A, K is a fuzzy predicate and ¼ is the fuzzy "min" conjunction.
- C_A is a fuzzy expression of the form:

  $$[C_{A_1} \wedge C_{A_2} \wedge \ldots \wedge C_{A_n} \wedge (L)_A]$$

  where $\wedge$ is the fuzzy "min" conjunction and L is a fuzzy expression constructed as a logical combination of:

- $Card_A$ lies in some numerical range;
- $Uni(A_i)$ for some i, 1≤i≤ n, and
- $Can(A_i, X)$ for some i, 1≤i≤ n, where X is a non-empty subset of $\{A_1,..., A_n\} - \{A_i\}$;

subscripted with the name of the item *A*,

then the named triple $A[\, S_A, V_A, C_A]$ is an M-adic *item* with *item name A*, S_A is called the *item semantics* of *A*, V_A is called the *item tuple integrity measure* of *A* and C_A is called the *item set integrity measure* of *A*. "$Uni(A_i)$" is a fuzzy predicate whose truth value is "the proportion of the members of the value set of item A_i that also occur in the value set of item *A*". "$Can(A_i, X)$" is a fuzzy predicate whose truth value is "in the value set of item *A*, the proportion of members of the value set of the set of items X that functionally determine members of the value set of item A_i,". "$Card_A$" means "the number of different values in the value set of item *A*". The subscripts identify the item's components to which that measure applies. Given an item *A* and tuple X, if $V_A(X) = 1$ then this does *not* imply that X is invalid in the value set of *A*; if $V_A(X) = 0$ then X is invalid in the value set of *A*. Likewise for C_A. The measures are *not* measures of validity. A value of unity does *not* imply validity. An item's semantics specifies what *should be* in an implementation, and the two integrity measures are measures of invalidity of what *is* in an implementation.

For example, an application may contain an association whereby each *cost-price* is associated with a *sales-tax* amount as determined by the prevailing *tax-rate*. This association could be represented by the knowledge item:

[cost-price, sales-tax, tax-rate][
$\lambda xyz\bullet[\, S_{cost\text{-}price}(x) \wedge S_{sales\text{-}tax}(y) \wedge S_{tax\text{-}rate}(z) \wedge (y = x \times z)]\bullet,$
$\lambda xyz\bullet[\, V_{cost\text{-}price}(x) \wedge V_{sales\text{-}tax}(y) \wedge V_{tax\text{-}rate}(z) \wedge K_2(x, y, z)\,]\bullet$
$[\, C_{cost\text{-}price} \wedge C_{sales\text{-}tax} \wedge C_{tax\text{-}rate} \wedge$
(Can(*cost-price*, {*sales-tax*, *tax-rate*}) ∧
Can(*sales-tax*, {*cost-price*, *tax-rate*}) ∧
Can(*tax-rate*, {*cost-price*, *sales-tax*}) $)_{[cost\text{-}price,\ sales\text{-}tax,\ tax\text{-}rate]}$]]

where:

$$K_2(x,y,z)=\begin{cases}0 & \text{if } x\neq 0 \quad \text{and} \quad y\neq 0\\ \dfrac{x}{x+100\times|z\times x-y|} & \text{otherwise}\end{cases}$$

Items make it difficult to analyse the structure of the whole application because, for example, two rules that share the same basic wisdom may be expressed in terms of quite different components; this could obscure their common wisdom. To make the inherent structure of knowledge clear 'objects' are introduced as item building operators [4].

Object names are written in bold italics. Suppose that the conceptual model already contains the item "*part*" which represents spare parts, and the item "*cost-price*" which represents cost prices; then the information "spare parts have a cost price" can be represented by "*part/cost-price*" which may be built by applying the "***costs***" object to *part* and *cost-price*:

part/cost-price = ***costs***(*part, cost-price*)

Suppose that the conceptual model already contains the item "*part/sale-price*" which represents the association between spare parts and their corresponding selling price, and the item "*mark-up*" which represents the data thing a universal mark-up factor; then the rule "spare parts are marked up by a universal mark up factor" can be represented by *[part/sale-price, part/cost-price, mark-up]* which is built by applying the "***mark-up-rule***" object to the items "*part/sale-price*", "*part/cost-price*" and "*mark-up*":

[part/sale-price, part/cost-price, mark-up] =
mark-up-rule(*part/sale-price, part/cost-price, mark-up*)

The conceptual model contains items. A fundamental set of data items in the conceptual model is called the *basis*. The remaining items in the conceptual model are built by applying object operators to the other items in the conceptual model. As for items, objects may either be represented informally as "o-schema" or formally as typed λ-calculus expressions.

In [2] the composition of items and objects using a "join" operator is described. Join is extended here to include the measures of integrity. Decomposition is defined in terms of join. Knowledge base normalisation is defined in terms of decomposition [5]. Normalisation removes hidden relationships from the conceptual model. Hidden relationships can present a maintenance hazard [6]. Knowledge base normalisation simplifies the estimation of knowledge decay [7].

Item join provides the basis for item decomposition. The definition of "item composition" follows. Given two items:

$A[\,S_A, V_A, C_A\,]$ and
$B[\,S_B, V_B, C_B\,]$

Suppose that S_A has n variables, that is *A* is an n-adic item. Suppose that S_B has m variables, that is *B* is an m-adic item. Some of the components of *A* and *B* may be identical. Suppose that k pairs of components of *A* and *B* that are identical are identified, where $k \geq 0$. Let E be an ordered set of components where each is one of these identical pairs of components of both *A* and *B*. E may be empty. To ensure that the definition is well defined the order of the components in the set E is the same as order in which they occur as components of *A*. Suppose the semantics expressions of the components from item *A* (or item *B*) that are in the set E are expressed in terms of a total of p variables. Let *A** be an n-adic item that is identical to item *A* except for the order of its variables. The last p variables in *A** are those variables in *A* that belong to the components of *A* in the set E. Let *B** be an m-adic item that is identical to item *B* except for the order of its variables. The first p variables in *B** are those variables in *B* that belong to the components of *B* in the set E. Let π be a permutation that turns the ordered set of variables of *A** into the ordered set of variables of *A*. Let π' be a permutation that turns the ordered set of variables of *B** into the ordered set of variables of *B*. Suppose that 'x' is an (n - p)-tuple of free variables, 'y'is a p-tuple of free variables and 'z' is an (m - p)-tuple of free variables. Then the item with name $A \otimes_E B$ is the *composition* of *A* and *B* on E and is defined to be the item:

$$(A \otimes_E B)[\,\lambda xyz\bullet[S_A(\pi\,(x,y)) \wedge S_B(\pi'(y,z))]\bullet,$$
$$\lambda xyz\bullet[V_A(\pi\,(x,y)) \wedge V_B(\pi'\,(y,z))]\bullet, C_{A \otimes_E B}\,]$$

where $C_{A \otimes_E B}$ is defined as follows. Suppose that C_A is an expression of the form $c_A \wedge G$ where c is that part of C_A that carries the subscript '*A*' where any occurrence of the predicate Card are equated to "true", and G is that part of C_A that carries subscripts other than '*A*'. Likewise suppose that C_B is an expression of the form $d_B \wedge H$. Then:

$$C_{A \otimes_E B} = (c \wedge d)_{A \otimes_E B} \wedge (G \wedge H)$$

The set E is *a* set of identical pairs of components of *A* and *B*. If E is the set of *all* identical pairs of components of *A* and *B* then $A \otimes_E B$ is written as $A \otimes B$.

Given two n-adic items *A* and *B* with the same set of components that are not necessarily in the same order, *A* and *B* are *weakly equivalent*, written $A \cong_w B$, if there exists a permutation π such that:

$$(\forall x_1 x_2 \ldots x_n)[S_A(x_1,x_2,\ldots,x_n) \leftrightarrow S_B(\pi\,(x_1,x_2,\ldots,x_n))]$$

where the x_i are the n_i variables associated with the i'th component of A. The composition $A \otimes_E B$ is a *monotonic composition* if $A \otimes_E B$ is *not* weakly equivalent with either A or B.

The $\otimes$ operator forms the basis of decomposition in which each item may be replaced by a set of simpler items. An item I is *decomposable* into the set of items $D = \{I_1, I_2, ..., I_n\}$ if: I_i has non-trivial semantics for all i, $I = I_1 \otimes I_2 \otimes ... \otimes I_n$, where each composition is *monotonic*. If item I is decomposable then it will not necessarily have a unique decomposition [4]. A knowledge base is *normal* if it contains no decomposable items [1].

3. KNOWLEDGE BASE IMPLEMENTATION

The semantics of an item $A[S_A, V_A, C_A]$ is a function that recognises the members of its value set. The value set is a conceptual notion in the system design. So the value set of the item A—as in the definition of an M-adic item above—at time τ is:

$$\gamma^{\tau}(A) = \{y_1^1 ... y_{m_1}^1 ... y_{m_n}^n : S_A(y_1^1, ..., y_{m_1}^1, ..., y_{m_n}^n) \text{ at } time\ \tau\}$$

A *knowledge base implementation* is a set of knowledge items and a set of stored relations and data domains representing some information and data items. Some information and data items are associated with actual stored data, and some are not. Knowledge items are not normally associated with actual stored data. If an item is associated with actual stored data then it is a *real item*; otherwise it is a *virtual item*. The set of tuples in the implementation of the *real* item A is denoted by $\lambda^{\alpha}(A)$ where α is the time of the most recent modification to those tuples. Knowledge items may be used to derive tuples for virtual data and information items. For example, suppose that the real data item *mark-up* has a stored data value mark-up, and that the real information item *part/cost-price* has a stored relation part/cost-price. Then the knowledge item *[part/sale-price, part/cost-price, mark-up]*—or an "if-then" implementation of it—may be used to *derive* tuples in the relation for the virtual item *part/sale-price*. Further, the knowledge item *[part/sale-price, part/tax-payable, tax-rate]* could then enable the tuples in the relation for the virtual item *part/tax-payable* to be derived. This is illustrated in Fig. 1. If a virtual item A_i is a component of a knowledge item A where the tuples (or data values) associated with A_i are derived from $\{ \lambda^{\alpha_j}(A_j) : A_j \text{ is a component of } A, j \neq i \}$ using the knowledge A then A_i is *derivable* and those tuples (or data values) are called the *derived set* which is denoted by $\lambda^{\beta}(A_i)$ where β is the time at which the derivation is performed.

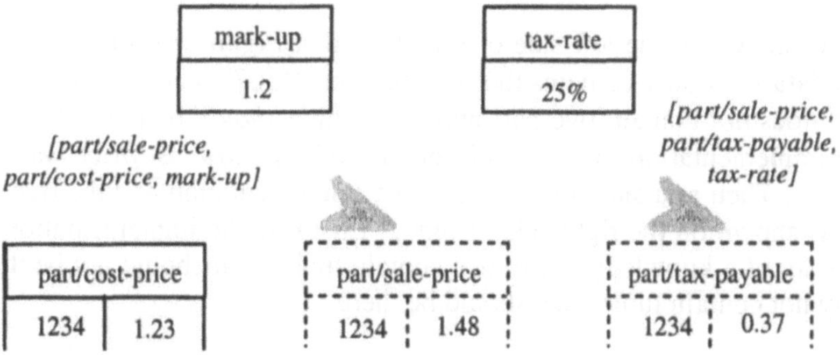

Fig. 1. **Real and virtual items**

$\lambda^{\alpha}(part)$

part
part-number
1234
2345
2468
3456
3579
4567

$\Lambda^{\tau}(part)$

part
part-number
1234
2345
2456
2468
3456
3579
4680

$\lambda^{\alpha}(part/cost\text{-}price)$

part/cost-price	
part-number	dollar-amount
1234	1.20
2345	2.40
2468	3.60
3456	4.80
3579	5.10
4567	6.30

$\Lambda^{\tau}(part/cost\text{-}price)$

part/cost-price	
part-number	dollar-amount
1234	1.20
2345	2.60
2456	0.60
2468	3.80
3456	4.80
3579	5.20
4680	0.80

Fig. 2. **The implementation and the true set**

This definition is recursive. In Fig. 1 only part/cost-price, mark-up and tax-rate are stored. This example shows how the decay of the virtual item *part/tax-payable* is determined by the decay of those three real items *and* by the decay of those two knowledge items. So if any of those three real items or either of those two knowledge items has decayed in some way then that calculation *may* yield an incorrect result.

For a knowledge base, its implementation may have decayed because *updates* that should have been performed were not, or *modifications* that should not have been performed were. The corruption of a knowledge base by such modifications is not considered here. The failure to perform updates is considered. So *updates* are changes that should have been performed on the implementation of real items or knowledge items. In addition, incorrect values may be attributed to a knowledge base implementation because the derived tuples for some virtual items were calculated prior to required updates being performed [8]. At time α the *true set* for a—real or virtual—item A is the set of tuples that should be associated with A at time α; it is denoted by $\Lambda^{\alpha}(A)$. In other words, the implementation is what *is* either stored or derived in the knowledge base, the true set is what *should be* either stored or derived.

Suppose that the implementation of the real data item *part* was stored at time α. Then at a subsequent time τ the implementation and the true set may be as shown on the left side of Fig. 2. In that Figure the implementation for the data item *part* contains the part number "4567" that should *not* be there, and does *not* contain two part numbers which *should* be there. Suppose that the implementation for the real information item *part/cost-price* was stored at time α. Then at a subsequent time τ the implementation and the true set may be as shown on the right side of Fig. 2. Likewise the implementation and the true set of a knowledge item may contain tuples that should not be there, and may not contain tuples that should be there.

4. KNOWLEDGE DECAY

At time τ, $\Lambda^{\tau}(A)$ and $\lambda^{\alpha}(A)$, $\alpha \leq \tau$, may not be the same. The implementation of a real item is "correct" as long as its tuples have been correctly stored and maintained [9]. The derived set of a virtual item is "correct" if the knowledge used to derive the tuples for that item has been correctly maintained *and* the stored data used by that knowledge has been correctly maintained. In reality we may hope that the implementation is correct, and expect that it is incorrect. To measure the extent that the implementation or the derived set are the same as the true set, let $p_{X/Y}$ be the proportion of those elements in set X that are also in set Y. Then the *difference measure*:

$$\Delta(A, B) = \sqrt{p_{A/B} \times p_{B/A}}$$

is unity if both sets are identical and is zero if one set contains no elements from the other; the square root ensures that this measure retains linearity with measured proportion. For example, if each set contains exactly half of the members of the other set then the value of this measure is 0.5. The value of the difference measure is *not* necessarily equal to the proportion of valid members in either set because the difference measure takes account of those elements that are not in each set but should be there. The *decay* of a real or virtual item A at time τ is:

$$\delta_A(\tau) = \Delta(\lambda^{\tau}(A), \Lambda^{\alpha}(A))$$

where $\tau \geq \alpha$ and the difference measure Δ is as defined above. $0 \leq \delta_A(\tau) \leq 1$. If $\delta_A(\tau) = 1$ then item A is valid. If $\delta_A(\tau) = 0$ then the set of tuples associated with item A contains no tuples that it should contain and A has decayed completely.

If we know precisely what knowledge decay has occurred then we can usually rectify it [6]. In practice we tend to have some loose expectation ε of the decay δ. For example, suppose the knowledge item *[part/sale-price, part/cost-price, mark-up]* is built by applying the knowledge object ***mark-up-rule*** to the three items *part/sale-price*, *part/cost-price* and *mark-up*.

That knowledge item may be used to derive tuples for the information item *part/sale-price*. We may expect that "within a year the whole part/cost-price relation will be out of date". So our expectation for the decay of the *part/cost-price* item may be represented by a function with a linear decay of one year's extent. Also, we may expect that "as the 'types' of parts are redesignated, the contents of the part/type relation will decay decreasingly over time so that in a year roughly half of the relation will be out of date and in a 'very long time' the whole relation will be out of date". So our expectation for the decay of the *part/type* item is represented by a function with an exponential decay with a half-life of one year. The decay estimates for these two examples are:

$$\varepsilon_{\text{part/cost-price}}(\tau) = \begin{cases} 1-\tau & \text{if } 0 \le \tau \le 1 \\ 0 & \text{otherwise} \end{cases}$$

$$\varepsilon_{\text{part/type}}(\tau) = 2^{-\tau} \quad \text{for} \quad \tau \ge 0$$

If an object has decayed then such decay will contribute to the decay of any item generated by that object. But objects do not have a value set or an implementation. The decay of the item *A*, generated using object ***B***, *A*=***B***(*C*, *D*, *E*, *F*) may be analysed completely in terms of the decay of items *C*, *D*, *E* and *F* and the decay of object ***B***. In other words, if items *C*, *D*, *E* and *F* are valid then the decay of item *A* will be attributable entirely to the decay of object ***B***. So the *decay* of an object is the decay of any item generated by that object when applied to a set of valid items.

5. PROPAGATING DECAY ESTIMATES

It would be convenient if:

$$\varepsilon_{\boldsymbol{ob}(cc,\, dd)}(\tau) = \varepsilon_{\boldsymbol{ob}}(\tau) \times \varepsilon_{cc}(\tau) \times \varepsilon_{dd}(\tau)$$

but this product rule is *not* valid in general because the decay of the components—in the above example the components are *cc* and *dd*—may be logically dependent. This product rule is valid if the decay of the object ***ob*** and the decay of the two component items are all independent. The decay of X is *independent* of the decay of Y if $(\varepsilon_X(\tau) \mid \varepsilon_Y(\tau)) = \varepsilon_X(\tau)$. The decay of X is *determined by* the decay of Y if $(\varepsilon_X(\tau) \mid \varepsilon_Y(\tau)) = \varepsilon_Y(\tau)$.

Suppose that object ***ob*** is applied to a set of n component items C = {*cc*, D} where *cc* is a component item and D is a set of n-1 component items. The general rule for propagating decay estimates through an object operator is:

$$\models \varepsilon_{\boldsymbol{ob}(C)}(\tau) = \varepsilon_{\boldsymbol{ob}}(\tau) \times (\varepsilon_C(\tau) \mid \varepsilon_{\boldsymbol{ob}}(\tau))$$
$$= \varepsilon_C(\tau) \times (\varepsilon_{\boldsymbol{ob}}(\tau) \mid \varepsilon_C(\tau))$$

where $(\, \varepsilon_C(\tau) \mid \varepsilon_{\boldsymbol{ob}}(\tau)\,)$ is "an estimate of the decay of the set of n component items C at time τ given that the estimate of the decay of object ***ob*** at time τ is $\varepsilon_{\boldsymbol{ob}}(\tau)$." If the knowledge base has been normalised then $(\, \varepsilon_C(\tau) \mid \varepsilon_{\boldsymbol{ob}}(\tau)\,) = \varepsilon_C(\tau)$. To propagate decay estimates across a set of component items, suppose that the set C is a set of n component items as above. The general recursive rule for propagating decay estimates over such a set is:

$$\models \varepsilon_{\{cc,\, D\}}(\tau) = \varepsilon_{cc}(\tau) \times (\, \varepsilon_D(\tau) \mid \varepsilon_{cc}(\tau)\,)$$

where $(\, \varepsilon_D(\tau) \mid \varepsilon_{cc}(\tau)\,)$ is "an estimate of the decay of the set of n-1 component items D at time τ given that the estimate of the decay of the component item *cc* at time τ is $\varepsilon_{cc}(\tau)$." In general $(\, \varepsilon_D(\tau) \mid \varepsilon_{cc}(\tau)\,) \neq \varepsilon_D(\tau)$ even if the knowledge base has been normalised. Now suppose that item *cc* is virtual and that it is derivable from the set of items D using knowledge item ***ob***(*cc*, D), ie that Can(*cc*, D) = 1 in ***ob***(*cc*, D). Then the decay of item *cc* depends on the decay of object ***ob*** and on the decay of the items in the set D. These decay estimates are propagated by:

$$\models \varepsilon_{cc}(\tau) = \varepsilon_{\boldsymbol{ob}}(\tau) \times (\, \varepsilon_D(\tau) \mid \varepsilon_{\boldsymbol{ob}}(\tau)\,)$$

If the knowledge base has been normalised then $(\, \varepsilon_D(\tau) \mid \varepsilon_{\boldsymbol{ob}}(\tau)\,) = \varepsilon_D(\tau)$.

The three rules above for propagating decay estimates follow from the definition of item decay. These three rules lead to complex expressions for decay estimates due to the quantity of conditional expressions—ie expressions involving "|". But the quantity of these conditional expressions may be reduced.

If the knowledge base has been decomposed [10] and if the sub-item relationships have been reduced to sub-type relationships between data items then the object operators and the basis items in the conceptual model are independent with the possible exception of sub-item relationships between data items [5]. So if the knowledge base has been decomposed and there are no sub-item relationships between data items then all the conditional expressions may be removed [1]. For example, if the knowledge base has been decomposed and there are no sub-item relationships between data items then the decay estimate for the virtual information item *part/tax-payable* is:

$$\begin{aligned} \varepsilon_{part/tax\text{-}payable}(\tau) &= \varepsilon_{\boldsymbol{tax\text{-}rule}}(\tau) \\ &\qquad \times (\, \varepsilon_{\{part/sale\text{-}price,\ tax\text{-}rate\}}(\tau) \mid \varepsilon_{\boldsymbol{tax\text{-}rule}}(\tau)\,) \\ &= \varepsilon_{\boldsymbol{tax\text{-}rule}}(\tau) \times \varepsilon_{\{part/sale\text{-}price,\ tax\text{-}rate\}}(\tau) \\ &= \varepsilon_{\boldsymbol{tax\text{-}rule}}(\tau) \times \varepsilon_{part/sale\text{-}price}(\tau) \\ &\qquad \times (\, \varepsilon_{tax\text{-}rate}(\tau) \mid \varepsilon_{part/sale\text{-}price}(\tau)\,) \end{aligned}$$

$$= \varepsilon_{\textbf{tax-rule}}(\tau) \times \varepsilon_{part/sale\text{-}price}(\tau) \times \varepsilon_{tax\text{-}rate}(\tau)$$
$$= \varepsilon_{\textbf{tax-rule}}(\tau) \times \varepsilon_{\textbf{mark-up-rule}}(\tau)$$
$$\times (\varepsilon_{\{part/cost\text{-}price,\ mark\text{-}up\}}(\tau) \mid \varepsilon_{\textbf{mark-up-rule}}(\tau))$$
$$\times \varepsilon_{tax\text{-}rate}(\tau)$$
$$= \varepsilon_{\textbf{tax-rule}}(\tau) \times \varepsilon_{\textbf{mark-up-rule}}(\tau)$$
$$\times \varepsilon_{part/cost\text{-}price}(\tau) \times \varepsilon_{mark\text{-}up}(\tau) \times \varepsilon_{tax\text{-}rate}(\tau)$$

If sub-item relationships are present or if the knowledge base has *not* been normalised then the calculations become more involved. For example, suppose the *supervisor* data item is a sub-item of the *person* data item. Consider the real *person/supervisor* item; the implementation of which is populated with 2-tuples (person-id, person-id) where the second person is the "supervisor" of the first. Suppose that this item is built by applying the ***super*** information object to the data items *person* and *supervisor*:

person/supervisor = ***super***(*person, supervisor*)

then the decay estimate of the *person/supervisor* information item will be:

$$\varepsilon_{\textbf{super}(person,\ supervisor)}(\tau)$$
$$= \varepsilon_{\{person,\ supervisor\}}(\tau) \times (\varepsilon_{\textbf{super}}(\tau) \mid \varepsilon_{\{person,\ supervisor\}}(\tau))$$
$$= \varepsilon_{person}(\tau) \times (\varepsilon_{supervisor}(\tau) \mid \varepsilon_{person}(\tau)) \times \varepsilon_{\textbf{super}}(\tau)$$
$$= \varepsilon_{person}(\tau)^2 \times \varepsilon_{\textbf{super}}(\tau)$$

where $(\varepsilon_{\textbf{super}}(\tau) \mid \varepsilon_{\{person,\ supervisor\}}(\tau)) = \varepsilon_{\textbf{super}}(\tau)$ assuming that the knowledge base has been normalised and the decay of the ***super*** operator is independent of the decay of the items to which it is applied; and where $(\varepsilon_{supervisor}(\tau) \mid \varepsilon_{person}(\tau)) = \varepsilon_{person}(\tau)$ because the decay of *supervisor* is assumed, quite reasonably, to be determined by the decay of *person*.

6. CONCLUSION

Decay is the degradation of integrity over time [11]. In a unified knowledge representation, data, information and knowledge are all represented in a single formalism. Two measures of knowledge integrity are included in a unified knowledge representation. A join operator is defined that enables items in the unified representation to be joined together to form other items. Item join preserves the validity of the two measures of integrity. Decomposition is defined in terms of join. Knowledge base normalisation is defined in terms of decomposition. Normalisation removes hidden relationships from the conceptual model. Hidden relationships can present a maintenance hazard. The representation of a knowledge base using the unified representation, and the normalisation of that representation simplifies the estimation of knowledge decay.

7. REFERENCES

1. Debenham, J.K. "*Knowledge Engineering*", Springer-Verlag, 1998.
2. Debenham, J.K. "Knowledge Simplification", in *proceedings 9th International Symposium on Methodologies for Intelligent Systems ISMIS'96*, Zakopane, Poland, June 1996.
3. Date, C.J., "*An Introduction to Database Systems*" (4th edition) Addison-Wesley, 1986.
4. Debenham, J.K. "Knowledge Object Decomposition", in *proceedings 12th International FLAIRS Conference*, Florida, May 1999, pp203—207.
5. Debenham, J.K. "Understanding Expert Systems Maintenance", in *proceedings Sixth International Conference on Database and Expert Systems Applications DEXA'95*, London, September 1995.
6. Barr, V. "Applying Reliability Engineering to Expert Systems" in *proceedings 12th International FLAIRS Conference*, Florida, May 1999, pp494—498.
7. Mayol, E. and Teniente, E. "Addressing Efficiency Issues During the Process of Integrity Maintenance", in *proceedings Tenth International Conference on Database and Expert Systems Applications DEXA'99*, Florence, September 1999, pp270—281.
8. Katsuno, H. and Mendelzon, A.O., "On the Difference between Updating a Knowledge Base and Revising It", in *proceedings Second International Conference on Principles of Knowledge Representation and Reasoning, KR'91*, Morgan Kaufmann, 1991.
9. Debenham, J.K. "From Conceptual Model to Internal Model", in *proceedings Tenth International Symposium on Methodologies for Intelligent Systems ISMIS'97*, Charlotte, October 1997, pp227—236.
10. Debenham, J.K. "Representing Knowledge Normalisation", *in proceedings Tenth International Conference on Software Engineering and Knowledge Engineering SEKE'98*, San Francisco, US, June 1998 pp132—135.
11. Tayar, N. "A Model for Developing Large Shared Knowledge Bases" in *proceedings Second International Conference on Information and Knowledge Management*, Washington, November 1993, pp717—719.

AN INFORMATION-THEORETIC APPROACH TO THE PRE-PRUNING OF CLASSIFICATION RULES

Max Bramer
University of Portsmouth, Portsmouth, UK

Abstract: The automatic induction of classification rules from examples is an important technique used in data mining. One of the problems encountered is the overfitting of rules to training data. In some cases this can lead to an excessively large number of rules, many of which have very little predictive value for unseen data. This paper is concerned with the reduction of overfitting. It introduces a technique known as *J-pruning*, based on the *J-measure*, an information theoretic means of quantifying the information content of a rule and applies this to two rule induction methods: one where the rules are generated via the intermediate representation of a decision tree and one where rules are generated directly from examples.

Keywords: Knowledge Discovery, Data Mining, Classification Rules, Decision Trees

1. INTRODUCTION

The growing commercial importance of knowledge discovery and data mining techniques has stimulated new interest in the automatic induction of classification rules from examples, a field in which research can be traced back at least as far as the mid-1960s [1].

Most work in this field to date has concentrated on generating classification rules in the intermediate form of a decision tree using variants of the TDIDT (Top-Down Induction of Decision Trees) algorithm [2]. An alternative approach, which generates classification rules directly from the examples, is Prism [3,4].

A problem that arises with all methods of generating rules is that of *overfitting* of the rules to the training data. In some cases this can result in excessively large rule sets and/or rules with very low predictive power for previously unseen data.

This paper describes a method for reducing overfitting in classification rules known as *J-Pruning*. The method makes use of the value of the *J-measure*, an information theoretic means of quantifying the information content of a rule. The rules are *pre-pruned*, i.e. pruned as they are being generated.

Results are presented for a range of datasets using both TDIDT and Prism. The use of J-pruning leads in all cases to a reduction in the number of rules generated and in many cases to an increase in predictive accuracy.

2. AUTOMATIC INDUCTION OF CLASSIFICATION RULES FROM EXAMPLES

2.1 Basic Terminology

It is assumed that there is a universe of *objects*, each of which belongs to one of a set of mutually exclusive *classes*. Objects are described by the values of a number of their *attributes*. There is a two-dimensional table of examples, known as a *training set*, each row of which (an *instance*) comprises the values of the attributes and the corresponding classification for a single object. The aim is to develop classification rules that enable the class to which any object in an unseen *test set* of further instances belongs to be determined from the values of its attributes. It will be assumed that the rules are to be in propositional form, each comprising a conjunction of *terms*, such as

IF x=a AND y=b AND z>34.5 AND w=k THEN Class=3

A more detailed description is given in [5].

2.2 Top-Down Induction of Decision Trees

Many systems have been developed to derive classification rules of the above kind from a training set. Most (but not all) do so via the intermediate form of a decision tree constructed using a variant of the TDIDT (top-down induction of decision trees) algorithm given in Figure 1 below.

The induced decision tree can be regarded as a set of classification rules, one corresponding to each branch.

The most widely used criterion for selecting attributes at step (a) is probably *Information Gain*. This uses the information-theoretic measure

IF all cases in the training set belong to the same class
THEN return the value of the class
ELSE

(a) Select an attribute A to *split* on *
(b) Sort the instances in the training set into non-empty subsets, one for each value of attribute A
(c) Return a tree with one branch for each subset, each branch having a descendant subtree or a class value produced by applying the algorithm recursively for each subset in turn.

* When selecting attributes at step (a) the same attribute must not be selected more than once in any branch.

Figure 1. The TDIDT Tree Generation Algorithm

entropy to choose the attribute which maximises the expected gain of information from applying the additional test. This is the approach adopted in well-known systems such as C4.5 [2].

2.3 The Prism Algorithm

The Prism classification rule generation algorithm was developed by Cendrowska [3], primarily as a means of avoiding the generation of unnecessarily complex rules, which it was argued is an unavoidable but undesirable consequence of the use of a tree representation. The need to fit rules into such a representation requires them all to begin with a test on the value of the same attribute, even though that attribute may be irrelevant to many or most of the rules.

The Prism algorithm induces classification rules directly from a training set one rule at a time. Each rule is generated term-by-term, by selecting the attribute-value pair that maximises the probability of a chosen outcome class.

Reference [4] introduced a revised form of the Prism algorithm, incorporating a number of new features. The version of the algorithm used for the experiments described in this paper (PrismTCS) will be described in detail in Section 5.1.

2.4 Dealing With Clashes

Clashes occur during the classification tree/rule generation process whenever an algorithm is presented with a subset of the training set which contains instances with more than one classification, but which cannot be processed further. Such a subset is known as a ‘clash set’.

The principal cause of clashes is the presence of inconsistent data in the training set, where two or more instances have the same attribute values but different classifications. In such cases, a situation will inevitably occur during tree/rule generation where a subset with mixed classifications is reached, with no further attributes available for selection.

If this occurs at step (a) of the TDIDT algorithm the simplest way of dealing with the clash (and the method assumed in this paper) is to treat all the instances in the clash set as if they belong to the class that contains the largest number of them and generate a rule (i.e. a branch of the classification tree) accordingly.

Clashes in Prism are resolved in the following way. First the largest class for the subset of instances in the clash set is determined. If this largest class is the one for which a rule is being generated, the induced rule is treated as complete. If not, the rule is discarded and those instances in the clash set that have that classification are removed from the training set.

2.5 Overfitting of Rules to Data

The principal problem with TDIDT, Prism and other algorithms for generating classification rules is that of *overfitting*. Beyond a certain point, specialising a rule by adding further terms can become counter-productive. The generated rules give a perfect fit for the instances from which they were generated but in some cases are too specific to have a high level of predictive accuracy for other instances. Another consequence of excessive specificity is that there is often an unnecessarily large number of rules. A smaller number of more general rules may have greater predictive accuracy on unseen data, at the expense of no longer correctly classifying some of the instances in the original training set. Alternatively, a similar level of accuracy may be achieved with a more compact set of rules.

2.6 Pruning Classification Rules to Reduce Overfitting

One approach to reducing overfitting, known as *post-pruning*, which is often used in association with decision tree generation, is to generate the whole set of classification rules and then remove a (possibly substantial) number of rules and terms, by the use of statistical tests or otherwise. An empirical comparison of a number of such methods is given in [6]. An important practical objection to post-pruning methods is that there is a large computational overhead involved in generating rules only then to delete a high proportion of them, especially if the training sets are large.

Pre-pruning a set of classification rules (or a decision tree) involves terminating some of the rules (branches) prematurely as they are being generated. Each incomplete rule such as

IF x = 1 AND z = yes AND q > 63.5 .... THEN ...

corresponds to a subset of instances currently 'under investigation'.

If not all the instances have the same classification the rule would normally be extended by adding a further term, as described previously. When following a pre-pruning strategy the subset is first tested to determine whether or not a termination condition applies. If it does not, a further term is generated as usual. If it does, the rule is *pruned*, i.e. it is treated as if no further attributes were available and a clash had occurred (see Section 2.4).

Reference [7] reports on experiments with four possible termination conditions for pre-pruning rules as they are generated by TDIDT, e.g. truncate each rule as soon as it reaches 4 terms in length. The results obtained clearly show that pre-pruning can substantially reduce the number of terms generated and in some cases can also increase the predictive accuracy. Although they also show that the choice of pre-pruning method is important, it is not clear that (say) the same length limit should be applied to each rule, far less which of the termination conditions is the best one to use or why. There is a need to find a more principled choice of termination condition to use with pre-pruning, if possible one which can be applied completely automatically without the need for the user to select any 'threshold value' (such as the maximum number of terms for any rule). The *J-measure* described in the next section provides the basis for a more principled approach to pre-pruning.

3. THE J-MEASURE

3.1 Measuring the Information Content of a Rule

The *J-measure* was introduced into the rule induction literature by Smyth and Goodman [8] as an information theoretic means of quantifying the information content of a rule that is soundly based on theory.

Given a rule of the form **If Y=y, then X=x**, using the notation of [8], the (average) information content of the rule, measured in bits of information, is denoted by J(X;Y=y). The value of this quantity is given by the equation

$$J(X;Y=y) = p(y).j(X;Y=y)$$

Thus the J-measure is the product of two terms:

- p(y) The probability that the hypothesis (antecedent of the rule) will occur - a measure of *hypothesis simplicity*
- j(X;Y=y) The *j-measure* (note the small letter 'j') or *cross-entropy* - a measure of the *goodness-of-fit* of a given rule.

The cross-entropy term is defined by the equation:

$$j(X;Y=y) = p(x \mid y).\log_2(\frac{p(x \mid y)}{p(x)}) + (1 - p(x \mid y)).\log_2(\frac{(1 - p(x \mid y))}{(1 - p(x))})$$

The maximum value of the J-measure can be shown to be $\frac{\log_2 e}{e}$, which is approximately 0.5307 bits.

Further information on the J-measure and its uses is given in [8].

In what follows, it will be taken as a working hypothesis that a rule with a high J value (i.e. high information content) is also likely to have a high level of predictive accuracy for previously unseen instances.

3.2 A J-measure Interpretation of Overfitting

The results given in [7] strongly suggest that, beyond a certain point, adding further terms to rules can become counter-productive because of overfitting. Analysing successive forms of a rule using the J-measure clarifies why this happens.

Taking the l*ens24* dataset for illustration, one of the rules generated is

IF tears=2 AND astig=1 AND age=3 AND specRx=1 THEN class=3

This has a J-value of 0.028 and seems a reasonable rule. However, by looking at the way the rule develops term-by-term a different picture emerges.

Reference [8] gives a formula for Jmax, an upper bound on the J value of any rule that can be obtained by *specialising* a given rule by adding further terms. After just one term, the rule and corresponding J and Jmax values were

IF tears=2 THEN class=3 (J=0.210, Jmax=0.531)

In general, specialising a rule by adding further terms may either increase or decrease the value of J (i.e. the information content). However the value of

Jmax gives the maximum J value that any possible specialisation of the rule may achieve. In this case Jmax = 0.531, so it seems appropriate to continue developing the rule. Adding the second term gives

IF tears=2 AND astig=1 THEN class=3 (J= 0.161, Jmax=0.295)

The J value has gone down from 0.210 to 0.161, but has the potential to increase again, possibly up to 0.295 by further specialisation. Adding the third and fourth terms completes the picture.

IF tears=2 AND astig=1 AND age=3 THEN class=3
(J= 0.004, Jmax=0.059)
IF tears=2 AND astig=1 AND age=3 AND specRx=1 THEN class=3
(J= 0.028, Jmax=0.028)

The combined effect of adding the three final terms has been to lower the J value (information content) of the rule by almost a factor of 10. If we assume that the J measure is a reliable indicator of the information content and thus the predictive accuracy of a rule, it would have been better to truncate the left-hand side of the rule after a single term. This would have led to more misclassified instances for the training data, but may have led to better predictive accuracy on unseen data.

4. USING J-PRUNING WITH TDIDT

4.1 J-Pruning

There are several ways in which J values can be used to aid classification tree generation. One method, which will be called *J-pruning*, is to prune a branch as soon as a node is generated at which the J value is less than that at its parent.

Looking at this in terms of partially completed rules, say there is an incomplete rule for the *lens24* dataset

(1) IF tears=2 AND astig=2 ....

Splitting on attribute specRx (which has two values) would add an additional term, making the incomplete rule

(2) IF tears=2 AND astig=2 AND specRx=1 ....
or

(3) IF tears=2 AND astig=2 AND specRx=2 ....

All the instances corresponding to branch (2) have the same classification, so the rule is completed with that classification in the usual way. However the instances corresponding to branch (3) have more than one classification.

The J-pruning technique now involves a comparison between the J-value of (3) and the J-value of (1). If the former is smaller, the rule is truncated and the instances are all classified as belonging to the class to which the largest number of instances belong. If not, the TDIDT algorithm continues by splitting on an attribute as usual.

The difficulty in implementing the above method is that the value of J depends partly on the class specified in the rule consequent, but when the partial rules (incomplete branches) are generated there is no way of knowing which class that will eventually be. A branch may be extended by TDIDT to have a large descendent subtree, obtained by subsequent splittings on attributes, with many leaf nodes each of which has its own classification.

If the rules had been truncated at (1) there are 3 possible ways in which all the instances could have been assigned to a single class. These are listed below with the corresponding values of J and Jmax

IF tears=2 AND astig=2 THEN class=1 (J = 0.223, Jmax = 0.431)
IF tears=2 AND astig=2 THEN class=2 (J = 0.084, Jmax = 0.084)
IF tears=2 AND astig=2 THEN class=3 (J = 0.063, Jmax = 0.236)

There are 3 possible ways in which the instances corresponding to (3) could be assigned to a single class:

IF tears=2 AND astig=2 AND specRx=2 THEN class=1
(J=0.015, Jmax=0.108)
IF tears=2 AND astig=2 AND specRx=2 THEN class=2
(J=0.042, Jmax=0.042)
IF tears=2 AND astig=2 AND specRx=2 THEN class=3
(J=0.001, Jmax=0.059)

If there are only two classes the value of J is the same whichever is taken. When there are more than two classes an effective heuristic is to use the largest of the possible J values in each case. Thus the J values for branches (1) and (3) are taken to be 0.223 and 0.042 respectively.

Since the value for (3) is lower than for (1), J-pruning takes place and branch (3) is truncated.

Table 1 shows the results obtained using J-pruning with a variety of datasets and the comparative figures for unpruned rules. The results were obtained using 10-fold cross-validation [7] in each case. The Information Gain attribute selection criterion is used throughout. The number of attributes and the percentage size of the largest class are also included for information.

Table 1. Comparison of Unpruned and J-pruned Rules for TDIDT

Dataset	Largest Class %	No. of Attributes	Number of Rules (No Pruning)	Accuracy (%) (No Pruning)	Number of Rules (With J-pruning)	Accuracy (%) (With J-pruning)
agaricus_lepiota	52	22	24.0	100.00	16.0	99.41
breast-cancer	66	9	93.2	89.84	66.5	91.27
chess	95	7	20.0	99.38	6.2	96.44
contact_lenses	88	5	16.0	92.55	8.3	92.64
genetics	52	60	357.4	89.22	25.9	78.15
lens24	63	4	8.4	70.00	6.2	70.00
monk1	50	6	37.8	83.91	14.4	67.76
monk2	62	6	88.4	43.82	21.3	55.66
monk3	51	6	26.5	86.92	12.5	90.90
soybean	13	35	106.9	88.74	29.6	76.87
vote	61	16	29.2	91.67	11.1	94.00
zoo	41	16	13.8	97.00	10.9	89.18
AVERAGE			68.5	86.09	19.1	83.52

The reduction in the number of rules is clearly considerable for many of the datasets (e.g. 357.4 to 25.9 for *genetics* and from 106.9 to 29.6 for *soybean*). On average the number of rules is reduced from 68.5 to only 19.1 for the 12 datasets. This again confirms that the basic (unpruned) form of TDIDT leads to substantial overfitting of rules to the instances in the training set. The predictive accuracy is higher with J-pruning for 5 of the datasets, lower for 6 and unchanged for one (the smallest dataset, *lens24*). On average the predictive accuracy is reduced by 2.5% but this may not be as important in practice as the substantial reduction in the number of rules and corresponding gain in simplicity of the classification rules generated.

The method of using the J-measure for pre-pruning adopted here has limitations that relate directly to the use of the decision tree representation imposed by TDIDT and are difficult to overcome in that framework.

The method prunes a branch as soon as a node is generated at which the J value is less than that at its parent. It would have been better if that branch had been pruned at the parent node instead, but doing so would also have removed all other descendant branches, possibly with damaging results.

The use of a decision tree representation for rules has previously been identified as itself a major cause of overfitting [3,4]. An example is given in [3] of two rules with no attribute in common which are equivalent to a complex decision tree almost all branches and terms of which are redundant.

It may prove more effective to incorporate J-pruning or other pre-pruning techniques into an algorithm such as Prism, which generates classification rules directly rather than through the intermediate representation of a decision tree.

5. ADDING J-PRUNING TO PRISM

5.1 PrismTCS

The version of Prism described in this paper is a modified form known as PrismTCS (standing for Prism with Target Class, Smallest first), which has been found to produce smaller sets of classification rules than the original form of the algorithm, with a similar level of predictive accuracy. In that form the training set is restored to its original state before the rules are generated for each class, thus requiring the full training set to be processed once for each of the classes.

(1) Find the class with fewest instances in the training set (ignoring any with none). Call this the *target class* TC.

(2) Calculate the probability that class = TC for each possible attribute-value pair *

(3) Select the attribute-value pair with the maximum probability and create a subset of the training set comprising all instances with the selected combination (for all classes)

(4) Repeat 2 and 3 for this subset until it contains only instances of class TC. The induced rule is then the conjunction of all the attribute-value pairs selected in creating this subset

(5) Remove all instances covered by this rule from the training set

Repeat 1-5 until there are no instances remaining in the training set

* Any attribute that is part of an attribute-value pair already selected should not be used again for the same rule

Figure 2. The PrismTCS Rule Generation Algorithm

Instead PrismTCS makes use of a *target class,* which varies from one rule to the next as shown in Figure 2.

With this form of the algorithm the full training set only needs to be processed once however many classes there are.

5.2 Using the J-measure to Prune Prism Classification Rules

At each stage of rule generation the J-value of the incomplete rule is calculated and recorded. If at any stage adding an additional term would lead to a decrease in the J-value, the term is discarded and the clash handling method described in Section 2.4 is invoked. This method is known as *J-pruning*.

The following table shows the number of rules generated and the corresponding predictive accuracy of PrismTCS with and without J-pruning for twelve datasets. The results were obtained using 10-fold cross-validation in each case.

It can be seen that the number of rules generated for the unpruned algorithm is on average significantly smaller for PrismTCS than for TDIDT. Nevertheless the use of J-Pruning with PrismTCS reduces the number of rules by more than one-third, with a substantial reduction from 87.7 rules to only 25.1 for *genetics* and a halving of the number of rules from 37.3 to 16.9 for *monk2*, in both cases accompanied by an increase in predictive accuracy. The predictive accuracy is larger for the J-pruned rule sets in seven cases and smaller for only three. On average there is a small increase in predictive accuracy despite the substantially reduced number of rules.

Table 2. Comparison of Unpruned and J-pruned Rules for PrismTCS

Dataset	Largest Class %	No. of Attributes	Number of Rules	Accuracy (%)	Number of Rules	Accuracy (%)
			No Pruning		With J-Pruning	
agaricus_lepiota	52	22	11.9	100.00	11.9	100.00
breast-cancer	66	9	37.8	93.99	33.2	95.28
chess	95	7	7.9	99.38	3.6	97.98
contact_lenses	88	5	8.6	88.73	6.6	89.82
genetics	52	60	87.7	90.88	25.1	93.48
lens24	63	4	6.5	55.00	6.4	58.33
monk1	50	6	14.0	87.56	10.8	88.46
monk2	62	6	37.3	50.18	16.9	59.71
monk3	51	6	15.2	85.32	13.6	83.65
soybean	13	35	64.9	90.63	51.5	92.98
vote	61	16	21.6	92.33	11.0	91.00
zoo	41	16	10.4	92.09	9.7	92.09
AVERAGE			27.0	85.51	16.69	86.90

6. CONCLUSIONS

This paper has demonstrated the potential value of using the information-theoretic J-measure as the basis for reducing overfitting by pre-pruning rules as they are generated. The J-pruning technique illustrated works well in practice for a range of datasets, both with the decision tree representation of TDIDT and even more successfully with PrismTCS, an algorithm that directly generates classification rules from examples. Unlike many other possible measures, the J-measure has a sound theoretical foundation as a measure of the information content of rules.

REFERENCES

[1] Hunt, E.B., Marin J. and Stone, P.J. (1966). Experiments in Induction. Academic Press

[2] Quinlan, J.R. (1993). C4.5: Programs for Machine Learning. Morgan Kaufmann

[3] Cendrowska, J. (1987). PRISM: an Algorithm for Inducing Modular Rules. International Journal of Man-Machine Studies, 27, pp. 349-370

[4] Bramer, M.A. (2000). Automatic Induction of Classification Rules from Examples Using N-Prism. In: Research and Development in Intelligent Systems XVI. Springer-Verlag, pp. 99-121

[5] Bramer, M.A. (1997). Rule Induction in Data Mining: Concepts and Pitfalls. Data Warehouse Report, No. 10, pp. 11-17 and No. 11, pp. 22-27

[6] Mingers, J. (1989). An Empirical Comparison of Pruning Methods for Decision Tree Induction. Machine Learning, 4, pp. 227-243

[7] Bramer, M.A. (2002). Using J-Pruning to Reduce Overfitting in Classification Trees. In: Research and Development in Intelligent Systems XVIII. Springer-Verlag, pp. 25-38.

[8] Smyth, P. and Goodman, R.M. (1991). Rule Induction Using Information Theory. In: Piatetsky-Shapiro, G. and Frawley, W.J. (eds.), Knowledge Discovery in Databases. AAAI Press, pp. 159-176

A USER-CENTERED VISUAL APPROACH TO DATA MINING

THE SYSTEM D2MS

Tu Bao Ho, Trong Dung Nguyen, Duc Dung Nguyen
Japan Advanced Institute of Science and Technology
Tatsunokuchi, Ishikawa 923-1292, Japan

Abstract: We present a human-centered approach to model selection in machine learning and data mining that emphasizes and facilitates the active participation of the user in the knowledge discovery process with quantitative and qualitative evaluation of patterns/models. The key idea of such a model selection is it would result from a combination of a quantitative evaluation of model characteristics and performance metrics with a qualitative evaluation of patterns/model by the user. We develop data mining methods integrated with visualization tools in the user-centered visual system D2MS (Data Mining with Model Selection). We finally present a case-study of D2MS in mining stomach cancer data.

Key words: data mining, user-centered, visualization, model selection.

1. INTRODUCTION

The problem of *model selection* in machine learning and data mining—choosing appropriate learned models or algorithms and their settings for obtaining such models in a given application—is non-trivial and difficult because it requires empirical comparative evaluation of discovered models and meta-knowledge on models/algorithms.

Finding interesting patterns/models hidden in data is the objective of data mining. The interestingness of discovered patterns/models can be seen as a function of four criteria: validity, simplicity, usefulness, and novelty. Among these components, data mining systems can judge only the validity and simplicity of discovered patterns/models (e.g., the accuracy and support of rules), but only the user can evaluate their usefulness and novelty. However, it can be observed that the support for the user in evaluation has received inadequate attention in the data mining community [1].

Though visualization techniques have progressed dramatically in the last decade, it can be seen that visual knowledge discovery still remains in its infancy [2], [3], [6]. Most data mining systems do not yet take advantage of visualization techniques, or visualization techniques still usually reside at the beginning and at the end of the knowledge discovery process [4].

In this paper we present a user-centered approach to data mining with visualization support for model selection, and the visual data mining system D2MS (Data Mining with Model Selection) that provides visualization integrated into the KDD process. We illustrate the approach and D2MS by a case-study in medical application.

2. VISUALIZATION SUPPORT FOR USER-CENTERED MODEL SELECTION

Recognizing the importance of the user in the knowledge discovery process [1], we have focused on a user-centered approach to knowledge discovery. Fig. 1 illustrates the basic idea of this approach in which the user plays a central role in the knowledge discovery process with the support of visualization tools.

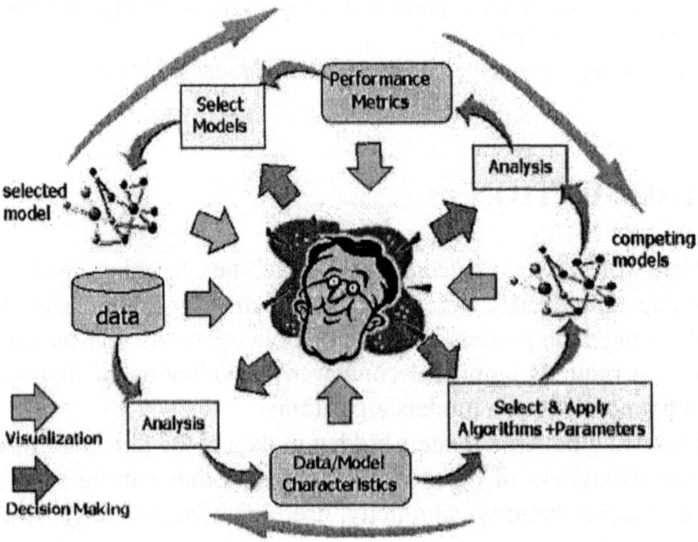

Fig. 1: The key idea of user-centered data mining with support for model selection and visualization

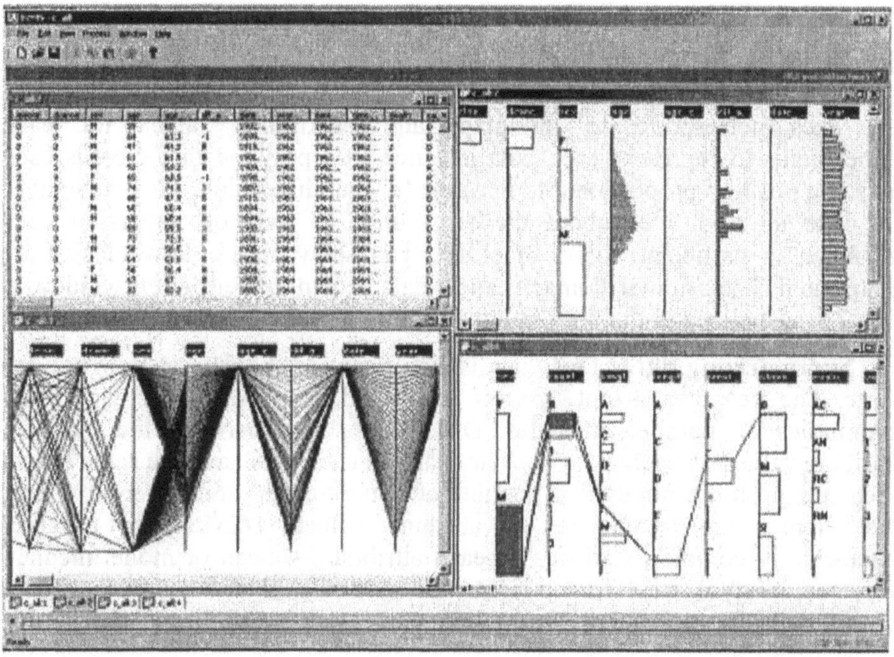

Figure 2. Data visualization in D2MS: The top-left window shows the dataset, the bottom-left window shows the original data view, the top-right window shows summarizing data view, and the bottom-right window shows the querying data view.

This user-centered approach requires an active participation of the user in the learning/mining process with both quantitative and qualitative evaluation of patterns/models. We have developed the user-centered visual data mining system D2MS to support such an active participation of the user in which the visualization module is linked to all other modules relating to model selection [5]. This visualization module consists of a data visualizer, a rule visualizer, and a tree visualizer. These visualizers are integrated to most methods available in D2MS for preprocessing, data mining, and postprocessing. We describe each visualizer with focus on its techniques and how it is linked to the steps in the KDD process.

2.1 Data Visualization

D2MS improves parallel coordinates [2] in several ways to adapt them to the knowledge discovery context. It is because when viewing a large dataset with many attributes, particularly categorical attributes, the advantage of parallel coordinates may lose as many polylines or their parts are partially overlapped, and certain kinds of summarization might be needed. Also, the user often needs to see subsets of the dataset in terms of cases and/or attributes.

Viewing original data. The basic idea of viewing a p-dimensional dataset by parallel coordinates is to use p equally spaced axes—which are parallel to one of the screen axes and correspond to attributes and the ends of the axes correspond to minimum and maximum values for each dimension—to represent each data instance as a polyline that crosses each axis at a position proportional to its value for that dimension. This view gives the user a rough idea about the distribution of data on values of each attribute; in particular colors of classes can show clearly how classes are distributed. The original stomach cancer data shown in the top-left window in Fig. 2 is visualized in the bottom-left window.

Summarizing data. This view is significant as the dataset may be very large. The key idea is not to view original data points but to view their summaries on parallel attributes. D2MS uses bar charts in the place of attribute values on each axis. The bar charts in each axis have the same height (depending on the number of possible attribute values) and different widths that signify the frequencies of attribute values. D2MS also provides interactively common statistics on each attribute as mean or mode, median, variance, boxplot, etc. The top-right window in Fig. 2 shows the summaries of the stomach cancer data.

Querying data. This view serves the hypothesis generation and hypothesis testing manually. It allows the user to view subsets of the dataset determined by queries. There are three types of queries: (i) based on a value of the class attribute where the query determines the subset of all instances belonging to the indicated class; (ii) based on a value of a descriptive attribute where the query determines the subset of all instances having this value, (iii) based on a conjunction of attribute-values pairs where the query determines the subset of all instances satisfied this conjunction. The subset of instances matched a query is visualized in viewing data mode and in summarizing data mode. The gray regions on each axis show the proportions of specified instances on values of this attribute as visualized in the bottom-right window in Fig. 2.

2.2 Rule Visualization

A rule is a pattern related to several attribute-values and a subset of instances. The importance in visualizing a rule is how this local structure is viewed in its relation to the whole dataset, and how the view supports the user's evaluation of the rule interestingness. D2MS's rule visualizer allows the user to visualize rules in the form *antecedent→consequent* where *antecedent* is a conjunction of attribute-value pairs, *consequent* is a conjunction of attribute-value pairs in case of association rules, and is a value of the class attribute in case of prediction rules. A rule is simply displayed by a subset of parallel coordinates included in *antecedent* and *consequent*. The D2MS's rule visualizer has the following functions:

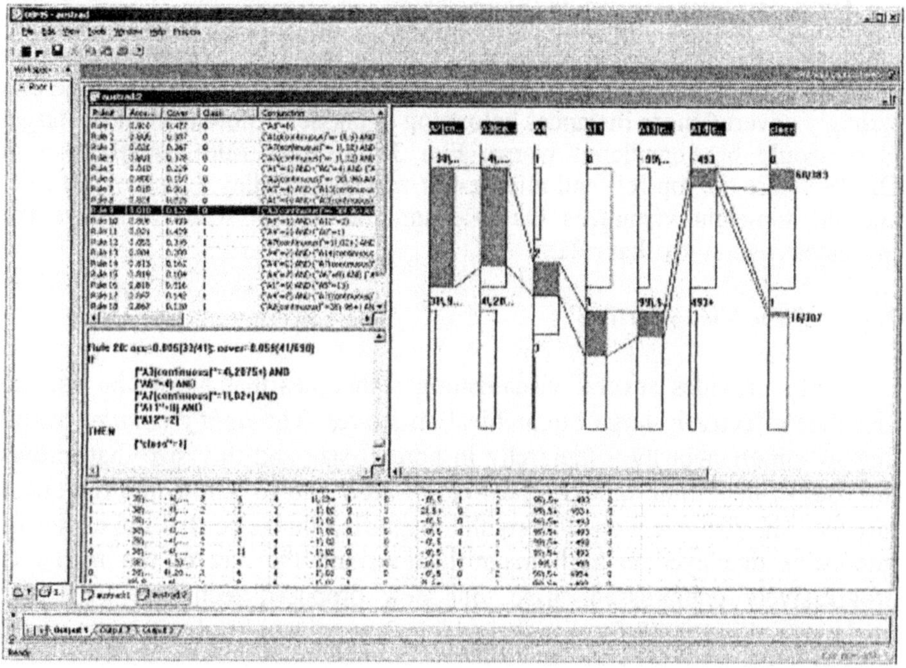

Figure 3. Rule Visualization in D2MS: The top-left window shows the list of discovered rules with a highlighted rule, the middle-left window shows this rule content, the top-right window visualizes the rule by parallel coordinates, the bottom window shows the set of instances covered by the rule.

Viewing rules. Each rule is displayed by polylines that goes through the axes containing attribute-values occurred on the antecedent part of the rule leading to the consequent part of the rule that are displayed with different color. In the case of prediction rules, the ratio associated with each class in the class attribute corresponds to the number of instances of the class covered by the rule over the total number of instances in the class.

Viewing rules and data together. The subset of instances covered by a rule is visualized together with the rule by parallel coordinates or by summaries on parallel coordinates. From this subset of instances, the user can see the set of rules each of them cover some of these instances, or the user can smoothly change the values of an attribute in the rule to see other related possible rules. These possible operations facilitate the user in evaluating the quality of this rule: a rule is good if instances covered by it are not recognized by other rules, and vice-versa. The rules for a class can be displayed together, and all instances covered by these rules are displayed.

Rule visualization in model selection. There are several ways that support the user in evaluating the quality of the rule together with other measure such as coverage and accuracy of the rule. For example, two rules predicting a target class having the same support and confidence but the one wrongly covered more instances belonging to classes different from the target class would be considered worse. Fig. 3 illustrates rule visualization in D2MS where the top-left and middle-left windows display a discovered rule, and the top-right visualizes the rule and the bottom window shows the instances covered by that rule.

2.3 Tree Visualization

D2MS provides several visualization techniques that allow the user to visualize effectively large hierarchical structures. The *tightly coupled views* display simultaneously a hierarchy in normal size and tiny size that allows the user to determine quickly the field-of-view and to pan to the region of interest. The *fish-eye view* distorts the magnified image so that the center of interest is displayed at high magnification, and the rest of the image is progressively compressed. Also, our new proposed technique *T2.5D* is implemented in D2MS for visualizing very large hierarchical structures.

Different modes of viewing hierarchical structures. The D2MS tree visualizer provides multiple-views of trees or hierarchical structures.

- *Tightly coupled views*: The global view (on the left) shows the tree structure with nodes in same small size without labels and therefore it can display a tree fully or a large part of it, depending on the tree size. The detailed view (on the right) shows the tree structure and nodes with their labels associated with operations to display node information. The global view is associated with a field-of-view or panner (a wire-frame box) that corresponds to the detailed view. These two views are tightly coupled as the field-of-view can be moved around in the global view in order to pan the detailed view. Also, when the detailed view is scrolled the position of the field-of-view will be updated accordingly. The user can resize windows for these views, and the field-of-view shape and size will be automatically changed. The top-left and top-right windows in Figure 3 show the tightly coupled views of D2MS for the stomach cancer data.

- *Customizing views*: Initially, according to the user's choice, the tree is either displayed fully or with only the root node and its direct sub-nodes. The tree then can be collapsed or expanded partially or fully from the root or from any intermediate node.

• *Tiny mode with fish-eye view*: Note that no current visualization technique allows us to display efficiently the entire tree when it has, says, ten thousands nodes. The tightly coupled views are extended with three viewing modes according to the user's choice: normal size, small size and tiny size. The tiny mode uses much more efficiently the space to visualize the tree structure, on which the user can determine quickly the field-of-view and pan to the region of interest. It allows the user to be able to see the tree structure while focusing on any particular part so that the relationship of parts to the whole can be seen and the focus can be moved to other parts in a smooth and continuous way.

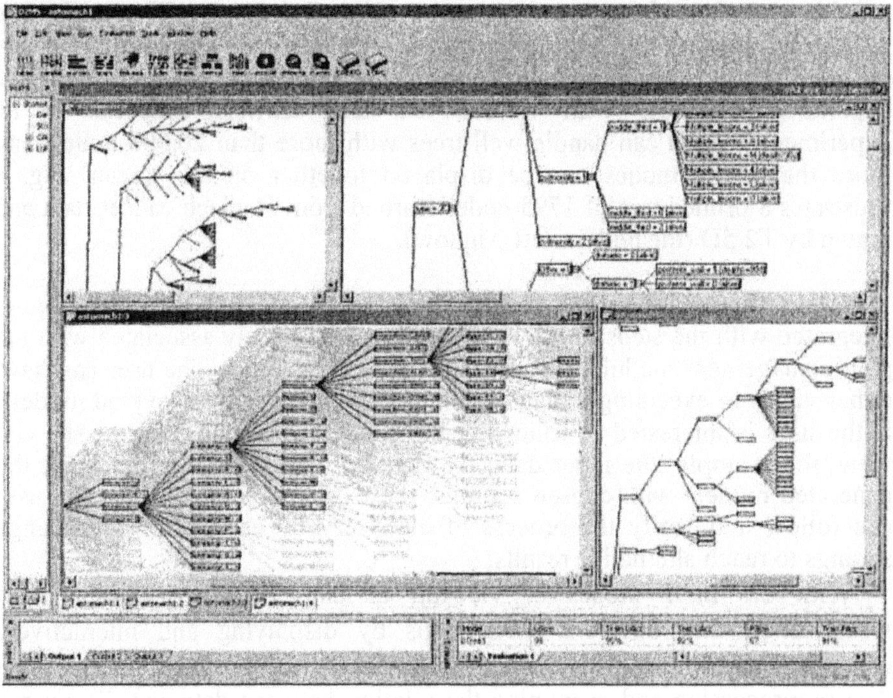

Figure 4. Multiple views of trees: Tightly coupled, fish-eye, overall, and T2.5D views.

• *Trees 2.5 Dimensions.* The user might find it difficult to navigate a very large hierarchy, even with tightly coupled and fish-eye views. To overcome this difficulty, we have been developing a new technique called T2.5D (stands for Trees 2.5 Dimensions) [5]. Different from tightly-coupled and fish-eye views that can be seen as location-based views, T2.5D can be seen as a relation-based view in the sense that highlighted parts of a tree are relations determined by queries. The starting point of T2.5D is the observation that a large tree consists many subtrees that are not usually and necessarily viewed simultaneously. The key idea of T2.5D is to represent a large tree in a virtual 3D space (subtrees are overlapped to reduce occupied space) while each subtree of interest is displayed in a 2D space.

To this end, T2.5D determines the fixed position of each subtree (its root node) in two axes X and Y, and in addition, it computes dynamically a Z-order for this subtree in an imaginary axis Z.

A subtree with a given Z-order is displayed "above" its siblings those have higher Z-orders. When visualizing and navigating a tree, at each moment the Z-order of all nodes on the path from the root to a *node in focus* in the tree is set to zero by T2.5D. The *active wide path* to a node in focus, which contains all nodes on the path from the root to this node in focus and their siblings, is displayed in the front of the screen with highlighted colors to give the user a clear view. Other parts of the tree remain in the background to provide an image of the overall structure. With Z-order, T2.5D can give the user an impression that trees are drawn in a 3D space. The user can easily change the active wide path by choosing another node in focus. We have experimented T2.5D with various real and artificial datasets. In an experiment, T2.5D can handle well trees with more than 20,000 nodes, and more than 1,000 nodes can be displayed together on the screen. Fig. 4 illustrates a pruned tree of 1795 nodes learned from stomach cancer data and drawn by T2.5D (the bottom-left window).

Tree Visualization in Model Selection. In D2MS, visualization is integrated with the steps of the KDD process and closely associated with the plan management module in support for model selection. The user can have either views in executing a plan or comparative views of discovered models. If the user is interested in following the execution of one plan, he/she can view, for example, the input data, the derived data after preprocessing, the generated models with chosen settings, the exported results. Thus, the user can follow and verify the process of discovery by each plan, and change settings to reach alternative results.

With the three modes of viewing of data, D2MS integrates data visualization into different KDD steps by displaying and interactively changing these views of data at any time. Data visualization supports doing data preprocessing and examining the relation between data and discovered knowledge. In the first step of collecting data and formulating the problem, the user can and often need to view the original dataset and its summarization. The visual analysis of collected data may help the user to identify important or redundant attributes or new attributes to be added. The data visualization has shown to be significant in the data preprocessing step that consists of functions on data cleaning, integration, transformation and reduction. Many discretization algorithms provide alternative solution of dividing a numerical attribute into intervals, where the visual data query on the discretized attribute and the class attribute can give insights for decision.

The data visualization is also very significant in data mining step with data query mode, and particularly in the evaluation step in its synergistic combination with rule and tree visualization. If the user is interested in comparative evaluation of competing models generated by different plans, he/she can have multiple views on these models. The user can compare performance metrics of all activated plans that are always available in the summary table. Whenever the user highlights a row in the table, the associated model will be automatically displayed. Several windows can be opened simultaneously to display competing models in forms of trees, concept hierarchies, or rule sets. For example, two rules predicting a target class having the same support and confidence but the one wrongly covered more instances belonging to classes different from the target class would be considered worse (Figure 6).

3.ACTIVE PARTICIPATION OF THE USER IN MINING STOMACH CANCER DATA

3.1 The dataset

The stomach cancer dataset collected at the National Cancer Center (NCC) in Tokyo during the period 1962-1991 is a very precious source for the research. It contains data of 7,520 patients described originally by 83 numeric and categorical attributes. These include information on patients, symptoms, type of cancer, longitudinal and circular location, metastasis, pre-operative complication, post-operative complication, etc.

One problem is to use of attributes containing patient information before operation to predict the patient status after the operation. The domain experts are particularly interested in finding predictive and descriptive rules for the class of patients who "death within 90 days" after operation among totally 5 classes ("alive", "death after 5 years", "death after 90 days", "death within 90 days", "unknown"). This class has only 302 available cases from the total 6,712 cases in the dataset (4%). We face here with the problem of mining *minority classes in imbalanced datasets* that is very popular in medicine.

3.2 Mining stomach cancer data with D2MS

The task of extracting patterns/models from unbalanced datasets in general, and from the class "death within 90 days" in particular, is very difficult because of such a class distribution and there is no sharp boundary between this target class and the others. The NCC experts evaluate discovered patterns/models by three criteria of "acceptability", "novelty", and "utility" with points from 1 (lowest) to 5 (highest).

We first applied well-known and popular data mining methods such as CBA [7], C4.5 [8] and its commercial version See5 to this task. However, the obtained results were far from expectation. We could not find a trade off between support and confidence to discover rules. Moreover, discovered rules usually cover less than a half of patients of the target class. Also, it happens that the found rules are often acceptable (5 points) in terms of validity but not new (1 point) to the domain experts and thus are not interesting to them.

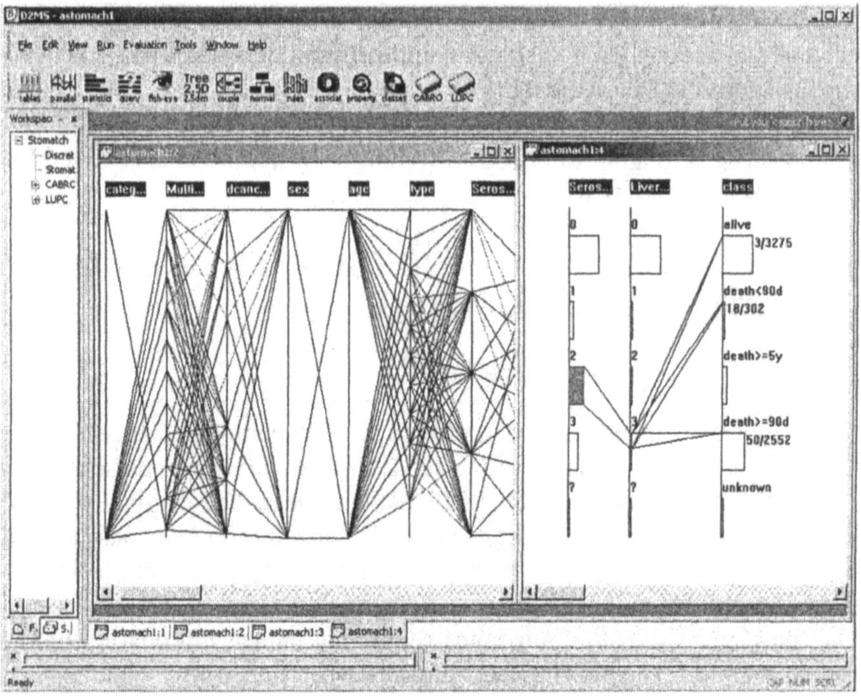

Figure 5. Data visualization supports finding unusual phenomena.

LUPC (Learning Unbalanced Positive Class) is our data mining method implemented in D2MS [5] to deal with the problem of mining in unbalanced datasets. It can find efficiently prediction and description rules by allowing the user (1) to vary its parameters and search strategies to detect possible rules with different values of support and accuracy, (2) to impose constraints on discovered patterns/models.

The visualization tools in D2MS allow the us to examine interactively the data and to gain better insight into complex data. The summarizing and querying modes can suggest hypotheses to be investigated. An illustration of identifying unusual phenomena is shown in Fig. 5. It is known that patients who have symptoms of "liver metastasis" of all levels 1, 2, or 3 will not be able to survive. Also, "serosal invasion = 3" is a typical symptom of the class "death within 90 days". With the visualization tools, we found several unusual events such as 5 of 2329 patients in class "alive" have heavy metastasis of level 3; as well 1 and 8 of them are of metastasis level 2 and 1, respectively. Moreover, the querying data allow us to verify some significant combination of symptoms such as "liver metastasis = 3" and "serosal invasion = 3" as shown in Fig. 5.

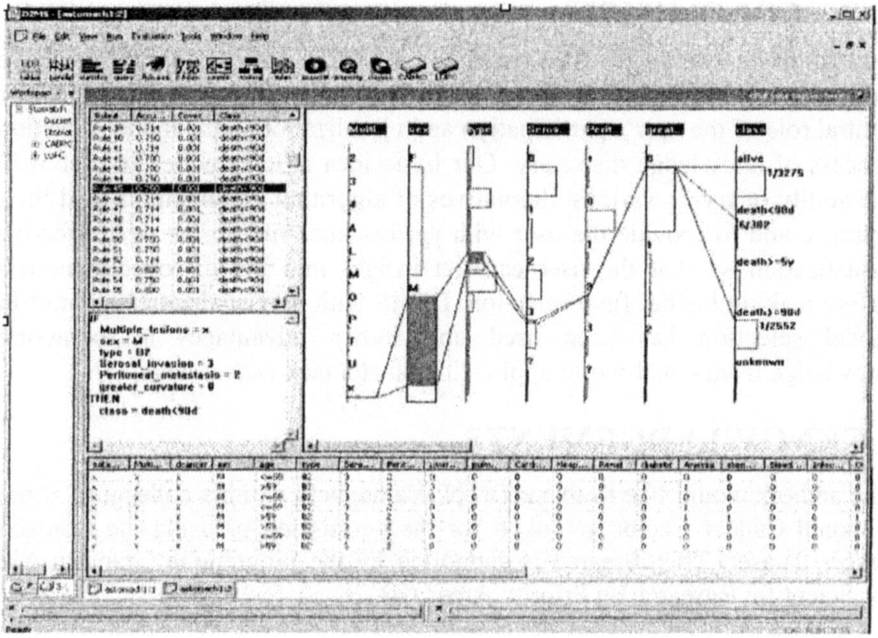

Figure 6. Rule visualization supports the user in evaluating discovered knowledge.

Using visual interactive D2MS we have tried different trials with varying parameters and constraints to find only rules that do not contain the characterized attribute "liver metastasis" and/or its combination with other two typical attributes "Peritoneal metastasis", "Serosal invasion" (Fig. 6). Below is a rule with accuracy 100% discovered by D2MS that brings new and *irregular* patterns in the class "death with 90 days".

```
Rule 8:   accuracy = 1.0 (4/4), cover = 0.001 (4/6712)
IF        category = R AND sex = F AND proximal_third = 3 AND
          middle_third = 1
THEN      class = death within 90 days
```

Thank to the supported interaction with D2MS we can also discover *rare* patterns. D2MS allow us examine effectively the hypothesis space and identify rare rules with any small given support or confidence. An example is to find rules in class "alive" that contain the symptom "liver metastasis". Such patterns are certainly rare and influence the human decision making. We found events in the class "alive" such as male patients getting "liver metastasis" at serious level 3 who can survive with the accuracy of 50%.

```
Rule 1:   accuracy = 0.500 (2/4); cover = 0.001(4/6712)
IF        sex = M AND type = B1 AND liver_metastasis = 3 AND
          middle_third = 1
```

THEN class = alive

4. CONCLUSION

We have presented the visualization techniques in the knowledge discovery system D2MS for supporting model selection. We emphasize the central role of the user's participation and visualization in the model selection process of knowledge discovery. Our basic idea is to provide the user with the ability of trying various alternatives of algorithm combinations and their settings, and to provide the user with performance metrics as well effective visualization so that the user can get insight into the discovered models before making his/her final selection. D2MS with its visualization support in model selection has been used and shown advantages in extracting knowledge from a real-world application on stomach cancer data.

ACKNOWLEDGEMENTS

The authors would like to thank Dr. N. Yamaguchi and his colleagues at the National Cancer Center in Tokyo for the permission of using the stomach cancer dataset. This research is supported by the programme Grand-in-Aid for Scientific Research on Priority Areas (B).

REFERENCES

[1] Brachman, R. and Anand, T., "The Process of Knowledge Discovery in Databases", in *Advanced in Knowledge Discovery and Data Mining*, Fayyad, U. et al. (Eds.), Morgan Kaufmann, 1996, 38-57.

[2] Card, S. K., Mackinlay, J. D., and Shneiderman, B., *Readings in Information Visualization,* Morgan Kaufmann, 1999.

[3] Fayyad, U.M., Grinstein. G.G., and Wierse, A. *Information Visualization in Data Mining and Knowledge Discovery, Morgan Kaufmann,* 2002.

[4] Han, J. and Cercone, N., *Visualizing the Process of Knowledge Discovery, J. of Electronic Imaging*, No. 4, 404-420, 2000.

[5] Ho, T.B., Nguyen, T.D., Nguyen, D.D., and Kawasaki, S., "Visualization Support for User-Centered Model Selection in Knowledge Discovery and Data Mining", *International Journal of Artificial Intelligence Tools*, Vol. 10, No. 4, 691-713, 2001.

[6] Keim D. A. and Kriegel H.P., "Visualization Techniques for Mining Large Databases: A Comparison", *J. IEEE Transactions on Knowledge and Data Engineering*, 923-938, 1996.

[7] Liu, B., Hsu, W., and Ma, Y., "Integrating Classification and Association Rule Mining", *Fourth Int. Conf. on Knowledge Discovery and Data Mining KDD'98,* 80-86, 1998.

[8] Quinlan, R., C4.5: *Programs for Machine Learning*, Morgan Kaufmann, 1993.

ONTOCOPI
Methods and Tools for Identifying Communities of Practice

Harith Alani, Kieron O'Hara and Nigel Shadbolt
Intelligence, Agents, Multimedia Group
Dept. of Electronics and Computer Science
University of Southampton

Abstract: The paper describes ONTOCOPI, a tool for identifying communities of practice (COPs) by analysing ontologies of the relevant working domain. COP identification is currently a resource-heavy process largely based on interviews. ONTOCOPI attempts to uncover informal COP relations by spotting patterns in the formal relations represented in ontologies, traversing the ontology from instance to instance via selected relations. Experiments to determine particular COPs from an academic ontology are described, showing how the alteration of threshold and temporal settings, and the weights applied to the ontology's relations affect the composition of the identified COP.

Key words: ontologies, communities of practice, network analysis, distributed knowledge management, corporate memory

1. INTRODUCTION

Communities of practice (COPs) are informal self-organising groups of individuals interested in a particular practice. Membership is not often conscious; members will typically swap war stories, insights or advice on particular problems or tasks connected with the practice (Wenger 1998). An example of a COP might be the set of people in an organisation who do the same (or overlapping) jobs. They understand each other's problems, both with the job itself and with liaison with the outside world. A *de facto* community gradually emerges from their discussions and interests.

COPs can therefore take on a number of important roles for organisations. They may (a) act as corporate memories, (b) transfer best practice, (c) provide mechanisms for situated learning of the practice, and (d) act as foci for innovation. For individuals, the COP promotes the smooth integration of the practice with daily working life. For an example where COPs have been exploited in knowledge management, see the experience of Schlumberger (Smith and Farquhar 2000).

However, COPs are difficult to identify within organisations – an essential first step to understanding the knowledge resources of an organisation (Wenger 1999, McDermott 1999). In this paper we describe ONTOCOPI, the ONTOlogy-based Community Of Practice Identifier, a tool which uses ontology-based network analysis to support the task of COP identification. As a first cut proxy for a COP, we look for the set of most similar instances to a selected instance in the knowledge-base (i.e the instances that have most in common). ONTOCOPI was built as part of the Advanced Knowledge Technologies (AKT 2001) project.

Considerations of space in this paper preclude a deep discussion of the theory underlying ONTOCOPI. For such a discussion see (O'Hara et al 2002).

The structure of the paper is as follows. Section 2 will briefly examine the issues relating to the use of ontologies of working domains to identify COPs, while section 3 will then set out the principles underlying ONTOCOPI. Sections 4 and 5 will then discuss the current and future refinements of ONTOCOPI's performance.

2. EXPLOITING ONTOLOGIES FOR COMMUNITIES OF PRACTICE

ONTOCOPI is a tool for *ontology-based network analysis* (ONA). By an ontology we refer to the classification structure and the knowledge-base of instantiations. If an ontology represents the objects and relations in a domain of work, then it can be analysed to extract the connections between entities in that domain. A COP is defined by certain relations between entities relating to that practice, and so the aim of ONTOCOPI is to extract patterns of such relations.

The advantage of using an ontology to analyse such networks is that relations have semantics or types. Hence certain relations – the ones relevant to the COP – can be favoured in the process of analysis. During the analysis the weight of the contribution made by the important relations is high, while that of the less important ones can be made relatively low, or zero.

We discuss ONA in more detail in (O'Hara et al 2002). There are some important points to note here, though. First, the effectiveness of ONA for COP identification is dependent to a large extent on the content on the ontology and the properties of the COP. The choice of ontology therefore is an important step.

The essence of a COP is that it is an informal set of relations; ontologies will be wholly or largely made up of formal relations. By 'formal' here we mean relations that are determinate, fixed and cheap to establish/monitor, such as the relation of being a member of a group, being the author of a paper, having a particular telephone number. By 'informal' we mean relations that are often indeterminate and expensive to establish, such as a tendency to have a drink together after work. The ONTOCOPI hypothesis is that such informal relations can be inferred from the presence of formal relations. For instance, if A and B have no formal relation, but they have both authored papers (formal relation) with C, then that indicates that they might share interests (informal relation).

3. ONTOCOPI

The AKT ontology is implemented in Protégé 2000 (Eriksson et al 1999). ONTOCOPI plugs into Protégé and uses the ontology as its raw material. For more on the AKT ontology, see (O'Hara et al 2002). The user interface is shown in *Figure 1*. The left hand panel shows the ontology, to allow the user to select a class; second on the left displays the class instances, allowing an instance to be selected. Top right shows the available relations. The user selects the relations that he feels will be important in COP identification, and gives these weights depending on their relative importance (this can be done automatically – see below); selected relations and weights are displayed in the middle right panel. Controls at the bottom right allow the user to determine threshold and temporal settings.

When the user clicks the 'Get COP' button, a spreading activation search on the ontology moves from the selected instance to other instances connected to it by the selected relations, up to a maximum number of links set as part of the threshold settings (see Section 3.2). Weights of linked instances are calculated and results are displayed in the third column. Currently there is no restriction of the type of object that can appear in a COP. One may want to find the COP of a person, and the COP may largely be made up of instances of the class 'person'. However, it may be desired to find the COP associated with, say, a particular journal, or subject area, or research group; type restrictions would prevent a search being done on such items.

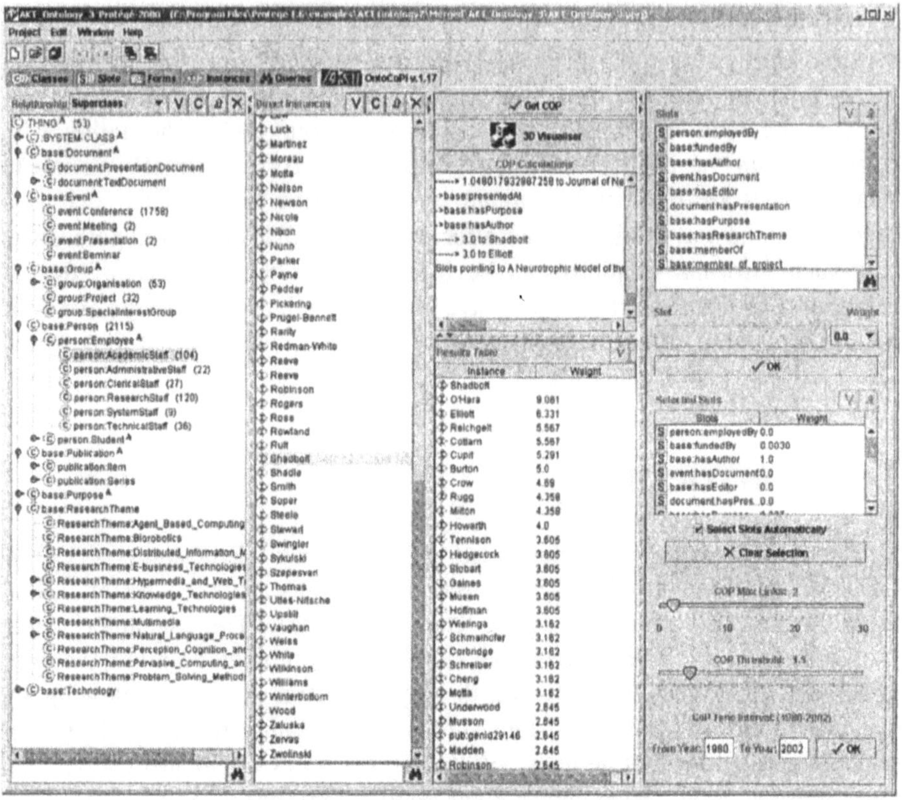

Figure 1. ONTOCOPI's User Interface

3.1 Relation and Weight Selection

Selecting the relations and weights can be manual or automatic. The system allows the user to select the relationships of interest, and weight them as needed. For example if the user is interested in peoples' collaboration on projects and co-authorships, then the relations *memberOfProject*, *hasAuthor*, and *publishedIn* can be selected. The user can then set weights for these relations to increase or decrease their impact on the COP to be identified. The less weight a relation is given, the less its impact will be.

The advantage of this approach is that users have total control on which relationships to traverse and how they should be weighted. But the user needs to know what the relationships represent, and have an idea of how important they are for his purposes. The effect of a relation's weight on the results is not only proportional to the weight of the other selected relations, but also on the number of these relations in the ontology. In other words, the more a relation is used, the greater its effect on results because it will be traversed more often than other relations.

The system can also select relations and calculate their weights automatically based on the frequency of use of these relations in the ontology, which is taken as an indication of the level of importance of those relations to that ontology, and whether the ontology is good or weak in providing information related to certain relationships. Ontologies are normally unevenly populated. Our experience shows that when an ontology is populated with instances, certain relations will normally be used more than others; some relations might not be used at all (i.e. the slot has been created but not filled in for any instance). This is normally due to the unavailability of certain information, or that different information has different levels of importance reflected in the amount of effort given to collecting and adding it to the ontology. This approach of selecting relations bypasses problems about user uncertainty, but equal frequency of use may only be a partial measure of its relevance to a user's interests.

3.2 The Algorithm

The expansion algorithm generates the COP of the selected instance (this is a person in our experiments, but could be any type of object) by identifying the set of close instances and ranking them according to the weights of their relations. It applies a breadth first, spreading activation search, traversing the semantic relations between instances (ignoring directionality) until the link threshold is reached. Starting with a weight of 1 for all instances, it transfers weights to all other instances following a set of weighted relations. The pseudocode is given in *Figure* 2; where n is the number of links traversed to reach the instance starting from the primary instance.

Consider the example in *Figure 3*. Assume we need to identify the COP of the query instance *A*, using the relationships *hasAuthor*, *memberOf* and *attended*, with the weights 1.0, 0.6, and 0.3 respectively. All instances will have an initial weight of 1. Activation will spread from the query instance to neighbouring instances in the network, up to a given number of links. In the first expansion, the query instance *A* will pass on weight to all the instances it is connected to. The amount of weight passed equals the weight of the instance multiplied by the weight of the traversed relationship. In this case, *A* passes 1*0.6 to *D*, and 1*1 to *H*. These will be added to their initial weights of 1. In return, these instances will pass their total weights to all their neighbours, so *D* for example will pass (1+1*0.6)*0.6 to *B* and *A*. Expansion will stop when the link paths are exhausted or the link threshold is reached (in the algorithm, locking/unlocking instances prevent feedback loops continuing till the link threshold is reached). Results are then raised to the power 1/n to normalise them according to their link-distance, where *n* is the minimum number of links traversed to reach the instance starting from the query instance. Instances therefore accumulate weight based on the number of relevant relations they have with the initial instance.

```
Initialise all instances weights to 1
Create a relationship-array of selected relationships and weights
Set query instance as the current instance
Mark current instance as unlocked and add it to an instance-array
Loop to the maximum number of links to traverse
  Search for the first unlocked instance in instance-array
  If found:
    Mark instance as locked
    Set instance as the current instance
    Get all instances connected to current instance with a
          relationship in the relationship-array
    Loop to number of connected instances
      If instance not in instance-array (new instance)
         Weight of instance = initial weight + current instance
                              weight * weight of connecting
                              relationship
         Mark instance as unlocked and add it to instance-array
      If instance already in instance array
         Weight of instance = instance weight + current instance
                              weight * weight of connecting
                              relationship
    End loop
  If not found then exit
End loop
Normalise all weights to the power 1/n
Rank instance-array according to instance final weights
```

Figure 2. The ONTOCOPI Algorithm in Pseudocode

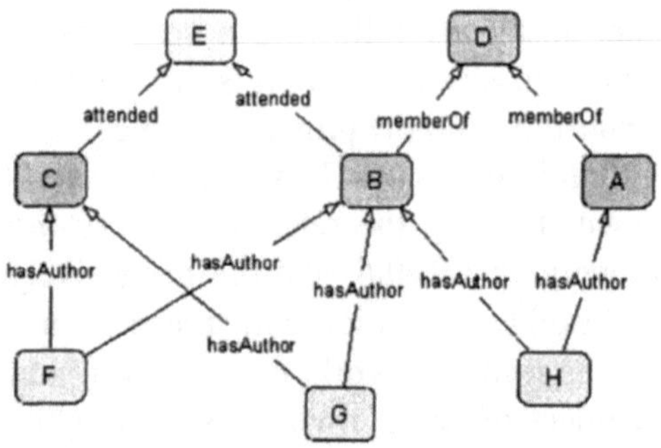

Figure 3. Example Ontology Network

The number of links to expand has an important effect on the COP results. The algorithm attempts to identify the instances with most in common with the query instance within a boundary defined by the given link-threshold. If expansion is limited to one link only then all identified instances will have a direct relation to the query instance. As the number of links increases, so will the number of instances which only have an indirect link with the query instance.

The number of indirectly-linked instances will also increase if *hubs* appear in the connected network. Hubs are highly-connected instances, and are very influential. They often score high ranks in the identified COPs as they receive high weights accumulated from their many connections. The drawback of this is that a high percentage of a hub's weight can be propagated to some of its connected instances which in turn will earn an 'unjustified' high rank in the COP. One possible approach to take is to compensate the weight to be passed from an instance based on the number of connections the instance has. The more connections an instance has, the more general it is considered to be, and hence the less weight it can transfer.

In terms of its intellectual roots, the ONTOCOPI algorithm takes ideas derived from the literature on similarity measures and applies them to the context of ONA. It builds on an approach introduced by Paice (1991) where relevance values of instances increase with the number of semantic paths leading to these instances. The algorithm however is different to Paice's in that relationship direction is ignored, since ontological relationships can be represented bi-directionally (e.g. *has-author* vs *authored-by*).

Furthermore, ONTOCOPI's algorithm allows an instance to transfer some weight back to its "source" instance, to ease a problem that arises when applying Paice's method to a dense ontology, were some instances have large number of connections. If activation is spread over more than few links, reaching heavily connected instances, then such instances will receive disproportionately high weights accumulated from their large number of connections. Hence a one-step backwards weight transfer is introduced in our algorithm to give extra weight back to source instances. We are experimenting with other alternatives, such as applying a weight-transfer cost for each instance based on its number of connections.

4. REFINING THE PICTURE

Getting the COP right will depend on the ontology, on the purposes of the user, and on the domain. Even if there are rules of thumb that emerge from study, experiments would still need to be carried out in any new domain to establish the network properties of the ontology. In this section, we discuss some of the experiments tried on the AKT ontology.

Lets assume the user would like to identify the COP of *Shadbolt*, an instance of the class *Academic Staff*. He can select relations and weight them manually, or go for the automatic selection. The selected relations and their weights will be displayed in the *Selected Slots* table on the right panel. Link and weight thresholds are set with slide bars. The weight threshold is used to filter out any instance with a final weight less than the given value. This is used to reduce the amount of noise in the results set, which often occurs when expanding to a high number of links, or if the initial instance has low connectivity (i.e. not much information is available about the selected instance). The weight threshold also allows the user to control the display of results to, for example, only highly ranked entities if the interest is to identify strongly related entities only. We can describe the results of a set of experiments with ONTOCOPI using different settings to identify the COP of *Shadbolt* based on the AKT ontology. Note that only the first 20 results of each experiment are displayed.

4.1 Using Automatic Settings

The extent of the identified COP is dependent on the number of links to expand from the COP query instance. Here we first use a 2 link-threshold to identify the immediate COP of *Shadbolt*; the automatic relations selector was used, which sets the highest weight of 1 to the relationship *hasAuthor*, which is the reason why the highly ranked people in *Shadbolt's* COP are in general the ones with the highest number of joint publications with him. It can be seen from *Figure 4*(a) that the closest person to *Shadbolt* was found to be *O'Hara*, *Shadbolt's* trusty lieutenant, who works in the same department, and has co-authored more than 30 papers with him.

Instance	Weight
Shadbolt	
O'Hara	30.218
Hall	27.517
Intelligence, Agent...	22.36
Elliott	20.346
De Roure	18.45
Jennings	15.617
Carr	14.937
Davis	14.816
Lewis	14.169
Hamad	12.986
Crowder	12.258
Heath	11.162
Luck	10.574
Hill	9.038
Wills	9.023
Dobie	8.762
Glaser	8.739
Moreau	8.387
Hitchcock	6.89

(a)

Instance	Weight
Shadbolt	
O'Hara	8.061
Elliott	6.331
Reichgelt	5.587
Cottam	5.567
Cupit	5.291
Burton	5.0
Crow	4.69
Rugg	4.358
Milton	4.358
Howarth	4.0
Tennison	3.605
Hedgecock	3.605
Stobart	3.605
Oaines	3.605
Musen	3.605
Hoffman	3.606
Wielinga	3.162
Schmalhofer	3.162
Corbridge	3.162

(b)

Figure 4. Shadbolt's COP, Automatic Selection (a) 2 links (b) 4 links

Increasing the link threshold to 4, with the relation settings unchanged, gives the COP shown in *Figure 4*(b). More instances have now been reached as the range of analysis is extended. Instances have now accumulated higher weights as more weights are passed around and new paths are explored. This COP is wider than before and it includes instances that are indirectly connected to the query instance through other instances, for example the supervisors of someone's co-authors. Hence we see new people with less direct connections coming into the picture because of their connections with others; in this way we can see that the COP identified with a higher link threshold can make suggestions for COP membership that the unaided subject would be less likely to come up with.

4.2 Using Manual Settings

To identify more specific types of COP, the user can select the relations of interest and weigh them manually. For example to identify the COP of *Shadbolt* based on his co-authors, project collaborators, and co-workers, then the relationships *hasAuthor*, *memberOfProject*, and *memberOf* can be selected. Using the relationship weights of 0.2, 0.9 and 0.3 respectively, the resulting COP will be as in *Figure 5*.

Instance	Weight
Shadbolt	
O'Hara	3.399
ANNA: Acquisition t...	2.8
AKT: Advanced Knc...	2.8
Elliott	2.262
Luo	2.0
Jennings	2.0
Wills	2.0
Harris	2.0
Carr	2.0
De Roure	2.0
Dasmahapatra	2.0
Alani	2.0
Meng	2.0
Gibbins	2.0
Walker	2.0
Hall	2.0
Reichgelt	1.949
Cottam	1.949
Glaser	1.876

Figure 5. Shadbolt's COP, manual selection

This COP differs from the one identified in the previous section as some of the instances in this COP (all the ones with a weight of 2) have no joint papers with *Shadbolt*, but are all members of the same project, group, and department. The results will obviously be slightly different if the weights of the selected relationships change. For example people with more joint publications with *Shadbolt* will get higher values if the weight of *hasAuthor* is increased.

Specifying certain relationships to be used by ONTOCOPI needs some understanding of their semantics. It is our intention to facilitate this task by allowing the user to select the main concepts of interest from which the system can select and weight relevant relationships automatically.

4.3 Temporally-based COP Identification

Previous examples identified COPs using default temporal boundaries (from 1980 till 2002). Temporal limits can be applied to restrict COPs to certain intervals. *Figure 6* shows the COPs of *Shadbolt* in three different periods, focusing on co-authorship relations. *Hedgecock*, *Underwood*, and *Stobart* were highly ranked in (a) but were excluded from the COP in (b). Others such as *Reichgelt*, *Burton*, *Rugg* were some of the most relevant to Shadbolt's COP in (a) but faded gradually when their ranks dropped in (b) and disappeared completely in (c). There are always new people in the COP replacing the fading ones, for example *O'Hara*, *Cottam*, and *Elliott* appeared in (b) and maintained very high ranks throughout (b) and (c).

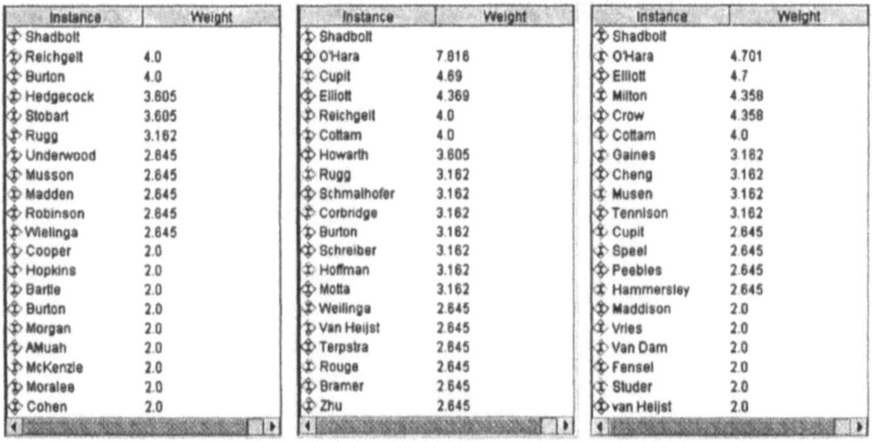

Instance	Weight
Shadbolt	
Reichgelt	4.0
Burton	4.0
Hedgecock	3.605
Stobart	3.605
Rugg	3.162
Underwood	2.645
Musson	2.645
Madden	2.645
Robinson	2.645
Wielinga	2.645
Cooper	2.0
Hopkins	2.0
Bartle	2.0
Burton	2.0
Morgan	2.0
AMuah	2.0
McKenzie	2.0
Moralee	2.0
Cohen	2.0

Instance	Weight
Shadbolt	
O'Hara	7.816
Cupit	4.69
Elliott	4.369
Reichgelt	4.0
Cottam	4.0
Howarth	3.605
Rugg	3.162
Schmalhofer	3.162
Corbridge	3.162
Burton	3.162
Schreiber	3.162
Hoffman	3.162
Motta	3.162
Weilinga	2.645
Van Heijst	2.645
Terpstra	2.645
Rouge	2.645
Bramer	2.645
Zhu	2.645

Instance	Weight
Shadbolt	
O'Hara	4.701
Elliott	4.7
Milton	4.358
Crow	4.358
Cottam	4.0
Gaines	3.162
Cheng	3.162
Musen	3.162
Tennison	3.162
Cupit	2.645
Speel	2.645
Peebles	2.645
Hammersley	2.645
Maddison	2.0
Vries	2.0
Van Dam	2.0
Fensel	2.0
Studer	2.0
van Heijst	2.0

(a) (b) (c)

Figure 6. Shadbolt's COPs, (a) 1985-90, (b) 1991-7, (c) 1998-2002

The Proustian *Figure 7* shows the time-related ranks of certain people in *Shadbolt's* co-authorship-based COP, displaying how people fade out of the COP while others move in. The rate of change in a COP depends of course on the movements of these individuals. For example *Reichgelt* climbed from 4th in 1987 to top in 1991, then dropped until he disappeared for good in 1995. A new person, *Elliott*, joined this COP in 1995 and started to climb and secure higher positions but also began to fade after 1998.

Time-based COP identification can be improved if more temporal information is available. Ontologies tend to lack temporal information due to the difficulty in capturing such information and the complexity of representing it. Some of the results of time-based COPs cannot be very accurate due to information loss. For example even though the date when papers were published is captured in the AKT ontology, it is not known when the work on these papers actually began, or when they were submitted. As COPs are highly variable through time, it would be useful to be able to filter out relations that did not obtain in particular relevant periods; however, such information must be present in the ontology in the first place.

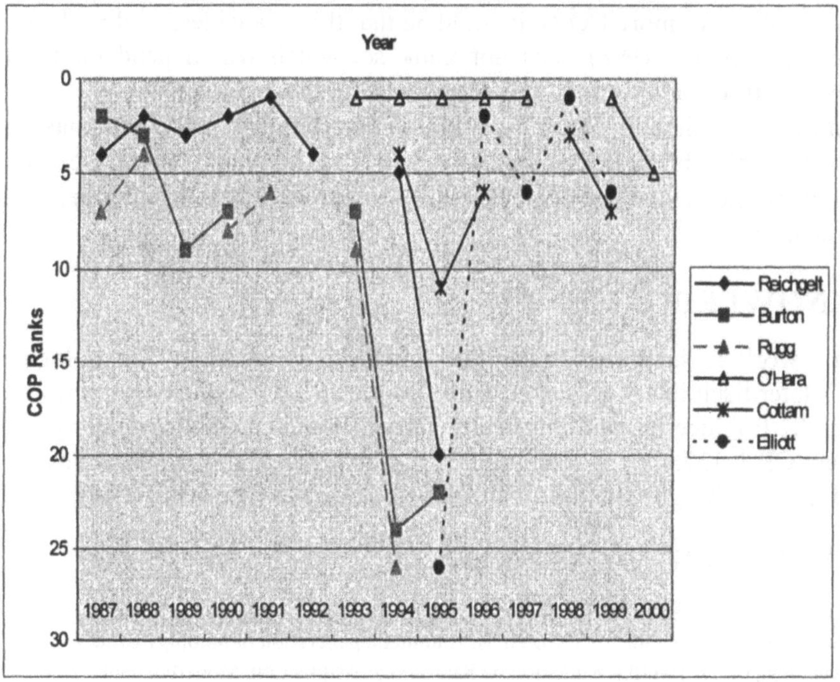

Figure 7. Changing Ranks in Shadbolt's COPs

5. DISCUSSION

By using ontologies, ONTOCOPI makes itself sensitive to the semantics of the relations out of which networks are built. As a support tool for COP identification, it has the scope to cut down search spaces radically.

This contrasts with similar work investigating networks of semi-formal relations between people or within systems. For instance, the analysis of networks of pages and hyperlinks to identify hubs and authoritative sites on the web in order to improve search engine results (e.g. Page et al 1999) is based on the number and direction of links between web pages, but the significance of such links is lost after a page is authored. Work related to ONTOCOPI is discussed in more depth in (O'Hara et al 2002).

We have discussed ONTOCOPI's ontology-based analysis techniques; we should also express the following caveats (cf. O'Hara et al 2002).

1. ONTOCOPI makes an explicit assumption that (some) informal COP relations can be inferred from the formal ones in an ontology.
2. In any new domain, a range of trials would have to be carried out to determine the interesting link thresholds and relation weights.
3. Note the problem of *brokers* or *boundary objects* (people or objects who exist in two COPs). In cases such as these the COPs identified may be the *union* of two or more COPs. It could be that this is a widespread problem, though Wenger (1998) does not think so. Much will depend on what possible filtering information is represented in the ontology.

Future research will focus on ways of filtering out noise and making search more flexible. Further scenarios will also be employed to ascertain which other knowledge management tasks can exploit ONA (e.g. coreference identification).

ACKNOWLEDGEMENTS

This work is supported under the Advanced Knowledge Technologies (AKT) Interdisciplinary Research Collaboration (IRC), which is sponsored by the UK Engineering and Physical Sciences Research Council under grant number GR/N15764/01. The AKT IRC comprises the Universities of Aberdeen, Edinburgh, Sheffield, Southampton and the Open University.

REFERENCES

AKT, The AKT Manifesto, 2001, http://www.aktors.org/publications/Manifesto.doc

Eriksson H, Fergerson R, Shahr Y, Musen M. Automatic generation of ontology editors. Proceedings of the Twelfth Workshop on Knowledge Acquisition, Modelling and Management (KAW'99); 1999; Banff. Canada.

McDermott R., Why information technology inspired but cannot deliver knowledge management, California Management Review, 1999; 41

O'Hara K, Alani H, Shadbolt N. Identifying communities of practice: analysing ontologies as networks to support community recognition. Proceedings of the World Computer Congress; 2002; Montreal. Canada.

Page L, Brin S, Motwani R, Winograd T. The PageRank Citation Ranking: Bringing Order to the Web. Stanford University working paper SIDL-WP-1999-0120; 1999.

Paice C.D. A thesaural model of information retrieval. Information Processing and Management 1991, 27(5):433-447

Smith R.G., Farquhar A. The road ahead for knowledge management: an AI perspective. AI Magazine, Winter 2000, 17-40

Wenger E, *Communities of Practice: Learning, Meaning and Identity*. Cambridge University Press, Cambridge, 1998.

Wenger E., Communities of practice: the key to knowledge strategy. Knowledge Directions: The Journal of the Institute for Knowledge Management, 1999, 1:48-93

THE JESSTAB APPROACH TO PROTÉGÉ AND JESS INTEGRATION

Henrik Eriksson
Department of Computer and Information Science
Linköping University
SE-581 83 Linköping, Sweden
her@ida.liu.se

Abstract Communication with performance systems is becoming increasingly important for ontology development and knowledge-modeling tools. Such tools can benefit from tight integration with inference engines. JessTab is an extension to the Protégé framework that allows developers to take advantage of the Jess performance system. JessTab supports declarative mapping of sections of Protégé knowledge bases to the Jess knowledge representation and adds functionality for operations on ontologies and knowledge bases.

Keywords: Knowledge acquisition, knowledge engineering, ontologies, expert-system shells

1. Introduction

Development environments for ontology definition and knowledge modeling require integration with other types of software. For example, it is important to communicate with other programs and to control external programs. Furthermore, it is sometimes desirable for external programs to control a development environment (e.g., to open an ontology editor and to focus on a particular part of the ontology). The ability to integrate development environments with other software is a critical factor for using these systems in a wide range of organizations and a key to widespread acceptance of such environments.

The Protégé (Grosso et al., 1999) development tool provides an application programmer interface (API) for this type of integration. However, this API is based on low-level concepts. It allows calls to and from the environment implementation language (Java). There is no support for integration with declarative languages and there are no shells suitable for implementation of problem solvers.

Protégé is essentially a stand-alone tool in the sense that it produces output (i.e., ontologies and knowledge bases) that other programs can read. Protégé assumes that the performance engine runs as a separate program, perhaps on a different platform. This separation is advantageous in most situations because the development and run-time environments are typically different. However, there are several situations in which tight integration with a performance system would be useful.

In many situations it is useful to create programs that perform operations on ontologies or modify the knowledge base in certain ways. A developer might want to define rules that match patterns in the knowledge base and trigger actions, such as filling in information derived from other values and making adjustments that refine the knowledge base. Alternatively, a developer might want to run problem-solving methods in the Protégé environment to enable immediate testing.

JessTab is an approach to integrate two popular systems—Jess and Protégé. The JessTab implementation allows developers to create knowledge bases in Protégé that work together with Jess programs and rule bases. It creates a declarative mapping between the knowledge representation schemes supported by these tools. This mapping unifies the Protégé and Jess formats by mapping sections of the knowledge base to the Jess fact base. JessTab can propagate automatically modifications to mapped Protégé instances on Jess.

We found that having an integrated performance component in a tool such as Protégé has several advantages. Developers can use the performance component as a macro language for manipulating of knowledge bases. Rules and functions can automate repetitive tasks (e.g., during maintenance), and can ensure consistency. Furthermore, it is possible to use JessTab as an object-oriented extension to Jess by using the ontology representation supported by Protégé. In this approach, Protégé is an extension to Jess.

In the remainder of this paper, we shall describe the background in terms of Protégé and Jess, and present the JessTab approach in detail. Finally, we discuss the potential uses of JessTab and considers directions for future research in this area.

2. Background

Before discussing the JessTab extension, let us first examine the current Protégé-2000 implementation, the axiom-language extension to Protégé (which is a complementary extension), and the Jess language and its implementation.

2.1. Protégé-2000

Protégé-2000 is a tool that supports knowledge acquisition and the development of knowledge bases (Grosso et al., 1999). It includes an ontology editor and a system for generating and custom tailoring forms for data entry by domain specialists. The Protégé-2000 user interface consists of several *tabs* that provide different views of the knowledge base. For example, there are tabs for ontology editing, form layout, knowledge entry, and knowledge-base search. Protégé-2000 is implemented as an open-source Java application.

An important feature of Protégé-2000 is the possibility to extend its functionality through plug-in modules. By defining *slot-widget* plug-ins, developers can extend the functionality of data-entry widgets (e.g., by implementing new interaction modes). The mechanism for *tab-widget* plug-ins allows developers to add new tabs to the Protégé-2000 user interface. Developers often use this plug-in API to implement project-specific tabs that provide unique views of the knowledge base.

2.2. PAL: The Protégé Axiom Language

PAL is a language for expressing constraints in Protégé knowledge bases. It is based on first-order predicate logic. PAL allows developers to define constraints that can be checked by the PAL interpreter. Once the knowledge base under development is in a reasonably coherent state, the developer can invoke the PAL engine to check the consistency with respect to the constraints. PAL then reports any constraint violations to the developer. PAL is implemented as a tab-widget plug-in to Protégé.

The main difference between JessTab and PAL is that JessTab allows developers to use Jess as a programming language and inference engine. PAL, however, is not a programming language in the sense that it can be used to define inferences and behaviors. Developers invoke PAL explicitly to perform constraint checking. The result of this process is a report (rather than a behavior). Unlike Jess, PAL is custom tailored for expressing constraints for checking knowledge bases.

Jess and PAL are complementary languages in the sense that PAL can be used to test the integrity of a knowledge base, whereas Jess can be used to implement operations on the knowledge base. Because Jess is Turing complete, it is possible to use it to implement custom-tailored constraint checkers as well as programs that modify the knowledge base.

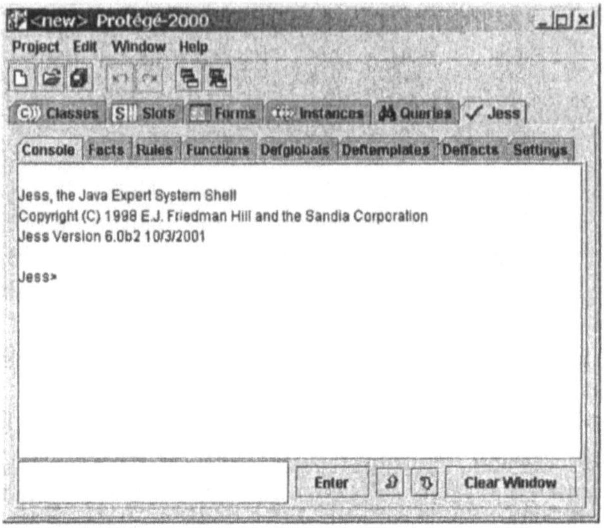

Figure 1. Jess console window as a Protégé-2000 tab.

2.3. Jess

Jess (Friedman-Hill, 1997; Watson, 1997) is a reimplementation of a subset of CLIPS (NASA, 1991) in Java. Jess implements some additional functionality not provided by CLIPS. Like CLIPS, reasoning in Jess is based on a list of known *facts* and a set of *rules* that match on these facts in its fact base.

Facts are basically a list of known values, such as `(temperature outdoor 25)`, and the preconditions of the rules are patterns with wildcards and conditional expressions, such as `(temperature ? ?t&:(> ?t 20))`. Rules can assert new facts when they fire, which in turn could result in other rules firing. Jess uses the Rete algorithm to ensure efficient pattern matching and rule activation (Forgy, 1982). Jess supports both forward chaining and backward chaining.

3. The JessTab Approach

JessTab provides a Jess console window in the Protégé environment (see Figure 1). Developers can easily switch between the Jess read-evaluate-print dialogue and the normal graphical interaction with Protégé. To make Jess development in the Protégé environment easier, JessTab implements graphical inspectors for Jess facts and definitions (rules, functions, defglobals, deftemplates, and deffacts).

In addition to the graphical tools, JessTab extends the Jess and Protégé functionality in five important areas:

1 Mapping instances to facts. JessTab maps Protégé knowledge bases consisting of instances to facts in the Jess fact list.

2 Functions for knowledge-base operations. JessTab adds several functions to Jess that allow Jess programs to query and manipulate Protégé knowledge bases.

3 Functions for ontology reflection and operations. JessTab adds functions that examine and modify the Protégé ontology.

4 Mirroring Jess definitions in Protégé knowledge bases. Instances represent Jess definitions, such as rules and functions.

5 Support for methods and message handlers in Jess. Currently under development.

The remainder of Section 3 covers basic integration of Jess with Protégé instances (Areas 1–2) while Section 4 discusses issues related to ontology integration (Areas 3–4).

3.1. Mapping Protégé Knowledge Bases to Jess Facts

A core component of Protégé–Jess integration is the *mapping* mechanism. This approach makes it possible to mark classes in the ontology for mapping to Jess facts. By using the expression `(mapclass <class-name>)`, developers can map all instances of the specified class to Jess facts. The mapclass expression applies to direct as well as indirect instances (i.e., instances of subclasses). An alternative to the class-mapping mechanism is to map a specific instance to a fact through the expression `(mapinstance <instance>)`. An important design goal for the JessTab mapping mechanism is to enable Jess rules to pattern match on mapped instances. We can then write rules that fire when the appropriate conditions in the Protégé knowledge base are met.

Let us consider an example. Mapping the class `Person`, which has a single instance representing "John" age 20, results in a Jess fact with the format `(object (is-a Person) (name "John") (age 20))`. This fact represents the instance with its slot values for `name` and `age`.[1]

[1]The fact in this example is simplified for clarity; the actual fact holds additional information about the instance.

JessTab asserts facts based on a certain pattern (template). The pattern starts with `object` and it always contains the class name and a direct reference to the Protégé object. As shown in the example, the slot–value pairs of the instance are also part of the fact. The mapping mechanism asserts a fact for every instance (of a mapped class). Creating a new instance of the class `Person`, for example, will result in the assertion of a new fact matching the instance.

Our motivation for designing this type of mapping to facts is that it enables developers to define Jess rules that pattern match on mapped instances in many ways. For example, it is possible to write rules that match on instances regardless of their class by using a wildcard for the `is-a` property. The pattern `(object (is-a ?) (name "John"))` matches every (mapped) instance that has a slot *name* with the value "John".

The mapping from instances to facts in unidirectional in the sense that changes to the Jess fact list, such as assertions of facts, are *not* propagated back to the Protégé knowledge base. However, it is possible to make changes to the knowledge base from Jess by calling functions that operate on knowledge-base constructs.

3.2. Knowledge Base Operations from Jess

JessTab provides several functions for retrieving information from Protégé knowledge bases and for modifying them. There are functions for getting slot values from instances, for defining new classes, and for instantiating classes. Whenever possible, these functions are compatible with their corresponding CLIPS counterparts (if any).

Let us consider how we can use JessTab to create Protégé classes and instances from Jess. Just as in CLIPS, developers can use the `defclass` construct[2] to create a new class and attach slots to it. The `make-instance` function allows us to create an instance of a specified class in the knowledge base and, optionally, provide initial slot values for it. Using `defclass` and `make-instance` we can now experiment with creating instances and then map them to facts. The following example illustrates how we can create a class `Person` and create a person instance named "John":

```
Jess> (defclass Person (is-a :THING)
          (slot name (type string))
          (slot age (type integer)))
```

[2] Jess also implements an alternative format for `defclass` (Friedman-Hill, 1997). Advanced developers can use this format to specify communication with native Java classes.

```
TRUE
Jess> (make-instance john of Person (name "John") (age 20))
<External-Address:SimpleInstance>
Jess> (mapclass Person)
Person
```

The `mapclass` expression marks the `Person` class as mapped, and it will assert facts of the (direct and indirect) instances of `Person`. After the `mapclass` operation, we can check the resulting Jess fact:

```
Jess> (facts)
f-0   (object (is-a Person) (is-a-name "Person")
        (OBJECT <External-Address:SimpleInstance>)
        (age 20) (name "John"))
For a total of 1 facts.
```

This fact represents the instance of the class `Person` we created. In addition to the class name and the slot–value pairs, the fact contains a reference to the actual Protégé instance (the Java object representing it). This reference is useful when defining rules that perform operations on the object in the action part. The `is-a-name` value is a string version of the class name, which is useful in some rule patterns.

Because the class Person is marked as mapped, changing a Protégé slot value results in a change of the corresponding fact. We use the `slot-set` function to change the age to 21:

```
Jess> (slot-set john age 21)
Jess> (facts)
f-1   (object (is-a Person) (is-a-name "Person")
        (OBJECT <External-Address:SimpleInstance>)
        (age 21) (name "John"))
For a total of 1 facts.
```

When we change a fact property, Jess actually retracts the old fact and asserts a new version of it (i.e., the fact number changes). This behavior is normal Jess semantics.

Creating a second instance adds a new fact to the Jess list of facts:

```
Jess> (make-instance sue of Person (name "Sue") (age 22))
<External-Address:SimpleInstance>
Jess> (facts)
f-1   (object (is-a Person) (is-a-name "Person")
        (OBJECT <External-Address:SimpleInstance>)
        (age 21) (name "John"))
f-4   (object (is-a Person) (is-a-name "Person")
        (OBJECT <External-Address:SimpleInstance>)
        (age 22) (name "Sue"))
For a total of 2 facts.
```

Because the mapping of the class `Person` is reactive, JessTab asserts a new fact automatically when we create a new instance.

We can now write a Jess rule that pattern matches on the facts. The following rule prints the name for every person of the age 21 or older:

```
Jess> (defrule twentyone
         (object (is-a Person)
             (name ?n) (age ?a&:(>= ?a 21)))
       =>
         (printout t "The person " ?n
                     " is 21 or older" crlf))
TRUE
Jess> (run)
The person John is 21 or older
The person Sue is 21 or older
2
Jess>
```

This rule format allows us to write rules that perform object matching in several different ways. For example, we can write rules with constraints or wildcards for the class name. The action part of the rules can perform reasoning tasks, such as asserting new facts and making changes to slot values. Note that the format of these rules is similar to the CLIPS rule format for pattern matching on objects (as of CLIPS version 6.0).

To perform active modification of the knowledge base, we need functions for accessing and modifying values in Protégé. The functions slot-get and slot-set allow us to retrieve and change slot values, respectively. For example, the expression (slot-get sue age) will return the age slot value for the instance sue. The expression (slot-set sue age 23) will set the slot value for age to 23. Continuing the previous example, we can define a generalized rule that changes the age from 22 to 23 for every person:

```
Jess> (defrule changeage
       ?o <- (object (is-a Person) (age 22))
       =>
        (slot-set ?o age 23))
TRUE
```

There are also functions for getting and setting facet values (i.e., slot properties). You can use expressions (facet-get <class-name> <slot-name> <facet-name>) and (facet-set <class-name> <slot-name> <facet-name> <new-value>) to access the facets.

4. Ontology Integration

JessTab allows Jess programs to integrate with Protégé ontologies in a fundamental way. There are several ways in which Jess programs can examine and manipulate ontologies. Let us consider four aspects briefly:

1 Ontology reflection. It is possible for Jess programs to reflect on the makeup of Protégé ontologies. Built-in functions, such as `class-subclasses`, can discover the structure of ontologies. These functions enable us to develop Jess programs that analyze ontologies.

2 Meta-level objects. Protégé provides advanced support for meta-level objects (Eriksson et al., 1999). For example, classes are instances of metaclasses. Slots and facets are instances as well. JessTab supports these meta-level objects by allowing programs to create new classes by instantiating a metaclass (e.g., with the `make-instance` function).

3 Mapping metaclasses. Because classes behave as instances (of a metaclass) in most aspects, it is possible to map them to facts just as regular instances. Thus, by mapping classes to facts, we can apply Jess rules to Protégé classes. For example, it is possible to write rules that pattern match certain classes in a large ontology and modify them.

4 Definition mirroring. JessTab mirrors Jess definitions in the Protégé ontology. For example, Jess defrules are mirrored as an instance of the system class `:JESS-RULE` in Protégé. These mirror instances contain a textual representation of the Jess definition (i.e., the source code). Thus, Jess programs can reflect the structure of themselves by inspecting the mirror instances (e.g., by mapping them to facts and applying rules). Furthermore, it is possible to save these mirror instances together with the rest of the knowledge base, and to reinsert them during reload from files.

In summary, the meta-level objects in Protégé fit well together with Jess.[3] JessTab enables Jess programs to inspect and modify ontologies just like instances, which result in a superior expressive power for rules operating on the ontology.

5. Discussion

During its development, the scope of Protégé been has broadened from an environment that mainly supported knowledge acquisition from domain experts through generating knowledge-acquisition tools to a general tool for ontology and knowledge base development with an open architecture (Eriksson and Musen, 1993; Grosso et al., 1999). The advan-

[3]Note that CLIPS does not support metaclasses or other meta-level objects at all.

tage of today's Protégé is the combined power of the plug-in components and the possibility to custom tailor the environment by developing your own components.

A practical goal for JessTab is that it should be a useful tool for projects originating from both the Protégé and Jess communities. For the Protégé user, the JessTab extension adds a performance engine to Protégé and support for a declarative mapping between Protégé and Jess to this tool-box. For the the Jess developer, JessTab makes it possible to take advantage of Protégé as a graphical development environment and to use third-party plug-ins (tabs) added to Protégé.

A development tool and a performance system working together is a powerful combination, and one which developers can use in several ways. The approach of combining graphical environments and reasoners is not new. In the mid-1980s, hybrid tools such as KEE featured graphical development environments (Fikes and Kehler, 1985). These tools, however, did not have the richness and flexibility of current knowledge-modeling tools and they lacked the suppleness of the Java-based Jess engine. JessTab enables developers to use the performance system for ontology and knowledge base development (e.g., by using Jess to query and modify ontologies). There are also recent tools that have performance counterparts, such as OntoEdit (which uses Ontobroker (Decker et al., 1999)), WebODE (Arpírez et al., 2001), WebOnto (Domingue, 1998), and Ontosaurus (Swartout et al., 1996) (which uses Loom (MacGregor, 1991)).

The current JessTab implementation opens interesting possibilities for future development. One potential extension is to make Protégé a Jess development environment by taking advantage of the graphical capabilities of Protégé. This approach would require a tight integration between graphical editing in Protégé and Jess definitions and structures. Some JessTab users have requested a different mapping between Protégé instances and Jess facts. A generalized mapping mechanism that allows users to define their own mappings, perhaps as Jess rules, would permit custom `mapclass` and `mapinstance` operations. An extension currently under development is support for CLIPS-like message handlers and methods. This approach will bring Jess and JessTab closer to a full object system.

One major advantage of the Protégé–Jess combination is that developers can use other Protégé plug-ins and other Jess extensions and interfaces. For example, Jess and JessTab enable developers to use Protégé for development of software agents. The Java Agent Development Framework (JADE) (Bellifemine et al., 2001) can communicate with Jess, which in turn communicates with Protégé using JessTab. Using this approach, developers can get Protégé ontology support for JADE agents by using Jess rules. Jess rules can create Protégé instances based on messages from agents. Furthermore, Jess rules can create and send agent messages based on the content of Protégé knowledge bases.

Another possibility is to use Protégé and Jess for the development of semantic-web applications (Berners-Lee et al., 2001). Protégé supports encoding of ontologies in the resource description framework (RDF) format (Lassila, 1998). Thus, Jess can operate on such ontologies through JessTab. Used in this fashion, the Protégé–Jess combination is a building block for the semantic web.

6. Conclusion

JessTab allows developers to write Jess programs that manage Protégé ontologies and knowledge bases. Furthermore, the Jess inference engine enables developers to apply rule-based reasoning to Protégé definitions. The Protégé meta-object protocol makes it is possible to apply this reasoning to meta-level objects and to use JessTab to make structural changes and extensions to classes, slots, and facets.

The JessTab project contributes to the understanding of how ontology editors and performance systems can work together. This understanding includes the mapping from the Protégé knowledge representation to the Jess representation and the use of Jess definitions as system classes in Protégé ontologies. In practice, JessTab contributes to the Protégé community by enabling the use of Jess under Protégé. JessTab also supports the Jess community by allowing the use of Protégé as an object-oriented extension to Jess and by providing a tool for using Protégé as a graphical front-end to Jess.

JessTab is a solid basis for further development of the Protégé–Jess integration. Examples of such potential integration projects are the representation of Jess problem solvers in ontologies and detailed modeling of Jess definitions (e.g., rules) in knowledge bases. Furthermore, the JessTab approach is a road map for integrating Protégé and other performance systems.

Acknowledgments

The JessTab user community contributed with testing, bug reports, and suggestions for further improvements. Ray Fergerson and Ernest Friedman-Hill provided Protégé-2000 and Jess support, respectively. Samson Tu provided valuable insights in the problem of transferring information from Protégé-2000 and to Jess via Java.

References

Arpírez, J. C., Corcho, O., Fernández-López, M., and Gómez-Pérez, A. (2001). WebODE: A workbench for ontological engineering. In *Proceedings of K-CAP 2001*, Victoria, B.C., Canada.

Bellifemine, F., Poggi, A., and Rimassa, G. (2001). Developing multi-agent systems with a FIPA-compliant agent framework. *Software: Practice and Experience*, 31(2):103–128.

Berners-Lee, T., Hendler, J., and Lassila, O. (2001). The semantic web. *Scientific American*, 284(5):34–44.

Decker, S., Erdmann, M., Fensel, D., and Studer, R. (1999). Ontobroker: Ontology based access to distributed and semi-structured information. In *Preceedings of DS-8: Semantic Issues in Multimedia Systems*, pages 351–369.

Domingue, J. (1998). Tadzebao and WebOnto: Discussing, browsing, and editing ontologies on the web. In *Proceedings of the Eleventh Banff Knowledge Acquisition for Knowledge-Based Systems Workshop*, Banff, Canada. Also available as `http://ksi.cpsc.ucalgary.ca/KAW/KAW98/domingue/`.

Eriksson, H., Fergerson, R. W., Shahar, Y., and Musen, M. A. (1999). Automatic generation of ontology editors. In *Proceedings of the Twelfth Workshop on Knowledge Acquisition, Modeling, and Management*, pages 4.6.1–4.6.20, Banff, Canada. Also available as `http://sern.ucalgary.ca/KSI/KAW/KAW99/papers/Eriksson1/`.

Eriksson, H. and Musen, M. A. (1993). Metatools for knowledge acquisition. *IEEE Software*, 10(3):23–29.

Fikes, R. and Kehler, T. (1985). The role of frame-based representation in reasoning. *Communications of the ACM*, 29(9):904–920.

Forgy, C. L. (1982). Rete: A fast algorithm for the many pattern/many object pattern match problem. *Artificial Intelligence*, 19(1):17–37.

Friedman-Hill, E. J. (1997). Jess, the Java expert system shell. Technical Report SAND98-8206, Sandia National Laboratories. Also available as `http://www.prod.sandia.gov/cgi-bin/techlib/access-control.pl/1998/98820\%6-r.pdf`.

Grosso, W. E., Eriksson, H., Fergerson, R. W., Gennari, J. H., Tu, S. W., and Musen, M. A. (1999). Knowledge modeling at the millennium (The design and evolution of Protégé-2000). In *Proceedings of the Twelfth Workshop on Knowledge Acquisition, Modeling, and Management*, Banff, Canada. Also available as `http://sern.ucalgary.ca/KSI/KAW/KAW99/papers/Grosso1/kmatm.pdf`.

Lassila, O. (1998). Web metadata: A matter of semantics. *IEEE Internet Computing*, 2(4):30–37.

MacGregor, R. (1991). Inside the LOOM classifier. *SIGART Bulletin*, 2(3):70–76.

NASA (1991). *CLIPS Reference Manual.* Software Technology Branch, Lyndon B. Johnson Space Center, NASA, Houston, TX.

Swartout, B., Patil, R., Knight, K., and Russ, T. (1996). Toward distributed use of large-scale ontologies. In *Proceedings of the Tenth Banff Knowledge Acquisition for Knowledge-Based Systems Workshop*, pages 32.1–32.19, Banff, Canada. Also available as `http://ksi.cpsc.ucalgary.ca/KAW/KAW96/swartout/Banff_96_final_2.html`.

Watson, M. (1997). *Intelligent Java Applications for the Internet and Intranets*, chapter 8. Morgan Kaufmann Publishers, San Francisco, CA.

IMPLEMENTING CONSTRAINT SOLVERS IN B-PROLOG

Neng-Fa Zhou
Department of Computer and Information Science
CUNY Brooklyn College & Graduate Center
New York, NY 11210-2889, USA
zhou@sci.brooklyn.cuny.edu

Abstract Constraint Logic Programming (CLP) defines a family of programming languages that extend Prolog to support constraint solving over certain domains. Current state-of-the-art CLP systems are based on abstract machines or language constructs that are good for certain domains and propagation algorithms but are either not sufficiently expressive or inefficient for some other domains and propagation algorithms. B-Prolog provides a construct, called *action rules*, for programming interactive agents such as constraint propagators. As far as constraint propagation is concerned, an agent maintains dynamically a certain level of consistency for a constraint. This paper presents constraint solvers implemented in action rules for six domains, namely, finite-domains, Boolean, trees, lists, sets, and floating-point intervals. Some of the solvers such as the finite-domain and set solvers are competitive in performance with the fastest solvers available now.

Keywords: Constraint propagation, constraint solving, constraint logic programming, and action rules.

1. Introduction

Constraint Logic Programming (CLP) defines a family of programming languages that extend Prolog by replacing unification of Herbrand terms with constraint solving over certain domains [11, 26]. Various abstract machines and language constructs have been proposed for implementing constraint solvers. Most languages are designed for a particular domain. For example, there are extended WAMs [2] for constraint solving over finite-domains [1, 9], reals [25], and floating-point intervals [29]. The drawback of these languages is a lack of flexibility and extendibility. CHR (Constraint Handling Rules) [17] is a high-level language for implementing propagation-based constraint solvers. However, a fast compiler for CHR is yet to be implemented. Now, constraint solvers implemented in CHR are an order of magnitude slower than constraint interpreters implemented in low level languages.

B-Prolog [38, 40] provides a powerful language construct, called *action rules*, for programming interactive agents. An action rule specifies a pattern for agents, an action that the agents can carry out, and an event pattern for events that can activate the agents. An agent is like a sub-goal in Prolog that behaves in an event-driven manner. An agent can be suspended when certain conditions on it are satisfied and can be activated to take its actions when certain events are posted. The action rule language combines goal-oriented and event-driven execution models, and is suitable for programming interactive agents such as constraint propagators. As far as constraint propagation is concerned, an agent maintains dynamically a certain level of consistency for a constraint.

The merits of action rules over most other languages are: (1) it is high-level and therefore easy to learn and use; (2) it is flexible and facilitates implementation of various kinds of propagation algorithms; (3) it is efficient because it is compiled; and (4) it provides a convenient platform for end-users to program problem-specific algorithms.

This paper presents constraint solvers implemented in action rules for six domains, namely finite-domains, Boolean, trees, lists, sets, and floating-point intervals. For each domain, the representation scheme of domain variables and sample propagation rules are given.

2. Action Rules in B-Prolog

An *action rule* takes the following form:

```
<Agent> <Condition> {<Event>} '=>' <Action>
```

where `Agent` is an atomic formula that represents a pattern for agents, `Condition` is a sequence of conditions on the agents, `Event` is a set of patterns for events that can activate the agents, and `Action` is a sequence of actions performed by the agents when they are activated.

All conditions in `Condition` must be in-line tests. The event set `Event` together with the enclosing braces is optional. If an action rule does not have any event patterns specified, then the rule is called a *commitment rule*. A set of built-in events is provided for programming constraint propagators and interactive graphical user interfaces. For example, `ins(X)` is an event that is posted when the variable `X` is instantiated and `dom(X,E)` is posted when an inner element `E` is excluded from the domain of the finite-domain variable `X`. A user program can create and post its own events and define agents to handle them. A user-defined event takes the form of `event(X,T)` where `X` is a variable, called a ***suspension variable***, that connects the event with its handling agents, and `T` is a Prolog term that contains the information to be transmitted to the agents. If the event poster does not have any information to be transmitted to the agents, then the second argument `T` can be omitted. The built-in action `post(E)` posts the event `E`.

When an agent is created, the system searches in its definition for a rule whose agent-pattern ***matches*** the agent and whose conditions are satisfied. This kind of rules is said to be ***applicable*** to the agent. Notice that since one-directional matching rather than full-unification is used to search for an applicable rule and no variable in the conditions can be instantiated, the agent will remain the same after an applicable rule is found.

The rules in the definition are searched sequentially. If there is no rule that is applicable, the agent will fail. After an applicable rule is found, the agent will behave differently depending on the type of the rule.

If the rule found is a commitment rule in which no event pattern is specified, the actions will be executed. The agent will commit to the actions and a failure of the actions will lead to the failure of the agent. A commitment rule is similar to a clause in concurrent logic languages, but an agent can never be blocked while it is being matched against the agent pattern.

If the rule found is an action rule, the agent will be suspended until it is ***activated*** by one of the events specified in the rule. When the agent is activated, the conditions are tested ***again***. If they are met, the actions will be executed. A failure of any action will cause the agent to fail. The agent does not vanish after the actions are executed, but instead turns to wait until it is activated again. So, besides the difference in event-handling, the action rule "`H,C,E => B`" is similar to the guarded clause "`H :- C | B, H`", which creates a clone of the agent after the action `B` is executed.

Let `post(E)` be the selected sub-goal. After `E` is posted, all agents waiting for `E` will be activated. In practice, for the sake of efficiency, events are postponed until before the execution of the next non-inline call. At a point during execution, there may be multiple events posted that are all expected by an agent. If this is the case, then the agent has to be activated once for each of the events.

There is no primitive for killing agents explicitly. As described above, an agent never disappears as long as action rules are applied to it. An agent vanishes only when a commitment rule is applied to it.

Suspension variables

A suspension variable is a variable to which there are suspended agents and some other information attached. Suspension variables are useful for implementing user-defined domains. The call

```
susp_attach_term(X,T)
```

attaches the term T to the variable X. The formerly attached term to X, if any, will be lost after this operation. This operation is undone automatically upon backtracking. In other words, the originally attached term will be restored upon backtracking. The call

```
susp_attached_term(X,T)
```

gets the current term T attached to the variable X. In this paper, we use the notation `X^attached` for the term attached to X.

Suspension variables are similar to attribute variables [24], but do not rely on goal expansion to define the behaviors associated with them. Whenever a suspension variable X is bound to another term, which may be another variable, the event `ins(X)` will be posted. The user can specify the action to be taken after a suspension variable is bound, but not the action to be taken before unification takes place.

The following example illustrates the use of suspension variables:

```
create_fd_variable(X,D) =>
     susp_attach_term(X,D),
     check_member(X,D).

check_member(X,D),var(X),{ins(X)} => true.
check_member(X,D) => member(X,D).
```

This is a simple implementation of finite-domain variables. The agent `check_member(X,D)` is suspended when X is a variable. When X is instantiated, the agent is activated to check whether the value assigned to X is a member of D. In a real implementation, unification of two finite-domain variables should be considered as well.

3. Implementing Constraint Solvers in Action Rules

In the CLP family, CLP(X) is a language that supports constraint solving over the domain X. Most CLP systems introduce new operators for expressing constraints rather than extending the unification operator. In this paper, we use self-explainary mathematical symbols for constraints. Operators are usually generic and their interpretation depends on the types of the constraint expressions. For this reason, the users are required to provide the information about the types of variables.

The type of each variable can be known from its domain declaration or can be inferred from its context. The domain of a variable is declared by a call as follows:

```
V :: D
```

where `V` is a variable and `D` is a range `L..U` of values, where `L` is the lower bound and `U` is the upper bound. One of the bounds can be omitted if it is unknown, but not both. The type of `V` is determined by the bounds. For example, `1..3` denotes a set of integers from 1 to 3, `1..` a set of positive integers, `[]..[_,_,_]` a set of lists of up to three elements, `{}..{a,b,c}` a set of all subsets of `{a,b,c}`, and `0.0..` a set of non-negative floating-point numbers. For finite-domain variables, `D` can be a list of ground terms. So, `V :: [a,b,c]` says that `X` can be `a`, `b`, or `c`.

We only consider propagation-based solvers. Constraint propagation, which is a technique originated in Artificial Intelligence [28, 36] for solving constraint satisfaction problems, works as follows: Whenever the constraint store is changed, e.g., new constraints are added or the domain of a variable in some constraint is updated, it propagates the change to other constraints to attempt to exclude those no-good values from the domains of variables that can never be a part of a solution. Constraint propagation is an iterative procedure that continues until no further change can be made to the constraint store.

For most problems, propagation alone is inadequate for finding a solution, and the *divide-and-conquer* or *relaxation* method is usually necessary for finding a solution. The call

```
indomain(V)
```

finds a value for `V` either by enumerating the values in `V`'s domain or by splitting the domain. After a variable is instantiated, the propagation procedure will be invoked again.

In this section, we describe how to implement in action rules constraint solvers over six different domains, namely finite domain, Boolean, trees, lists, sets, and floating-point intervals.

3.1. CLP(FD)

CLP(FD), the member of the CLP family that supports finite-domain constraints, may be the most successful member in the CLP family. A large number of applications ranging from design, scheduling, to configuration have been developed [15, 37], and many implementation methods have been explored [1, 7, 9, 19, 33, 39].

A finite domain variable is represented as a suspension variable with an attached term of the following form:

```
fd(First,Last,Size,Elms)
```

The arguments refers to, respectively, the *first* element, the *last* element, the number of remaining elements, and a data structure that represents the elements in the domain. The last argument may be a bit vector or a hashtable that tells the status of each element in the domain.

An event will be posted whenever the domain of a variable is updated. For a domain variable X, instantiating X posts the event ins(X), updating the bound of the domain posts bound(X) if the domain contains only integers, and excluding any inner element E from the domain posts the event dom(X,E).

Action rules extend delay clauses [39] and can be used to implement various kinds of propagation algorithms for finite-domain constraints. The following shows the implementation of the arc consistency rule for the constraint X = Y+C where X and Y are integer domain variables and C is an integer:

```
'X=Y+C_arc'(X,Y,C):-
    'X in Y+C_arc'(X,Y,C),
    C1 is -C,
    'X in Y+C_arc'(Y,X,C1).

'X in Y+C_arc'(X,Y,C),var(X),var(Y),{dom(Y,Ey)} =>
    Ex is Ey+C,
    fd_exclude(X,Ex).
'X in Y+C_arc'(X,Y,C) => true.
```

The propagator 'X in Y+C_arc'(X,Y,C) maintains arc consistency for X in the constraint. Whenever an element Ey is excluded from the domain of Y, it excludes Ex, the counterpart of Ey, from the domain of X.

3.2. CLP(Boolean)

CLP(Boolean) can be considered as a special case of CLP(FD) [10] where each variable has a domain of two values. We use 0 to denote *false*, and 1 to denote *true*. A Boolean expression is composed of constants (0 or 1), Boolean domain variables, basic relational constraints, and the operators. Since constraints can be operands in a Boolean expression, it is possible to use a Boolean variable to indicate the satisfibility of a constraint. For example, the constraint (X = Y) <=> B says that X and Y are equal iff B is equal to 1. This technique, called *reification*, is useful for implementing global constraints such as cardinality constraints.

It is possible to implement various kinds of propagators with different powers in action rules. For example, for the constraint `(X = Y) <=> B`, one simple propagator is to delay the evaluation until either B is ground or both X and Y become ground. A more powerful propagator would add the constraint `B = 0` once the domains of `X` and `Y` are known to be disjoint.

3.3. CLP(Tree)

Prolog can be considered as a CLP language over trees. The unification `T1=T2` finds a valuation, called *unifier*, for the variables in the terms such that `T1` and `T2` become identical after each variable is replaced with its substitute. Prolog does not support disequality constraints over trees. The built-in `T1\=T2` is equivalent to not(T1=T2), which may fail even if `T1` and `T2` represent two different terms. For instance, the query

```
f(X) \= f(Y), X=a, Y=b
```

fails in Prolog. Prolog-II [12] and many others support disequality constraints over trees. These systems delay the evaluation of disequality constraints until the variables in the terms are instantiated sufficiently [6]. Since action rules extend the delay constructs, it is possible to implement disequality constraints over trees in a similar way.

3.4. CLP(List)

CLP(List) hasn't received as much attention as CLP(FD) and now few systems support constraints over lists. Nevertheless, CLP(List) is becoming popular as it is found useful in string processing such as the analysis of bio-sequences [16] and the processing of XML documents. Propagation rules for list constraints are yet to be explored. In Prolog-III, which may be the only CLP language that supports list constraints now, a concatenation constraint is delayed until the lengths of the participating lists are fixed. In [16], an implementation of a pattern language is given that adopts the backtracking algorithm. We propose a solver for CLP(List) that integrates propagation with string pattern matching.

For list domains, the following notations are used. `E1+E2` denotes the concatenation of `E1` and `E2`, `V^[I..J]` the sublist of `V` from the `I`th to the `J`th positions where `I` and `J` can be variables, `V^[I]` the `I`th element, and `|V|` the length of `V`.

A list domain variable `V` can be represented as a suspension variable with an attached term of the following form:

```
list(Length,Value,IndexTable,SuperLists)
```

where the arguments have the following meanings: Length is an integer domain variable that indicates the length of V. Value the prefix of V that is already known. Value evolves from a variable to a complete list with a fixed length while information about V is accumulated. IndexTable is a hashtable that facilitates the access of particular list elements. For each element E at the Ith position in Value, there is a pair (I,E) in IndexTable. SuperLists represents a list of super lists of which V is a sublist. For each super list SL of V, there is an element (Start,SL) in SuperLists where Start indicates the starting position of V in SL. This representation of list domains facilitates translating list constraints into finite-domain constraints.

The sublist constraint A^[I..J] = B is interpreted as follows: B becomes a sublist of A whose starting position in A is I and whose length is equal to J-I+1. Whenever an element of B becomes sufficiently instantiated, the matching algorithm is invoked to reduce the possible values for I and J. For example, suppose A is the list [b,c,a,a,d,a] and B's current value is the incomplete list [B1,_|_]. Once B1 is bound to a, the set of possible starting positions for B in A is narrowed to [3,4].

The concatenation constraint A+B = C entails the following: A is a sublist of C starting at 1, B is a sublist of C starting at |A|+1, and |A|+|B| = |C|.

The call indomain(V) searches for a value that is a sublist of all the super lists of V. The accumulated constraints on V are used to guide the string pattern matching algorithm.

3.5. CLP(Set)

CLP(Set) is a member in the CLP family where each variable can have a set as its value. We consider only finite sets of ground terms. CLP(Set) is well suited for some optimization problems that are hard to model in CLP(FD) [18, 3]. CLP(Set) is also found useful in some other application areas such as program analysis [22] and computational linguistics [32]. Systems that support set constraints include Eclipse [18], Mozart Oz [31] and the ILOG solver [34].

One of the key issues in implementing set constraints is how to represent set domains. Let N be the size of the universal set. Then the domain of a set variable has 2^N sets. Because the domain size is exponential in the size of the universal set, it is unrealistic to enumerate all the values in a domain and represent them explicitly. One method is to use intervals to represent set domains [18, 34]. We adopt the same method, but instead of using constant sets to represent the bounds we use finite-domain variables [41].

A set-domain variable V is represented as a suspension variable with an attached term of the following form:

```
set(Low,Up,Card,Univ)
```

where Low and Up are two finite-domain variables that represent respectively the lower and upper bounds, Card is another finite-domain variable that represents the cardinality, and Univ is a term that represents the universal set.

The representation scheme for set domains facilitates the manipulation of bounds. It takes constant time to add an element to or remove an element from a set domain. Constraint propagators update the bounds when related domains are updated. For example, the following shows one of the rules for dynamically maintaining the interval consistency for the subset constraint $A \subseteq B$:

```
propagate_inclusion_low(A,B),
        A^attached = set(ALow,AUp,ACard,AUniv),
        {dom(ALow,E)} =>
        add(E,B).
```

Whenever an element is added to the lower bound of A, it adds the element to B.

3.6. CLP(F-Interval)

Interval arithmetic, which is an arithmetic defined on sets of intervals, has become a rich source of methods for scientific computing [27]. Cleary first introduced interval arithmetic into Prolog [8]. Since then, several systems have been implemented (e.g., [4, 5, 23, 29]). In BNR-Prolog [5], a propagation method similar to the one used in CLP(FD) is used to reduce the set of values for variables. In Newton [4], a propagation method inspired by the Newton's root finding method is used to speed-up the convergence process. All the systems require the modification of the underlying abstract machines. In this subsection, we illustrate how to implement interval arithmetic with action rules.

An interval domain variable V is represented as a suspension variable with the following attached term float(Low,Up), where Low and Up are floating-point numbers that denote respectively the lower and upper bounds of the domain. Whenever a bound is updated, the event bound(V) is posted.

Just as for integer constraints, there are many different ways of implementing propagation rules. For instance, the following propagator maintains interval consistency on X for the constraint X=Y+Z:

```
x_is_y_plus_z(X,Y,Z),{bound(Y),bound(Z)} =>
```

```
Low is min(Y)+min(Z),
Up is max(Y)+max(Z),
X in Low..Up.
```

The call `X in Low..Up` narrows the bounds of `X` if the current lower bound is less than `Low` or the current upper bound is greater than `Up`.

The interval arithmetic is a rigorous theory that provides the definitions of all the computable functions in the floating-point arithmetic. All the definitions can be translated into action rules.

4. Concluding Remarks

This paper presents six constraint solvers in action rules, a language construct available in B-Prolog. These solvers illustrate the power of the language. The solvers for finite-domains, Boolean, trees and sets have been incorporated into B-Prolog, and the solvers for lists and floating-point intervals are to be included in B-Prolog in the future. The results are very encouraging. The finite-domain solver is one of the fastest. It is about four times as fast as the solver in Sicstus Prolog and is even faster than GNU-Prolog, a native compiler that has the reputation as the fastest CLP(FD) system. The reader is referred to *www.probp.com/fd_evaluation.htm* for the comparison results. The set constraint solver is significantly faster than Conjunto in Eclipse. The high performance is attributed not only to the fast finite-domain constraint solver but also to the new representation scheme for domains that facilitates updates of bounds. Further work needs to be done on improving the compiler and deploying domain-specific optimization techniques in the solvers.

References

[1] A. Aggoun and N. Beldiceanu: Overview of the CHIP Compiler System, In *Proc. of the 8th International Conference on Logic Programming*, pp.775-789, MIT Press, 1991.

[2] H. Ait-Kaci : *Warren's Abstract Machine*, The MIT Press, 1991.

[3] F. Azevedo and P. Barahona: Modeling Digital CIrcuits Problems with Set Constraints, *Proc. Computational Logic - CL 2000*, LNAI 1861, 2000.

[4] F. Benhamou, D. McAllester, P. van Hentenryck, CLP(Intervals) Revisited, *Proc. International Symposium on Logic Programming*, pp.124-138, 1994.

[5] F. Benhamou and W.J. Older, Applying Interval Arithmetic to Real, Integer, and Boolean Constraints, *Journal of Logic Programming*, 1996.

[6] M. Carlsson: Freeze, Indexing, and other Implementation Issues in the WAM, *Proc. 4th International Conference on Logic Programming*, 40-58,1987.

[7] M. Carlsson, G. Ottosson, and B. Carlson: An Open-ended Finite Domain Constraint Solver, *Proc. Programming Languages and Logic Programming*, pp.191-206, 1997.

[8] J.G. Cleary, Logical Arithmetic, *Future Generation Computing*, Vol. 2, pp.125-149, 1987.

[9] P. Codognet and D. Diaz: Compiling Constraints in clp(FD), *Journal of Logic Programming*, 27(3), pp.185-226, 1996.

[10] P. Codognet and D. Diaz: Boolean Constraints Solving Using clp(FD), *Journal of Automatic Theorem Proving*, 1996.

[11] J. Cohen: Constraint Logic Programming Languages, *Communications of ACM*, Vol.33, No.7, pp.52-68, 1990.

[12] A. Colmerauer.: Equations and In-equations on Finite and Infinite Trees, *Proc. of the International Conference on Fifth Generation Computer Systems (FGCS'84)*, ICOT, 85-99, 1984.

[13] A. Colmerauer.: An Introduction to Prolog-III, *Communications of ACM*, Vol.33, No.7, 1990.

[14] M. Dincbas, P. van Hentenryck, H. Simonis, A. Aggoun, T. Graf, and F. Berthier: The Constraint Logic Programming Language CHIP, In *Proceedings of the Fifth Generation Computer Systems*, pp.693-702, ICOT, 1988.

[15] M. Dincbas, H. Simonis, P. van Hentenryck: Solving Large Combinatorial Problems in Logic Programming. *Journal of Logic Programming*, 8(1), pp.75-93, 1990.

[16] I. Eidhammer, D. Gilbert, I. Jonassen, and M. Ratnayake: A Constraint Based Structure Description Language for Biosequences, *Constraints, An International Journal*, 2001.

[17] T.W. Fruhwirth: Theory and Practice of Constraint Handling Rules, *Journal of Logic Programming*, Vol.37, pp.95-138, 1998.

[18] C. Gervet: Interval Propagation to Reason about Sets: Definition and Implementation of a Practical Language, *Constraints, An International Journal*, vol.1, pp.191-246, 1997.

[19] W. Harvey and P.J. Stuckey: Improving Propagation by Changing Constraint Representation, *Constraints, An International Journal*, to appear.

[20] P. van Hentenryck: *Constraint Satisfaction in Logic Programming.* MIT Press, 1989.

[21] P. van Hentenryck and V. Saraswat (eds.), Strategic Directions in Constraint Programming, *ACM Computing Survey*, Vol.28, No.4, pp.701-728, 1996.

[22] N. Hentze and J. Jaffar: Set Constraints and Set-Based Analysis, *Proc. Principle and Practice of Constraint Programming*, A. Borning, ed., LNCS, pp.281-298, Springer-Verlag, 1994.

[23] T. Hickey, Q. Ju, and M.H. Van Emden, Interval arithmetic: From principles to implementation, *Journal of the ACM*, Vol. 48 , No. 5, pp.1038-1068, 2001.

[24] C. Holzbaur: Meta-structures Vs. Attribute Variables in the Context of Extensible Unification, *Proc. PLLP'92*, LNCS 631, pp.260-268, 1992.

[25] J. Jaffar, S. Michaylov, P. Stuckey and R. Yap, An Abstract Machine for CLP(R), *Proc. SIGPLAN'92 Conf. on Programming Language Design & Implementation (PLDI)*, San Francisco, 1992.

[26] J. Jaffar and M. J. Maher, Constraint Logic Programming: A Survey, *Journal of Logic Programming*, 1994.

[27] R.B. Kearfott and V. Kreinovich: *Applications of Interval Computations*, Kluwer, 1996.

[28] V. Kumar: Algorithms for Constraint Satisfaction Problems: A Survey. *AI Magazine*, 13(1), pp.32-44, 1992.

[29] J.H.M Lee and T.W. Lee: A WAM-based Abstract Machine for Interval Constraint Logic Programming, *Proc. IEEE International Conference on Tools with Artificial Intelligence*, pp.122-128, 1994.

[30] A.K. Mackworth: Constraint Satisfaction, In *Encyclopedia of Artificial Intelligence*, John Wiley & Sons, 205–211, 1986.

[31] T. Muller: *Constraint Propagation in Mozart*, PhD Thesis, Programming Systems Lab, Universit Saarlandes, *http://www.ps.uni-sb.de/˜ tmueller/thesis/*, 2001.

[32] L. Pacholski and A.Podelski: Set Constraints: A Pearl in Research on Constraints, In *Proc. 3rd International Conference on Constraint Programming*, 1997.

[33] J.F. Puget and M. Leconte: Beyond the Glass Box: Constraints as Objects, *Proc. International Logic Programming Symposium*, pp.513-527, 1995.

[34] J.F. Puget: Finite Set Intervals, in *Proc. Workshop on Set Constraints*, CP'96, 1996.

[35] E. Shapiro: The Family of Concurrent Logic Programming Languages, *ACM Comput. Surveys*, vol.21, no.3 pp.412-510, 1989.

[36] E. Tsang: *Foundations of Constraint Satisfaction*, Academic Press, 1993.

[37] M.G. Wallace, Practical Applications of Constraint Programming, *Constraints Journal*, vol.1 no.1, Kluwer, 1996.

[38] N.F. Zhou: Parameter Passing and Control Stack Management in Prolog Implementation Revisited, *ACM Transactions on Programming Languages and Systems*, 18(6), 752-779, 1996.

[39] N.F. Zhou: A High-Level Intermediate Language and the Algorithms for Compiling Finite-Domain Constraints, *Proc. Joint International Conference and Symposium on Logic Programming*, 70-84, MIT Press, 1998. A revised version is available from: *http://www.sci.brooklyn.cuny/˜ zhou/pappers/arule.pdf*.

[40] N.F. Zhou: *B-Prolog User's Manual (Version 6.1)*, *http://www.probp.com*, 2001.

[41] N.F. Zhou and J.Schimpf: Implementation of Propagation Rules for Set Constraints Revisited, submitted for publication, 2002.

APPLICATION OF UNCERTAIN VARIABLES TO DECISION MAKING IN A CLASS OF DISTRIBUTED COMPUTER SYSTEMS

Z. Bubnicki
Institute of Control and Systems Engineering
Wroclaw University of Technology
Wyb. Wyspianskiego 27, 50-370 Wroclaw, POLAND
email: bubnicki@ists.pwr.wroc.pl

Abstract: The paper is concerned with a class of uncertain distributed systems described by a set of relations containing unknown parameters. The purpose of the paper is to present an application of so called uncertain variables to decision making in the systems under consideration. In the first part of the paper, a problem of the decision making in the distributed system in which the knowledge of the system as a whole is decomposed into two levels is considered. In the second part it is shown how to apply the uncertain variables in the determination of computational tasks allocation in a set of parallel processors.

Key words: distributed systems, parallel processing, uncertain systems

1. INTRODUCTION

The paper concerns a class of distributed systems described by a set of relations between the variables characterizing the decisions and their effects (a relational knowledge representation). For the decision making in such a class of systems the algorithms of learning have been proposed [1]. The purpose of this paper is to present an application of so called *uncertain variables* to the decision making in the same class of distributed systems. The uncertain variable $\bar{x}$ is defined by a certainty distribution $h_x(x) = v(\bar{x} \,\tilde{\in}\, x)$, i.e. the certainty index v that "$\bar{x}$ is approximately equal to x". The certainty distribution is given by an expert and describing his/her knowledge of the approximate values of the variables [2, 3, 4].

2. DECISION MAKING PROBLEM

Let us consider a distributed system with a structure presented in Fig.1 where $u_j \in U_j$, $x_j \in X_j$ $(j \in \overline{1,k})$, $y \in Y$ are real number vectors. The lower and upper level subsystems are described by relations

$$R_j(u_j, x_j; c_j) \subseteq U_j \times X_j\,, \quad j \in \overline{1,k} \tag{1}$$

$$R(x_1, ..., x_k, y; b) \subseteq X_1 \times ... \times X_k \times Y\ , \tag{2}$$

respectively. The set of relations forms the knowledge representation of our system with the input $u = (u_1,..., u_k)$ **(relational knowledge representation)**. The unknown parameters b and c_j are assumed to be values of uncertain variables $\bar{b}$ and $\bar{c}_j$ described by the certainty distributions $h_b(b)$ and $h_{cj}(c_j)$, respectively. The decision problem consists in finding u^* maximizing the certainty index that the set of all possible y approximately belongs to the set $D_y \subset Y$ given by a user. The problem may be decomposed into two levels.

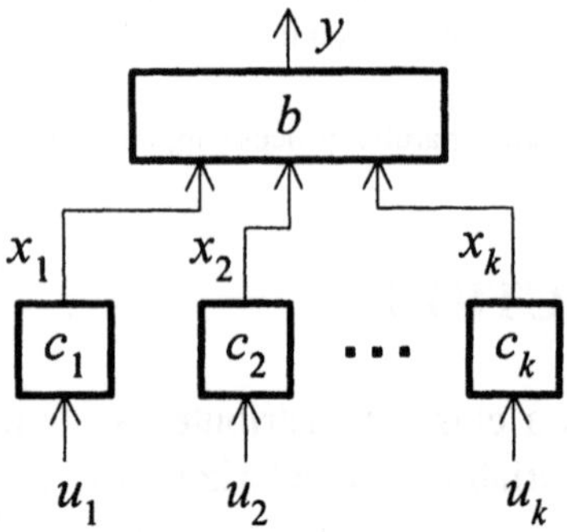

Figure 1. Two-level system

1. **Upper level problem**: Given $R(x_1,...,x_k, y; b)$, $h_b(b)$ and D_y, find

$$x^* = \arg\max_x \; v[D_y(x;\bar{b}) \,\tilde{\subseteq}\, D_y] \stackrel{\Delta}{=} v(x)$$

where $x = (x_1,..., x_k)$ and $D_y(x;\bar{b})$ is the set of all possible y for the fixed

x. It may be shown [1, 2] that

$$v(x) = \max_{b \in D_b(x)} h_b(b)$$

where $D_b(x) = \{b \in B : (x, y) \in R(x, y; b) \rightarrow y \in D_y\}$.

2. **Lower level problem**: Given $R_j(u_j, x_j; c_j)$, $h_{cj}(c_j)$ and D_{xj}, find u_j^* maximizing $v(\bar{x}_j \,\tilde{\in}\, D_{xj})$; $j \in \overline{1,k}$. The sets D_{xj} are such that $D_{x1} \times D_{x2} \times ... \times D_{xk} \subseteq D_x$ where D_x is the set of solutions x^* of the upper level problem. The solution is analogous to that for the upper level.

3. TASK ALLOCATION

The approach presented in the previous section may be applied to a problem of the tasks allocation in the group of parallel processors with uncertain execution times. We assume that the global computational task to be distributed may be decomposed into N separate parts (programs or parts of programs) which may be executed simultaneously by the separate processors. Each partial task is characterized by an upper bound of the execution time τ_j for j-th processor ($j = 1, 2, ..., k$), and τ_j is assumed to be the same for each partial task. The decision problem consists in the determination of the numbers of the partial tasks $n_1, n_2, ..., n_k$ assigned to the processors taking into account the execution time $T = \max\{T_1, T_2, ..., T_k\}$ where T_j is the execution time for j-th processor; $n_1 + ... + n_k = N$. If N is sufficiently large, we can determine the decisions $u_j \in R^+$ (any positive numbers) and then obtain n_j by rounding off u_j to the nearest integer. To apply the notation in the previous section let us denote $T_j \triangleq x_j$, $T \triangleq y$, $\tau_j \triangleq c_j$. Then the knowledge representation of our distributed system is as follows: $x_j \le c_j u_j$, $y = \max\{x_1, x_2, ..., x_k\}$. The unknown parameters c_j are assumed to be values of uncertain variables $\bar{c}_j$ described by the certainty distributions $h_{cj}(c_j)$ given by an expert estimating the execution times for the partial tasks. The **decision problem** may be formulated as follows: Given α and $h_{cj}(c_j)$, $j \in \overline{1,k}$, find the allocation $u^* = (u_1^*, u_2^*, ..., u_k^*)$ maximizing the certainty index of the property: " the user's requirement is approximately satisfied ", i.e. " the approximate value of the execution time $T = y$ is less than α ". Then

$$u^* = \arg\max_u v(T \tilde{\leq} \alpha)$$

where "$T \tilde{\leq} \alpha$"="$D_T(u) \tilde{\subseteq} [0,\alpha]$", $D_T(u)$ is the set of possible values T for the fixed u and $v[T \tilde{\leq} \alpha] = v[(T_1 \tilde{\leq} \alpha) \wedge ... \wedge (T_k \tilde{\leq} \alpha)] = \min v_j(u_j)$ where

$$v_j(u_j) = v[T_j \tilde{\leq} \alpha] = \max_{c_j \in D_{cj}(u_j)} h_{cj}(c_j) \qquad (3)$$

and $D_{cj}(u_j)$ is described by the inequality $c_j \leq \alpha u_j^{-1}$.

The procedure of the determination of u^* is then the following:
1. To determine $v_j(u_j)$ according to (3). 2. To determine $u_1^*, u_2^*, ..., u_k^*$ by solving the maximization problem

$$\max_{u_1, ..., u_k} \min\{v_1(u_1), ..., v_k(u_k)\}$$

subject to constraints $u_1 + ... + u_k = N$. 3. To round off the values u_j^* and to obtain the number n_j^*.

Numerical examples and simulations showed a significant influence of the parameters in the certainty distributions on the final results.

NOTES

This work was supported by the Polish State Committee for Scientific Research under Grant No. 4 T11C 001 22

4. REFERENCES

1. Bubnicki Z. Knowledge validation and updating in a class of uncertain distributed knowledge systems. Proc. of 16th World Computer Congress, vol. IIP; 2000 August 21-25; Beijing. Beijing: Publ. House of Electr. Industry, 2000
2. Bubnicki, Z. Uncertain variables and their applications for a class of uncertain systems. International Journal of Systems Science 2001; 32:651-59
3. Bubnicki, Z. Uncertain variables and their application to decision making. IEEE Transactions on SMC, Part A: Systems and Humans 2001; 31:587-96
4. Bubnicki, Zdzislaw, *Uncertain Logics, Variables and Systems*. London, Berlin: Springer-Verlag, 2002 (in press).

LEARNING FUZZY DECISION TREES FROM SEQUENTIAL AND INCOMPLETE DATA

G. Chen, Ruqian Lu, Z. Jin
Institute of Mathematics, Chinese Academy of Sciences
No. A1, Nansijie, Zhongguancun, Beijing 100080, P.R. China
cg@amss.ac.cn , rqlu@math08.ac.cn, zhijin@math03.math.ac.cn
Tel: +86-10-62554389

Abstract: In this paper we present a way of constructing and using fuzzy decision trees for machine learning from sequential and incomplete data. We develop a theory and technique for processing such data. At first, we introduce a decision tree with fuzzy attributes and class the properties of fuzzy attributes and classes, where we will introduce the fuzzy division of objects in classes in a different way than that used in the literature. Then we will also introduce properties of fuzzy attribute value to enrich the fuzziness of our decision trees.

Keywords: fuzzy decision trees, tendency detection, sequential and incomplete data

1. INTRODUCTION

Fuzzy decision trees have been used in machine learning and data analysis to solve the problem of incomplete data and noisy data [2, 3, 5]. When using the technique of fuzzy decision trees, the fuzziness of decision-making may be introduced at different points such as: a) The values of attributes may be fuzzy, b)The matching of attribute values may be fuzzy, c) The division of objects in classes may be fuzzy, d) The branching of a node in different arcs may be fuzzy. In literature, the properties b) and d) are often used to define a fuzzy decision tree. For example, Chang and Pavlidis[1] introduced a fuzzy decision tree such that each non-leaf node I has a k-tuple decision function f_i from the sample set X to $[0,1]^k$ and k ordered sons. In

Janikow's fuzzy decision trees[2], an example can match more than one condition and the example may eventually fall into many of the leaves.

2. FUZZY DECISION TREE

A fuzzy decision tree with the goal classes ($g_1, g_2, \ldots, g_L$), the attributes ($a_1, a_2, \ldots, a_n$), and the dictionary of fuzziness *DOF*=(*C, D, F, M, Q*), is a tree, called *FDT*, with the following properties: 1) It is finite, 2) Each leaf of the tree corresponds to a membership vector $m=(m_1, m_2, \ldots, m_L)$, where L is the number of classes, and where each m_i is a value from [0,1], denoting the degree to which this leaf node belongs to the ith class, 3) Each branch is attached with a fuzzy expression c_i, where c_i belongs to F of *DOF*.

Let there be in total L different classes which form a set G. The membership vector of an object with regard to these classes is a L-dimensional vector, of which each component is a real number in [0,1]. Let *ob[i]* be the ith component of the membership vector of the object *ob*. This *ob[i]* denotes the membership degree of *ob* with regard to the ith class g_i. Further let the appearance maximum $apmax(g_i, X)$ and the appearance minimum $apmin(g_i, X)$ of the ith class g_i with regard to the object set X be

$$apmax(g_i, X)=Max\{ob[i] \mid ob \text{ is an object of } X\}$$

$$apmin(g_i, X)=Min\{ob[i] \mid ob \text{ is an object of } X\}$$

then the following sum:

$$H(X,G)=\sum\{ apmax(g_i, X)\times \log apmin(g_i, X) \mid \text{for all } i\}$$

is called the fuzzy entropy of the set X with regard to the set G of classes.

3. TENDENCY DETECTION WITH FDT

The length of a finite sequence *a*, length(*a*), is the number of its elements minus one. The average height of the sequence *a*, high(*a*), whose elements are real numbers, is the mean value of these values.

Let $SVL=(a_0, a_1, \ldots, a_N)$ be a sequence. We say that a_1 is its head and a_N its tail. Further we define the tendency of change *TOC*, of the sequence *SVL* as follows:

$$TOC=(a_N-a_0)/N$$

We call the tendency positive if *TOC* is positive, otherwise we call it negative. Length, average height and tendency of change are the three parameters which characterize the state of a sequence. We use a unified name tendency for all of the three together.

Now we have transformed the problem of classifying exact value sequences into one of classifying fuzzy value sequences. The question remaining is how to compare vectors (sequences) of unequal length and how to use them in the decision procedure.

4. CONSTRUCTING FUZZY DECISION TREES

Since one-way adjusted value sequences are rather frequently met in the practice. We are going to first process this kind of incomplete data. Here we also allow fuzzy values. Since the fuzzy value sequences are usually not of equal length, we will not use the method of vector comparison or vector clustering. Rather, we will try to construct a new kind of fuzzy decision trees which also apply to one-way-adjusted fuzzy value sequences. However, before we go into the details, we should differentiate between two issue: (1) To construct a fuzzy decision tree by using incomplete data. (2) To test an example consisting of incomplete data. In the following we will only discuss the issue of constructing a decision tree for one-way adjusted data.

Algorithm 1. (Construction of Fuzzy Decision Trees for Pre-adjusted Sequences).

1. Let X be the set of all examples and $ihr > 0$ be some threshold value. Each example is a fuzzed data sequence as described in algorithm 1. Let A and B two empty sets of open and closed nodes, respectively.
2. Construct a decision tree T with only one node, i.e. the root (X, Z) where X is the set of all examples, Z is the length of the longest fuzzy value sequence among all examples, i.e., Z $=max$ *{|seq|| seq is the fuzzy value sequence of some example from X}*
   Put (X, Z) in the set A.
3. Let (X',Z') be an open leaf node. If all examples of X' belong to the same set of classes (for a precise meaning of this statement see step 3 of algorithm 1), or if Z equals to zero, then fetch this node from A and put it into B. Call the vector
   $M = Mean\{m_i | m_i \text{ is the membership vector of some example from } X\}$
   as the membership vector of (X,Z). The average is taken for each component separately. Do the same for all nodes of such kind.
4. Stop the algorithm if A becomes empty.
5. Fetch a node (X', Z') from A and put it into B. Let $i = Z\text{-}Z'+1$.
6. If there is no non-empty subset X'' of X', where no sequence has an *i-th* item, then go to step 9. Otherwise build the vector
   $M = mean\{m_i | m_i \text{ is the membership vector of some example from } X\}$
   The average is separately taken for each component.

7. If $X'=X''$ then define M be its membership vector and Go to step 3.
8. Otherwise, call M the complement vector of (X',Z'). Let X'=X'-X''.
9. Let the different fuzzy values *FR* of the *i-th* items of all examples of the set X' be $(d_1, d_2, ..., d_G)$. Construct *G* branches from the node (X', Z'), marked with the label $(d_1, d_2, ..., d_G)$, respectively. Call the endpoints of these branches $(X'_j, Z'\text{-}1)$ respectively, for j =1 , ...,G, where the ith item of the fuzzy value sequence of each example from X^j is equal to d_j . We put all of them in *A*.
10. Go to step 3.

5. CONCLUSION

We have present here our work on how detect temporal tendencies in form of fuzzy decision trees. A major part of this research has been contributed to the solution of the problem, that the temporal knowledge and data we collect is often incomplete.

6. REFERENCE

[1] Chang, R.L.P. and Pavlids, T. Fuzzy decision trees. In Proceedings of the IEEE Transactions on Systems, Man, and Cybernetics, pages 360-367, 1976.

[2] Janikow, C.Z.. Fuzzy processing in decision trees. In Proceedings of the sixth International Symposium on Artificial Intelligent, pages 360-367, 1993.

[3] Janikow, C.Z.. Fuzzy decision trees, issues and methods. IEEE Transactions on Systems, Man, and Cybernatics, 1997.

[4] Lu,R. and Jin,Z. Domain modeling-based software engineering, Kluwer Academic Publishers. August 2000

[5] M.Umato and et al. Fuzzy decision trees by fuzzy ID3 algorithm and its application to diagonosis systems. In Proceedings of the third IEEE Conference onFuzzy Systems, pages 2113-2118, 1994.

HARNESSING THE INTERNET INTO A KNOWLEDGE FRAMEWORK

Richard Longworth
Capilano College, Vancouver, Canada rlong@capcollege.bc.ca
iGEN Knowledge Solutions, Vancouver, Canada rlong@igeninc.com

Abstract: This paper identifies a critical problem for learners and teachers: the information overload associated with the Internet, and why it is not an effective tool for learning. The paper identifies two current learning theories, constructivism and multiple intelligences. It suggests a solution based on recent technology advances using XML, DOM, and the RDF framework. The proposed solution gives learners and teachers a way to retrieve information from the Internet, and to create an on-line knowledge framework for all learners..

1. THE PROBLEM: INFORMATION OVERLOAD

Excessive information on the Internet is particularly irksome for educators and students. So much raw material is received that, in most cases, it overwhelms the learner. The result is "negative information which causes the reader to know less because it cannot be integrated, applied, and transformed into knowledge"[4].

Acquiring information is not the same as knowledge. "We can mass produce information through the Internet, but we cannot mass produce knowledge which is created by individual minds "[6]. Jace Hargis identifies two pedagogical short-comings related to the seemingly infinite resources on the Internet. "The first is information overload and lack of useful instructional format, the second is the effective design and evaluation of different learning formats"[2].

A solution is to leverage the mass of information that is available on the Internet to create better knowledge frameworks.

2. DEFINING A PEDAGOGICAL FRAMEWORK

In order to develop a new model for knowledge acquisition, we need to acquaint ourselves with current learning theories.

One modern approach is the constructivist framework. It implies that the knowledge received is not passively absorbed but integrated, or constructed, in a unique way by the learner.

Dirk Rodenberg suggests that learning must provide the context defined by the learner's experience, into which new content must be integrated. These cognitive models provide a ground onto which new information is integrated, which in turn extends and reshapes these models. Further, Rodenberg argues that the cognitive load that learners can carry is based on their level of expertise [5].

Thus learning is best accomplished when students are able to think about a topic and to "provide an opportunity of alternate sources, reconciling any differences and forming a reliable coherent individualized model of the topic in question"[5]. The basic premise of constructivism is that the learner must construct knowledge; the teacher cannot necessarily supply it.

3. A POTENTIAL SOLUTION

Some recent attempts to make the web smarter include work by Rob Barrett at the Almaden Research Center (Web Browsing Intelligence), and by Pattie Maes and her colleagues at MIT Multimedia Labs (collaborative filtering and intelligent agents) [3]. The acceptance of this work directs future software towards more personalization and more user-centred applications. Our solution is geared towards personalized services in a framework of XML, DOM and RDF.

XML

XML-based technology provides a means for identifying content. It gives meaning to the information, and if organized correctly, substantially reduces information overload. The XML-world speaks of XML Documents for specific constituents. Since our domain is knowledge, it will be named "XML General Knowledge Document." Here is our XML Document:

XML General Knowledge Document

```
<Knowledge>
   <Subject>
      <Topic>
```

<Title>

<Author>

<Reference>

<Language>

<Date>

<Comprehension>
<Level>

<Readability>

<CognitiveKeys>

<Content>

.... with suitable end tags

Most of the tags (elements) are self-explanatory, however some need annotation.

Knowledge is our root element. The nested elements include

- a Reference that identifies any credible sources such as World Encyclopedia or the Smithsonian Institute
- Language to identify the written content language.

The important Comprehension element contains nested elements to aid the learner at his/her comprehension level

- Level has three possible values: "Introductory" or "Intermediate" or "Advanced"
- Readability is based on either the Gunning-Fogg or Flesch-Kincaid index that identifies a grade level within a statistical norm.
- CognitiveKeys are key words and phrases (such as description, definition, outline, logical explanation) that correlate learning styles with Gardner's seven multiple intelligences [1] (verbal, visual, logical, kinesthetic, rhythmic, interpersonal, intra-personal).

DOM and RDF

The above schema can be enhanced through manipulating DOM objects using XPath and XPointers. We would be particularly interested in XPath to define the direction and destination through the object node, and XPointers to pick out partial content and reduce the excessive information.

RDF is a framework that provides an infrastructure for using and encoding metadata. Our XML General Knowledge Document is a product that would be accessed from the RDF. Since this framework works within the

XML domain, our General Knowledge Document would include a unique URI using a namespace convention.

4. APPLYING THE PROPOSED SOLUTION

4.1 A Curriculum Example

The learner wishes to enhance his/her knowledge of a topic by using the Internet. The learner sends a request identifying the Subject/Topic and any constraints (such as readability level, understanding level, and any cognitive keys) as a personalized request. An application program notifies a Search Engine of the Subject/Topic keyword search. The Search Engine, based on General Knowledge XML documents, finds sites meeting the Subject/Topic criteria. The URL and the XML document are returned and passed to the Application Server. The application program matches the learner's constraints against the XML tags. The Application Server alerts the Web Browser on the user-side of the matching filtered URL's.

The learner can now use the results of the refined search. User feedback is gathered and used for future intelligent agents and for data warehousing in a database server.

5. FUTURE POSSIBILITIES

Potential exists for disadvantaged learners; for personalized learning; for providing motivational resources; and for extending the model with technology enhancements.

Here are a few possibilities:

Adopting an XML Document allows us to use the same information across a variety of media, including speech synthesizers and Braille readers

Clustering on any CognitiveKeys would empower the learner to seek out his/her specific learning styles, for example, learning through "models" or "pictures" or "text"

Clustering on Level and Readability would empower the learner in the construction of a hierarchy of learning

Identifying personal preferences and behaviour patterns opening the potential of software agents

6. CONCLUSION

The problem defined in the introduction is the gap between learning and knowledge, and the difficulty of using the Internet as a meaningful information source. Using a constructivist approach to learning, we have suggested a way to turn the Internet into a learning framework, and a means of reducing information overload. The core solution is the XML General Knowledge Document. This involves the learner selecting keywords based on his/her level of knowledge and prior experiences; the effect is to open the possibility of constructing a hierarchy of learning that links new knowledge to existing patterns. The solution therefore offers repeated and relevant information which matches the experience of the learner, and provides a manner of learning through the Internet which is based on sound pedagogical principles.

7. REFERENCES

1. Gardner, Howard (1995). Multiple Intelligences. Arlington, Illinois: Skylight Training.

2. Hargis, Jace (Summer 2001). Can Students Learn Science Using the Internet? Journal of Research on Computing in Education. Volume 33 #4.

3. Maes Pattie. Agents that Reduce Work and Information Overload. Online: http://pattie.www.media.mit.edu/people/pattie/CACM-94/CACM-94.p1.html

4. Milton, B. B. (1989). Making Sense or Non-Sense: Key Issues in the Information Age. Canadian Vocational Journal 24, no 3 (February 1989).

5. Rodenberg, Dirk (December 1998). Shifting Perspectives in Education Technology. Online: http://horizon.unc.edu/TS/default.asp?show=article&id=59

6. Wurman, Richard (1989). Information Anxiety, New York: Bantam Doubleday Dell Publishing Group.

ANALOGY SUPPORTS FOR SOFTWARE REUSE AND KNOWLEDGE MANAGEMENT

Chung-Horng Lung[a], Gerald T. Mackulak[b], and Joseph E. Urban[c]
[a]Department of Systems and Computer Engineering
Carleton University, Ottawa, Canada
chlung@sce.carleton.ca

[b]Department of Industrial Engineering
Ariona State Univeristy, Tempe, AZ
mackulak@asu.edu

[c]Department of Computer Science & Engineering
Arizona State Univeristy, Tempe, AZ
joseph.urban@asu.edu

1. INTRODUCTION

Analogical reasoning is critical in problem solving and is fundamental in learning and cognitive development, because analogy is a key factor in hypothesis formation, explanation, and the definition of abstract concepts [1,2,4]. Many analogy theories have been proposed to solve the problem A:B::C:X. Given that A is related to B as C is related to some X, find that X. For example, car:engine::gear:tooth.

Software reuse is similar to analogical reasoning in some respects. To reuse an existing solution for a new problem, we are essentially solving a problem like p(X):s(X)::p(Y):s(X'), where problems p(X) and p(Y) are identical or analogous, and solutions s(X) and s(X') are identical or similar. It may or may not be easy to identify the similarities and differences between p(X) and p(Y). Software reuse can also be at different levels, such as software architectures or at the code level.

Knowledge management deals with the way of how to capture, organize, update, share, and use the knowledge. Knowledge management is closely coupled with analogy in that both areas discuss the transfer of knowledge from one problem (base) to another problem (target).

These three areas have many in common. All deals with similar dimensions, including representation, retrieval, elaboration, mapping, evaluation, integration, generalization, classification, and learning. Furthermore, analogy community advocates that rich representation must include syntactic, semantic, and pragmatic components [3,4]. Same ideas are used in software engineering discipline.

The objective of this paper is to present some crucial discoveries in analogy [1-4]. We have developed an approach based on analogy to support software modelling. A study in the manufacturing problem domain is briefly described. The study shows reuse from the discrete manufacturing domain to continuous manufacturing problem area. Compared with the base, the development time for the target problem artifacts is significantly reduced from days to hours. The result suggests researchers in software engineering and knowledge management may benefit more by exploring further in the analogy community.

2. ANALOGICAL REASONING

Here, we highlight two critical aspects of analogy, namely modelling of high-order relations and reasoning of semantic relations.

A often discussed area in various analogical reasoning theories is relations [1-4]. Relations between concepts, not just the representation of individual concepts, are the key in identifying analogy. Relational modelling in this paper emphasizes two aspects: higher-order relations and classification of semantic relations.

The central idea in Gentner's structure-mapping theory [3] is the principle of systematicity, which states that analogy is a mapping of systems of relations governed by higher-order relations with inferential import, rather than isolated predicates. Higher-order relations capture the relation of relations.

Take the analogy between the structure of our solar system and the atom system as an example. Several relations between the sun and a planet include distance, attract, more-massive, revolve-around, and hotter-than. Together, distance, attract, more-massive, and revolve-around form a higher-order relation:

CAUSE [distance(sun, planet), attract(sun, planet), more massive(sun, planet), revolve-around(planet, sun)]

This higher-order relation can be mapped to the atom system. Some solutions for the solar system can then be mapped to the atom system. Isolated relations, such as the sun is hotter-than the planet, are discarded in the mapping phase.

Next, the ability to readily compare relations means that relations are readily decomposed into more primitive elements [2]. People readily compare relations. This requires that relations can be decomposed into aspects in which they are the same and aspects in which they differ. Bejar et al. [1] presented a taxonomy of the semantic relations. Two of relation classes are closely related to object-oriented methods. They are class inclusion (Is-A) and part-whole (Has-A).

3. APPLICATION OF ANALOGY TO SOFTWARE REUSE AND KNOWLEDGE TRANSFER

The idea of software reuse through analogy is not new [5,6]. In order to support the modelling of higher-order relations, the approach comprises object modelling, functional modelling, relational modelling, and dynamic modelling. Object, functional, and dynamic modelling are similar to object-oriented methods. Specifically, the main artifacts adopted from those modelling phases include entity relationship diagram, data flow diagram, functional descriptions, and a rule-based Petri net representation. The artifacts can be replaced with other similar representation schemes.

Object Modelling. We start with a detailed comparison of the main components between the discrete and continuous manufacturing. The main purpose is to identify both similarities and differences. Both domains have similar material handling systems, whose primary operation is to move and store materials, parts, and products. In a continuous problem, the number of machines is fewer, but generally each machine is costly and performs more complex operations. Because the stations are more sophisticated in the continuous domain, planning for maintenance and equipment failure is more important than in the discrete domain. Another significant difference is the scheduling process due to the difference in product type and machine stations. As a result, simulation models needed for these two domains are also different. In the discrete domain, finite state machines and discrete event models are commonly used. In the continuous domain, difference equations or differential equations are needed.

Based on above comparison and observations, and the object model for discrete manufacturing, an entity relationship diagram (ERD) for the continuous domain is derived. Based on the analysis, entities queue and sensor, and their associated relationships are removed for the target domain.

Functional Modelling. The main artifact for the functional model is data flow diagrams (DFD). The DFD derived for the target share many similarities with that of the base. There are eight main processes in the base problem. Seven processes are derived from the discrete manufacturing and one (dealing with the queue) is removed. Five processes are repeated use without modifications. Two processes that deal with monitoring of product position is modified to deliver/remove materials and monitoring the product quality, respectively.

Dynamic modelling. Dynamic modelling includes modelling of high-order relations. Dynamic models capture more detailed and more specific information. Modelling of higher-order relations, on the other hand, conveys high-level cause-effect information. Currently, there is no appropriate technique or formal mechanism for modelling higher-order relations, i.e., relations of relations. In traditional OO modelling, we usually capture relations between classes or objects. Those types of relations represent low-order relations.

The idea is similar to the dynamic modelling in OO modelling languages like UML. Features in UML to model behavioural diagrams, e.g., use case diagram, sequence diagram, and collaboration diagram, represent collection of relations, which is conceptually similar to the structure of relations proposed in analogical reasoning. However, many OO applications focus on the solution space. To be effective, the problem space should be explicitly and clearly modelled. Moreover, we also need to represent the problem space beyond objects and lower-order relations. Improvements in representation will facilitate the identification of similarities and differences between p(X) and p(Y) as stated in the introduction.

Relational Modelling. Class inclusion (Is-A) and part-whole (Has-A) relations proposed in analogy are also widely used in OO modelling. Bejar et al. [1] listed five members for the Is-A class and ten members for the Has-A class, which might worth further exploring.

For this study, part-whole relations are examined in more detail. For instance, an engine is part of a car. Specifically, car:engine is in the Object:Component category [1]. However, there are differences beyond the part-whole level. For the continuous manufacturing, there also exist part-whole relations, but they fall into the Mass:Portion category as in the milk:skim milk example. The distinction between the two problems directs us to do further investigation. As a result, two different types of machine stations and control processes are identified for these two domains, albeit these two domains share a similar higher-order relation.

Part-whole relationships are widely used in OO modeling. There is confusion about the relationship [7]. In UML, composition is advocated as a special form of aggregation within which the parts are inseparable from the whole. The idea of separating composition from aggregation is similar to the classification of semantic relations. However, there exist more differences than just aggregation and composition. For example, *car:engine* and *department:company* are different even though they both share part-whole relationships. In the first case, car has one engine and only one. Other parts, e.g., transmission, are very different from engine. However, departments within a company share many similarities. In [1], both examples share part-whole relationship, but *car:engine* is classified as *Object:Component* and *company:department* belongs to *Collection:Member.*

4. CONCLUSION AND FUTURE DIRECTIONS

This article presented an analogy-based approach to support software ruse and knowledge transfer. A case study was briefly presented. We highlighted lessons that we can learn from analogy. Some important lessons include modelling of higher-order relations, comparison of semantic relations, and OO modelling. Software engineering is a people- and knowledge-intensive business that would benefit from the reuse of past experience. Other relevant methods reported in analogical reasoning could also be applied to software engineering.

5. REFERENCES

1. I.I. Bejar, R. Chaffin, S. Embretson, *Cognitive and Psychometric analysis of analogical problem solving*, Springer-Verlag, 1991.
2. R. Chaffin and D. Herrmann, "Relation Element Theory: a New Account of the Representation and Processing of Semantic Relations", *Memory and Learning: The Ebbinghaus Centennial Conf.*, 1987, pp. 221-245.
3. D. Gentner, "Structure-Mapping: a Theoretical Framework for Analogy", *Cognitive Science*, vol. 7, no. 2, 1983, pp. 155-170.
4. D. Helman, ed., *Analogical Reasoning*, Kluwer Academic Publishers, 1988.
5. C.-H. Lung and J.E. Urban, "An Expanded View of Domain Modeling for Software Analogy", *Proc. of Int'l Computer Software & Applications Conf,* 1995, pp. 77-82.
6. N.A.M. Maiden and A.G. Sutcliffe, "Requirements Engineering by Example: an Empirical Study", *Proc. of IEEE Int'l Symp. on Reqt. Eng.*, 1993, pp. 104-111.
7. A.L. Opdahl, et al. "Ontological Analysis of Whole-Part Relationships in OO-Models", *Info and Software Technology*, 43, 2001, pp. 387-399.

KNOWLEDGE MANAGEMENT SUPPORT FOR COOPERATIVE RESEARCH

Jun Ma and Matthias Hemmje
Fraunhofer-IPSI, Dolivostrasse 15, Darmstadt D-64293, Germany
{jun,hemmje}@ipsi.fhg.de, Tel:+49-6151-869-4884; +49-6151-869-844

Abstract: A prototype system designed for enhancing the cooperative research of groups and individuals in research institutes is provided. The main implementing techniques are introduced as well.

Keywords: knowledge management, knowledge filters, knowledge audit, knowledge reuse.

1. INTRODUCTION

A prototype system designed based on the research activities of Fraunhofer-IPSI for enhancing the cooperative research of groups and individuals is introduced. Compared with some known knowledge management (KM) systems [1,2,4-6], the design is human-centred and service-oriented, i.e. it is emphasized more to enhance working efficiency, decrease expense, avoid reinventing, reuse former working experience and strengthen co-research in innovative organizations by providing intelligent services. An outline of the main functions of the prototype system is shown in Fig. 1.

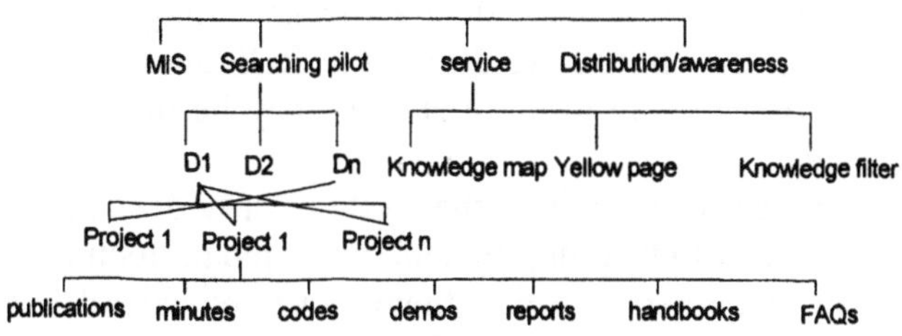

Figure 1. An outline of the prototype system.

2. THE MAIN IMPLEMENTATION TECHNIQUES

The design and implementation of the system mainly utilizes the databases recording the profiles of employees and groups as well as the documents describing the best practices and the projects carried out before. A personal profile consists of research interests, the projects participated, the roles in these projects, education and training as well as publications. A group profile describes the members in the group and the synergy relations with other partners. The descriptions of the projects and best practices in the system are presented in meta-documents that are classified into several categories according to application domains denoted by *D1, D2,..., Dn* and the types of documents shown in Fig. 1. These documents are organized in hierarchy based on the subclass-of relations defined on the categories. For each application domain, the learning materials is presented by a directed graph *Gi* (V,A) without directed cycles, where V consists of the names of the learning materials; $\forall u,v \in V$, $<u,v> \in A$ iff it is better for a learner to study *u* before to study *v*. Furthermore the learning materials are classified as the *elementary* and the *professional* based on their contents.

Some techniques used in the project are now introduced below.

1. Knowledge audit: When one wants to participate a project related to a domain *Di*, based on his/her profile, e.g. the courses leaned, and the corresponding directed graph *Gi*, the system helps him/her to find which knowledge is missing and how to schedule his/her study as well as recommends suitable learning materials to him/her.
2. Knowledge mapping: based on the profiles of individuals and groups, the system displays various relationships graphically, e.g., the technical and research synergy relations among individuals, groups and the partners inside and outside the institute. The detail information of the partners can be provided based on the *yellow pages* of the system as well.
3. Knowledge bases: The descriptions of the best practices and projects carried out before are presented in meta-documents, where meta-data are used to annotate the entities in a meta-document and the semantic relationships among the entities in the meta-document. An entity may be a demo, a literal report, and a piece of graphic and image. The semantic relationships among the entities are denoted in RDF and XML [8], while the documents corresponding to these entities may be dispersed across a number of servers.
4. Knowledge awareness/distribution: the system provides each group a shared file space that allows group members to upload documents and in the meantime informs others to access them. A shared calendar shows the schedules of group members in coming weeks. Based on the users' searching requirements and the personal profiles, e.g. publications, the roles in projects and the projects participated before, the system can also

recommend the experts in some application areas within organizations and partners.

In the following talk, we describe a knowledge filter in detail because for the time being knowledge filtering is done mainly by human, e.g. accepting the consensus of experts [7]. Our algorithm is different from some known collaborative filters, e.g. the algorithms provided in [3], in terms of multi-evaluation factors with different weights are synthetically considered.

The main usage of the knowledge filter is to rank files based on the comments of experts or peers. Then the knowledge filter will generate a synthetic comment in order to identify whether files should be added into the knowledge bases or the databases or other file systems. The algorithm for knowledge filtering collects the comments of experts on the Internet and produces the synthetic comment based on fuzzy computation and statistics. The detail algorithm is described below.

Let P represent a file, e.g., which is a proposal or business strategy. We design an m×n matrix to collect the comments for P from experts. Let U = $\{u_1, u_2, \ldots, u_n\}$, where u_i, $1 \le i \le n$, is an evaluation factor, such as, *originality, creativity, presentation, relativity* and so on. The comment set V = $\{v_1, v_2, \ldots, v_m\}$, where v_i is a comment, $1 \le i \le m$, e.g. *"bad", "normal", "good" and "excellent"*. If an expert chooses a comment v_i to evaluation factor u_j for P, then he/she gives a mark at the position *(i,j)* of the table. Following algorithm gives a synthetic comment by fuzzy and statistic computation to determine whether the knowledge is good enough to be added to knowledge bases. The detail will be discussed below.

Algorithm (synthetic comment computation)

Input:

1. A file P;
2. The evaluation factor set U=$\{u_1, u_2, \ldots, u_n\}$, where u_i, $1 \le i \le n$, is an evaluation factor;
3. The comment set V =$\{v_1, v_2, \ldots, v_m\}$, where v_i is a comment, $1 \le i \le m$.
4. A fuzzy vector X=$(x_1/u_1, x_2/u_2, \cdots, x_n/u_n)$, such that, $\sum_1^n x_i = 1$. $x_i \ge 0$, $i = 1,2,\ldots,n$. x_i represents the importance of the factor u_i in the evaluation.
5. The experts' comments on P.

Output: A synthetic comment of P.

Step 1. After collecting the comments from all referees for a file P, calculate following fuzzy sets:

$(\mu_{i1}/v_1, \mu_{i2}/v_2, \cdots, \mu_{im}/v_m)$, $0 \le \mu_{ij} \le 1$, $i = 1,2,\ldots n$; $j=1,2,\ldots m$; Where μ_{ij} = (the number of persons who give v_j to u_i)/ (total number of referees)× 100%. *N* fuzzy sets are represented in a matrix $E = (\mu_{ij})_{n\times m}$.

Step 2. Calculate following vector

$(y_1/v_1, y_2/v_2, \cdots, y_m/v_m)$ by following formula.

$$y_i = \bigvee_{i=1}^{n} (x_i \wedge \mu_{ij}),\ j = 1, 2, \cdots m.$$

Where $\vee$ and $\wedge$ represent a suitable operation, e.g. $a \vee b$ = max(*a*,*b*); and $a \wedge b$ = min(*a*,*b*);

Step 3. If y_k is of the maximum in set $\{ y_1, y_2, \ldots y_m \}$, then output v_k as the synthetic comment.

P will be added to knowledge base if v_k is good enough. The principle of the algorithm can be stated as follows. We do the statistics computation in the step 2, where the percentage of the comment v_j gotten in all given comments on evaluation factor u_i is calculated, $1 \le i \le n$ and $1 \le j \le m$. In step 3, based on the principle of fuzzy processing technique, a fuzzy vector X = $(x_1/u_1, x_2/u_2, \cdots, x_n/u_n)$ is used, where x_i represents the importance of evaluation factor u_i in the computation of a synthetic comment on a proposal P. x_i is as a weight value in the calculation of the mathematics expectation of each v_j, $1 \le j \le m$ also. Clearly the computation of mathematics expectation of v_i, $1 \le i \le m$, considers both the comments from all referees and the importance of each evaluation factor. We choose the one with the maximum mathematics expectation among all comments as the final comment on P.

In this paper we want to show many functions of KM systems can be designed and implemented based on the descriptions of the profiles of employees and groups; knowledge bases can be organized based on the meta-documents that describe the best practice and projects in the system. We also introduce a design of a knowledge filter. We want to show a service-oriented KM system can provide a convenient environment for researchers in their daily work.

References

[1] Borghoff U.M., and Pareschi R., Information Technology for Knowledge Management, Springer-Verlag press, 1998, 1-8.

[2] Caldwell N.H.M., Clarkson P.J., Rodgers P.A. and Huxor A.P., Web-Based Knowledge Management for Distributed Design, IEEE Intelligent systems, May/June 2000, 40-47.

[3] Collaborative Filters, http://www.acm.org/chi95/Electronic/documents/papers.

[4] Kim K.H., and Paik S.K. Practical Experiences and Requirements on Workflow, Proceedings on Coordination Technology for Collaborative Applications, Wolfram Conen and G.Neumann (Eds) ,Singapore, Springer-Verlag press, 1997, pp145-160.

[5] Kappel G., Schott S.R. and Retschitzegger W., Proceedings on Coordination in Workflow Management Systems A Rule-Based Approach, Coordination Technology for Collaborative Applications, Eds. Wolfram Conen, G.Neumann ,Singapore, Springer-Verlag press, 1997, 100-119.

[6] Nonaka I. and Takeuchi H., The knowledge Creating Company: How Japanese Companies Create the Dynamics of Innovation, New York: Oxford Univ. Press, 1995.

[7] O'Leary D.E, Enterprise knowledge management, IEEE on Computer, March, 1998, 54-61.

[8] RDF and XML, www.w3.org/TR.

AN EXTENDED POSSIBILITY-BASED FUZZY NESTED RELATIONAL DATABASE MODEL AND ALGEBRA

Z. M. Ma and F. Mili
Department of Computer Science and Engineering , Oakland University, Rochester, MI 48309

1. INTRODUCTION

In order to enhance the expressive power of relational database model, non-first normal (NF^2 or nested) relational database model has been introduced, where attribute values may be atomic or set-valued and even relations themselves [1], on one hand. On the other hand, Fuzzy values have been employed to model information imprecision in databases since Zadeh [4] proposed the theory of fuzzy sets. A NF^2 relational database model with fuzzy information accommodates imprecision and complexity of the real world objects simultaneously. Based on similarity relation, a fuzzy NF^2 relational database model is introduced in [3] and two restructuring operations: *Merge* and *Unmerge* are emphatically given. In this paper, an extended possibility-based fuzzy NF^2 relational database model is introduced, where the fuzziness of data comes from possibility distributions over universes of discourse and as resemblance relation [2]. We give database model and define fuzzy nested algebra.

2. DATABASE MODEL

A fuzzy NF^2 relational schema is a set of attributes (A1: D1, A2: D2, ..., An: Dn), where attribute domain Di ($1 \leq i \leq n$) can be one of the following: (1) The set of atomic values, denoted *dom*; (2) The set of null values, denoted *ndom*, where null values may be *unk*, *inap*, *nin*, and *onul*; (3) The set of fuzzy subset, denoted *fdom*; (4) The power set of the set in (1), denoted *sdom*; (5)

The set of relation values. The corresponding attribute value, say ai, is a tuple of the form <ai1, ai2, ..., aim> which is an element of Di1 × Di2 × ... × Dim (m > 1 and $1 \leq i \leq n$), where each Dij ($1 \leq j \leq m$) may be a domain in (1), (2), (3), and (4) and even the set of relation values. Formally, the attribute domain of A_i ($1 \leq i \leq n$) is represented as follows.

$$\tau_i = dom \mid ndom \mid fdom \mid sdom \mid \langle B_1 : \tau_{i1}, B_2 : \tau_{i2}, \ldots, B_m : \tau_{im}\rangle$$

where B1, B2, …, Bm are attributes.

A relation *r* over fuzzy NF^2 schema ($A_1 : \tau_1, A_2 : \tau_2, \ldots, A_n : \tau_n$) is a subset of Cartesian product $\tau_1 \times \tau_2 \times \ldots \times \tau_n$. A tuple in *r* with the form of <a1, a2, ..., an> consists of n components. Each component ai ($1 \leq i \leq n$) may be an atomic value, null value, set value, fuzzy value, or another tuple.

The semantic relationships between two fuzzy data include equivalence, inclusion, intersection, and irrelevancy, which can be assessed with semantic inclusion degree proposed in [2].

Let π_A and π_B be two fuzzy data on U = {$u_1, u_2, \ldots, u_n$}. Let *Res* be a resemblance relation on U and α ($0 \leq \alpha \leq 1$) be a threshold corresponding to *Res*. The semantic inclusion degree of π_A and π_B $SID_\alpha(\pi_A, \pi_B)$ based on α, which means π_A semantically includes π_B, is defined as

$$SID_\alpha(\pi_A, \pi_B) = \sum_{i=1}^{n} \min_{u_i, u_j \in D} (\pi_B(u_i), \pi_A(u_j)) / \sum_{i=1}^{n} \pi_B(u_i)$$

For a given threshold β, we have (1) π_A includes π_B iff $SID_\alpha(\pi_A, \pi_B) \geq \beta$, (2) π_A and π_B are equivalent to each other iff $SID_\alpha(\pi_A, \pi_B) \geq \beta$ and $SID_\alpha(\pi_B, \pi_A) \geq \beta$, and (3) π_A and π_B are irrelevant to each other iff $SID_\alpha(\pi_A, \pi_B) < \beta$ and $SID_\alpha(\pi_B, \pi_A) < \beta$. The notion of equivalence degree for two fuzzy data is hereby given as follows.

The semantic equivalent degree of π_A and π_B $SE_\alpha(\pi_A, \pi_B)$, denoting the degree that π_A and π_B are equivalent to each other, is hereby defined.

$$SE_\alpha(\pi_A, \pi_B) = \min(SID_\alpha(\pi_A, \pi_B), SID_\alpha(\pi_B, \pi_A))$$

Two fuzzy data π_A and π_B are considered α-β-redundant iff $SE_\alpha(\pi_A, \pi_B) \geq \beta$. The equivalent degree of two crisp data (atomic or set-valued) is 1.0 if they are equal to each other. The elimination of duplicate could be achieved by merging π_A and π_B and producing a new fuzzy data π_C. We define the following merging operation according to Zadeh's extension principle [5].

$$\pi_C = \pi_A \cup_f \pi_B = \{\pi_C(w)/w \mid (\exists\, \pi_A(u_i)/u_i)(\exists\, \pi_B(v_j)/v_j)(\pi_C(w) = \mathrm{Max}(\pi_A(u_i), \pi_B(v_j)) \wedge (w = u_i|_{\pi C(w) = \pi A(ui)} \vee w = v_j|_{\pi C(w) = \pi B(vj)}) \wedge Res(u_i, v_j) \geq \alpha \wedge u_i, v_j \in U \wedge 1 \leq i, j \leq n) \vee (\exists\, \pi_A(u_i)/u_i)(\forall\, \pi_B(v_j)/v_j)(\pi_C(w) = \pi_A(u_i) \wedge w = u_i \wedge Res(u_i, v_j) < \alpha \wedge u_i, v_j \in U \wedge 1 \leq i, j \leq n) \vee (\exists\, \pi_B(v_j)/v_j)(\forall\, \pi_A(u_i)/u_i)(\pi_C(w) = \pi_B(v_j) \wedge w = v_j \wedge Res(u_i, v_j) < \alpha \wedge u_i, v_j \in U \wedge 1 \leq i, j \leq n)\}$$

Informally, any two tuples in a nested relation are redundant, if, for pair of the corresponding attribute values, the equivalence degree is greater than or equal to the threshold value. If the pair of the corresponding attribute values is simple, the equivalence degree is one for two values. For two values of structured attributes, however, the equivalence degree is one for structured attributes. Two redundant tuples t and t' are written $t \equiv t'$.

3. RELATIONAL ALGEBRA OPERATIONS

Union and *Difference*: Let r and s be two union-compatible fuzzy nested relations. Then

$$r \cup s = min(\{t \mid t \in r \vee t \in s\}) \text{ and } r - s = \{t \mid t \in r \wedge (\forall v \in s)(t \not\equiv v)\}$$

Here, the operation *min* () means to remove the fuzzy redundant tuples in r and s. Of course, the threshold value should be provided for the purpose.

Cartesian Product. Let r (R) and s (S) be two fuzzy nested relations. Then $r \times s$ is a fuzzy nested relation with the schema $R \cup S$.

$$r \times s = \{t \mid t(R) \in r \wedge t(S) \in s\}$$

Projection. Let r (R) be a fuzzy nested relation and $S \subset R$.

$$\Pi_S(r) = min(\{t \mid (\forall v \in r)(t = v(S)\})$$

Here, an attribute in S may be of the form $B.C$, in which B is a structured attribute and C is its component attribute.

Selection. In classical relational databases, the selection condition is of the form X θ Y, where X is an attribute, Y is an attribute or a constant value, and $\theta \in \{=, \neq, >, \geq, <, \leq\}$. In order to implement fuzzy query for fuzzy relational databases, "θ" should be fuzzy, denoting $\approx$, $\not\approx$, $\succ$, $\prec$, $\succeq$, and $\preceq$. In addition, X is only a simple attribute or the simple attribute of a structured attribute but Y may be (a) a constant, crisp or fuzzy one, (b) a simple attribute, or (c) a simple component attribute of a structured attribute, having the form A. B, where A is a structured attribute and B is its simple component attribute.

The fuzzy comparison operations are defined as follows. (a) $X \approx Y$ iff $SE_\alpha(X, Y) \geq \beta$, where β is a selected cut (the followings are the same); (b) $X \not\approx Y$ iff $SE_\alpha(X, Y) < \beta$; (c) $X \succ Y$ iff $X \not\approx Y$ and min (Supp (X)) > min (Supp (Y)); (d) $X \succeq Y$ iff $X \approx Y$ or $X \succ Y$; (e) $X \prec Y$ iff $X \not\approx Y$ and min (Supp (X)) < min (Supp (Y)); (f) $X \preceq Y$ iff $X \approx Y$ or $X \prec Y$.

Depending on Y, the following situations can be identified for X θ Y. Let X be the attribute A_i: τ_i in a fuzzy nested relation.

(1) $A_i\ \theta\ c$, where c is a crisp constant. According to τ_i, $A_i\ \theta\ c$ is as follows: if τ_i is *dom*, then $\theta \in \{=, \neq, >, <, \geq, \leq\}$; if τ_i is *fdom*, then $\theta \in \{\approx, \not\approx, \succ, \prec, \succeq, \preceq\}$; if τ_i is *ndom*, $A_i\ \theta\ c$ is a null comparison and regarded as the special fuzzy comparison; if τ_i is *sdom*, $A_i\ \theta\ c$ is a element-set comparison. Then $A_i\ \theta\ c$ if c and any element in the value of Ai of a tuple satisfy the "θ".

(2) $A_i\ \theta f$, where f is a fuzzy value: if τ_i is *dom*, *fdom*, or *ndom*, $A_i\ \theta f$ is a fuzzy comparison and $\theta \in \{\approx, \not\approx, \succ, \prec, \succeq, \preceq\}$; if τ_i is *sdom*, $A_i\ \theta f$ is a fuzzy set comparison. Then $A_i\ \theta f$ if f and any element in the value of Ai of a tuple satisfy the fuzzy "θ", where $\theta \in \{\approx, \not\approx, \succ, \prec, \succeq, \preceq\}$.

(3) A_i θ A_j, where A_j: τ_j is a simple attribute and $i \neq j$: if τ_i and τ_j are all *dom*, A_i θ A_j is a traditional comparison; if τ_i and τ_j are *dom* and *fdom*, *fdom* and *fdom*, or *ndom* and *fdom*, A_i θ A_j is a fuzzy comparison; if τ_i and τ_j are *dom* and *ndom*, A_i θ A_j is a null comparison; if τ_i and τ_j are *dom* and *sdom*, A_i θ A_j is a element-set comparison; if τ_i and τ_j are *fdom* and *sdom*, A_i θ A_j is a fuzzy set comparison; if τ_i and τ_j are all *ndom*, A_i θ A_j is a null-null comparison. Then A_i θ A_j if they have the same null values on the same universe of discourse; if τ_i and τ_j are *ndom* and *sdom*, A_i θ A_j is a null-set comparison and regarded as the special element-set comparison; if τ_i and τ_j are *sdom* and *sdom*, A_i θ A_j is a set-set comparison and regarded as the special element-set comparison.

(4) A_i θ A_j. B, where A_j is a structured attribute ($i \neq j$) and B is a simple attribute. The situations are the same as those in above case (3).

Let Q be a predicate denoting the selection condition. The selection operation for a fuzzy nested relation r is defined as $\sigma_Q(r) = \{t \mid t \in r \wedge Q(t)\}$

We do not give the definitions of two restructuring *Nest* and *Unnest* in the database model because of the space limitation.

4. CONCLUSION

In this paper, we introduced fuzzy data into nested relational databases to model complex objects and imprecise and uncertain information. The fuzzy data here is extended possibility-based fuzzy data expressed by possibility distribution over a universe of discourse and meanwhile a resemblance relation on the universe is in effect. We gave the structure of fuzzy nested relational model and the approach for assessing fuzzy data redundancies. On the basis, the algebra is defined for manipulating fuzzy and complex data.

REFERENCES

[1] M. Levene, *The Nested Universal Relation Database Model*, Lecture Notes in Computer Science No. 595, Springer-Verlag, Berlin, 1992.

[2] Z. M. Ma, W. J. Zhang and W. Y. Ma, Semantic Measure of Fuzzy Data in Extended Possibility-Based Fuzzy Relational Databases, *International Journal of Intelligent Systems*, 15 (8) (2000) 705-716.

[3] A. Yazici, A. Soysal, B. P. Buckles and F. E. Petry, Uncertainty in a Nested Relational Database Model, *Data & Knowledge Engineering*, 30 (1999) 275–301.

[4] L. A. Zadeh, Fuzzy Sets, *Information and Control*, 8 (3) (1965) 338-353.

[5] L. A. Zadeh, The Concept of a Linguistic Variable and Its Application to Approximate Reasoning (Parts 1, 2, and 3), *Information Science*, 8 (1975) 119-248, 301-357; 9 (1975) 43-80.

REAL-TIME MEETING SCHEDULING MODEL BY COMPUTER SUPPORTED COOPERATIVE WORK

Goran Martinović[1], Leo Budin[2]
[1] *Faculty of Electrical Engineering, Josip Juraj Strossmayer University of Osijek, Kneza Trpimira 2b, 31000 Osijek, Croatia (Phone:+38531224766; Fax:+38531208905; E-mail:goran.martinovic@etfos.hr);* [2] *Faculty of Electrical Engineering and Computing, University of Zagreb, Unska 3, 10000 Zagreb, Croatia (Phone:+38516129936; E-mail: leo.budin@fer.hr)*

Abstract: Computer supported cooperative work (CSCW) implies a group of people doing work supported by the computer system and modern networking technologies. The proposed real-time CSCW meeting scheduling model includes a group, jobs, cooperation and scheduling. Availability, experience, knowledge, interests and the internal infrastructure present group members. Real-time properties of jobs are execution time, deadline, period and interarrival time. The scheduling problem consists of assigning jobs to members of the previously formed groups. The described model represents a prerequisite for harder real-time requests in CSCW.

Keywords: Computer Supported Cooperative Work, Human, Meeting, Scheduling

1. INTRODUCTION

The importance of knowledge and information in the globalization process, but also the need for cooperation in problem solving increase constantly. Real-time problems are rather extensive. A human represents an active component in CSCW. CSCW combines understanding of the way people work in groups with enabling technologies of computer networking, and associated hardware, software, services and techniques, as in [1] and [2].

The paper includes significant organization and timing parameters of CSCW meeting scheduling. The model is focused on the properties of group members meetings at which they cooperate. Group members possess both knowledge and capabilities. Group effectiveness is mostly determined by the member cooperation, as in [6]. That cooperation has a goal to better understand tasks, allocate resources and develop the cooperative strategy, as in [3].

2. MEETING SCHEDULING IN CSCW

Scheduling in the CSCW system can be presented by group G, job that has to be done by the group J, cooperation enabling carrying out of the job C and scheduling procedure S:

$$(G,J,C,S) \tag{1}$$

Group G, according to (2) consists of n members:

$$G=\{M_1,M_2,...,M_n\} \tag{2}$$

Every member M_i of the group G can be shown as in (3):

$$M_i=\{A_i,e_i,s_i,l_{Pi},l_{Gi},D_i,I_i,CS_i\}, \text{ where:} \tag{3}$$

A_i – member availability according to the schedule
e_i – an experience level of a group member
s_i – a special knowledge level of a group member
l_{Pi} – a personal interest level of a group member
l_{Gi} – a general interest level of a group member
D_i – the law of statistical distribution of group member's availability
I_i – internal ordering of group member's infrastructure
CS_i – credits given to a member

Job J that should be carried out by the group consists of m tasks:

$$J=\{T_1,T_2,...,T_m\} \tag{4}$$

Every task can be presented in a general case as in (5). c_j is the worst case execution time, t_{dj} is the deadline, p_j is the period for a periodic task, t_{ia} is the interarrival time for an aperiodic task and H/S determines a hard or a soft deadline.

$$T_j=(c_j,t_{dj},p_j,t_{iaj},H/S) \tag{5}$$

A condition for the group to execute a job is that members must cooperate. The cooperation or meeting is denoted by C. Out of the total number of meetings q, the k-th meeting C_k can be shown as in (6), where μ represents organization and infrastructure properties (7), and τ timing properties.

$$C_k = \{\mu_k, \tau_k\} \tag{6}$$

$$\mu_k = \{GM_k, H_k, O_k, e_k, s_k, l_{Pk}, I_k, P_k, CS_k\}\text{, where} \tag{7}$$

GM_k – a set of members participating in the meeting
H_k – a set of meeting hosts
O_k – a level of meeting organization
e_k – the expected experience level of group members. The experience indicator e_i of a future group member (8) must be as in (9).

$$\bar{e}_k = \sum_{k=1}^{z} \frac{e_k}{z} \tag{8}$$

$$e_i \geq \bar{e}_k \tag{9}$$

s_k is the expected level of special knowledge and must be $s_i \geq \bar{s}_k$. l_{Pk} is the allowed level of personal interests of members and must be $l_{Pi} \leq \bar{l}_{Pk}$. I_k is the level of infrastructure ordering of a potential member I_i. It must be $I_i \geq \bar{I}_k$. P_k is the meeting priority level and CS_k is a number of involved champions. Expression (10) shows meeting timing parameters, as in [4].

$$\tau_k = \{t_{ck}, t_{rk}, c_k, t_{sk}, t_{dk}, t_{xk}, t_{Kk}, p_k, t_{iak}\}\text{, where:} \tag{10}$$

t_{ck} – planned duration of the meeting
t_{rk} – meeting prolongation time
c_k – real duration of the meeting, corresponds to sum of t_{ck} and t_{rk}
t_{sk} – meeting start time or imagined calendar time of the meeting start
t_{dk} – meeting deadline
t_{xk} – time to decide whether to accept or cancel the meeting
t_{Kk} – a relative position of the meeting in the schedule
p_k – period of the meeting being carried out
t_{aik} – interarrival time between consecutive meetings of the same groups

Real-time meeting scheduling by CSCW is shown in Figure 1. It represents a resource scheduling to users. However, resources represent a job to be done, and the users of these resources are group members. It incorporates the following: definition of job and member parameters, selection of members, scheduler implementation and scheduling according to a relevant parameter, as in [4] and [5].

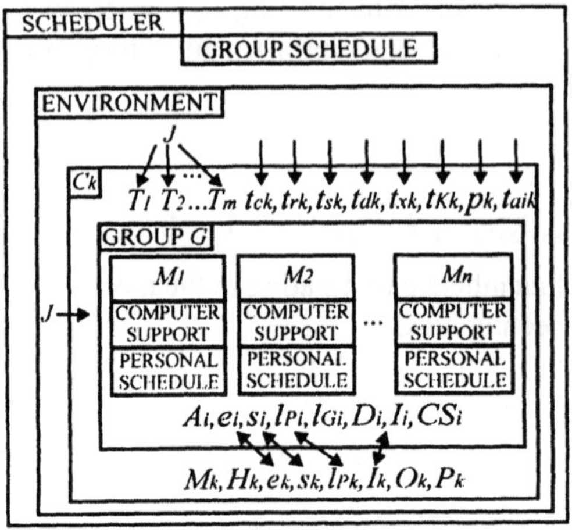

Figure 1. CSCW Meeting Scheduler

3. CONCLUSION

The meeting scheduling is presented by the parameters of the group and its members, parameters of jobs that should be executed, properties of cooperation between group members, and the scheduling procedure. Scheduling is based on the cooperation schedule in the calendar format. Special attention is given to a human as a group member. Humans cooperate in problem solving because of their capabilities. The described model represents a precondition for harder real-time requests in CSCW.

REFERENCES

[1] Borghoff U.M., J.H. Schlichter, Computer Supported Cooperative Work, Introduction to Distributed Applications, Springer – Verlag, 2000.

[2] Greenberg S., E. Chang, Computer Support for Real-Time Collaborative Work, Congressus Numerantium, 75, 1990, pp.247-262.

[3] Li D., L. Zhou, R.R. Muntz, A New Paradigm of User Intention Preservation in Real-Time Collaborative Editing Systems, Proc. of 7th IEEE Int. Conf. on Paralell and Distributed Systems, ICPADS'00, 2000, pp.401-408.

[4] Martinović G., Ž. Hocenski, L. Budin, A Tool for Evaluation of Scheduling Algorithms in Real-Time Systems, 5th WSES/IEEE Int. Conf. CSCC 200, Rethimnon, Crete Island, Greece, 2001, pp.173–179.

[5] Sandusky R.J., Infrastructure Management as Cooperative Work: Implications for Systems Design, ACM GROUP 97, Phoenix, AZ, USA, 1997, pp.91-100.

[6] Sen S., E. H. Durfee, A Formal Study of Distributed Meeting Scheduling, Proc.Conf. on Organizational Comp. Systems, Atlanta, GA, USA, SIGOIS ACM, 1995, pp. 55-68.

THE NED IIS PROJECT - FOREST ECOSYSTEM MANAGEMENT

W.Potter, D.Nute, J.Wang, F.Maier, M.Twery*, M.Rauscher*, P. Knopp*, S.Thomasma*, M.Dass, H.Uchiyama
*Artificial Intelligence Center, University of Georgia; *USDA Forest Service*

Abstract: For many years we have held to the notion that an Intelligent Information System (IIS) is composed of a unified knowledge base, database, and model base. The main idea behind this notion is the transparent processing of user queries. The system is responsible for "deciding" which information sources to access in order to fulfil a query regardless of whether this involves a data retrieval, an inference, a computational method, a problem solving module, or some combination of these. The NED IIS project is an effort to develop a robust, intelligent, goal-driven forest ecosystem management system to help forest managers plan and achieve wildlife, ecological, water, landscape, and timber goals. NED, using a blackboard architecture dominated by semi autonomous intelligent agents, integrates a core database, domain knowledge, meta-knowledge, and a GUI with external (possibly distributed) legacy and special purpose (heterogeneous) information sources. The current version of NED is NED-2. NED-2 is still under construction, however a prototype incorporating the major components of the architecture has been completed and demonstrated.

Key words: Intelligent Information Systems, Blackboard Architecture, Agents

1. INTRODUCTION

The development of NED began in 1987 among researchers within the USDA Northeastern Forest Experiment Station. One of the ideas put forward was to develop a computer system that would combine all the existing independently produced growth and yield models developed by scientists within the Station. Early efforts focused on developing a decision-support system for management problems at the stand level (a stand is a localized area with similar overstory and understory, i.e., trees and brush). As more complex problems involving multiple resources were identified, the concept of NED expanded to include landscape scales as well (multiple stands grouped into management units as well as entire forests). A primary motivation of the project was to develop a single, easy-to-use system to provide summary information and expert prescriptions for any forest type.

The current version under development is NED-2; the focus of this poster. For the resource manager, NED uses an original prescription design system to incorporate management goals for multiple objectives, analyze current forest conditions, recommend management alternatives, and predict future conditions under different alternatives. This is the key facet of NED and is called the NED process. NED is designed to include a long-term, landscape-level view of the forest as an interconnected ecosystem. Recommendations for potential treatments provide options from which a manager may choose.

The NED decision process is goal driven. When we build and project treatment plans, our purpose is always to find a way to satisfy the management goals we have adopted. In building different management scenarios for comparison, the manager must analyze different points in the future with respect to different plans to determine how well the goals have been achieved. The manager may decide that the process needs to be repeated several times in order to refine the treatments and timings of the treatments. In addition, some situation may change in the future which requires the initial goals to be re-evaluated and possibly new plans to be analyzed.

2. THE NED-2 ARCHITECTURE

The central organizing principle for NED-2 is the blackboard. We selected a blackboard architecture over other existing approaches (e.g., federated database, hierarchical mediator/wrapper, ontology-based, or descriptive logic approaches) for several reasons including: 1) due to the nature and history of the NED project, a rapid prototyping approach where functionality could easily be added, deleted, and changed was considered necessary, 2) the original NED style of user interaction needed to be maintained due to the existing/expanding user base, and 3) not all external information sources were known ahead of time but the flexibility for integrating new sources was considered necessary. Note that new sources are accessed via a wrapper to ensure proper integration but the important facet of integration is the meta-knowledge maintained that represents specific functionality, it's relationship to existing components, and the details for NED/source interaction.

Prolog provides the primary implementation platform for the knowledge components (knowledge models, agents, meta-knowledge, inference engine environment, blackboard, and wrappers). The user interface is currently implemented in Visual C++. The core NED-2 database is implemented in

Access. Simulators and other non-NED modules are integrated into NED-2 via their wrappers (written in Visual C++, Prolog, or Visual Basic for example) and are written in various programming languages (e.g., fortran).

An interesting aspect of the NED-2 architecture is the inclusion of the core database "on the blackboard". To NED-2, the core database values appear as prolog facts for all intents and purposes although the database is actually an external component. The idea is to allow forest managers to maintain their management unit data in a standard database format as well as give NED-2 full access to the data. Managers may elect to integrate special purpose yet external databases to NED-2 but these would be handled as an external source and need a wrapper plus associated meta-knowledge in order to be integrated.

Knowledge based models consist of rule sets written in Prolog and are used in conjunction with one of the NED-2 inference engines. Standard forward and backward chaining inference engines, a fuzzy backward chaining inference engine, a certainty factor based engine, and a defeasible inference engine have all been developed for NED-2.

Meta-knowledge is also required for some knowledge models. For example, the current NED-2 prototype includes a knowledge model for wildlife habitat requirements based on research for the Northeastern United States. Alternative wildlife models are being developed for the Great Lakes region and for the Southeastern United States. A meta-knowledge base allows NED-2 to select the appropriate wildlife model to use for a management unit.

The output from NED-2 analyses can be displayed using external modules such as a Geographical Information System (e.g., ArcView), a stand visualization system, landscape visualization tools, or hypertext. Only plans and years that have been simulated can be examined using these tools.

The report generation agent consults the NED-2 database or the blackboard to determine which reports the user has requested or needs based on the goals specified. It also consults any corresponding meta-knowledge to determine the format for each requested report and the data that each report requires. The agent then collects the data from the blackboard and builds a set of linked hypertext documents containing the reports. When it is time to display the reports to the user, the agent starts the user's default Web browser and directs it to the entry page for the hyper-document containing the reports.

NED-2 includes special agents that develop plans for completing complex tasks. For example, the NED-2 user may request that all selected reports be generated. A report-planning agent responds to this type of request. Reports can only be generated for the baseline year or for some future year that has been simulated according to one or more treatment plans. The report-planner determines whether a baseline has been generated and whether any treatment plans have been simulated. If not, it informs the user that no report can be generated and the cause. If a baseline has been generated but no treatment plans have been simulated, then the report-planning agent assumes that all reports are to be generated for the baseline. If multiple years of simulated data are available, the report-planner opens a dialog box where the user can select from the treatment plans and years that have been simulated.

Once the treatment plan and year have been identified, the report-planner consults the NED-2 database or blackboard to determine which reports the user has selected (or needs). This information will have been stored in the database by the report selection user interface module or on the blackboard by some other agent. The report-planner determines which of the requested reports require goal satisfaction analysis or other kinds of data analysis before the reports can be written. It then formulates a plan for performing any required analysis and putting the results into HTML reports. This plan is then placed on the blackboard as a complex request that replaces the original simple request for reports. The other NED-2 agents can respond to individual requests embedded in such a plan as readily as they can respond to an individual request. The difference is that if a request is embedded in a plan, the responding agent will not attempt to satisfy the request until the earlier steps in the plan have been completed.

3. SUMMARY

In this poster we have presented a brief overview of the NED Intelligent Information System. NED uses a blackboard architecture and intelligent agents to control user requests and decision making related to forest ecosystem management. As can be seen, much of the design and development of NED-2 has been driven by practical necessity. The intelligent agents provide a variety of functions to aid the forest manager achieve specified goals. In addition, agents manage various internal processing activities to provide the user with seamless, transparent access to internal and external (heterogeneous) information sources. The external sources may be knowledge bases designed to draw conclusions, databases that use different underlying data models (relational, hierarchical, or even flat file), and models used to predict future conditions or visualize a future estimation of stand characteristics for example. The type of information source is actually of only minor concern. The functionality that the source brings to NED-2 is the major element. Increasing NED-2's ability to help forest managers make sound decisions about the management of forested lands is our primary goal.

ELABORATION AND EXPLOITATION OF LESSONS LEARNED

Holitiana Rakoto[1,2], Philippe Clermont[1], Laurent Geneste[1]
[1]Ecole Nationale d'Ingénieurs de Tarbes - 47, avenue Azereix – BP 1629 – 65000 Tarbes
[2]ALSTOM Transport - Rue du Docteur Guinier – BP 4 -65600 Séméac
email : holitiana.rakoto@transport.alstom.com, clermont@enit.fr, laurent@enit.fr

1. INTRODUCTION

The production centre Alstom Transport in Tarbes, France, designs, industrialises and ensures the maintenance of several high technology equipment (such as power modules, command platforms...) of the traction part of trains, metros or tramways. A study has been launched on the problem of defining an architecture for the Return on Experience (RoE) and its integration into operational industrial processes such as design, integration or validation. The first part of this paper shows several ways that have been developed in several firms and organisations in order to handle the RoE and proposes a synthesis of their key elements. The second part aims at defining an alimentation process for the RoE and the third part proposes several considered functions for the exploitation part of the RoE.

2. SURVEYING APPROACHES

A study has been led about European and French approaches [1]. On the WWW, we can find forty approaches maintained by various government and other organizations [2]. Two main problems appear with such systems : the use of textual representation of experiences and the gap concerning experiences integration into processes they are intended to support [3]. From the Roe process [4] we have brought out some elements that compose the process (figure 1). These help us to position our approach.

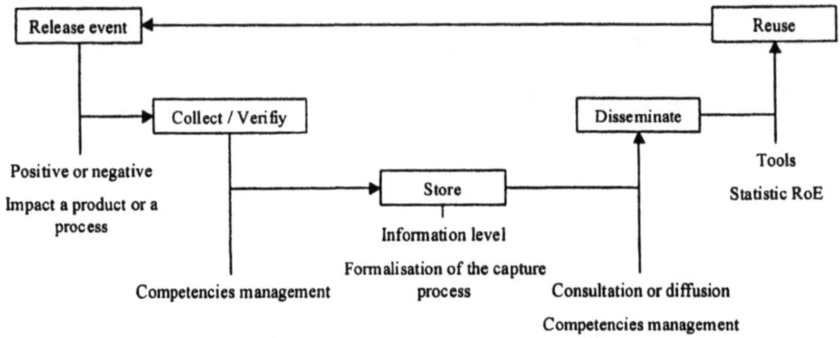

Figure 1 : Key elements of RoE process.

We distinguish three levels of information : rough information, experience and rule. Our approach in Alstom Transport is to take into account simultaneously all these levels order to develop a methodology as complete as possible. We detail in the next section the alimentation the suggested RoE process which integrates alimentation and exploitation sub-process.

3. ROE PROCESS

We show in figure 2 the detail of decomposition of the alimentation sub-process. Since the event reveals an unexpected failure, as soon as it is detected, a solving process is set up. This process corresponds to a sequence of activities defined by a workflow that will lead , in the best situation, to a resolution of the problem that caused the event.

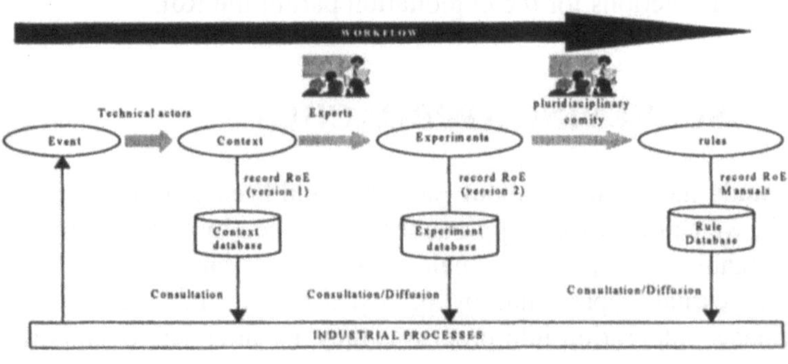

Figure 2 : RoE process and industrial processes.

The solving problems process involves several experts and during the process, it is necessary to capitalise the results of the expertise. This contributes to the elaboration of the database called "Experiments" in figure 3.

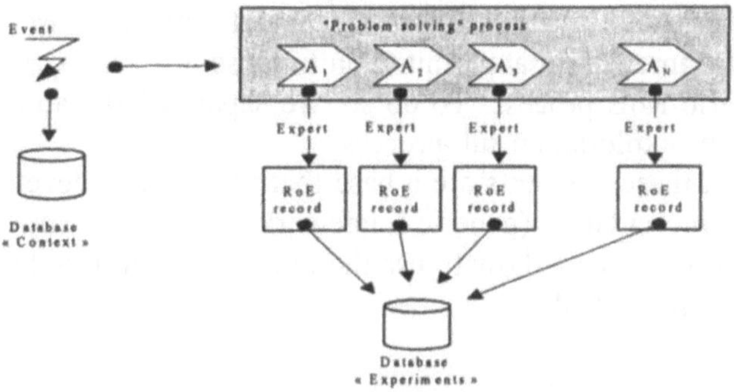

Figure 3 : Process of experiments capitalisation.

Each activity of the "solving problems" process feeds the database "Experiments" with RoE records that contains the expert analysis produced during the activity. This structure enables to define a net product - expertise which nodes are the RoE records. When the solving process is achieved, it may be judicious to build rules that will be systematically applied in future similar products developments. The elaboration of such rules involves one or several experts who, according to a set of previous experiments, will propose decisions in order to avoid future problems.

When a set of experiments and rules is formalised and memorised, it is important to facilitate its exploitation of this technical patrimony by the actors of the company.

For the consultation of the experiments database, we propose the set up of a search engine based on keywords in the corresponding database. For the dispatching of informations, the general idea is to exploit the informations contained in the experiments database in order to prevent a past error to be made again. Case based reasoning mechanisms [5], seem to be very suitable to help this exploitation task and a study is under way to develop tools of this kind [6]. We also consider to favour the construction of rules by defining some mechanisms of extraction and of generalisation.

For the consultation of the rule base, the set up of knowledge manuals available through hypertext on the intranet of the company is the considered solution. For the diffusion of the rule base, a solution is to integrate a systematic use of rules in the product development cycle.

3.1 Conclusion and future work

We present, in this paper, the RoE problematic and several approaches that have been considered to solve the problem. From these considerations and an experience in the Alstom Transport company we propose the definition of framework that permit to unify these different approaches and to build a generic RoE process. To do so, we separated the alimentation sub-process and the exploitation sub-process.

Of course, these elements are a base that we want to develop both in its conceptual representation (generic framework for the RoE structuration) and in its applicative aspects (how to use the representation in order to guide the set up of an efficient RoE).

4. REFERENCES

[1] P. clermont, L. Geneste, H. Rakoto, "Elaboration and exploitation of Return on Experience", ALCAA 2001, Biarritz, France, 2001.

[2] D. W. Aha, R. Weber, lessons learned links. Available at http://www.aic.nrl.navy.mil/~aha/lessons, 1999.

[3] D.W. Aha, I. Becerra-Fernandez, R. Weber, "Intelligent lessons learned systems", International Journal of Expert Systems research & Applications, Vol. 20, N°1, 17-34, 2001.

[4] U. Reimer, "Implementing a Knowledge Pump in your Organisation", First International Conference on Pratical Aspects of Knowledge Management, Workshop on The Lessons Learned Cycle, http://www.xlog.ch/pakm/procdocu.html , 1996.

[5] J. Kolodner, « Case-based reasonning », Morgan Kaufmann Publishers , San Mateo, 1993.

[6] L. Geneste, M. Ruet, Experience based configuration, 17th International Conference on Artificial Intelligence, IJCAI'01, Workshop on Configuration, Seattle, Washington, USA, 4-10 august 2001

A HYBRID EXPERT SYSTEM SUPPORTING DIAGNOSIS OF HEART DISEASES

Abdel-Badeeh M. Salem and Rania A. HodHod
Faculty of computer & Information Sciences
Ain Shams University, Abbassia, Cairo, Egypt
e-mail:absalem@asunet.shams.edu.eg
e-mail:rania_adel@hotmail.com

Abstract: In this paper, we have developed a hybrid expert system prototype used for supporting diagnosis of heart diseases. The system merges uncertainty management techniques and case-based reasoning. The system is able to give appropriate diagnosis for 4 heart diseases namely; mitral stenosis, left-sided heart failure, stable angina pectoris and essential hypertension with the corresponding certainty factor. The system has been implemented in visual prolog for windows and has trained set of 42 cases for Egyptian cardiac patients and has been tested by another 13 different cases. Each case contains 33 significant attributes resulted from the statistical analysis performed to 110 cases.

Keywords: ***Expert Systems, Case-Based Reasoning, Uncertainty, Medical Informatics.***

1. INTRODUCTION

There are many problems concerning the building of medical expert systems, such as dealing with uncertainty, fuzzy terms and doctors' heuristic knowledge. To overcome these problems, hybrid expert systems allow for the synergistic combination of more than one inference technique with more strength and less weakness than either one alone [1, 2]. In this paper, we developed a hybrid expert system prototype that merges case-based reasoning methodology (CBR) [3] and uncertainty management techniques [4] for supporting diagnosis for 4 heart diseases. One of the main advantages of CBR is dealing with situations where solutions are not clear cut and its ability to reason from old experiences or cases. In addition to its ability to overcome the problems addressed in rule based expert systems e.g. knowledge acquisition, performance experience, adaptive solutions and maintaining.

2. KNOWLEDGE ACQUISITION & REPRESENTATION

The knowledge has been collected from expert doctors in heart domain from EL-Maadi Military Egyptian hospital, health insurance Egyptian institute, El-Azhar University doctors and medical reference books [4].

Knowledge was collected for these diseases only: Mitral Stenosis (MS), Left-Sided Heart Failure (LSHF), Stable Angina Pectoris (SAP) and Essential Hypertension (EHT). Knowledge was represented using the concept of frames (where each frame represents one case). There were 110 collected cases each comprises 207 attributes.

The architecture of the developed system consists of two knowledge structures (KS). Case memory KS represents the episodic memory and contains the demographic and clinical data. Similarity rules KS, which are used to support retrieving of cases from the case memory. In addition to a working database contains the case specific data and explanation mechanism.

3. CASE INDEXING & RETRIEVAL

One-way to assign importance values to case features is to have a human expert assign them as the case library is being built. Another way is to do a statistical evaluation of a known corpus of cases to determine which dimension predicts different outcomes and/or solutions best. Both methods are applied to assign importance values to different features. Figure1 illustrates a sample of the assigned values of the different features. The features of the input case are assigned as indices characterizing the case. These indices are used to retrieve several closest match cases from the case memory. The system uses the nearest-neighbor algorithm, which determines how similar two cases are by comparing their features [3].

4. SYSTEM VERIFICATION & RESULTS

System verification includes the following tests [6]: (a) check case retrieval accuracy, (b) check retrieval consistency, (c) check for case duplication and (d) global tests.

(a) Check case retrieval accuracy, which means that if the case-base is queried with one of its cases, it should give the same case with distance measure, equals 100%. Figure2 shows the distance measure against the case identification number, where it is clear that only one case hits the value 1.0 which is the query case

(b) Check retrieval consistency, which means that if exactly the same search has been performed twice, the same source cases should be retrieved with the same accuracy.

(c) Check for case duplication in which a case should exactly match itself, but should not be identical to other cases.

(d) Global tests that are important to verify the overall performance of the system. The steps of this test are as follows: (1) did the system retrieve a useful set of cases? (2) Was the retrieval time acceptable?. Table 1 shows the answer to the above questions, for 5 patients.

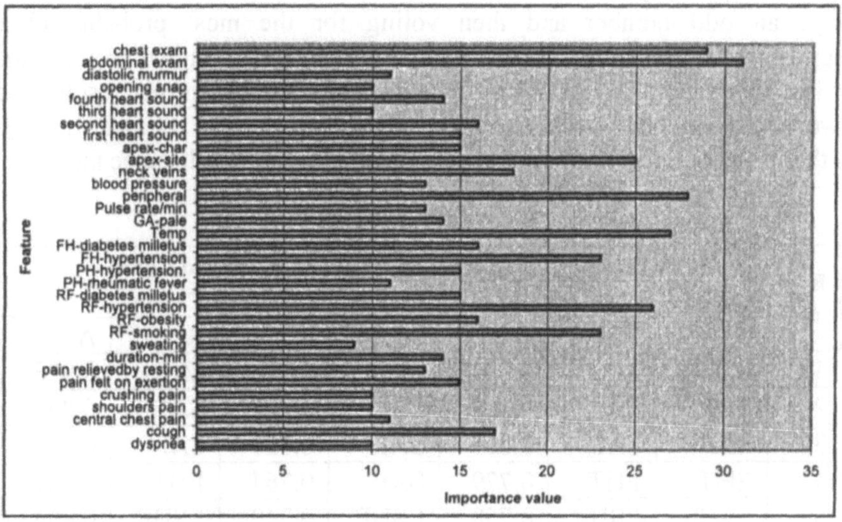

Figure 1: Importance values of different features

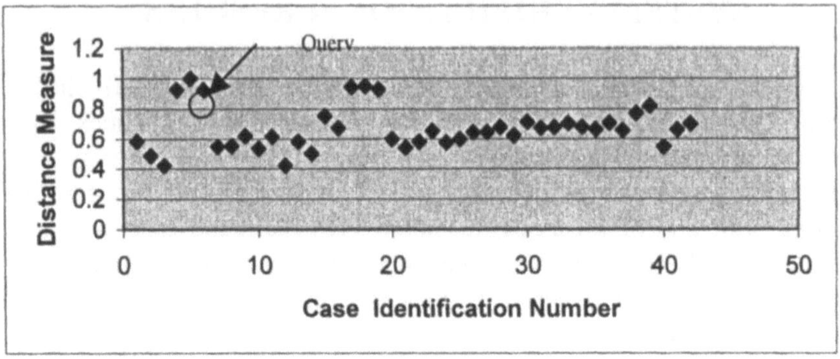

Figure 2:Check of retrieval accuracy

From the Table 1 the answer of the first question is yes. In experiments 1, 2, 3 and 5 the resulted diagnosis of all the closest retrieved cases are the same so this estimates that the query case has the same diagnosis, which is true. But, in experiment 4 there is a confused answer where essential hypertension (EHT) and stable angina pectoris (SAP) are two different diagnoses suggested for the query case. We overlapped this by using K-Nearest Neighbor algorithm, where K represents number of retrieved cases which is always an odd number and then voting for the most probable class (diagnosis) takes place, so there will be 1 vote for stable angine pectoris and 2 votes for essential hypertension tension which is the correct result. The answer of the second question, concerning the acceptable retrieval time, is less than 1 second to get all cases sorted according to their distance measure.

Table 1: Global system verification check

Exp .#	**Input Case** (Query)	**Result(R) & Accuracy(A) of the Retrieved Cases**					
		Case 1		**Case 2**		**Case 3**	
		R	A	R	A	R	A
1	MS	MS	0.984	MS	0.978	MS	0.923
2	SAP	SAP	0.869	SAP	0.868	SAP	0.847
3	SAP	SAP	0.829	SAP	0.821	SAP	0.820
4	EHT	EHT	0.779	SAP	0.764	EHT	0.756
5	LSHF	LSHF	0.758	LSHF	0.740	LSHF	0.694

5. CONCLUSION

In this paper, a hybrid medical expert system that supports diagnosis of four heart diseases is presented. Knowledge structure is represented via formalism integrating cases and rules. The system was successful in getting correct estimation to thirteen different patients (cases). The system was verified by conducting several tests in order to measure retrieval accuracy, retrieval consistency, case duplication and the overall system performance. System verification shows that both the system and the methodology are successful to estimate a correct diagnosis for heart disease patient. Cardiologists evaluate the system performance by testing it practically where the system succeeded in estimating the correct diagnosis for 13 foreign cases. For future work, more cases will be added to the case memory and it will be clinically tested.

5. REFERENCES

[1] D.E. Brown, J.J. Pomykalski, Truszkowski, "Expert Systems", Wiley Encyclopedia for Electrical and Electronics Engineering, 1999.

[2] I. Hatzilgeroudis, J. Prentzas, "HYMES: A Hybrid Modular Expert System with Efficient Inference and Explanation", in Proceedings of the 8th Panhellenic Conference on Informatics, Nicosia, Cyprus, 2001.

[3] J. L. Kolodner (Ed.), Case-Based Reasoning, Morgan Kaufmann Publishers: California, 1993.

[4] J. Macleod (Ed.), Davidson's Principles and Practice of Medicine, The English language book society and Churchill Livingstone, thirteenth edition, 1981.

[5] D. A. Waterman (Ed.), A Guide to Expert Systems, Reading, MA: Addison-Wisley, 1986.

[6] I. Watson (Ed.), Applying case-based reasoning: Techniques for Enterprise Systems. Morgan kauffmann Publishers: California, 1997.

IDSIS: INTELLIGENT DOCUMENT SEMANTIC INDEXING SYSTEM[21]

Zhongzhi Shi Bin Wu Qing He Xiujun Gong Shaohui Liu Yi Zheng
Shizz@ics.ict.ac.cn
Key Laboratory of Intelligent Information Processing ,
Institute of Computing Technology ,Chinese Academy of Sciences

Abstract: With rapid growth of the Internet, how to get information from this huge information space becomes an even important problem. In this paper, An Intelligence Document Semantic Indexing System : IDSIS is proposed. Some new technologies are integrated in IDSIS to obtain good performance. IDSIS is composed of four key procedures. A parallel, distributed and configurable Spider is used for information gathering; A multi-hierarchy document classification approach combining the information gain initially processes gathered web documents; A swarm intelligence based document clustering method is used for information organization; A concept-based retrieval interface is applied for user interactive retrieval. IDSIS is a concept-associated document semantic indexing system for information retrieval on Internet.

Keywords: document classification, document clustering, semantic indexing, concept space

1. INTRODUCTION

Large quantities of textual data available for example on the Internet pose a continuing challenge to applications that help users in making sense of the data. We describe here a new approach to automatic text classifying, clustering, indexing and topic retrieval. It is designed to overcome a fundamental problem that plagues existing retrieval techniques that try to

[21] This research supported by NSFC grant 60073019, 90104021, 60173017 and NSFB grant 4011003.

match words of queries with words of documents. The problem is that users want to retrieve on the basis of conceptual content, and individual words provide unreliable evidence about the conceptual topic or meaning of a document. There are usually many ways to express a given concept. The literal terms in a user's query may not match those of a relevant document. In addition, most words have multiple meanings, so terms in a user's query will literally match terms in documents that are not of interest to the user. The proposed approach tries to overcome the deficiencies of term matching retrieval by treating the unreliability of observed term document association data as a statistical problem.

2. ARCHITECHURE OF IDSIS

An automatic document collector is one of the fundamental components of IDSIS. The main task performed by this component is the automatic gathering of Web documents, which are usually stored locally for further processing. A parallel and distributed spider is employed in this system [3]. The documents collected by spider are processed by text analyzer including parsing and extracting the informative words for classification, concept clustering, semantic index generating and so on. Text classifier learned knowledge from pre-labeled documents and then classified the newly documents. An innovative and multi-layer classification model is used [4]. With the increase of Internet documents, the volumes of some directors become larger. To decrease the search space for retrieval by directory, we provide a document Clustering algorithm based on Swarm Intelligence and k-Means: CSIM [6]. CSIM gives the class description for each cluster. With the assistance of concept space, the system could help the searchers to find most relevant terms and retrieve most relevant documents by using these terms. In our system, we incorporate these two methods to generate concept space. We use Chen's[2] method to generate the concept space of specific domain and use HowNet [7] to generate the concept of general domain. By building the concept semantic space, IDSIS can broad or locate what they most want. Users can not only browse all documents belong some directory, but also gives the association concepts with the class concept in the directory way. IDSIS will return its association concepts and documents related the few words provided by users. Meanwhile, users may also filter some documents by setting the documents' class. Limited by the paper length, we only briefly introduce two parts of IDSIS. They are text classification and clustering.

3. TEXT CLASSIFICATION: INFORMATION INITIAL PROCESSING

After the web pages are crawled by Spiders, they will be classified automatically. To calculate term weight, the TF.IDF approach[5] consider two factors: TF (term frequency) and IDF (inverse document frequency). We introduces the concept of Information Gain from Information Theory, i.e., the document collection D is regarded as an information source according with some probability distribution, and the amount of information provided by one term (the importance of the term) in text classification can be obtained by considering the information gain between the information entropy of document collection and the conditional entropy of the term, then we can combine this amount of the information into the formula of calculating term weight.

The amount of information of term T_k can be calculated using the following formula: $IG_k=H(D)-H(D/T_k)$, Where H(D) is the entropy of the document collection D: $H(D) = -\sum_{d_i \in D} P(d_i) \times \log_2 P(d_i)$, $H(D/T_k)$ is the conditional entropy of term T_k: $H(D \mid T_k) = -\sum_{d_i \in D} P(d_i \mid T_k) \times \log_2 P(d_i \mid T_k)$, $P(d_i)$ is the conditional probability of the document d_i: $P(d_i) = \frac{wordfreq\ (d_i)}{\sum_i wordfreq\ (d_i)}$, where wordfreq($d_i$) is the sum of all the term frequencies in d_i. Then TF.IDF formula can be revised as follows:

$$W_{ik} = \frac{tf_{ik} \times \log(N / n_k + 0.01) \times IG_k}{\sqrt{\sum_{k=1}^{m} (tf_{ik})^2 \times [\log(N / n_k + 0.01) \times IG_k]^2}} \qquad (1)$$

We also propose an approach of multi-hierarchy text classification based on VSM, i.e., all classes are organized as a tree according to some given hierarchical relations. The basic insight supporting our approach is that classes that are attached to the same node have a lot more in common with each other than else classes, so the models of these classes will be based on a small set of features. In the test phase, we collect 21,430 documents downloaded from some famous web sits in China such as SINA, FM365 as training set. The corporation collects 11062 documents as testing set. There are 34 classes. The average precision is 84.20%.

4. TEXT CLUSTERING: SEMANTIC INFORMATION ORGANIZATION

We propose a document Clustering algorithm based on Swarm Intelligence and k-Means: CSIM in this paper. Swarm Intelligence is defined as any attempt to design algorithms or distributed problem-solving devices inspired by the collective behavior of the social insect colonies and other animal societies [1]. The main idea of CSIM is that: firstly, documents are denoted by Vector Space Model, and each vector regarded as a data object is randomly projected onto a plane. Secondly, each simple agent(ant) perceive the swarm similarity of current object within the local region by formula (2), and compute the picking-up or dropping probability, and act according to this probability. Clusters will visually form on the ant-work plane through simple agents' collective actions. Then, clusters results are collected from the plane by a recursive algorithm. Finally, an iterative partitioning phase is employed to further optimize the results. A formula of measuring the swarm similarity between a pair of documents is showed as formula (2).

$$f(d_i) = \sum_{Oj \in Neigh(r)} \left[1 - \frac{10*(1 - sim(d_i, d_j))}{\alpha} \right] \quad (2)$$

where $Neigh(r)$ denotes the local region, it is usually a rounded area with a radius r. $d(o_i, o_j)$ denotes the distance of document vector o_i with o_j in the space of attributes. It is usually cosine distance. The parameter α is defined as swarm similarity coefficient. The functions to compute picking-up or dropping probability are two lines with a slope k.

5. CONCLUSIONS

In this paper, an all-sided solution for information retrieval on Internet (IDSIS) is proposed. Concept search is a trend of information retrieval. IDSIS partially realized a concept-associated search by efficient information organization. IDSIS covers all procedures of information retrieval on internet, i.e. information gathering, information organization and information querying.

6. REFERENCES

[1]. E.Bonabeau, , M.Dorigo, & G.Theraulaz, Swarm Intelligence: From Natural to Artificial Systems, Oxford Univ. Press, New York, 1999

[2]. H. Chen, K. J. Lynch, K. Basu, and D. T. Ng. Generating, integrating, and activating thesauri for concept-based document retrieval. IEEE EXPERT, Special Series on Artificial Intelligence in Text-based Information Systems, 8(2):25-34, April 1993.

[3]. Dong Mingkai, Tian Qijia, Shi Zhongzhi, Web Spider Based on Intelligent Agent. SCI2001, Orlando, P292-296, 2001.

[4]. Shaohui Liu, Mingkai Dong, Haijun Zhang, Rong Li, Zhongzhi Shi, An Approach of Multi-hierarchy Text Classification, 2001 International Conferences on Info-tech and Info-net PPOCEEDINGS,Conferences C:95-100

[5]. G. Salton, B. Buckley. Term-weighting Approaches in Automatic Text Retrieval. Information Processing and Management, 1998, 24(5) : 513-523

[6]. Wu Bin Zheng Yi Liu Shaohui Shi Zhongzhi,CSIM: A Document Clustering Algorithm Based On Swarm Intelligence, To be appeared In Proceedings of Congress on Evolutionary Computation,2002

[7]. Zhendong Dong, Qiang Dong, HowNet, http://www.keenage.com

AN APPLICATION OF ASSEMBLY STRUCTURE IN WELDING ESTIMATE OF WELDING OBJECT IN MANUFACTURING DESIGN

Zhihua Zhang*, I. Nagasawa**, M. Mochizuki**, H. Yamaguchi*** and M. Umeda**

**Sanyo Women's College, **Kyushu Institute of Technology, ***Choryo Design Ltd. Co., Japan*

Abstract: Welding vessel objects such as heat-exchanger, oil-tank and other civil-used pressure vessels are comparatively large size products. Design works for such products not only concern with the geometric data, more important aspect is to treat with the design knowledge used in design process. But traditional CAD systems generally depend on shape-oriented approaches and pay less attention on the features of design and dealing with design knowledge. Therefore, there has been a considerable growth of interest toward knowledge-based design support systems. We have proposed a design object model for manufacturing design of welding vessels. In this model, the assembly structure of a design object is represented by the essential design elements and their dependencies. This paper discusses its application and focus on welding estimate of a welding object and dealing with design knowledge related.

Key words: Knowledge-based CAD, Design Object Model, Welding Estimate.

1. INTRODUCTION

In recent years, considerations of product development are remarkably increased such as the globalization of business, environmental problems, corresponding to new technologies, etc. Especially in the design business of welding vessels, it is mainly concerned about getting high reliability and low cost for high competition in a competitive worldwide manufacturing market, but it is very difficult to make a harmonized demand on quality, performance, economic efficiency and safety in design and production. So, how to improve the intelligent productivity of design work becomes more urgent. Till then, division and standardization on design activities are advanced in this field. Also for design automation, problems-oriented design support systems have been developed. But most of them directly coded the design procedures for particular product type in system structure. Modification is need whenever the design-plan changes because lack of integrated management abilities of design information. Therefore, we proposed a design object model, assembly structure [1], which centrally manages the design information such as cutting, welding, assembling, etc., and construction of design support system based on the model has also been discussed [2]. This paper focuses on welding estimate of a welding object and dealing with the related design knowledge.

2. DESIGN OBJECT MODEL

Welding vessel objects such as heat-exchanger, oil-tank and other pressure vessels are comparatively large size products. Generally, a welding vessel object is composed from tubes or/and globular body with nozzles, which usually manufactured by cutting, bending and welding steel plates or half-product parts like flanges. Much production is an article-ordered production with high performance and high reliability, also must fills to decided laws and safety standards. The design flow of such a product is usually divided as concept design, basic design, manufacturing design phases in our research.

2.1 Assembly Structure

In this model, the assembly structure of a design object is represented as assembly objects and their dependencies. It is able to centrally manage the design information generated in whole design process with related model.

- *Assembly Object* described by combination of *Functional Elements* based on the essential design operation units designed by designers, which not only include the form information of object but a designer who performed correlation with semantic processing or a functional operate in design.
- *Dependency Relation* used to describe the dependencies between assembly objects, such as part-of, dimension setting, machining process, etc.

In design, functional elements do interaction with others to embody its function and generally operated as a conceptual entity than form feature. An assembly object has attributes to identify its characteristics in design.

2.2 Assembly Structure Module

The stepwise refinement feature of design operation has been considered in the model. This is also helpful to represent the objects, for example, the welding lines. In design, a designer does it in a manner of succeeding determination. That is to say, it is firstly assigned as an empty-structured assembly object but owns design meaning, and then to be substituted alternatively by the compound assembly object that has a concrete assembly structure. We called it *Assembly Structure Module*. It is generally dealt with equally as a *functional element* and can be implemented as an abstract class from a viewpoint of software. The detailed structure of a module is determined in accordance with the progress of design operation.

3. OPERATION OF ASSEMBLY STRUCTURE

The assembly structure of a design object is constructed by using the following three types of design operations.

- *Primitive Operation* is a series of operations for constructing the data structure of a design object, editing the attributes of an assembly object and the dependencies between assembly objects in design.
- *Basic Operation* is the design operations related to manufacturing such as the end-cutting, hole-making and grooving, etc. of assembly objects.
- *Macro Operation* is a combination operation of primitive operations and basic operations to complete a series of design operations automatically if it is necessary.

4. APPLICATION OF ASSEMBLY STRUCTURE

Several applications of assembly structure model are available such as generation of manufacturing documents and 3D design information. Here, we focus on welding estimate of vessels because it is important for evaluate a design plan from aspects of cost and necessary for product makers.

Welding Estimate is to calculate the required cost of a welding vessel before manufacturing such as man-hours and material expense. Generally, long time is required for the job because there are many parts and processing points of a product, especially in case of large size. In many cases, a designer analogises by the actual achievements and experiences and diagrammatise it in a general view to support estimate. For example, by making the graph of model patterns and weight relation of a product, the estimate of alike product can be done by reverse reference of the graph. Although this method can estimate quickly, but cannot take out an exact estimate especially the product constitution changed. To solve the problem, as an application of assembly structure model, it is sufficient to manage manufacturing information such as man-hours related to cut processing, grooving and welding processing of a product into design models as the attributes of related object. By tracing the objects and evaluating the design attributes, the estimate can be sufficient done. Furthermore, factors like structure complexity and size of a design object, the estimate on man-hours of cutting and welding process is related to the design knowledge, which are systematically arranged according to different processing methods, especially for the public standards and the actual design know-how of specific factory. Design knowledge is deal with specific tools, which provide designers a simple knowledge process language based on the concept of data flow and some solutions search methods.

5. CONCLUSION

Traditional problem-oriented CAD systems mainly depend on shape-oriented approaches and pay less attention on the features of design operation and how to deal with design knowledge used in design process. We proposed the Assembly Structure, which provide a framework to centrally manage the design information in whole process. And the application of the model on welding estimate has been discussed. By adopting the techniques, systems can not only promote the intellectual productivity of design business, but also can cope with the new design more flexibly in product development. As future subject, it is necessary to systematize the design knowledge of welding vessel objects such as welding and structure standards that used in actual works. Additional research subject is to develop the related knowledge base for support system and test the ideas and approaches by construct a welding estimate support system so as to get the overall evaluation.

REFERENCE

1. Z. Zhang, I. Nagasawa, M. Mochizuki, H. Yamaguchi and M. Umeda: *A Design Object Model for Manufacturing Design of Welding Vessel Objects*, Transactions of IPSJ, Vol.41, No.1, pp123-135 (2000).
2. Z. Zhang, I. Nagasawa, M. Mochizuki, H. Yamaguchi and M. Umeda *A Design Support System for Manufacturing Design of Welding Vessel Objects*The Proceedings of IFIP 16th WCC on ITBM-2000 pp.658-666 (August 2000)
3. Jami J. Shah and Mary T. Rogers: *Assembly Modeling as a Feature-Based Design,* Research in Engineering Design (USA), Vol.5, No.3-4, pp.218- 237 (1993).
4. V. Allada and S. Anand: *Feature-based modeling approaches for integrated manufacturing: state-of- the-art survey and future research direction.*Int. J. Computer Integrated Manufacturing, Vol.8, No.6 pp.411-440 (1995).
5. Japan Standard Society: the JIS handbook, Weld (1992).

Author index

MIX
Papier aus verantwortungsvollen Quellen
Paper from responsible sources
FSC® C105338

If you have any concerns about our products,
you can contact us on
ProductSafety@springernature.com

In case Publisher is established outside the EU,
the EU authorized representative is:
Springer Nature Customer Service Center GmbH
Europaplatz 3, 69115 Heidelberg, Germany

Printed by Libri Plureos GmbH
in Hamburg, Germany